VEGAN COOKBOOK BEGINNERS 2022:

800+ AFFORDABLE PLANT-BASED HEALTHY, DELICIOUS RECIPES FOR YOUR VEGAN DIET.

Introduction

Veganism is a result of living that seeks to reject, as far as is possible and practicable, all shape of animal exploitation and cruelty. Sounds difficult? It's not!

A vegan diet is composed entirely of vegetables, grains, fruits, beans, legumes, and nuts. There are many reasons people decided to go vegan – from the health benefits to environmental concerns.

It excludes all foods of animal origin. This includes meat, dairy products, and eggs. Vegans generally avoid wearing leather, wool or silk. Vegans are also committed to the philosophy that animals should not be subject to human-based experimentation. Those who practice veganism for health reasons avoid foods that contain cholesterol and saturated fats, such as eggs, meat, poultry, shellfish, etc. Foods of plant origin contain fiber, vitamins, minerals, and antioxidants beneficial in preventing disease. There are many reasons to follow a vegan diet, some of which include:

The vegan diet is high in fiber and low in fat and calories. It is also very healthy. Health benefits of veganism include weight loss, lower blood pressure, lower cholesterol, and lower risk of developing diabetes type 2.

Protective against heart disease with its high fiber content and low saturated fat content. Vegan diets are also suitable for lowering blood pressure, reducing the risk for strokes and protecting against certain types of cancers.

Strengthens and builds bones and muscles with its high protein content. Vegan diets also contain essential amino acids, which are not readily available from plant-based proteins. Decreases risk of osteoporosis and certain cancers.

Veganism is especially good for the environment and helps to stop global warming. Animal agriculture requires enormous amounts of water and energy to grow feed crops for the animals.

A vegan lifestyle involves living life without cruelty towards other living things. A vegan lifestyle is a healthy way of living and can help stop cruelty to animals. By following a vegan diet, you can enjoy many of the same foods as non-vegans without having to worry about what has been involved in the process of producing them.

A vegan cookbook is a book that contains recipes without the use of any animal products. There are many sources because a person would want to try vegan cooking. A cookbook that contains only vegan recipes will help you learn more about different types of food and learn how to make new, exciting foods. There are so many kinds of food you can make, from easy meals for busy people to delicious desserts. You can try out new recipes and new ingredients as you cook. This book can be a great way to introduce other people to veganism and educate them about the benefits of a vegan lifestyle. You could get ideas for unique dishes and new ingredients, making everyone happy when they taste them. This book will also give you delicious recipes for those special events, like a birthday party, or Christmas dinner, and so much more.

So, what are you waiting for? Start cooking with this Vegan Cookbook. You'll love it and will never want to go back to regular cooking. You'll be surprised at how easy it is... and too good to be true!

Breakfast

1. Buckwheat Porridge with Apples and Almonds

Preparation time: 15 minutes
Cooking time: 10 minutes
Servings: 3
Ingredients:

- 1 cup buckwheat grouts, toasted
- 3/4 cup water
- 1 cup rice milk
- 1/4 teaspoon sea salt
- 3 tablespoons agave syrup
- 1 cup apples, cored and diced
- 3 tablespoons almonds, slivered
- 2 tablespoons coconut flakes
- 2 tablespoons hemp seeds

Directions:

1. In a saucepan, bring the buckwheat grouts, water, milk and salt to a boil. Immediately turn the heat to a simmer; let it simmer for about 13 minutes until it has softened.
2. Stir in the agave syrup. Divide the porridge between three serving bowls.
3. Garnish each serving with the apples, almonds, and coconut and hemp seeds. Bon appétit!

Nutrition:
Calories: 377 Fat: 8.8g. Carbohydrates: 7.0g Proteins: 10.6g.

2. Coconut Quinoa Mix

Preparation time: 10 minutes
Cooking time: 8 hours
Servings: 2
Ingredients:

- ½ cup quinoa
- 1 cup water

1. In your slow cooker, mix quinoa with water, coconut milk, maple syrup and salt, stir well, cover and cook on Low for 8 hours.
2. Divide into 2 bowls, sprinkle berries on top and serve for breakfast.

- ½ cup coconut milk
- 1 tablespoon maple syrup
- A pinch of salt
- 1 tablespoon berries

Directions:

3. Enjoy!

Nutrition:
Calories: 261 Fat: 5g Fiber: 7g Carbohydrates: 12g Proteins: 5g.

3. Carrots and Zucchini Oatmeal

Preparation time: 10 minutes
Cooking time: 8 hours
Servings: 2
Ingredients:

- ½ cup steel cut oats
- 1 cup coconut milk
- 1 carrot, grated
- ¼ zucchini, grated
- A pinch of nutmeg, ground
- A pinch of cloves, ground
- ½ teaspoon cinnamon powder
- 2 tablespoons brown sugar
- ¼ cup pecans, chopped
- Cooking spray

Directions:

1. Oil your slow cooker with cooking spray, add oats, milk, carrot, zucchini, nutmeg, cloves, cinnamon and sugar, toss, cover and cook on Low for 8 hours.
1. Divide into 2 bowls, sprinkle pecans on top and serve.
2. Enjoy!

Nutrition:
Calories: 200 Fat: 4g Fiber: 8g Carbohydrates: 11g Proteins: 5g

4. Banana & Blueberry Oats

Preparation time: 10 minutes
Cooking time: 6 hours
Servings: 2
Ingredients:

- 1/2 cup steel cut oats
- ¼ cup quinoa
- ½ cup blueberries
- 1 banana, mashed
- A pinch of cinnamon powder
- 2 tablespoons maple syrup
- 2 cups water
- Cooking spray
- ½ cup coconut milk

Directions:

1. Oil your slow cooker with cooking spray, add oats, quinoa, blueberries, banana, cinnamon, maple syrup, water and coconut milk, stir, cover and cook on Low for 6 hours.
2. Divide into 2 bowls and serve for breakfast.
3. Enjoy!

Nutrition:
Calories: 200 Fat: 4g Fiber: 5g Carbohydrates: 8g Proteins: 5g

5. Peanut Butter Oatmeal

Preparation time: 10 minutes
Cooking time: 8 hours
Servings: 2
Ingredients:

- 1 banana, mashed
- 1 and ½ cups almond milk
- ½ cup steel cut oats
- 2 tablespoons peanut butter
- ½ teaspoon vanilla extract
- ½ teaspoon cinnamon powder
- ½ tablespoon chia seeds

Directions:

1. In your slow cooker, mix almond milk with banana, oats, peanut butter, vanilla extract, cinnamon and chia, stir, cover and cook on Low for 8 hours.
2. Stir oatmeal one more time, divide into 2 bowls and serve.
3. Enjoy!

Nutrition:
Calories: 222 Fat: 5g Fiber: 6g Carbohydrates: 9g Proteins: 11g

6. Coconut Raisins Oatmeal

Preparation time: 10 minutes
Cooking time: 8 hours
Servings: 2
Ingredients:

- ½ cup water
- ½ cup coconut milk
- ½ cup steel cut oats
- ½ cup carrots, grated
- ¼ cup raisins
- A pinch of cinnamon powder
- A pinch of ginger, ground
- A pinch of nutmeg, ground
- ¼ cup coconut flakes, shredded
- 1 tablespoon orange zest, grated
- ½ teaspoon vanilla extract
- ½ tablespoon maple syrup
- 2 tablespoons walnuts, chopped

Directions:

1. In your slow cooker, mix water with coconut milk, oats, carrots, raisins, cinnamon, ginger, nutmeg, coconut flakes, orange zest, vanilla extract and maple syrup, stir, cover and cook on Low for 8 hours.
2. Add walnuts, stir, divide into 2 bowls and serve for breakfast.
3. Enjoy!

Nutrition:
Calories: 200 Fat: 4g Fiber: 6g Carbohydrates: 8g Proteins: 10g

7. Banana Oats

Preparation time: 10 minutes
Cooking time: 0 minutes
Servings: 2
Ingredients:

- ½ cup cold brewed coffee
- 2 dates, pitted
- 2 tablespoons cocoa powder
- 1 cup rolled oats

- 1 and ½ tablespoons chia seeds

Directions:

1. In a blender, combine the 1 banana with the ¾ almond milk and the rest of the ingredients, pulse, divide into bowls, and serve breakfast.

8. Berry Oats

Preparation time: 5 minutes
Cooking time: 0 minute
Servings: 2
Ingredients:

- ½ cup rolled oats
- 1 cup almond milk
- ¼ cup chia seeds
- 2 teaspoons maple syrup

9. Sun-dried Tomatoes Oatmeal

Preparation time: 10 minutes
Cooking time: 25 minutes
Servings: 4
Ingredients:

- 3 cups water
- 1 cup almond milk
- 1 tablespoon olive oil
- 1 cup steel-cut oats
- ¼ cup sun-dried tomatoes, chopped

Directions:

10. Cauliflower Fritters

Preparation time: 10 minutes
Cooking time: 50 minutes
Servings: 4
Ingredients:

- 30 ounces canned chickpeas, drained and rinsed
- 2 and ½ tablespoons olive oil
- 1 small yellow onion, chopped
- 2 cups cauliflower florets chopped
- 2 tablespoons garlic, minced

Directions:

1. Lay out half of the chickpeas on a baking sheet lined with parchment pepper, add 1 tablespoon oil, season with salt and pepper, toss and bake at 400 degrees F for 30 minutes.

11. Blueberries Quinoa

Preparation time: 5 minutes
Cooking time: 0 minutes
Servings: 4
Ingredients:

- 2 cups quinoa, almond milk
- ½ teaspoon cinnamon powder
- 1 tablespoon maple syrup
- 1 cup blueberries

12. Avocado and Olive Paste on Toasted Rye Bread

Preparation time: 5 minutes
Cooking time: 0 minute
Servings: 4
Ingredients:

- 1 avocado, halved, peeled and finely chopped
- 1 tbsp. green onions, finely chopped
- 2 tbsp. green olive paste
- 4 lettuce leaves
- 1 tbsp. lemon juice

Nutrition:
Calories: 451 Fat: 25g Fiber: 9.9g

- 1 cup berries, pureed

Directions:

1. In a bowl, combine the oats with the milk and the rest of the ingredients except 1 tbsp. of yogurt, toss, divide into bowls, top with the yogurt and serve cold for breakfast.

Nutrition:
Calories: 420 Fat: 30g Proteins: 6.4g

1. In a pan, scourge water with the milk, bring to a boil over medium heat.
2. Meanwhile, pre-heat pan with the oil over medium-high heat, add the oats, cook them for about 2 minutes and transfer m to the pan with the milk.
3. Stir the oats, add the tomatoes and simmer over medium heat for 23 minutes.
4. Divide the mix into bowls, sprinkle the red pepper flakes on top and serve for breakfast.

Nutrition:
Calories: 170 Fat: 17.8g Proteins: 1.5g

2. Transfer the chickpeas to a food processor, pulse well and put the mix into a bowl.
3. Heat a pan with the ½ tablespoon oil over medium-high heat, add the garlic and the onion and sauté for 3 minutes.
4. Add the cauliflower, cook for 6 minutes more, transfer this to a blender, add the rest of the chickpeas, pulse, pour over the crispy chickpeas mix from the bowl, stir and shape medium fritters out of this mix.
5. Heat a pan with the rest of the oil over medium-high heat, add the fritters, cook them for 3 minutes on each side, and serve breakfast.

Nutrition:
Calories: 333 Fat: 12.6g Proteins: 13.6g

- ¼ cup walnuts, chopped

Directions:

1. In a bowl, scourge quinoa with the milk and the rest of the ingredients, toss, divide into smaller bowls, and serve breakfast.

Nutrition:
Calories: 284 Fat: 14.3g Proteins: 4.4g

Directions:

1. Crush avocados with a fork or potato masher until almost smooth. Add the onions, green olive paste and lemon juice. Season with salt and pepper to taste. Stir to combine.
2. Toast 4 slices of rye bread until golden. Spoon 1/4 of the avocado mixture onto each slice of bread, top with a lettuce leaf and serve.

Nutrition:

Calories: 291 Fat: 13g Proteins: 3g

13. Veggie Casserole

Preparation time: 25 minutes
Cooking time: 45 minutes
Servings: 4
Ingredients:

- 1 lb. okra, trimmed
- 3 tomatoes, cut into wedges
- 3 garlic cloves, chopped
- 1 cup fresh parsley leaves, finely cut

14. Maple Flavored Oatmeal

Preparation time: 5 minutes
Cooking time: 25 minutes
Servings: 2
Ingredients:

- 2 tbsp. Maple Syrup
- 1 cup Oatmeal
- ½ tsp. Cinnamon
- 2 ½ cup Water
- 2/3 cup Soy Milk
- 1 tsp. Vegan Butter

Directions:

15. Country Breakfast Cereal

Preparation time: 5 minutes
Cooking time: 40 minutes
Servings: 6
Ingredients:

- 1 cup brown rice
- ½ cup raisins, seedless
- 1 tsp cinnamon, ground
- ¼ Tbsp butter

16. Oatmeal Fruit Shake

Preparation time: 10 minutes
Cooking time: 0 minutes
Servings: 2
Ingredients:

- cup oatmeal
- 1 apple, cored
- 1 banana, halved
- 1 cup baby spinach

17. Amaranth Banana Breakfast Porridge

Preparation time: 10 minutes
Cooking time: 25 minutes
Servings: 8
Ingredients:

- 2 cup amaranth
- 2 cinnamon sticks
- 4 bananas, diced
- 2 Tbsp chopped pecans
- 4 cups water

18. Breakfast Quinoa with Figs

Preparation time: 5 minutes
Cooking time: 15 minutes
Servings: 4
Ingredients:

- 2 cups water
- 1 cup white quinoa
- 1 cup dried figs

Directions:

1. In a deep ovenproof baking dish, combine okra, sliced tomatoes, olive oil and garlic. Add in salt and black pepper to taste and toss to combine. Bake in a prepared oven at 350 F for 45 minutes. Garnish with parsley and serve.

Nutrition:
Calories: 302 Fat: 13g Proteins: 6g

1. Boil oatmeal and water in a medium-sized saucepan over medium-high heat.
2. Next, lower the heat and cook for further 13 to 15 minutes while keeping the pan covered.
3. Take pan from the heat and fluff this mixture with a fork.
4. Cover the pan again. Set it aside for 5 minutes.
5. Then, stir in all the remaining ingredients to the oatmeal mixture until everything comes together.
6. Serve and enjoy.

Nutrition:
Calories: 411 Proteins: 14.7g Fat: 6.6g

- 2 ¼ cups water

Directions:

1. Combine rice, butter, raisins, and cinnamon in a saucepan. Add 2 ¼ cups water. Bring to boil.
2. Cover and simmer for 40 minutes.
3. Fluff with fork.

Nutrition:
Calories: 160 Proteins: 3g Fat: 1.5g

- 2 cups coconut water
- 2 cups ice, cubed
- ½ tsp ground cinnamon
- 1 tsp pure vanilla extract

Directions:

1. Blend all ingredients to a blender until smooth.

Nutrition:
Calories: 270 Fat: 1.5g Proteins: 5g

Directions:

1. Combine the amaranth, water, and cinnamon sticks, and banana in a pot. Cover and simmer around 25 minutes.
2. Remove from heat and discard the cinnamon. Places into bowls, and top with pecans.

Nutrition:
Calories: 330 Fat: 6g Proteins: 10g

- 1 cup walnuts
- 1 cup almond milk
- ½ tsp. cinnamon
- ¼ tsp. cloves

Directions:

1. Rinse quinoa under cool water.

2 Combine it with water, cinnamon, and cloves. Bring to boil.

3 Simmer covered for 10-15 minutes.

19. Spiced Quinoa Porridge

Preparation time: 30 minutes
Cooking time: 30 minutes
Servings: 4
 Ingredients:

- ¾ cup uncooked quinoa
- 1/8 teaspoon ground cardamom
- 1½ cups water
- ½ teaspoon ground cinnamon
- ¼ teaspoon ground ginger
- 1/8 teaspoon ground cloves
- 2 tablespoon ground sunflower seeds

20. Fruit Cup

Preparation time: 15 Minutes
Cooking time: 0 minute
Servings: 4
Ingredients:

- 2 cups melon
- 2 cups strawberries
- 2 cups grapes, sliced in half
- 2 cups peaches, sliced
- 3 tablespoons lime juice

21. Simple Vegan Breakfast Hash

Preparation time: 10 minutes
Cooking time: 25 minutes
Servings: 4
Ingredients:
For Potatoes:

- 1 large sweet potato
- 3 medium potatoes
- 1 tablespoon onion powder
- 2 teaspoons sea salt
- 1 tablespoon garlic powder
- 1 teaspoon ground black pepper
- 1 teaspoon dried thyme
- 1/4 cup olive oil

For Skillet Mixture:

- 1 medium onion
- 5 cloves of garlic

22. Peanut Butter Granola

Preparation time: 10 Minutes
Cooking time: 47 minutes
Servings: 4
Ingredients:

- 4 cups oats
- 1/3 cup of cocoa powder
- ¾ cup peanut butter
- 1/3 cup maple syrup
- 1/3 cup avocado oil
- 1½ teaspoons vanilla extract
- ½ cup cocoa nibs
- 6 ounces dark chocolate

Directions:

4 Add dried figs, nuts, and milk.

Nutrition:
Calories: 420 Fat: 20g Proteins: 11g

- 2 tablespoons maple syrup
- ¼ cup fresh strawberries, hulled and sliced

Directions:

1 Put water, quinoa and spices in a medium pan over medium heat.

2 Bring to a boil and reduce the heat to low.

3 Simmer, for 20 minutes and remove from the heat.

4 Stir in the sunflower seeds, maple syrup and strawberries to serve.

Nutrition:
Calories: 169 Fat: 15.4g Proteins: 7.5g

- ½ teaspoon ground ginger
- 3 teaspoons lime zest
- ¼ cup coconut flakes, toasted

Directions:

1 Toss the fruits in lime juice, ginger.

2 Sprinkle the lime zest on top.

3 Top with the coconut flakes.

Nutrition:
Calories: 65 Fat: 1.6g Proteins: 1g

- ¼ teaspoon salt
- ¼ teaspoon black pepper
- 1 teaspoon olive oil

Directions:

1 Switch on the oven, then set it to 450 degrees F and let it preheat.

2 Meanwhile, take a casserole dish, add all the ingredients for the potatoes, toss, and then cook for 20 minutes, stirring halfway.

3 Meanwhile, take a skillet pan, place it over medium heat, add oil and when hot, cook onion and garlic, for 5 minutes, season well.

4 When potatoes have roasted, add garlic and cooked onion mixture, stir, and serve.

Nutrition:
Calories: 212 Fat: 10g Proteins: 3g

1 Preheat your oven to 300 degrees F.

2 Spray a baking sheet with cooking spray.

3 In a medium saucepan add oil, maple syrup, and peanut butter.

4 Cook for 2 minutes on medium heat, stirring.

5 Add the oats and cocoa powder, mix well.

6 Spread the coated oats on the baking sheet.

7 Bake for 45 minutes, occasionally stirring.

8 Garnish with dark chocolate, cocoa nibs, and peanut butter.

Nutrition:
Calories: 134 Fat: 4.7g Proteins: 6.2g

23. Apple Chia Pudding

Preparation time: 10 minutes
Cooking time: 5 minutes
Servings: 4
Ingredients:
Chia Pudding:

- 4 tablespoons chia seeds
- 1 cup almond milk
- ½ teaspoon cinnamon

Apple Filling:

- 1 large apple
- ¼ cup water
- 2 teaspoons maple syrup

- Pinch cinnamon
- 2 tablespoons golden raisins

Directions:
1. In a sealable container, add cinnamon, chia seeds and almond milk, mix well.
2. Seal the container and refrigerate overnight.
3. In a medium pot, combine all apple pie filling ingredients and cook for 5 minutes.
4. Serve the chia pudding with apple filling on top.

Nutrition:
Calories: 387 Fat: 2.9g Proteins: 6.6g

24. Pumpkin Spice Bites

Preparation time: 10 minutes
Cooking time: 0 minutes
Servings: 2
Ingredients:

- ½ cup pumpkin puree
- ½ cup almond butter
- ¼ cup maple syrup
- 1 teaspoon pumpkin pie spice
- 1 1/3 cup rolled oats
- 1/3 cup pumpkin seeds

- 1/3 cup raisins
- 2 tablespoons chia seeds

Directions:
1. In a sealable container, add everything and mix well.
2. Seal the container and refrigerate overnight.
3. Roll the mixture into small balls.
4. Serve.

Nutrition:
Calories: 212 Fat: 4.4g Proteins: 7.3g

25. No-Bake Vegan Protein Bar

Preparation time: 20 minutes
Cooking time: 0 minute
Servings: 5
Ingredients:

- 1/3 cup amaranth
- 3 tbsp. vanilla vegan protein powder.
- 2 tbsp maple syrup.
- 1 cup almond butter.
- 3 tbsp. dark vegan chocolate.

Directions:
1. In 8 x 8-inch baking pan, place parchment paper and set aside.
2. Pop your amaranth by heating a big pot over medium-high heat.
3. Include about 2-3 tbsp amaranth at a time and right away cover. Shake over the heat to move the grain around.
4. Not every single grain will pop.
5. Do not blend any scorched grain with the completely popped grain. Set aside.
6. Mix in almond butter and maple syrup. Then add protein powder and stir.
7. Include popped amaranth a little at a time until you have a loose "dough" texture.
8. Transfer the mixture to the baking meal and press down to form an even layer. Lay parchment paper or plastic wrap on the top.
9. Transfer to freezer to set for 10-15 minutes or until firm to the touch. Lift out and slice it into nine bars.

Nutrition:
Calories: 215 Fat: 15g Proteins: 10.7g

26. Orange Pumpkin Pancakes

Preparation time: 15 minutes
Cooking time: 10 minutes
Servings: 4
Ingredients:

- 10 g ground flax meal
- 45 ml water
- 235 ml unsweetened soy milk
- 15 ml lemon juice
- 60 g buckwheat flour
- 60 g all-purpose flour
- 8 g baking powder
- 2 tsp finely grated orange zest
- 25 g white chia seeds
- 120 g organic pumpkin puree
- 30 ml melted and cooled coconut oil
- 5 ml vanilla paste

- 30 ml pure maple syrup

Directions:
1. Combine ground flax meal with water. Place aside for 10 minutes. Combine almond milk and cider vinegar. Place aside for 5 minutes.
2. Mix buckwheat flour, all-purpose flour, baking powder, orange zest, and chia seeds.
3. Whisk almond milk, along with pumpkin puree, coconut oil, vanilla, and maple syrup.
4. Heat large non-stick skillet over medium-high heat. Brush the skillet gently with some coconut oil.
5. Pour 60ml of batter into skillet. Cook the pancake for 1 minute. Flip.
6. Cook 1 1/2 minutes more. Slide the pancake onto a plate. Repeat with the remaining batter.

Nutrition:
Calories: 301 Fat: 12.6g Proteins: 8.1g

27. Sweet Potato Slices with Fruits

Preparation time: 15 minutes
Cooking time: 10 minutes
Servings: 2
Ingredients:

- 1 sweet potato

Topping:

- 60 g organic peanut butter.
- 30ml pure maple syrup.
- 4 dried apricots, sliced.
- 30 g fresh raspberries.

Directions:

1. Peel and slice sweet potato into 1/2 cm thick slices.
2. Place the potato slices in a toaster on high for 5 minutes. Toast your sweet potatoes TWICE.
3. Arrange sweet potato slices onto a plate.
4. Spread the peanut butter over sweet potato slices.
5. Drizzle the maple syrup over the butter. Top each slice with an equal number of sliced apricots and raspberries. Serve.

Nutrition:
Calories: 300 Fat: 16.9g Proteins: 10.3g

28. Energizing Daily Tonic

Preparation time: 15 minutes
Cooking time: 0 minute
Servings: 2
Ingredients:
Base:

- 2-4 tbsp. vegan protein powder.
- 1 tbsp. maca powder.
- 1 tsp. ashwagandha powder.
- 1 tsp. mushroom blend powder.
- 1 tsp. astragalus powder.
- 1/4 cup pecans.
- 2 Brazil nuts.
- Pinch of stevia powder.

- 1-2 tbsp. maple syrup or dates

Add-ons:

- 1 tbsp. cacao powder.
- 1 tbsp. ground coffee.
- 1/2 tsp. vanilla extract.

Directions:

1. Blend all the base active ingredients except the maple syrup up until smooth, velvety and tasty. Include 1 to 2 tablespoons of maple syrup or a small handful of dates, if you desire it sweeter.
2. Sprinkle with apple pie spice, if utilizing, and enjoy!

Nutrition:
Calories: 160 Fat: 5.5g Proteins: 0.8g

29. Strawberry Maple Scones

Preparation time: 10 minutes
Cooking time: 15 minutes
Servings: 6
Ingredients:

- 2 cups oat flour.
- 1/3 cup almond milk.
- 1 cup of strawberries.
- A handful of dried currants.
- 5 tbsp. coconut oil.
- 5 tbsp. of maple syrup.
- 1 tbsp. baking powder.
- 1 1/2 tsp. vanilla extracts
- 1 tsp. cinnamon.

Directions:

1. Include the coconut oil and with a pastry cutter or fork, cut and blend the coconut oil into the oat flour mix until a crumbly dough form. Mix in strawberry pieces, currants and slowly include in all the wet ingredients. Slowly blend the dry and wet components.
2. On a prepared baking sheet with parchment paper, form a circle out of the dough - it must have to do with 1 inch thick. Cut into eight triangular pieces and bake for 15-17 minutes. Delight in with jam, nut butter!

Nutrition:
Calories: 342 Carbohydrates: 48g Proteins: 4.1g

30. Spinach Tofu Scramble with Sour Cream

Preparation time: 10 minutes
Cooking time: 20 minutes
Servings: 4
Ingredients:
Sour cream:

- 75 g raw cashews
- 30 ml lemon juice
- 5 g nutritional yeast
- 60 ml water 1 pinch salt

Tofu scramble:

- 15 ml olive oil.
- 1 small onion
- 1 clove garlic.
- 400 firm tofu
- 1/2 tsp. ground cumin.
- 1/2 tsp. curry powder.
- 1/2 tsp. turmeric.

- 2 tomatoes, diced.
- 30 g baby spinach

Directions:

1. Make the cashew sour cream; rinse and drain soaked cashews.
2. Place the cashews, lemon juice, nutritional yeast, water, and salt in a food processor.
3. Blend on high until smooth, for 5-6 minutes.
4. Transfer to a bowl and place aside. Make the tofu scramble, heat olive oil in a skillet.
5. Add onion and cook 5 minutes over medium-high.
6. Add garlic, and cook stirring, for 1 minute.
7. Stir in crumbled tofu to coat with oil.
8. Add the cumin, curry, and turmeric. Cook the tofu for 2 minutes.
9. Cook tomatoes for 2 minutes.
10. Add spinach and cook, tossing until completely wilted, about 1 minute. Transfer tofu scramble on the plate.

11   Top with a sour cream and serve.

Nutrition:

31. Amaranth Quinoa Porridge

Preparation time: 10 minutes
Cooking time: 20 minutes
Servings: 3
Ingredients:

- 85 g quinoa.
- 70 g amaranth.
- 460 ml water.
- 115 ml unsweetened soy milk.
- 1/2 tsp. vanilla paste.
- 15 g almond butter.
- 30 ml pure maple syrup.
- 10 g raw pumpkin seeds.

32. Sweet Potato Toasts

Preparation time: 10 minutes
Cooking time: 10 minutes
Servings: 2
Ingredients:

- 2 large sweet potatoes
- 1/4-inch-thick slices.
- 1 tbsp. avocado oil.
- 1 tsp. salt 1/2 cup guacamole.
- 1/2 cup tomatoes, sliced.

33. Vacation Oven Roasted Seitan

Preparation time: 5 minutes
Cooking time: 20 minutes
Servings: 4
Ingredients:

- 1 cup of vital wheat gluten.
- 3 tbsp. nutritional yeast.
- 1 tsp. smoked paprika.
- 1 tsp. dried thyme
- 1 tsp. dried rosemary.
- 1 tbsp. garlic powder.
- 1 tsp. sea salt.
- 1/4 teaspoon dried sage.
- 1 tbsp. vegan Worcestershire sauce.
- 1 tbsp. vegan BBQ Sauce.
- 2 tbsp. liquid amino
- 4 cups of Vegetable Broth

34. Korean Braised Tofu

Preparation time: 10 minutes
Cooking time: 5 minutes
Servings: 3
Ingredients:

- 1 onion
- 1 14-ounce block firm tofu
- 1 tbsp. sugar.
- 1/2 -1 tbsp. Korean chili powder.
- 3 tbsp. soy sauce.
- 4 tbsp. sake.
- 1 scallion cut into thin slices.
- Toasted sesame seeds.

Directions:

Calories: 411 Fat: 26g Proteins: 25g

- 10 g pomegranate seeds.

Directions:

1   Combine quinoa, amaranth, and water.
2   Bring to a boil over medium-high heat.
3   Reduce heat and simmer, for 20 minutes. Stir in milk and maple syrup.
4   Simmer for 6-7 minutes. Pull out from the heat, stir in vanilla, and almond butter.
5   Allow the mixture to stand for 5 minutes.
6   Divide the porridge between two bowls.
7   Top with pumpkin seeds and pomegranate seeds.

Nutrition:
Calories: 474 Fat: 13.3g Proteins: 17g

Directions:

1   Preheat your oven to 425° F.
2   Cover a baking sheet with parchment paper.
3   Rub the potato slices with oil and salt and place them on a baking sheet. Bake for 5 minutes in the oven, then flip and bake again for 5 minutes. Top the baked slices with guacamole and tomatoes.

Nutrition:
Calories: 134 Fat: 4.7g Proteins: 6.2g

Directions:

1   Mix your dry active ingredients in one bowl and your wet components.
2   Incorporate wet with the dry and knead for about 5 minutes.
3   Bring about 4 cups of veggie broth to a simmer on medium-high.
4   Most dishes require you to wrap your seitan in plastic wrap prior to simmering.
5   Roll out seitan dough into a log and simmer in the covered pot of vegetable broth for 45 minutes.
6   After 45 minutes prep your oven to 350° F and bake on baking tray for 20 minutes, flipping it after 10 minutes.

Nutrition:
Calories: 135 Fat: 0.5g Proteins: 21g

1   Situate onion slices on a non-stick skillet or frying pan, then leading with pieces of tofu.
2   Incorporate sugar, Korean chili powder, soy sauce, and sake. Put over tofu slices.
3   Cover the frying pan with a lid. Set heat to high and cook until boiling. Turn the heat to medium-high, and cook for another 5 minutes, baste with the sauce several times.
4   Take lid off, turn the heat back to high, and cook till the sauce has minimized.
5   Shut off heat, transfer to a serving plate, garnish with scallions and sesame seeds. Serve immediately.

Nutrition:
Calories: 149 Fat: 10g Proteins: 6g

35. Arugula Pesto and Zucchini on Rye Toast

Preparation time: 15 minutes
Cooking time: 5 minutes
Servings: 1
Ingredients:

- 2 slices of rye toast
- 1/2 of an avocado.
- 1/2 large zucchini.
- Bunch of watercress
- 1 garlic clove.

For arugula pesto:

- 2 big handfuls of arugulas.
- 1 cup pine nuts
- 1 large handful of spinach.
- Juice of 1 lime.
- 1 tsp. of sea salt.
- 3 tbsp. olive oil.

Directions:

1. Incorporate all the ingredients into a food mill and whip up till the pesto becomes velvety and smooth.
2. Sauté the zucchini by first cutting it into very thin horizontal pieces. Warm the roughly sliced garlic clove, olive oil, sprinkle of sea salt, and a couple of splashes of water to a small pan on medium heat.
3. If the zucchini begins to dry, include the zucchini and sauté for 7 minutes - slowly include water. Toast the bread, then spread out the pesto throughout the toast, add the zucchini and sliced avocado, and leading with watercress!

Nutrition:
Calories: 598 Fat: 39g Proteins: 6g

36. Baked Sweet Potato and Turmeric Falafel

Preparation time: 5 minutes
Cooking time: 20 minutes
Servings: 3
Ingredients:

- 1 sweet potato
- 1 14-ounce can of chickpeas
- 1/2 cup fresh cilantro
- 1 tsp. turmeric powder.
- 2 garlic cloves.
- 1 tbsp. ground cumin.
- 1 tbsp. ground coriander.
- Juice and passion of 1/2 a lemon.
- 1 tsp. sea salt.

Directions:

1. Ready your oven to 375° F. place the baked or steamed sweet potato into the food mill and pulse for about 10 seconds. Then, add in the staying ingredients into the food processor.
2. Pulse for another 15-20 seconds, up until the chickpeas have been broken down.
3. Then, on a parchment paper-lined baking sheet, dig the falafel mixture with an ice cream scooper and location on the sheet. Just ensure the falafels are no larger than 1-inch thick. Bake for 15-20 minutes.

Nutrition:
Calories: 50 Fat: 10g Proteins: 2.5g

37. Tomato Baked Chickpeas Over Avocado Toast

Preparation time: 15 minutes
Cooking time: 10 minutes
Servings: 2
Ingredients:

- 2 tbsp. olive oil.
- 2 shallots or 1/2 small onion.
- 2 garlic cloves, minced.
- 3 cups diced tomatoes, canned.
- 1 tbsp. dried Italian flavoring.
- 2 (14 ounces) cans chickpeas.
- A handful of plant-based ricotta.
- A handful of parsley or cilantro.
- Pieces of sourdough bread + avocado.

Directions:

1. Prepare oven to 400° F in a large skillet, warm the olive oil over medium heat. Cook shallot and garlic, stirring regularly, for about 7-10 minutes. Include the canned tomatoes, spices, chili flakes, and salt.
2. Lower heat to a simmer for 10 minutes.
3. Stir in the beans and mix well.
4. Cook tomato beans for 25-30 minutes.
5. Pull the baked beans out and spray with the ricotta. Put back in the oven. Continue cooking for another 5 minutes.
6. Leading with the parsley/cilantro and take pleasure in the baked beans as is or over toast!
7. Layer baked beans, onto the toast and after that the avocado. Top with sea salt, black pepper, and capture of lemon.

Nutrition:
Calories: 186 Fat: 25g Proteins: 4g

38. Vegetarian Casserole

Preparation time: 10 minutes
Cooking time: 15 minutes
Servings: 3
Ingredients:

- 1 tbsp olive oil.
- 1 onion carefully sliced.
- 3 garlic cloves, sliced.
- 1 tsp. smoked paprika.
- 1/2 tsp. ground cumin.
- 1 tbsp. dried thyme.
- 3 medium carrots, sliced.
- 2 medium sticks celery.
- 1 red pepper, sliced.
- 1 yellow pepper, sliced.
- 2 x 400 g can tomato.
- 1 vegetable stock.
- 2 courgettes.
- 2 sprigs fresh thyme.
- 250 g cooked lentils.

Directions:

1. Warmth 1 tbsp olive or rapeseed oil in a huge, overwhelming based dish. Include 1 finely slashed onion and cook delicately for 5 – 10 minutes.
2. Include 3 cut garlic cloves, 1 tsp smoked paprika, 1/2 tsp ground cumin, 1 tbsp dried thyme, 3 cut carrots, 2 finely cut celery sticks, 1 hacked red pepper and 1 cleaved yellow pepper and cook for 5 minutes.

39. Spicy Cauliflower Rice

Preparation time: 10 minutes
Cooking time: 22 minutes
Servings: 2
Ingredients:
- 1 cauliflower head, cut into florets
- 1/2 tsp cumin
- 1/2 tsp chili powder
- 6 onion spring, chopped
- 2 jalapenos, chopped
- 4 tbsp olive oil
- 1 zucchini
- 1/2 tsp paprika
- 1/2 tsp garlic powder
- 1/2 tsp cayenne pepper
- 1/2 tsp pepper
- 1/2 tsp salt

40. Overnight Blueberry Nut Pudding

Preparation time: 20 minutes
Cooking time: 0 minute
Servings: 4
Ingredients:
- 1 cup raw almonds
- ½ cup flaxseeds
- ¼ cup frozen blueberries
- 3 cups water
- 2 tbsp. Lemon juice
- 2 tsp. Glucomannan powder
- Optional: ¼ tsp. Vanilla extract
- Optional: ¼ tsp. Cinnamon

Directions:
1. Put the almonds and flaxseeds in a medium-sized heat-safe bowl.

41. Raspberry Chia Bowl

Preparation time: 25 minutes
Cooking time: 0 minute
Servings: 4
Ingredients:
- 1 cup raw cashews
- 1 tbsp. Chia seeds
- ½ cup frozen raspberries
- 3 cups water
- 2 tbsp. Lemon juice
- 1 tsp. Glucomannan powder
- 2 tbsp. Hemp seeds
- Optional: 1 tbsp. Coconut flakes
- Optional: ¼ tsp. Organic lemon zest

Directions:

3. Include two 400 g jars tomatoes, 250 ml vegetable stock, 2 thickly cut courgette and 2 sprigs new thyme and cook for 20 - 25 minutes.
4. Take out the thyme sprigs. Mix in 250 g cooked lentils and take back to a stew. Present with wild and white basmati rice, squash or quinoa.

Nutrition:
Calories: 144 Fat: 10g Proteins: 0.8g

Directions:
1. Preheat the air fryer to 370 F.
2. Crush cauliflower florets into the food processor.
3. Transfer cauliflower rice into the air fryer baking pan and drizzle with half oil.
4. Place pan in the air fryer and cook for 12 minutes, stir halfway through.
5. Heat remaining oil in a small pan over medium heat.
6. Add zucchini and cook for 5-8 minutes.
7. Add onion and jalapenos and cook for 5 minutes.
8. Add spices and stir well. Set aside.
9. Add cauliflower rice in the zucchini mixture and stir well.
10. Serve and enjoy.

Nutrition:
Calories: 254 Fat: 28g Proteins: 4.3g

2. Boil 3 cups of water, then pour it onto the almonds and flaxseeds.
3. Stir in the glucomannan powder and lemon juice, as well as the optional ingredients, if desired.
4. Put the hot almond mixture in a heat-safe blender and process until all ingredients are combined into a smooth mixture.
5. Stir in the blueberries and put mixture into a canning jar or an airtight container. Set aside to cool down.
6. Seal the jar or container once the mixture is cool and refrigerate for a few hours or until the next morning before serving.

Nutrition:
Calories: 233 Fat: 19.7g Proteins: 8.4g

1. Put the raw cashews and chia seeds in a medium-sized heat-safe bowl.
2. Bring the 3 cups of water to a boil, then add it to the ingredients in the bowl.
3. Stir in the glucomannan powder and lemon juice.
4. Put the hot cashew mixture in a heat-safe blender and add the frozen raspberries and hemp seeds.
5. Pour the mixture into a canning jar or an airtight container and let it cool for about 15 minutes.
6. Seal the jar or cover the container after the mixture has cooled down and refrigerate it until the raspberry chia mixture is chilled.
7. Serve the raspberry chia bowl topped with the optional coconut flakes and lemon zest and enjoy!

Nutrition:
Calories: 142 Fat: 10g Proteins: 5.7g

42. Morning Oatmeal Bowl

Preparation time: 15 minutes
Cooking time: 0 minute
Servings: 1
Ingredients:

- 2 tbsp. Hemp seeds
- 2 tbsp. Pumpkin seeds
- 1 tbsp. Ground flax seed
- 1 cup unsweetened almond milk
- 1 tbsp. Lemon juice
- 6 drops stevia
- 1 tbsp. Coconut flakes
- Optional: ¼ tsp. Cinnamon

Directions:

1. Heat the almond milk in a medium-sized saucepan until it's almost boiling.
2. Turn off the heat, add all the remaining ingredients, and stir thoroughly. Note that, if desired, the optional cinnamon can either be incorporated or saved as a topping ingredient.
3. Set the saucepan aside for about 5 minutes to let the mixture cool down.
4. Serve the morning oatmeal cooled or still warm in a bowl and enjoy!

Nutrition:
Calories: 302 Fat: 25g Proteins: 13g

43. Tofu Frittata

Preparation time: 10 minutes
Cooking time: 40 minutes
Servings: 2
Ingredients:

- 1 (12 oz package) extra-firm tofu (drained)
- 1 tbsp. Nutritional yeast
- ¼ cup coconut flour
- ½ cup full-fat coconut milk
- ½ tsp. Glucomannan powder
- 1 tsp. Dried basil
- 1 tsp. Dried oregano
- 1 tsp. Curry powder
- ½ cup button mushrooms (diced)
- ½ medium green onion (diced)
- ¼ cup black olives (seeded, chopped)

Directions:

1. Prep the oven to 350°f/175°c and line a medium-sized casserole dish with parchment paper.
2. Blend tofu, nutritional yeast, coconut flour, coconut milk, glucomannan powder, and spices and season.
3. Process the ingredients into a smooth mixture and transfer the blended ingredients into the casserole dish.
4. Using a spoon, stir the diced mushrooms, green onion, and olives into the tofu mixture and flatten the surface.
5. Transfer the casserole dish to the oven.
6. Bake the tofu frittata for about 40 minutes, until the top of the frittata is golden brown
7. Pull out from the oven and set it aside.

Nutrition:
Calories: 347 Fat: 24g Proteins: 21g

44. Breakfast Crackers

Preparation time: 1 hour
Cooking time: 2 hours
Servings: 16
Ingredients:

- 1 cup flaxseeds
- 1 cup pumpkin seeds
- ½ cup sesame seeds
- 1 cup sunflower seeds
- 3 tbsp. Chia seeds
- 1 tsp. Sea salt
- 1 tsp. baking powder
- 1½ tsp. Glucomannan powder
- 3 cups water

Directions:

1. Prepare oven to 330°f/165°c and line a sheet pan with parchment paper.
2. Put the seeds, salt, baking powder, and glucomannan powder in a food processor and process the ingredients into a mixture with a course, sand-like consistency.
3. Transfer the mixture into a large bowl, add the water, and stir until all ingredients have mixed into a dough.
4. Spread the dough on the sheet pan, pressing it into a ¼-inch thick square.
5. Put the sheet pan into the oven and bake the dough for about 1 hour.
6. Take out from the oven, divide the square into 16 crackers, and set the sheet pan aside for about 30 minutes. Serve with guacamole.

Nutrition:
Calories: 172 Fat: 14g Proteins: 7g

45. Orange French Toast

Preparation time: 5 minutes
Cooking time: 30 minutes
Servings: 8 servings
Ingredients:

- 2 cups of plant milk (unflavored)
- Four tablespoon maple syrup
- 11/2 tablespoon cinnamon
- Salt (optional)
- 1 cup flour (almond)
- 1 tablespoon orange zest
- 8 bread slices

Directions:

1. Turn the oven and heat to 400-degree F afterwards.
2. In a cup, add ingredients and whisk until the batter is smooth.
3. Dip each piece of bread into the paste and permit to soak for a couple of seconds.
4. Put in the pan and cook until lightly browned.

5   Put the toast on the cookie sheet and bake for ten to fifteen minutes in the oven, until it is crispy.

46. Chocolate Chip Coconut Pancakes

Preparation time: 5 minutes
Cooking time: 30 minutes
Servings: 8 servings
Ingredients:

- 1 1/4 cup oats
- 2 teaspoons coconut flakes
- 2 cup plant milk
- 1 1/4 cup maple syrup
- 1 1/3 cup of chocolate chips
- 2 1/4 cups buckwheat flour
- 2 teaspoon baking powder
- 1 teaspoon vanilla essence
- 2 teaspoon flaxseed meal
- Salt (optional)

Directions:

47. Chickpea Omelet

Preparation time: 10 minutes
Cooking time: 30 minutes
Servings: 3 servings
Ingredients:

- 2 cup flour (chickpea)
- 1 1/2 teaspoon onion powder
- 1 1/2 teaspoon garlic powder
- 1/4 teaspoon pepper (white and black)
- 1/3 cup yeast
- 1 teaspoon baking powder

48. Apple-Lemon Bowl

Preparation time: 5 minutes
Cooking time: 15 minutes
Servings: 1-2 servings
Ingredients:

- 6 apples
- 3 tablespoons walnuts
- 7 dates
- Lemon juice
- 1/2 teaspoon cinnamon

49. Breakfast Scramble

Preparation time: 10 minutes
Cooking time: 30 minutes
Servings: 6 servings
Ingredients:

- 1 red onion
- 2 tablespoons soy sauce
- 2 cups sliced mushrooms
- Salt to taste
- 11/2 teaspoon black pepper
- 11/2 teaspoons turmeric
- 1/4 teaspoon cayenne
- 3 cloves garlic

50. Brown Rice Breakfast Pudding

Preparation time: 5 minutes
Cooking time: 15 minutes
Servings: 4 servings
Ingredients:

- 2 cups almond milk

Nutrition:
Calories: 129 Fat: 1.1g Carbohydrates: 21.5g Proteins: 7.9g

1   Put the flaxseed and cook over medium heat until the paste becomes a little moist.
2   Remove seeds.
3   Stir the buckwheat, oats, coconut chips, baking powder and salt with each other in a wide dish.
4   In a large dish, stir together the retained flax water with the sugar, maple syrup, vanilla essence.
5   Transfer the wet mixture to the dry ingredients and shake to combine
6   Place over medium heat the nonstick grill pan.
7   Pour 1/4 cup flour onto the grill pan with each pancake, and scatter gently.
8   Cook for five to six minutes, before the pancakes appear somewhat crispy.

Nutrition:
Calories: 198 Fat: 9.1g Carbohydrates: 11.5g Proteins: 7.9g

- 3 green onions (chopped)

Directions:
1   In a cup, add the chickpea flour and spices.
2   Apply 1 cup of sugar, then stir.
3   Power medium-heat and put the frying pan.
4   On each omelet, add onions and mushrooms in the batter while it heats.
5   Serve your delicious Chickpea Omelet.

Nutrition:
Calories: 399 Fat: 11.1g Carbohydrates: 11.5g Proteins: 7.9g

Directions:
1   Root the apples, then break them into wide bits.
2   In a food cup, put seeds, part of the lime juice, almonds, spices and three-quarters of the apples. Thinly slice until finely ground.
3   Apply the remaining apples and lemon juice and make slices.

Nutrition:
Calories: 249 Fat: 5.1g Carbohydrates: 71.5g Proteins: 7.9g

- 1 red bell pepper
- 1 large head cauliflower
- 1 green bell pepper

Directions:
1   In a small pan, put all vegetables and cook until crispy.
2   Stir in the cauliflower and cook for four to six minutes or until it smooth.
3   Add spices to the pan and cook for another five minutes.

Nutrition:
Calories: 199 Fat: 1.1g Carbohydrates: 14.5g Proteins: 7.9g

- 1 cup dates (chopped)
- 1 apple (chopped)
- Salt to taste
- 1/4 cup almonds (toasted)
- 1 cinnamon stick

- Ground cloves to taste
- 3 cups cooked rice
- 1 tablespoon raisins

Directions:
1 Mix the rice, milk, cinnamon stick, spices and dates in a small saucepan and steam when the paste is heavy.

51. Black Bean and Sweet Potato Hash

Preparation time: 10 minutes
Cooking time: 30 minutes
Servings: 4 servings
Ingredients:
- 1 cup onion (chopped)
- 1/3 Cup vegetable broth
- 2 garlic (minced)
- 1 cup cooked black beans
- 2 teaspoons hot chili powder
- 2 cups chopped sweet potatoes

52. Apple-Walnut Breakfast Bread

Preparation time: 15 minutes
Cooking time: 60 minutes
Servings: 8 servings
Ingredients:
- 11/2 cups apple sauce
- 1/3 cup plant milk
- 2 cups all-purpose flour
- Salt to taste
- 1 teaspoon ground cinnamon
- 1 tablespoon flax seeds mixed with 2 tablespoons warm water
- 3/4 cup brown sugar
- 1 teaspoon baking powder

53. Traditional Spanish Tortilla

Preparation time: 15 minutes
Cooking time: 10 minutes
Servings: 2
Ingredients:
- 3 tablespoons olive oil
- 2 medium potatoes, peeled and diced
- 1/2 white onion, chopped
- 8 tablespoons gram flour
- 8 tablespoons water
- Sea salt and ground black pepper, to flavor
- 1/2 teaspoon Spanish paprika

Directions:

54. Gingerbread Belgian Waffles

Preparation time: 15 minutes
Cooking time: 10 minutes
Servings: 3
Ingredients:
- 1 cup all-purpose flour
- 1 teaspoon baking powder
- 1 tablespoon brown sugar
- 1 teaspoon ground ginger
- 1 cup almond milk
- 1 teaspoon vanilla extract
- 2 olive oil

Directions:

2 Take the cinnamon stick down. Stir in the fruit, raisins, salt and blend.
3 Serve with almonds bread.

Nutrition:
Calories: 299 Fat: 1.1g Carbohydrates: 71.5g Proteins: 7.9g

Directions:
1 Put the onions in a saucepan over medium heat and add the seasoning and mix.
2 Add potatoes and chili flakes, then mix.
3 Cook for around 12 minutes more until the vegetables are cooked thoroughly.
4 Add the green onion, beans, and salt.
5 Cook for more 2 minutes and serve.

Nutrition:
Calories: 239 Fat: 1.1g Carbohydrates: 71.5g Proteins: 7.9g

- 1/2 cup chopped walnuts

Directions:
1 Preheat to 375-degree Fahrenheit.
2 Combine the apple sauce, sugar, milk, and flax mixture in a jar and mix.
3 Combine the flour, baking powder, salt, and cinnamon in a separate bowl.
4 Simply add dry ingredients into the wet ingredients and combine to make slices.
5 Bake for 25 minutes until it becomes light brown.

Nutrition:
Calories: 309 Fat: 9.1g Carbohydrates: 16.5g Proteins: 6.9g

1 Heat 2 tbsp. of the olive oil over a moderate flame. Now, cook the potatoes and onion; cook for about 20 minutes or until tender; reserve.
2 In a mixing bowl, thoroughly merge the flour, water, salt, black pepper and paprika. Add in the potato/onion mixture.
3 Warmth the remaining 1 tablespoon of the olive oil in the same frying pan. Pour 1/2 of the batter into the frying pan. Cook your tortilla for about 11 minutes, turning it once or twice to promote even cooking.
4 Redo with the remaining batter and serve warm.

Nutrition:
Calories: 379 Fat: 20.6g Carbohydrates: 4.2g Proteins: 5.6g

1. Warmth a waffle iron according to the manufacturer's instructions.
2. In a mixing bowl, thoroughly merge the flour, baking powder, brown sugar, ground ginger, almond milk, vanilla extract and olive oil.
3. Beat until everything is well blended.
4. Set 1/3 of the batter into the preheated waffle iron and cook until the waffles are golden and crisp. Repeat with the remaining batter.
5. Serve your waffles with blackberry jam, if desired. Bon appétit!

Nutrition:

Calories: 299 Fat: 12.6g Carbohydrates: 38.5g Proteins: 6.8g

55. Porridge with Banana and Walnuts

Preparation time: 10 minutes
Cooking time: 5 minutes
Servings: 4
Ingredients:

- 1 cup rolled oats
- 1 cup spelt flakes
- 2 cups unsweetened almond milk
- 4 tablespoons agave nectar
- 4 tablespoons walnuts, chopped
- 2 bananas, sliced

Directions:

1. In a nonstick skillet, fry the oats and spelt flakes until fragrant, working in batches.
2. Bring the milk to a boil and attach in the oats, spelt flakes and agave nectar.
3. Set the temperature to a simmer and let it cook for 6 to 7 minutes, stirring occasionally. Top with walnuts and bananas and serve warm. Bon appétit!

Nutrition:
Calories: 389 Fat: 11.6g Carbohydrates: 67.7g Proteins: 16.8g

56. Kid-Friendly Cereal

Preparation time: 10 minutes
Cooking time: 5 minutes
Servings: 5
Ingredients:

- 1 1/2 cups spelt flour
- 1/2 teaspoon baking powder
- 1 teaspoon cinnamon
- 1/2 teaspoon cardamom
- 1/4 teaspoon ground cloves
- 1/2 cup brown sugar
- 1/3 cup almond milk
- 2 teaspoons coconut oil, melted

Directions:

1. Begin by preheating your oven to 350F.
2. In a mixing bowl, thoroughly merge all the dry ingredients. Gradually, pour in the milk and coconut oil and mix to combine well.
3. Fill the pastry bag with the batter. Now, pipe 1/4-inch balls onto parchment-lined cookie sheets.
4. Bake in the warmth oven for about 13 minutes. Serve with your favorite plant-based milk.
5. Bon appétit!

Nutrition:
Calories: 203 Fat: 2.7g Carbohydrates: 39.7g Proteins: 4.4g

57. Classic Breakfast Burrito

Preparation time: 10 minutes
Cooking time: 5 minutes
Servings: 4
Ingredients:

- 1 tablespoon olive oil
- 16 ounces tofu, pressed
- 4 (6-inch) whole-wheat tortillas
- 1 1/2 cups canned chickpeas, drained
- 1 medium-sized avocado, pitted and sliced
- 1 tablespoon lemon juice
- 1 teaspoon garlic, pressed
- 2 bell peppers, sliced
- Sea salt and ground black pepper, to flavor
- 1/2 teaspoon red pepper flakes

Directions:

1. Warmth the olive oil in a frying skillet over medium heat. When it's hot, add the tofu and sauté for about 10 minutes, stirring occasionally to promote even cooking.
2. Divide the fried tofu between warmed tortillas; place the remaining ingredients on your tortillas, roll them up and serve immediately.
3. Bon appétit!

Nutrition:
Calories: 593 Fat: 23.7g. Carbohydrates: 71.7g Proteins: 30.4g

58. Homemade Toast Crunch

Preparation time: 10 minutes
Cooking time: 5 minutes
Servings: 8
Ingredients:

- 1 cup almond flour
- 1 cup coconut flour
- 1/2 cup all-purpose flour
- 1 cup sugar
- 1 teaspoon kosher salt
- 1 teaspoon cardamom
- 1/4 teaspoon grated nutmeg
- 1 tablespoon cinnamon
- 3 tablespoons flax seeds, ground
- 1/2 cup coconut oil, melted
- 8 tablespoons coconut milk

Directions:

1. Begin by preheating the oven to 340F. In a mixing bowl, thoroughly merge all the dry ingredients.
2. Gradually pour in the oil and milk; mix to combine well.
3. Set the dough into a ball and roll out between 2 sheets of a parchment paper. Cut into small squares and prick them with a fork to prevent air bubbles.
4. Bake in the warmth oven for about 15 minutes. Bon appétit!

Nutrition:
Calories: 330 Fat: 25.7g Carbohydrates: 24.7g Proteins: 4.8g

59. Autumn Cinnamon and Apple Oatmeal Cups

Preparation time: 10 minutes
Cooking time: 15 minutes
Servings: 9
Ingredients:

- 2 cups old-fashioned oats
- 1/2 teaspoon baking powder
- 1 teaspoon cinnamon
- 1/4 teaspoon grated nutmeg

- 1/4 teaspoon sea salt
- 1 cup almond milk
- 1/4 cup agave syrup
- 1/2 cup applesauce
- 2 tablespoons coconut oil
- 2 tablespoons peanut butter
- 1 tablespoon chia seeds
- 1 small apple, cored and diced

Directions:

1. Begin by preheating your oven to 360F. Spritz a muffin tin with nonstick cooking oil.
2. In a mixing bowl, thoroughly combine all the ingredients, except for the apples.
3. Fold in the apples and scrape the batter into the prepared muffin tin.
4. Bake your muffins for about 25 minutes or until a toothpick comes out dry and clean. Bon appétit!

Nutrition:
Calories: 232 Fat: 7.1g Carbohydrates: 36.3g Proteins: 7.1g

60. Spicy Vegetable and Chickpea Tofu Scramble

Preparation time: 10 minutes
Cooking time: 15 minutes
Servings: 2
Ingredients:

- 2 tablespoons oil
- 1 bell pepper, seeded and sliced
- 2 tablespoons scallions, chopped
- 6 ounces Cremini button mushrooms, sliced
- 1/2 teaspoon garlic, minced
- 1 jalapeno pepper, seeded and chopped
- 6 ounces firm tofu, pressed
- 1 tablespoon nutritional yeast
- 1/4 teaspoon turmeric powder
- Kala namak and ground black pepper, to taste
- 6 ounces chickpeas, drained

Directions:

1. Warmth the olive oil in a skillet. Once hot, sauté the pepper for about 2 minutes.
2. Now, add in the scallions, mushrooms and continue sautéing for a further 3 minutes or until the mushrooms release the liquid.
3. Then, add in the garlic, jalapeno and tofu and sauté for 5 minutes more, crumbling the tofu with a fork.
4. Add in the nutritional yeast, turmeric, salt, pepper and chickpeas; continue sautéing an additional 2 minutes or until cooked through. Bon appétit!

Nutrition:
Calories: 422 Fat: 23.8g Carbohydrates: 33g Proteins: 25.3g

61. Coconut Granola with Prunes

Preparation time: 30 minutes
Cooking time: 30 minutes
Servings: 10
Ingredients:

- 1/3 cup coconut oil
- 1/2 cup maple syrup
- 1 teaspoon sea salt
- 1/4 teaspoon grated nutmeg
- 1/2 teaspoon cinnamon powder
- 1/2 teaspoon vanilla extract
- 4 cups old-fashioned oats
- 1/2 cup almonds, chopped
- 1/2 cup pecans, chopped
- 1/2 coconut, shredded
- 1 cup prunes, chopped

Directions:

1. Begin by preheating your oven to 260F; line two rimmed baking sheets with a piece of parchment paper.
2. Then, thoroughly combine the coconut oil, maple syrup, salt, nutmeg, cinnamon and vanilla.
3. Gradually add in the oats, almonds, pecans and coconut; toss to coat well.
4. Scatter the mixture out onto the prepared baking sheets.
5. Bake and stir halfway through the cooking time, for about 1 hour or until golden brown.
6. Stir in the prunes and let your granola cool completely before storing. Store in an airtight container.
7. Bon appétit!

Nutrition:
Calories: 420 Fat: 15.2g Carbohydrates: 64.3g Proteins: 11.6g

62. Yogurt Carrot Griddle Cakes

Preparation time: 5 minutes
Cooking time: 25 minutes
Servings: 4
Ingredients:

- 1/2 cup oat flour
- 1/2 teaspoon baking powder
- 1 teaspoon coconut sugar
- 1/4 teaspoon ground allspice
- 1/4 teaspoon vanilla extract
- 1 large-sized carrot, trimmed and grated
- 1 cup banana, mashed
- 1/2 cup coconut yogurt
- 4 teaspoons coconut oil, at room temperature
- 4 tablespoons icing sugar
- 1 teaspoon ground cinnamon

Directions:

1. In a mixing bowl, thoroughly merge the flour, baking powder, coconut sugar, ground allspice and vanilla.
2. Gradually add in the carrot, banana and coconut yogurt.
3. Heat an electric griddle on medium and lightly slick it with the coconut oil.
4. Spoon about 1/4 of the batter onto the preheated griddle. Cook your cake for approximately 3 minutes until the bubbles form; flip it and cook on the other side for 3 minutes longer until browned on the underside.
5. Repeat with the remaining oil and batter. In a small bowl, merge the icing sugar and ground cinnamon.
6. Dust each griddle cake with the cinnamon sugar and serve hot. Enjoy!

Nutrition:

Calories: 254 Fat: 13.1g Carbohydrates: 34g Proteins: 3.4g

63. Raw Morning Pudding

Preparation time: 5 minutes
Cooking time: 25 minutes
Servings: 3
Ingredients:

- 2 1/2 cups almond milk
- 3 tablespoons agave syrup
- 1/2 teaspoon vanilla essence
- A pinch of flaky salt
- A pinch of grated nutmeg
- 1/4 teaspoon ground cardamom
- 1/4 teaspoon crystalized ginger
- 1/2 cup instant oats
- 1/2 cup chia seeds

Directions:

1. Add the milk, agave syrup and spices to a bowl and stir until everything is well incorporated.
2. Fold in the instant oats and chia seeds and stir again to combine well. Spoon the mixture into three jars, cover and place in your refrigerator overnight.
3. On the actual day, stir with a spoon and serve. Bon appétit!

Nutrition:
Calories: 364 Fat: 10.5g Carbohydrates: 61.4g Proteins: 9g

64. Baked Apple Pie Oatmeal

Preparation time: 5 minutes
Cooking time: 45 minutes
Servings: 5
Ingredients:

- 1 1/2 cups old-fashioned oats
- 1/2 teaspoon cinnamon
- 1/4 teaspoon grated nutmeg
- 1/4 teaspoon ground cloves
- 1/4 teaspoon sea salt
- 1 cup oat milk
- 1/2 cup canned applesauce
- 1/4 cup agave syrup
- 1 tablespoon chia seeds
- 1 tablespoon coconut oil
- 1/2 teaspoon almond extract
- 1/3 cup walnuts, chopped

Directions:

1. Start by preheating your oven to 370F. Spritz a casserole dish with a nonstick cooking spray.
2. In a mixing bowl, thoroughly combine all ingredients until everything is well incorporated.
3. Next, spoon the oatmeal mixture into the prepared casserole dish.
4. Bake in the warmth oven for about 35 minutes, until the center is set. Allow it to cool for before cutting and serving. Bon appétit!

Nutrition:
Calories: 345 Fat: 12g Carbohydrates: 51.4g Proteins: 10.8g

65. Easy Omelet with Tomato and Hummus

Preparation time: 5 minutes
Cooking time: 20 minutes
Servings: 2
Ingredients:

- 10 ounces silken tofu, pressed
- 4 tablespoons water
- 1 teaspoon balsamic vinegar
- 3 tablespoons nutritional yeast
- 2 teaspoons arrowroot powder
- 1/2 teaspoon turmeric powder
- Kala namak salt and black pepper
- 2 tablespoons olive oil

Topping:

- 2 tablespoons hummus
- 1 medium tomato, sliced
- 1 teaspoon garlic, minced
- 2 scallions, chopped

Directions:

1. In your blender or food processor, mix the tofu, water, balsamic vinegar, nutritional yeast, arrowroot powder, turmeric powder, salt and black pepper. Processes until you have a smooth and uniform paste.
2. In a nonstick skillet, heat the olive oil until sizzling. Pour in 1/2 of the tofu mixture and spread it with a spatula.
3. Cook for about 6 minutes or until set; flip and cook it for another 3 minutes. Slide the omelet onto a serving plate.
4. Repeat with the remaining batter. Place the topping ingredients over half of each omelet. Fold unfilled half of your omelet over the filling. Bon appétit!

Nutrition:
Calories: 324 Fat: 20.3g Carbohydrates: 18.4g Proteins: 18g

66. Grandma's Breakfast Waffles

Preparation time: 5 minutes
Cooking time: 20 minutes
Servings: 4
Ingredients:

- 1 cup all-purpose flour
- 1/2 cup spelt flour
- 1 teaspoon baking powder
- A pinch of salt
- 1/4 teaspoon ground cinnamon
- 1/4 teaspoon grated nutmeg
- 1/2 teaspoon vanilla extract
- 1 cup almond milk, unsweetened
- 2 tablespoons blackstrap molasses
- 2 tablespoons coconut oil, melted
- 1 tablespoon fresh lime juice

Directions:

1. Warmth a waffle iron according to the manufacturer's instructions.

2. In a mixing bowl, thoroughly merge the flour, baking powder, salt, cinnamon, nutmeg and vanilla extract.
3. In another bowl, mix the liquid ingredients. Then, gradually add in the wet mixture to the dry mixture.
4. Beat until everything is well blended.

67. Crunch Cereal with Almonds
Preparation time: 5 minutes
Cooking time: 20 minutes
Servings: 8
Ingredients:
- 1 cup spelt flakes
- 1 cup old-fashioned oats
- 1 1/2 cups almonds, roughly chopped
- 1/4 cup date syrup
- 7 tablespoons coconut oil, melted

Directions:

68. Grits with Fried Tofu and Avocado
Preparation time: 5 minutes
Cooking time: 30 minutes
Servings: 3
Ingredients:
- 3 teaspoons sesame oil
- 12 ounces firm tofu, cubed
- 1 small white onion, chopped
- 1/2 teaspoon turmeric
- 1/2 teaspoon red pepper flakes
- 3 cups water
- 1 cup stone-ground corn grits
- 1 thyme sprig
- 1 rosemary sprig
- 1 bay leaf
- 1/4 cup nutritional yeast
- 1 medium tomato, sliced
- 1 medium avocado, pitted, peeled and sliced

Directions:

69. Morning Kasha with Mushrooms
Preparation time: 5 minutes
Cooking time: 30 minutes
Servings: 2
Ingredients:
- 1 cup water
- 1/2 cup buckwheat groats, toasted
- Sea salt and ground black pepper, to flavor
- 2 tablespoons olive oil
- 1 cup button mushrooms, sliced
- 2 tablespoons scallions, chopped
- 1 garlic clove, minced
- 1 small avocado, pitted, peeled and sliced
- 1 tablespoon fresh lemon juice

Directions:

70. Tomato Tofu Scramble
Preparation time: 5 minutes
Cooking time: 15 minutes
Servings: 3
Ingredients:
- 2 tablespoons olive oil

5. Set 1/4 of the batter into the preheated waffle iron and cook until the waffles are golden and crisp. Repeat with the remaining batter.
6. Serve your waffles with a fruit compote or coconut cream, if desired. Bon appétit!

Nutrition:
Calories: 316 Fat: 9.9g Carbohydrates: 50.4g Proteins: 8.3g

1. Start by preheating your oven to 330F. Set a baking sheet with parchment paper or a Silpat mat.
2. In a mixing bowl, thoroughly combine all the ingredients until everything is well incorporated. Now, spread the cereal mixture onto the prepared baking sheet.
3. Bake for about 33 minutes or until crunchy. Allow it to cool fully before breaking up into clumps. Serve with a plant-based milk of choice. Bon appétit!

Nutrition:
Calories: 286 Fat: 14.7g Carbohydrates: 34.4g Proteins: 6.6g

1. Warmth the sesame oil in a wok over a moderately high heat. Now, fry your tofu for about 6 minutes.
2. Add in the onion, turmeric and red pepper and continue cooking until the tofu is crisp on all sides and the onion is tender and translucent.
3. In a saucepan, place the water, grits, thyme sprig, rosemary sprig and bay leaf and bring to a boil. Turn the heat to a simmer, secure and let it cook for approximately 20 minutes or until most of the water is absorbed.
4. Add in the nutritional yeast and stir to combine well.
5. Set the grits between serving bowls and top with the fried tofu/onion mixture. Top with tomato and avocado, salt to taste and serve immediately. Bon appétit!

Nutrition:
Calories: 466 Fat: 27g Carbohydrates: 29.4g Proteins: 26.6g

1. In a saucepan, bring the water and buckwheat to a boil. Set the heat to stew and continue to cook for about 20 minutes. Flavor with sea salt and ground black pepper to taste.
2. Then, heat the olive oil in a nonstick skillet, over medium-high heat. Sauté the mushrooms, scallions and garlic for about 4 minutes or until they've softened.
3. Spoon the kasha into two serving bowls: top each serving with the sautéed mushroom mixture.
4. Garnish with avocado, add a few drizzles of fresh lemon juice and serve immediately. Bon appétit!

Nutrition:
Calories: 446 Fat: 29g Carbohydrates: 43.1g Proteins: 9.6g

- 2 garlic cloves, minced
- 12 ounces extra-firm tofu
- 1 medium-sized tomato, diced
- 2 tablespoons nutritional yeast

- Kosher salt and ground black pepper, to flavor
- 1/2 teaspoon red pepper flakes, crushed
- A pinch of seaweed flakes
- 3 tablespoons soy milk, unsweetened
- 1 medium-sized avocado, pitted, peeled and sliced

Directions:

1. Warmth the olive oil in a skillet. Then, sauté the garlic, tofu and tomato, crumbling the tofu with a fork, for about 8 minutes

71. Spring Onion Flat Bread

Preparation time: 10 minutes
Cooking time: 30 minutes
Servings: 3
Ingredients:

- 1 cup all-purpose flour
- 1/2 teaspoon baking powder
- 1/4 teaspoon sea salt
- 1/2 cup warm water
- 1 cup spring onions, chopped
- Sea salt and ground black pepper, to flavor
- 1/2 teaspoon garlic powder
- 1/2 teaspoon cayenne pepper
- 1/2 teaspoon dried thyme
- 3 teaspoons olive oil

72. Chocolate Granola Bars

Preparation time: 10 minutes
Cooking time: 40 minutes
Servings: 12
Ingredients:

- 1 1/3 cups old-fashioned oats
- 1/2 cup fresh dates, pitted and mashed
- 1/2 cup dried cherries
- 1/3 cup agave syrup
- 1/3 cup almond butter, room temperature
- 2 tablespoons coconut oil, melted
- 1/2 cup almonds
- 1/2 cup walnuts
- 1/4 cup pecans
- 1/2 teaspoon allspice

73. Mexican-Style Omelet

Preparation time: 10 minutes
Cooking time: 15 minutes
Servings: 2
Ingredients:

- 2 tablespoons olive oil
- 1 small onion, chopped
- 2 Spanish peppers, deseeded and chopped
- 1/2 cup chickpea flour
- 1/2 cup water
- 3 tablespoons rice milk, unsweetened
- 2 tablespoons nutritional yeast
- Kala namak salt and black pepper, to flavor
- 1/2 teaspoon dried Mexican oregano

74. Breakfast Cranberry and Coconut Crisp

Preparation time: 10 minutes
Cooking time: 30 minutes
Servings: 10
Ingredients:

2. Add in the nutritional yeast, salt, black pepper, red pepper, seaweed flakes and soy milk. Continue to sauté an additional 2 minutes.
3. Divide the scramble between three serving plates, garnish with avocado and serve. Bon appétit!

Nutrition:
Calories: 399 Fat: 29.4g Carbohydrates: 17.3g Proteins: 23.3g

Directions:

1. Thoroughly merge the flour, baking powder and salt in a mixing bowl. Gradually add in the water until the dough comes together.
2. Add in the spring onions and spices and knead the dough one more time.
3. Divide the dough into three balls; flatten each ball to create circles.
4. Heat 1 tsp. of the olive oil in a skillet. Fry the first bread, turning it over to promote even cooking; fry it for about 9 minutes or until golden brown.
5. Redo with the remaining oil and dough. Bon appétit!

Nutrition:
Calories: 219 Fat: 5g Carbohydrates: 36.2g Proteins: 5.3g

- A pinch of salt
- A pinch of grated nutmeg
- 1/2 cup dark chocolate chunks

Directions:

1. In a mixing bowl, thoroughly combine the oats, dates and dried cherries.
2. Add in the agave syrup, almond butter and coconut oil. Stir in the nuts, spices and chocolate.
3. Set the mixture into a lightly greased baking dish. Transfer it to your refrigerator for about 30 minutes.
4. Set into 12 even bars and store in airtight containers. Enjoy!

Nutrition:
Calories: 229 Fat: 13.4g Carbohydrates: 27.9g Proteins: 3.1g

- 1/4 cup salsa

Directions:

1. Warmth the olive oil in a pan. Once hot, sauté the onion and peppers for about 3 minutes until tender and aromatic.
2. Meanwhile, whisk the chickpea flour with the water, milk, nutritional yeast, salt, black pepper and dried Mexican oregano.
3. Then, spill the mixture into the frying pan.
4. Cook for about 4 minutes. Turn it over and cook for an additional 3 to 4 minutes until set. Serve with salsa and enjoy!

Nutrition:
Calories: 329 Fat: 16.4g Carbohydrates: 35.2g Proteins: 12.9g

- 1/2 cup rye flakes
- 1/2 cup rolled oats
- 1/2 cup spelt flakes
- 1/2 cup walnut halves

- 1 cup flaked coconut
- 1/3 teaspoon salt
- 1/2 teaspoon ground cloves
- 1/2 teaspoon ground cardamom
- 1 teaspoon cinnamon
- 1 teaspoon vanilla extract
- 1/3 cup coconut oil
- 1/2 cup maple syrup
- 3 cups cranberries

Directions:

1. Warmth your oven to 340F. Spritz a baking pan with nonstick oil. Arrange the cranberries in the bottom of your pan.
2. Mix the remaining ingredients until everything is well incorporated. Spread the mixture over the cranberries.
3. Bake in the warmth oven for about 35 minutes or until the top is golden brown.
4. Serve at room temperature. Bon appétit!

Nutrition:
Calories: 209 Fat: 13.5g Carbohydrates: 26.2g Proteins: 3.5g

75. Authentic French toast with Strawberries

Preparation time: 10 minutes
Cooking time: 20 minutes
Servings: 5
Ingredients:

- 1 cup coconut milk
- 1/4 teaspoon sea salt
- 1/2 teaspoon ground cinnamon
- 1 teaspoon vanilla extract
- 1/2 teaspoon ground cardamom
- 1 French baguette, sliced
- 2 tablespoons peanut oil
- 2 ounces fresh strawberries, hulled and sliced

- 4 tablespoons confectioners' sugar

Directions:

1. In a mixing bowl, thoroughly merge the milk, salt, cinnamon, vanilla and cardamom.
2. Dip each slice of bread into the milk mixture until well coated on all sides.
3. Preheat the peanut oil in a frying pan over medium-high heat. Cook on each side, until golden brown.
4. Serve the French toast with the strawberries. Bon appétit!

Nutrition:
Calories: 296 Fat: 8.9g Carbohydrates: 45.3g Proteins: 8.9g

76. Easy Breakfast Wafers

Preparation time: 10 minutes
Cooking time: 20 minutes
Servings: 8
Ingredients:

- 1 1/4 cups rice flour
- 1/4 cup tapioca flour
- 1/2 cup potato starch
- 1/2 cup instant oats
- 1 teaspoon baking powder
- 1/2 teaspoon baking soda
- 1 pinch sea salt
- 1/2 teaspoon vanilla essence
- 1/2 teaspoon cinnamon
- 1 1/2 cups oat milk
- 1 teaspoon apple cider vinegar
- 1/3 cup coconut oil, softened
- 1/3 cup maple syrup

Directions:

1. Warmth a waffle iron according to the manufacturer's instructions.
2. In a mixing bowl, thoroughly merge the flour, potato starch, instant oats, baking powder, baking soda, salt, vanilla and cinnamon.
3. Gradually attach in the milk, whisking continuously to avoid lumps. Add in the apple cider vinegar, coconut oil and maple syrup. Whisk again to combine well.
4. Beat until everything is well blended.
5. Set 1/2 cup of the batter into the preheated iron and cook according to manufacturer instructions, until your wafers are golden. Repeat with the remaining batter.
6. Serve with toppings of choice. Bon appétit!

Nutrition:
Calories: 288 Fat: 11.11g Carbohydrates: 45.3g Proteins: 4.4g

77. Traditional Ukrainian Blinis

Preparation time: 10 minutes
Cooking time: 60 minutes
Servings: 6
Ingredients:

- 1 teaspoon yeast
- 1 teaspoon brown sugar
- 3/4 cup oat milk
- 1 cup all-purpose flour
- A pinch of salt
- A pinch of grated nutmeg
- A pinch of ground cloves
- 2 tablespoons olive oil

Directions:

1. Place the yeast, sugar and 2 tablespoons of the lukewarm milk in a small mixing bowl; whisk to combine and let it dissolve and ferment for about 10 minutes.
2. In a mixing bowl, combine the flour with the salt, nutmeg and cloves; add in the yeast mixture and stir to combine well.
3. Set the milk and stir until everything is well incorporated. Let the batter sit at a warm place.
4. Heat a small amount of the oil in a nonstick skillet over a moderate flame. Drop the batter, 1/4 cup at a time, onto the preheated skillet. Fry until bubbles form or about 2 minutes.
5. Flip your blini and continue frying until brown, about 2 minutes more. Repeat with the remaining oil and batter,
6. Serve with toppings of choice. Bon appétit!

Nutrition:
Calories: 138 Fat: 5.7g Carbohydrates: 17.9g Proteins: 3.4g

78. Old-Fashioned Cornbread

Preparation time: 10 minutes
Cooking time: 50 minutes
Servings: 10
Ingredients:

- 2 tablespoons chia seeds
- 1 1/2 cups plain flour
- 1 cup cornmeal
- 1 teaspoon baking powder
- 1 teaspoon baking soda
- 1 teaspoon kosher salt
- 1/3 cup sugar
- 1 1/2 cups oat milk
- 1/3 cup olive oil

Directions:

1. Start by preheating your oven to 420F. Now, spritz a baking pan with a nonstick cooking spray.
2. To make the chia "egg", mix 2 tablespoons of the chia seeds with 4 tablespoons of the water. Stir and let it sit.
3. In a mixing bowl, thoroughly merge the flour, cornmeal, baking powder, baking soda, salt and sugar.
4. Gradually add in the chia "egg", oat milk and olive oil, whisking constantly to avoid lumps. Set the batter into the prepared baking pan.
5. Bake your cornbread for about 25 minutes or until a tester inserted in the middle comes out dry and clean.
6. Let it stand before slicing and serving. Bon appétit!

Nutrition:
Calories: 388 Fat: 23.7g Carbohydrates: 39g Proteins: 4.7g

79. Breakfast Banana Muffins with Pecans

Preparation time: 10 minutes
Cooking time: 30 minutes
Servings: 9
Ingredients:

- 2 ripe bananas
- 4 tablespoons coconut oil, room temperature
- 2 tablespoons maple syrup
- 1/2 cup brown sugar
- 1 1/2 cups all-purpose flour
- 1/2 teaspoon baking powder
- 1/2 teaspoon baking soda
- 1/2 teaspoon salt
- 1/4 teaspoon grated nutmeg
- 1/4 teaspoon ground cardamom
- 1/3 teaspoon ground cinnamon
- 1/2 cup pecans, chopped

Directions:

1. Begin by preheating your oven to 350F. Coat 9-cup muffin tin with muffin liners.
2. In a mixing bowl, press the bananas; stir in the coconut oil, maple syrup and sugar. Beat in the flour, followed by the baking powder, baking soda and spices.
3. Stir to combine well and fold in the pecans. Set the mixture into the prepared muffin tin.
4. Bake your muffins in the preheated oven for about 27 minutes, or until a tester comes out dry and clean. Bon appétit!

Nutrition:
Calories: 258 Fat: 10.7g Carbohydrates: 37.8g Proteins: 3.1g

80. Grandma's Breakfast Gallete

Preparation time: 10 minutes
Cooking time: 30 minutes
Servings: 5
Ingredients:

- 1 cup all-purpose flour
- 1/2 cup oat flour
- 1 teaspoon baking powder
- 1 teaspoon baking soda
- 1/2 teaspoon kosher salt
- 1 teaspoon brown sugar
- 1/4 teaspoon ground allspice
- 1 cup water
- 1/2 cup rice milk
- 2 tablespoons olive oil

Directions:

1. Merge the flour, baking powder, and baking soda, salt, sugar and ground allspice using an electric mixer.
2. Gradually pour in the water, milk and oil and continue mixing until everything is well incorporated.
3. Heat a lightly greased griddle over medium-high temperature.
4. Set 1/4 of the batter into the preheated griddle and cook until your galette is golden and crisp. Repeat with the remaining batter.
5. Serve your galette with a homemade jelly, if desired. Bon appétit!

Nutrition:
Calories: 208 Fat: 7.7g Carbohydrates: 27.7g Proteins: 4.8g

81. Homemade Chocolate Crunch

Preparation ti0me: 10 minutes
Cooking time: 35 minutes
Servings: 9
Ingredients:

- 1/2 cup rye flakes
- 1/2 cup buckwheat flakes
- 1 cup rolled oats
- 1/2 cup pecans, chopped
- 1/2 cup hazelnuts, chopped
- 1 cup coconut, shredded
- 1/2 cup date syrup
- 1 teaspoon vanilla paste
- 1/2 teaspoon pumpkin spice mix
- 1/4 cup coconut oil, softened
- 1/2 cup chocolate chunks

Directions:

1. Start by preheating your oven to 330F. Set a baking sheet with parchment paper or a Silpat mat.
2. In a mixing bowl, thoroughly combine all the ingredients, except for the chocolate chunks. Then, spread the cereal mixture onto the prepared baking sheet.

82. Broiled Grapefruit with Cinnamon Pitas

Preparation time: 5 minutes
Cooking time: 15 minutes
Servings: 4
Ingredients:
- 2 whole-wheat pitas cut into wedges
- 2 tablespoons coconut oil, melted
- 1 tablespoon ground cinnamon
- 2 tablespoons brown sugar
- 1 grapefruit, halved
- 2 tablespoons pure maple syrup or agave

Directions:
1. Preheat the oven to 375°F. Line a baking sheet with parchment paper.

83. Veggie Bowls

Preparation time: 10 minutes
Cooking time: 5 minutes
Servings: 4
Ingredients:
- 1 tbsp. olive oil
- 1-pound asparagus, trimmed and roughly chopped
- 3 cups kale, shredded
- 3 cups Brussels sprouts, shredded
- 1/2 cup hummus
- 1 avocado, peeled, pitted, and sliced

For the dressing:
- 2 tbsp. lemon juice
- 1 garlic clove, minced
- 2 tsp. Dijon mustard

84. Avocado and Apple Smoothie

Preparation time: 5 minutes
Cooking time: 0 minutes
Servings: 2
Ingredients:
- 3 cups spinach
- 1 green apple, cored and chopped
- 1 avocado, peeled, pitted, and chopped
- 3 tbsp. chia seeds
- 1 tsp. maple syrup

85. Pumpkin Pancakes

Preparation time: 5 minutes.
Cooking time: 15 minutes.
Servings: 4
Ingredients:
- 2 cups unsweetened almond milk
- 1 teaspoon apple cider vinegar
- 2(1/2) cups whole-wheat flour
- 2 tablespoons baking powder
- 1/2 teaspoon baking soda
- 1 teaspoon sea salt
- 1 teaspoon pumpkin pie
- 1/2 cup canned pumpkin purée

3. Bake for about 33 minutes or until crunchy. Fold the chocolate chunks into the warm cereal mixture.
4. Allow it to cool fully before breaking up into clumps. Serve with a plant-based milk of choice. Bon appétit!

Nutrition:
Calories: 372 Fat: 19.9g Carbohydrates: 43.7g Proteins: 8.2g

2. Spread pita wedges in a single layer on a baking sheet and brush with melted coconut oil.
3. In a small bowl, merge the cinnamon and brown sugar and sprinkle over the pita wedges.
4. Bake in preheated oven until the wedges are crisp, about 8 minutes. Transfer the pita wedges to a plate and set them aside.
5. Turn the oven to broil. Drip the maple syrup over the top of the grapefruit, if using. Broil until the syrup bubbles and begins to crystallize, 3 to 5 minutes. Serve immediately.

Nutrition:
Calories: 451 Fat: 25.1g Fiber: 9.9g Carbohydrates: 55.4g Proteins: 9.3g

- 2 tbsp. olive oil
- Salt and black pepper to the taste

Directions:
1. Heat a pan put two tablespoon of oil over medium-high heat, and then adds the asparagus and sauté for 5 minutes, stirring often.
2. In a bowl, combine the other two tbsp. oil with the lemon juice, garlic, mustard, salt, and pepper and whisk well.
3. In a salad bowl, combine the asparagus with the kale, sprouts, hummus and avocado and toss gently.
4. Add the dressing, toss, and serve for breakfast.

Nutrition:
Calories: 323 Fat: 21g Fiber: 10.9g Carbohydrates: 24.8g

- 1 banana, frozen and peeled
- 2 cups of coconut water

Directions:
1. In your blender, blend the spinach with the apple and the rest of the ingredients. Pulse and divide into glasses and serve.

Nutrition:
Calories: 168 Fat: 10.1g Fiber: 6g Carbohydrates: 21g Proteins: 2.1g

- 1 cup water
- 1 tablespoon coconut oil

Directions:
1. Dip together the flour, baking powder, baking soda, salt and pumpkin pie spice.
2. In another large bowl, combine the almond milk mixture, pumpkin purée, and water, whisking to mix well.
3. Attach the wet ingredients to the dry ingredients and fold together until the dry ingredients are just moistened. You will still have a few streaks of flour in the bowl.

4. In a nonstick pan or griddle over medium-high heat, melt the coconut oil and swirl to coat. Pour the batter into the pan 1/4 cup at a time and cook until the pancakes are browned, about 5 minutes per side. Serve immediately.

86. Hot Breakfast Couscous Cereal

Preparation time: 10 minutes
Cooking time: 6 minutes
Servings: 4
Ingredients:

- 3/4 cup water
- 1/2 cup couscous
- 1/4 cup squeezed orange juice
- 1 tablespoon maple syrup (optional)
- 1 tablespoon frozen apple juice
- 1 teaspoon finely grated orange zest
- Dash ground cinnamon

87. Banana Quinoa

Preparation time: 10 minutes
Cooking time: 12 minutes
Servings: 4
Ingredients:

- 1 cup quinoa
- 2 cup almond milk
- 1 tsp. vanilla extract
- 1 tsp. maple syrup
- 2 bananas, sliced
- 1/4 tsp. ground cinnamon

Directions:

88. Avocado Milk Shake

Preparation time: 10 minutes
Cooking time: 0 minutes
Servings: 3
Ingredients:

- One avocado, peeled, pitted
- 2 tbsp. maple syrup
- 1/2 tsp. vanilla extract
- 1/2 cup vegetable cream
- 1 cup almond milk
- 1/3 cup ice cubes

89. Creamy Oatmeal with Figs

Preparation time: 10 minutes
Cooking time: 20 minutes
Servings: 5
Ingredients:

- 2 cups oatmeal
- 1 1/2 cup almond milk
- 1 tbsp. butter
- 3 figs, chopped
- 1 tbsp. maple syrup

Directions:

90. Baked Oatmeal with Cinnamon

Preparation time: 10 minutes
Cooking time: 25 minutes
Servings: 4
Ingredients:

- 1 cup oatmeal

Nutrition:
Calories: 420 Fat: 30.3g Fiber: 7.2g Carbohydrates: 35.3g
Proteins: 6.4g

Directions:
1. In a large casserole dish, attach all the ingredients and stir well. Cover in aluminum foil.
2. Transfer the dish to a microwave oven and cook for 5 to 6 minutes on high heat, stirring occasionally to prevent sticking.
3. Let sit for another 1 minute, covered.
4. Divide the cereal among bowls and serve hot.

Nutrition:
Calories: 170 Fat: 17.8g Fiber: 1.5g Carbohydrates: 3.8g
Proteins: 1.5g

1. Pour the almond milk into the saucepan and add quinoa.
2. Close the lid and cook it over medium heat for 12 minutes or until quinoa will absorb all liquid.
3. Then chill the quinoa for 10-15 minutes and place in the serving mason jars.
4. Add maple syrup, vanilla extract, and ground cinnamon.
5. Stir well.
6. Top quinoa with banana and stir it before serving.

Nutrition:
Calories: 279 Fat: 5.3g Fiber: 4.6g Carbohydrates: 48.4 g
Proteins: 10.7g

Directions:
1. Chop the avocado and put it in the food processor.
2. Add the maple syrup, vanilla extract, and heavy cream, almond milk, and ice cubes.
3. Blend the mixture until it smooth.
4. Set the cooked milkshake into the serving glasses.

Nutrition:
Calories: 291 Fat: 22.1g Fiber: 4.5g Carbohydrates: 22g
Proteins: 4.4g

1. Set almond milk into the saucepan. Attach oatmeal and close the lid.
2. Cook the oatmeal for 15 minutes. Then attach sliced figs and maple syrup.
3. Attach butter and mix up the oatmeal well.
4. Cook it for 5 minutes more.
5. Secure the lid and let the cooked breakfast rest for 10 minutes before serving.

Nutrition:
Calories: 222 Fat: 6g Fiber: 4.4g Carbohydrates: 36.5g
Proteins: 7.1g

- 1/3 almond milk
- 1 pear, chopped
- 1 tsp. vanilla extract
- 1 tbsp. Splenda
- 1 tsp. butter

- 1/2 tsp. ground cinnamon
- 1 tbsp. flax seed
- 3 tbsp. water

Directions:
1. Prepare the flax seed and water and then combine the. Let it sit for 5 minutes
2. In the big bowl merge up together oatmeal, milk, flax seed mixture, vanilla extract, Splenda, and ground cinnamon.

91. Almond Chia Porridge

Preparation time: 10 Minutes
Cooking time: 30 Minutes
Servings: 4
Ingredients:
- 3 cups organic almond milk
- 1/3 cup chia seeds, dried
- 1 tsp. vanilla extract
- 1 tbsp. maple syrup
- 1/4 tsp. ground cardamom

Directions:
1. Pour almond milk into the saucepan and bring it to boil.

92. Yogurt with Dates

Preparation time: 10 minutes
Cooking time: 0 minutes
Servings: 4
Ingredients:
- 5 dates, pitted, chopped
- 2 cups coconut yogurt
- 1/2 tsp. of vanilla extract
- 4 pecans, chopped

93. Tahini Shake

Preparation time: 5 minutes
Cooking time: 0 minute
Servings: 1
Ingredients:
- 1 frozen banana
- 2 tablespoons tahini
- 1/8 teaspoon sea salt
- 3/4 teaspoon ground cinnamon
- 1/4 teaspoon vanilla extract, unsweetened
- 2 teaspoons lime juice

94. Cashew-Ginger Soba

Preparation time: 5 Minutes
Cooking time: 20 Minutes
Servings: 2
Ingredients:
For the Bowls
- 7 ounces soba noodles
- 1 carrot
- 1 bell pepper
- 1 cup snow peas, or snap peas make sure to trimmed and sliced in half
- 2 tablespoons chopped scallions
- 1 cup chopped kale, spinach, or lettuce
- 1 avocado, thinly sliced
- 2 tablespoons cashews, chopped

For the Dressing
- 1 tablespoon grated fresh ginger

3. Melt butter and add it to the oatmeal mixture.
4. Then attach chopped pear and stir it well.
5. Transfer the oatmeal mixture to the casserole mold and flatten gently. Cover it with foil and secure edges.
6. Bake the oatmeal at 350F.

Nutrition:
Calories: 151 Fat: 3.9g Fiber: 3.3g Carbohydrates: 23.6g Proteins: 4.9g

2. Then chill the almond milk to room temperature (or appx. For 10-15 minutes).
3. Add vanilla extract, maple syrup, and ground cardamom. Stir well.
4. After this, add chia seeds and stir again.
5. Close the lid and let chia seeds soak the liquid for 20-25 minutes.
6. Transfer the cooked porridge into the serving ramekins.

Nutrition:
Calories: 150 Fat: 7.3g Fiber: 6.1g Carbohydrates: 18g Proteins: 3.7g

Directions:
1. Mix up all ingredients in the blender and blend until smooth.
2. Pour it into the serving cups.

Nutrition:
Calories: 215 Proteins: 8.7g Carbohydrates: 18.5g Fat: 11.5g Fiber: 2.3g

- 1 cup almond milk, unsweetened

Directions:
1. Put the whole shopping list: in the order in a food processor or a blender and then blend for 2 or 3 minutes on high speed until smooth.
2. Pour the smoothie into a glass and serve.

Nutrition:
Calories: 225 Fat: 15g Carbohydrates: 22g Proteins: 6g Fiber: 8g

- 2 tablespoons cashew butter or almond or sunflower seed butter
- 3 tbsp. of rice vinegar or apple cider vinegar
- 2 tablespoons tamari or soy sauce
- 1 teaspoon toasted sesame oil
- 2 to 3 tablespoons water (optional)

Directions:
1. Warm water in a large pot, and then add the noodles. Keep it at a low boil, lowering the heat and adding cold water to keep it just below the boiling point. The soba will take 6 to 7 minutes to cook. Drain it in a colander. You can rinse it with hot or cold water.
2. You can set the vegetables raw, in which case you just must cut them into pieces. If you want to cook them, heat a skillet to a medium-high temperature and brown the carrot with a little water, broth, and

olive oil or sesame oil. Once the carrot has softened slightly, attach the pepper. Then add the peas and shallots, to heat for a minute before turning off the heat.

3. Prepare the dressing by squeezing the grated ginger for its juice, then whipping the whole shopping list together: or by blending in a small blender, adding 2 or 3 tablespoons of water just enough to obtain a creamy consistency. To put aside.

95. Portobello Mushrooms

Preparation time: 5 Minutes
Cooking time: 8 Minutes
Servings: 4
Ingredients:

- 3 tablespoons low-sodium soy sauce
- 1 tablespoon grated ginger
- 3 cloves garlic, peeled and minced
- 3 tablespoons brown rice syrup (optional)
- Freshly ground black pepper, to taste
- 4 large Portobello mushrooms stemmed

Directions:

1. Mix the soy sauce, ginger, garlic, brown rice syrup (if desired) and pepper in a small bowl and toss to combine.

96. Black Bean Pizza

Preparation time: 10 Minutes
Cooking time: 10 Minutes
Servings: 2
Ingredients:

- 2 prebaked pizza crusts
- 1/2 cup Spicy Black Bean Dip
- 1 tomato, thinly sliced
- Pinch freshly ground black pepper
- 1 carrot, grated
- Pinch sea salt
- 1 red onion, thinly sliced
- 1 avocado, sliced

Directions:

1. Preheat the oven to 400F.

97. Pad Thai

Preparation time: 10 Minutes
Cooking time: 10 Minutes
Servings: 2
Ingredients:

- 7 ounces brown rice noodles
- 1 teaspoon olive oil, or one tablespoon vegetable broth or water
- 2 carrots, peeled or scrubbed, and julienned
- 1 cup thinly sliced Napa cabbage, or red cabbage
- 1 red bell pepper, seedless and thinly sliced
- 2 scallions, finely chopped
- 2 to 3 tbsp. fresh mint, finely chopped
- 1 cup bean sprouts
- 1/4 cup Peanut Sauce
- Fresh lime wedges
- 1/4 cup fresh cilantro, finely chopped
- 2 tablespoons roasted peanuts, chopped

4. Arrange your bowl, set with a layer of chopped kale or spinach (for hot noodles) or lettuce (for cold noodles), then the noodles topped with some extra tamari, then the vegetables.
5. Top with the dressing, sliced avocado and a sprinkle of chopped cashews.

Nutrition:
Calories: 392 Fat: 28g Carbohydrates: 31g Fiber: 10g Proteins: 12g

2. Arrange the mushrooms on a baking dish, stem side up. Sprinkle the mushrooms with the marinade and leave to rest for 1 hour.
3. Preheat the grill over medium heat.
4. Drain the liquid from the mushrooms. Don't forget to reserve the marinade.
5. Grill the mushrooms until tender, brushing both sides of the mushrooms with the remaining marinade, about 4 minutes per side.
6. Serve and enjoy your meal!

Nutrition:
Calories: 17 Fat: 0.1g Carbohydrates: 2.3g Proteins: 1.8g Fiber: 0.4g

2. Arrange the two crusts on a large baking sheet. Spread half of the spicy black bean sauce over each pizza crust. Then lay the tomato slices with a pinch of pepper if you like.
3. Sprinkle the grated carrot with sea salt and massage it lightly with your hands. Spread the carrot over the tomato and then add the onion.
4. Put the pizzas in the oven for 10-20 minutes or until they are ready according to your taste.
5. Top the cooked pizzas with sliced avocado and another sprinkle of pepper.

Nutrition:
Calories: 379 Fat: 13g Carbohydrates: 59g Fiber: 15g Proteins: 13g

Directions:

1. In a medium saucepan of boiling water, place the rice noodles and cover them. Let it sit until softened, about 10 minutes. Rinse, drain and set aside to cool.
2. Cook the oil in a large skillet over medium-high heat, sauté the carrots, cabbage and bell pepper until softened, 7 to 8 minutes. Add the shallots, mint and bean sprouts and cook for a minute or two, then remove from the heat.
3. Season the noodles with the vegetables and combine them with the peanut sauce.
4. Transfer to bowls and sprinkle with cilantro and peanuts. Serve with a lime wedge to squeeze onto the plate to increase the flavor.

Nutrition:
Calories: 660 Fat: 19g Carbohydrates: 110g Fiber: 10g Proteins: 15g

98. Ginger Smoothie

Preparation time: 5 minutes
Cooking time: 0 minute
Servings: 1
Ingredients:

- 1 frozen banana
- 2 cups baby spinach
- 2-inch piece of ginger, peeled, chopped
- 1/4 teaspoon cinnamon
- 1/4 teaspoon vanilla extract, unsweetened
- 1/8 teaspoon salt
- 1 scoop vanilla protein powder

99. Black Bean Taco

Preparation time: 15 Minutes
Cooking time: 5 Minutes
Servings: 3
Ingredients:
For the Black Bean Salad

- 1 (14-ounce) can black beans, drained and washed, or 11/2 cups cooked
- 1 cup corn kernels, fresh and blanched, or frozen and thawed
- 1/4 cup fresh cilantro, or parsley, sliced
- Zest and juice of 1 lime
- 1 to 2 teaspoons chili powder
- Pinch sea salt
- 11/2 cups cherry tomatoes halved
- 1 red bell pepper, seeded and chopped
- 2 scallions, chopped

For Tortilla Chips

- 1 large whole-grain tortilla or wrap
- 1 teaspoon olive oil
- Pinch sea salt
- Pinch freshly ground black pepper
- Pinch dried oregano
- Pinch chili powder

For Bowl

100. Kale Bowl

Preparation time: 5 Minutes
Cooking time: 20 Minutes
Servings: 4
Ingredients:

- 1 cup dry quinoa, rinsed
- 2 cups of water
- 6 ounces kale, stemmed and chopped
- One small tomato, chopped
- 3 teaspoons lemon juice or two teaspoons unseasoned rice vinegar
- 1/4 to 1/2 teaspoon salt
- 1/4 teaspoon freshly ground black pepper

Directions:

101. Mushroom Wraps

Preparation time: 15 Minutes
Cooking time: 0 Minutes
Servings: 2
Ingredients:

- 3 tablespoons soy sauce
- 3 tablespoons fresh lemon juice

- 1/8 teaspoon cayenne pepper
- 2 tablespoons lemon juice
- 1 cup of orange juice

Directions:

1. Put the whole shopping list: in the order in a food processor or a blender and then blend for 2 or 3 minutes on high speed until smooth.
2. Pour the smoothie into a glass and serve.

Nutrition:
Calories: 320 Fat: 7g Carbohydrates: 64g Proteins: 10g Fiber: 12g

- 1 cup fresh greens (lettuce, spinach, or whatever you like)
- 3/4 cup cooked quinoa, or brown rice, millet, or other whole grain
- 1/4 cup chopped avocado, or Guacamole
- 1/4 cup Fresh Mango Salsa

Directions:
To Make the Black Bean Salad
1. Merge all the materials together in a large bowl.
To Make Tortilla Chips
2. Brush the tortilla with olive oil, then sprinkle with salt, pepper, oregano, chili powder, and any other toppings you like. Cut it into eight like a pizza. Transfer the tortilla pieces to a small baking sheet lined with parchment paper and place them in the oven or toaster to toast or broil for 3-5 minutes, until golden brown.
To Make the Bowl
3. Place the vegetables in the bowl, garnish with the cooked quinoa and 1/3 of the black bean salad, avocado and salsa.

Nutrition:
Calories: 589 Fat: 14g Carbohydrates: 101g Fiber: 20g Proteins: 21g

1. In a medium saucepan, mix the quinoa and water. Bring to the boil. Cover the pot, reduce the heat to medium-low and simmer for 15-20 minutes until absorbed.
2. Remove from the heat, add the kale to the pot (do not mix) and set aside for about 5 minutes. Add the tomato, lemon juice, salt (if used) and pepper and combine gently.
3. In each of the 4 single-serving containers, collect 1 cup of quinoa. Allow to cool before closing the lids.

Nutrition:
Calories: 183 Fat: 3g Proteins: 8g Carbohydrates: 33g Fiber: 4g

- 1/2 tablespoons toasted sesame oil
- 2 Portobello mushroom caps cut into 1/4-inch strips
- 1 ripe Hass avocado pitted and peeled
- 2 cups fresh baby spinach leaves

- 1 medium red bell pepper cut down into 1/4-inch strips
- 1 ripe tomato, chopped
- Salt and freshly ground black pepper

Directions:
1. Combine the soy sauce, two tablespoons of lemon juice and the oil. Add the Portobello strips, mix to combine and marinate for 1 hour or overnight. Drain the mushrooms and set them aside.
2. Mash the avocado with the remaining spoonful of lemon juice.

102. Coconut Battered Cauliflower

Preparation time: 5 Minutes
Cooking time: 20 Minutes
Servings: 4
Ingredients:
- salt and pepper to taste
- 1 flax egg or one tablespoon flaxseed meal + 3 tablespoon water
- 1 small cauliflower, cut into florets
- 1 teaspoon mixed spice
- 1/2 teaspoon mustard powder
- 2 tablespoons maple syrup
- 1 clove of garlic, minced
- 2 tablespoons soy sauce
- 1/3 cup oats flour
- 1/3 cup plain flour
- 1/3 cup desiccated coconut

Directions:
1. In a mixing bowl, merge the oats, flour, and dried coconut. Season with salt and pepper to taste. To put aside.

103. Warm Salad

Preparation time: 10 Minutes
Cooking time: 15 Minutes
Servings: 4
Ingredients:
- Salt for salting water, plus 1/2 teaspoon (optional)
- 4 red potatoes, quartered
- 1-pound carrots, sliced into 1/4-inch-thick rounds
- 1 tablespoon extra-virgin olive oil (optional)
- 2 tablespoons lime juice
- 2 teaspoons dried dill
- 1/4 teaspoon freshly ground black pepper
- 1 cup Cashew Cream

Directions:
1. Boil the salted water in a large pot, then add the potatoes and cook for 8 minutes.

104. Chickpea and Artichoke Curry

Preparation time: 10 Minutes
Cooking time: 15 Minutes
Servings: 4
Ingredients:
- 1 teaspoon extra-virgin olive oil or two teaspoons vegetable broth
- 1 small onion, diced
- 2 teaspoons minced garlic (2 cloves)
- 1 (14.5-ounce) can of chickpeas, rinsed and drained

3. To assemble the rolls, place a tortilla on a work surface and spread with some avocado puree. Set with a layer of baby spinach leaves. In the lower third of each tortilla, set the strips of soaked mushrooms and a few strips of bell pepper. Splash with the tomato and salt and black pepper to taste. Roll up well and cut in half diagonally. Repeat with the remaining shopping list: and serve.

Nutrition:
Calories: 89 Fat: 8g Carbohydrates: 3g Fiber: 2g Proteins: 4g

2. In another bowl, put the flax egg and add a pinch of salt to taste. To put aside.
3. Season the cauliflower with a mixture of spices and mustard powder.
4. Dry the florets first in the flax egg, then in the flour mixture.
5. Air frying. Place inside the instant crisp Air Fryer, close the air fryer lid and cook at 400 ° F or 15 minutes.
6. Meanwhile, place the maple syrup, garlic and soy sauce in a saucepan and heat over medium heat. Wait for it to boil and turn the heat to low until the sauce has thickened.
7. After 15 minutes, remove the florets from the Instant Crisp Air Fryer and place them in the saucepan.
8. Stir to coat the florets and place them in the Instant Crisp Air Fryer and cook for another 5 minutes.

Nutrition:
Calories: 154 Fat: 2.3g Proteins: 4.69g Carbohydrates: 1.2g

2. Add the carrots and cook for another 8 minutes until the potatoes and carrots are crisp and tender.
3. Drain and return to the pot. Add the olive oil (if using), lime juice, dill, the remaining 1/2 teaspoon of salt (if using) and pepper and mix well to coat well.
4. Divide the vegetables evenly between four single-compartment containers or wide-mouthed glass pint jars and pour 1/4 cup of cream or pesto over the vegetables. Allow to cool before closing the lids.

Nutrition:
Calories: 393 Fat: 15g Proteins: 10g Carbohydrates: 52g Fiber: 9g

- 1 (14.5-ounce) can artichoke hearts, drained and quartered
- 2 teaspoons curry powder
- 1/2 teaspoon ground coriander
- 1/2 teaspoon ground cumin
- 1 (5.4-ounce) can of unsweetened coconut milk

Directions:
1. In a large skillet or saucepan over medium-high heat, heat the olive oil. Add the onion and garlic, then sauté for about 5 to 8 minutes.

2. Add the chickpeas, artichoke hearts, curry powder, coriander and cumin.
3. While adding the shopping list: stir to combine well.
4. Spill the coconut milk into the pot, mix well and bring to a boil. Cover the pot, lower the heat and let it simmer for 10 minutes.

105. Quinoa Nut Berry Porridge

Preparation time: 10 Minutes
Cooking time: 15 Minutes
Servings: 6
Ingredients:

- 1 cup water
- 1/8 tsp. sea salt
- 1 cup white quinoa
- 1 1/2 cup oat milk
- 1 cup mixed berries
- 1/2 cup sliced and toasted pecans
- 1 tbsp. agave

Directions:
1. Put the water and salt in a pot and bring to a boil.

106. Healthy Pancakes with Fruit

Preparation time: 10 Minutes
Cooking time: 5 Minutes
Servings: 6
Ingredients:

- 1 1/2 cups whole wheat flour
- 1/4 cup corn flour
- 1/4 cup oats or oat flour
- 1 tbsp. baking powder
- 1/2 tsp. salt
- 1/4 tsp. ground cinnamon
- 1/8 tsp. ground nutmeg
- 1/8 tsp. ground cardamom
- 1 3/4 cups oat milk
- 1/2 smooth applesauce
- 2 tbsp. agave
- 1 cup strawberries (for topping)
- Maple syrup (for topping)

Directions:

107. Sweet Potato Tofu Hash

Preparation time: 10 Minutes
Cooking time: 15 Minutes
Servings: 4
Ingredients:

- 8oz tofu
- 2 sweet potatoes
- 1 large beet
- 1/4 cup avocado oil
- 3/4 tsp. sea salt
- 3/4 tsp. black pepper
- 1 onion
- 4 cloves of garlic
- 1/2 tsp. chopped thyme
- 1/3 cup dairy-free heavy cream
- 2 green onions

Directions:
1. Drain tofu by wrapping it in several layers of paper towels and leaving it with a weight on top. Then

5. Divide the curry evenly between four wide mouth glass jars or single compartment containers. Allow to cool before closing the lids.

Nutrition:
Calories: 267 Fat: 12g Proteins: 9g Carbohydrates: 36g Fiber: 11g

2. Add quinoa and reduce to medium heat. Secure the pot and simmer for 16 minutes, or until quinoa is softened.
3. Stir in the milk and continue simmering, stirring every few minutes until the milk is thoroughly mixed in and quinoa are thick and soft. This will take around 10 minutes.
4. Take pot off heat and add your berries, nuts, and sweetener to taste.

Nutrition:
Calories: 225 Fat: 15g Carbohydrates: 22g Proteins: 6g Fiber: 8g

1. Warmth the oven to 200F to keep the pancakes warm.
2. Set all dry ingredients in a large bowl until thoroughly mixed.
3. In another bowl, whisk together your milk, applesauce, and agave.
4. Set wet ingredients into dry ingredients and mix until just incorporated.
5. Heat a griddle or pan to medium high heat, then spoon on 1/3 cup of batter per pancake. Cook for 2-4 minutes, or until the top looks bubbly and the edges are solid. Flip and cook for another 2-4 minutes. Repeat. Place already cooked pancakes in a cooking dish in the preheated oven to keep warm.
6. Serve the warm pancakes with your sliced strawberries and maple syrup!

Nutrition:
Calories: 304 Fat: 14g Fiber: 3.8g Carbohydrates: 27.5g Proteins: 17.8g

remove tofu and cut into even pieces about 1/2 inches large.
2. Peel potatoes and beet, then chop both into roughly 1/2 inch chunks.
3. Chop onion and garlic into fine pieces and set aside.
4. Chop green onions and set aside.
5. In a large bowl, mix potato and beet pieces with 1 tbsp. oil, 1/2 tsp. sea salt, and 1/2 tsp. black pepper.
6. Cover bowl with a heat-resistant lid or plate and microwave for 10 minutes, stirring every couple of minutes, until the potatoes and beet are soft.
7. While waiting for the potatoes to soften, heat a large pan over medium-high heat. Add 1 tbsp. olive oil and wait until heated.
8. Add to pan the tofu, soy sauce, 1/4 tsp. sea salt, and 1/4 tsp. black pepper. Leave for 4 minutes (or until one side is darkened) then flip pieces and

brown the other side for another 4 minutes. Transfer to a clean bowl and set to the side.

9. Heat 2 tbsp. olive oil in the hot pan over medium high heat until hot. Attach the onion, garlic, and thyme cook until the onion is translucent and soft, about 6 minutes.

10. Add to pan the microwaved veggies and creamer. Mix, then firmly press it all down into a thick

108. Pear Oatmeal Casserole

Preparation time: 25 Minutes
Cooking time: 15 Minutes
Servings: 6
Ingredients:

- 3 pears
- 2 cups oats
- 3/4 cups crushed pecans
- 1/2 cup raisins
- 1/4 cup maple syrup
- 1 1/2 tsp. ground cinnamon
- 1/2 tsp. ground ginger
- 1/4 tsp. ground nutmeg
- 1/4 tsp. cardamom
- 1/4 tsp. salt
- 2 cups oat milk
- 1 tbsp. vanilla extract
- 2 tbsp. melted coconut oil

109. Avocado Tofu Tacos

Preparation time: 15 minutes
Cooking time: 30 minutes
Servings: 4
Ingredients:

- 14oz firm tofu
- 1/4 tsp. sea salt
- 1/8 tsp. black pepper
- 2 tbsp. chili powder
- 2 cans chopped tomatoes
- 4 tsp. lime juice
- 1 tbsp. maple syrup
- 1 cup cilantro leaves
- 4 green onions
- 1 avocado
- 1 yellow onion
- 5 cloves garlic
- 1/2 cup canned green chilies
- 1/4 cup avocado oil
- 8 taco shells or corn tortillas
- 1 lime sliced, for serving

Directions:

1. Set tofu by wrapping in paper towels and leaving a weight on top. Let drain for at least 20 minutes, then cut in half lengthwise before slicing into strips roughly 1/2 inch wide. Pat on sea salt, pepper, and 1/2 tsp. chili powder.

2. Preheat oven to 500F and line a large baking pan with parchment paper.

110. Sweet Potato Breakfast

Preparation time: 20 minutes
Cooking time: 30 minutes
Servings: 4

pancake shape. Let it sit and cook for 2 minutes, then flip. Keep repeating for 8 minutes or until both sides are nicely browned.

11. Transfer the hash to a plate, then garnish with chopped green onions and serve.

Nutrition:
Calories: 466 Fat: 27g Carbohydrates: 29.4g Proteins: 26.6g

Directions:

1. Preheat oven to 350F. Use a 13x9 inch non-stick baking pan (or grease one with a little oil).

2. Cut pears into thin slices then evenly layer into the bottom of the pan.

3. Using a large mixing bowl, mix the oats, pecans, raisins, brown sugar, cinnamon, nutmeg, cardamom, and salt.

4. In a smaller bowl, whisk the milk, vanilla, and melted butter.

5. Attach the wet ingredients to the dry ingredients and mix thoroughly.

6. Spread the mixture evenly over the pears.

7. Bake for 30-40 minutes, or until firm all the way through. Can be eaten hot or cold and saved in the fridge for several days.

Nutrition:
Calories: 422 Fat: 23.8g Carbohydrates: 33g Proteins: 25.3g

3. Save 1 1/4 cups of juice from the canned tomatoes and discard the rest. Whisk the juice with 1 tbsp. lime juice and maple syrup. Set aside.

4. Chop cilantro, green onion, and avocado. Set aside.

5. Finely chop the onion, garlic, and green chilies then, in a mixing bowl, mix with 2 tbsp. oil, 2 tbsp. chili powder, and the tomatoes. Once mixed, pour onto the baking pan and cook for 20 minutes, then stir around and cook for another 20 minutes. It should be soft and slightly charred.

6. Bring 1 tbsp. oil heat in a large pan on the oven. Carefully add the tofu to the hot oil and cook for 4 minutes on each side, or until browned and crispy. Remove and let drain on paper towels.

7. When the tomatoes are done cooking, move the mix to the pan and add tomato juice and bring to a simmer. Add a pinch of salt and pepper.

8. After 6 minutes, or when the sauce begins to thicken, add tofu and cook another 5 minutes.

9. While waiting, mix 1 tbsp. oil, 1 tsp. lime juice, cilantro, scallions, and avocado. Make sure everything gets evenly covered.

10. Build your taco with a layer of tofu-tomato mixture then the avocado mixture. Garnish with sliced lime and enjoy!

Nutrition:
Calories: 589 Fat: 14g Carbohydrates: 101g Fiber: 20g Proteins: 21g

Ingredients:

- 4 sweet potatoes
- 1/4 cup pecans

- 1/4 cup shredded coconut
- 2 tbsp. maple syrup
- 1 cup canned pineapple pieces
- 2 tsp. cinnamon
- 1/4 tsp. salt

Directions:
1. Preheat oven to 350F.
2. Scrub any dirt off the potatoes before placing on a baking tray and cooking in the oven for an hour until the potatoes are soft. You can test this by inserting a skewer or fork.
3. While the potatoes are in the oven, set the nuts into slices and toast in a pan over medium heat until they brown, but be careful not to burn them.
4. Combine the toasted nuts with the shredded coconut and 1 tbsp. maple syrup. Mix thoroughly and set aside.

111. Apple Pie Pancake

Preparation time: 15 minutes
Cooking time: 30 minutes
Servings: 8
Ingredients:
- 4 apples
- 1/4 cup pecans
- 1 tsp. cinnamon
- 1 tbsp. coconut oil
- 1 tbsp. plus 1 teaspoon fresh lemon juice
- 1 1/2 cups all-purpose flour
- 2 tsp. baking powder
- 1/4 tsp. and 1/8 tsp. salt
- 1 can coconut milk
- 3 tbsp. maple syrup
- 1 1/4 tbsp. lemon juice
- 1 1/2 tsp. vanilla extract

Directions:
1. Preheat the oven to 375F.

112. Scrambled Tofu and Veggies

Preparation time: 5 minutes
Cooking time: 10 minutes
Servings: 4
Ingredients:
- 14 oz. tofu
- 1 bell pepper
- 1 shallot
- 1 1/2 tsp. avocado oil
- 3/4 tsp. sea salt
- 1/8 tsp. turmeric powder
- 1/8 tsp. black pepper
- 2 tbsp. basil leaves

Directions:

113. Healthy Tofu Tacos

Preparation time: 10 minutes
Cooking time: 40 minutes
Servings: 4
Ingredients:
- 1 lb. tofu
- 1 onion
- 1 bell pepper
- 1 sweet potato

5. When potatoes are done cooking, cut along each on lengthwise, but leaving the halves attached.
6. Scoop out the potato, leaving enough attached to the skin to form a solid shell.
7. In a large bowl, add the potato flesh, pineapple pieces, 1 tbsp. maple syrup, cinnamon, and salt. Stir until smooth, trying to mix up any large chunks.
8. Set the potato mixture back into the potato skin, evenly divided and place back on the baking tray.
9. Evenly spread the coconut mixture on top of the potatoes and put tray back in oven for 25 minutes until the coconut starts to brown.
10. Remove and serve!

Nutrition:
Calories: 215 Proteins: 8.7g Carbohydrates: 18.5g Fat: 11.5g Fiber: 2.3g

2. Peel apples and thinly slice, removing the seeds.
3. Chop pecans and add to apples. Add 1/2 tsp. cinnamon and toss to mix.
4. In an oven, melt oil, then cook the apple mixture. After the apples are soft, add 1 tbsp. maple syrup, 1 tsp. lemon juice, and a sprinkle of salt.
5. In a medium bowl, set together the flour, baking powder, 1/4 tsp. salt, and 1/2 tsp. cinnamon.
6. In a new, clean bowl, mix the coconut milk, 2 tbsp. maple syrup, 1 tbsp. lemon juice, and vanilla.
7. Attach wet ingredients to dry ingredients and mix until there are no lumps.
8. Add the batter to the pan with the apples, making sure to cover everything, then put pan in the device and bake for 35 minutes, or until fully cooked and browned.

Nutrition:
Calories: 660 Fat: 19g Carbohydrates: 110g Fiber: 10g Proteins: 15g

1. Wrap tofu in paper towels and let drain with a weight on top. Leave for at least 20 minutes.
2. Using your hands, break apart the tofu into small chunks.
3. Finely chop bell pepper and shallot.
4. Finely chop basil and set aside.
5. In a large pan, add oil over medium-high heat. Add bell pepper and shallot. Cook for about 5 minutes until soft.
6. Add tofu, salt, turmeric, and black pepper. Stir for another 5 or so minutes.
7. Serve and top with chopped basil.

Nutrition:
Calories: 420 Fat: 15.2g Carbohydrates: 64.3g Proteins: 11.6g

- 4 garlic cloves
- 2 tbsp. basil
- 1 tsp. thyme
- 2 tbsp. turmeric powder
- 1/4 cup nutritional yeast
- Salt
- Black pepper
- 4 wheat tortillas

- Salsa (for serving)

Directions:
1. Wrap tofu in paper towels and let drain with a weight on top. Leave for at least 20 minutes.
2. Using your hands, break apart the tofu into small chunks.
3. Preheat oven to 350F.
4. Finely chop onion, bell pepper, and potato.
5. In a large pan, cook onion, bell pepper, and potato for 10 minutes or until the potato become soft. Add water if needed to prevent sticking.
6. Finely chop garlic, basil, and thyme.

114. Spiced Vegan Sausage

Preparation time: 10 minutes
Cooking time: 20 minutes
Servings: 10
Ingredients:
- 1 tsp. sage
- 1/2 tsp. rosemary
- 8 oz. tempeh
- 2 tbsp. maple syrup
- 2 tbsp. whole wheat flour
- 1 tbsp. avocado oil
- 1 tbsp. red miso
- 1/4 tsp. pepper
- 1/8 tsp. red pepper flakes

Directions:
1. Preheat oven to 400F.

115. Multi-Grain Porridge

Preparation time: 5 minutes
Cooking time: 10 minutes
Servings: 4
Ingredients:
- 4 cups water
- 1/2 cup millet
- 1/2 cup white quinoa
- 1/4 cup amaranth
- 1/2 tsp. sea salt
- 1 cup oat milk
- 1/2 tsp. cinnamon powder
- 1/8 tsp. nutmeg powder
- 11/2 cups mixed berries
- 2 tbsp. maple syrup

116. Eggless Vegetable Quiche

Preparation time: 5 minutes
Cooking time: 35 minutes
Servings: 12
Ingredients:
- 2 cups chickpea flour
- 1/4 cup nutritional yeast
- 1 tsp. gluten-free baking powder
- 1/2 tsp. salt
- 1/4 tsp. turmeric powder
- 1/8 tsp. pepper
- 2 cups spinach
- 3 cloves garlic
- 2 cups water

7. Into the pan, add garlic, basil, thyme, and turmeric. Cook few minutes more.
8. Add the crumbled tofu, nutritional yeast, salt, and pepper to the pan.
9. Transfer the pan's contents to a baking tray and spread it evenly. Cook in the oven for 35 minutes, stirring occasionally.
10. Build your burrito by filling the tortilla with the tofu mixture and topping with salsa if desired. Set one end of the tortilla in then roll.
11. Serve with more salsa as a dip!

Nutrition:
Calories: 231 Proteins: 14.9g Carbohydrates: 3.2g Fat: 18g
Fiber: 1.1g

2. Chop sage and rosemary.
3. Crumble tempeh into a food processor and combine with the maple syrup, flour, oil, miso, sage, rosemary, pepper, and red pepper. Pulse until there are no large chunks.
4. Wet your hands to avoid sticking and mold the mixture into evenly sized patties.
5. Grease a large baking pan with parchment paper or non-stick oil and place the patties side by side.
6. Put pan in the oven for 15 minutes, then flip the patties and cook another 15 minutes.
7. Serve however you want!

Nutrition:
Calories: 17 Fat: 0.1g Carbohydrates: 2.3g Proteins: 1.8g
Fiber: 0.4g

Directions:
1. Rinse the millet, quinoa, and amaranth in cold water.
2. Boil water in a large pot. Take pot off heat and mix in millet, quinoa, amaranth, and salt. Cover pot and leave to soak for 8 hours or overnight.
3. When ready to cook, mix in milk, cinnamon, and nutmeg. Place over medium heat and simmer for 10 minutes, stirring every other minute.
4. Stir in fruit and maple syrup then serve. Keep in mind the porridge will thicken as it sits, so feel free to add more milk as needed.

Nutrition:
Calories: 150 Fat: 7.3g Fiber: 6.1g Carbohydrates: 18g
Proteins: 3.7g

- 1 tbsp. avocado oil

Directions:
1. Preheat the oven to 400F. Grease two pie tins with oil.
2. Whisk together the flour, yeast, baking powder, salt, turmeric, and pepper in a large mixing bowl.
3. Finely chop the spinach and garlic.
4. Add the greens and garlic to the dry ingredients, and then combine the water and olive oil to make a runny batter.
5. Divide the batter between the two pie tins and bake for 45 minutes.
6. Let cool, slice, and serve!

Nutrition:

Calories: 379 Fat: 13g Carbohydrates: 59g Fiber: 15g Proteins: 13g

117. Tomato Tofu Bake

Preparation time: 7 minutes
Cooking time: 10 minutes
Servings: 4
Ingredients:

- 2 packages of tofu
- 1 onion
- 1 bell pepper
- 3 cloves garlic
- 1 tbsp. avocado oil
- 1 tbsp. red pepper paste
- 1/4 tsp. turmeric powder
- 2 tbsp. tomato paste
- 1 can diced tomatoes
- 1 cup water
- 1/4 tsp. sea salt

Directions:

1. Set the tofu in paper towels and place a weight on top. Leave to drain for at least 20 minutes before slicing into even pieces.
2. Preheat the oven to 400F.
3. Finely chop the onion, bell pepper, and garlic.
4. Warmth oil in a large frying pan over medium heat. Attach the onion and cook for 5 minutes, or until onions turn transparent.
5. Add bell pepper and garlic. Cook for another 3 minutes.
6. Add red pepper paste and turmeric and cook until incorporated.
7. Add tomato paste stir for a minute or until it starts to darken.
8. Add tomatoes with juice, water, salt, and tofu into the pan and turn heat to medium-high.
9. Once the tomatoes start to bubble, transfer the contents of the pan to an oven-proof baking pan and cover with foil.
10. Cook for 15 minutes, then remove foil and cook for another 15 minutes.
11. Enjoy!

Nutrition:
Calories: 372 Fat: 19.9g Carbohydrates: 43.7g Proteins: 8.2g

118. Summer Fruit Smoothie

Preparation time: 5 minutes
Cooking time: 4 minutes
Servings: 2
Ingredients:

- 1 orange
- 2 cups spinach
- 1/2 cup water
- 2 cups frozen peach pieces
- 1 frozen banana
- 1/2 cup sliced strawberries
- 1 peach
- 1 kiwi
- 1/4 cup cashews
- 4 mint leaves

Directions:

1. Peel the orange and slice into fourths, then add to a blender with spinach and water. Blend on high until smooth.
2. Add the frozen peaches and banana, and then blend on high. If the mixture is too thick, attach a little more water until you get the desired consistency and are smooth.
3. Chop the fresh fruit into slices or cubes. Chop cashews and mint leaves.
4. Spoon out the smoothie into two bowls and top with equally divided chopped fruit and cashews. Sprinkle the mint on top and serve promptly.

Nutrition:
Calories: 219 Fat: 5g Carbohydrates: 36.2g Proteins: 5.3g

119. Quinoa Black Beans Breakfast Bowl

Preparation time: 15 minutes
Cooking time: 25 minutes
Servings: 1
Ingredients:

- 1/4 cup brown quinoa, rinsed well
- Salt to taste
- 1 tbsp. plant-based yogurt
- 1/2 lime, juiced
- 1 tbsp. chopped fresh cilantro
- 1 (5 oz.) can black beans, drained and rinsed
- 1 tbsp. tomato salsa
- 1/4 small avocado, pitted, peeled, and sliced
- 1 radish, shredded
- 1/4 tbsp. pepitas (pumpkin seeds)

Directions:

1. Cook the quinoa with 2 cups of slightly salted water in a medium pot over medium heat or until the liquid absorbs, 15 minutes.
2. Spoon the quinoa into serving bowls and fluff with a fork.
3. In a small bowl, merge the yogurt, lime juice, cilantro, and salt. Divide this mixture on the quinoa and top with beans, salsa, avocado, radishes, and pepitas.
4. Serve immediately.

Nutrition:
Calories: 131 Fat: 3.5g Carbohydrates: 20g Proteins: 6.5g

120. Corn Griddle Cakes with Tofu Mayonnaise

Preparation time: 15 Minutes
Cooking time: 35 Minutes
Servings: 1
Ingredients:

- 1 tbsp. flax seed powder + 3 tbsp. water
- 1 cup water or as needed
- 1 cup yellow cornmeal
- 1 tsp. salt
- 1 tsp. baking powder
- 1 tbsp. olive oil for frying
- 1 cup tofu mayonnaise for serving

Directions:

1. In a medium bowl, merge the flax seed powder with water and allow thickening for 5 minutes to form the flax egg.
2. Mix in the water and then whisk in the cornmeal, salt, and baking powder until soup texture forms but not watery.
3. Warmth a quarter of the olive oil in a griddle pan and pour in a quarter of the batter. Cook until set and golden brown beneath, 3 minutes. Bend the

121. Savory Breakfast Salad

Preparation time: 15-30 Minutes
Cooking time: 20 Minutes
Servings: 1
Ingredients:
For the sweet potatoes:
- Sweet potato: 2 smalls
- Salt and pepper: 1 pinch
- Coconut oil: 1 tbsp.

For the Dressing:
- Lemon juice: 3 tbsp.
- Salt and pepper: 1 pinch each
- Extra virgin olive oil: 1 tbsp.

For the Salad:
- Mixed greens: 4 cups

For **Servings:**

122. Almond Plum Oats Overnight

Preparation time: 15-30 Minutes
Cooking time: 10 Minutes
Servings: 1
Ingredients:
- Rolled oats: 60g
- Plums: 3 ripe and chopped
- Almond milk: 300ml
- Chia seeds: 1 tbsp.
- Nutmeg: a pinch
- Vanilla extract: a few drops
- Whole almonds: 1 tbsp. roughly chopped

123. High Protein Toast

Preparation time: 30 Minutes
Cooking time: 15 Minutes
Servings: 1
Ingredients:
- White bean: 1 drained and rinsed
- Cashew cream: 1/2 cup
- Miso paste: 1 1/2 tbsp.
- Toasted sesame oil: 1 tsp.
- Sesame seeds: 1 tbsp.
- Spring onion: 1 finely sliced
- Lemon: 1 half for the juice and half wedged to serve

124. Hummus Carrot Sandwich

Preparation time: 30 Minutes
Cooking time: 25 Minutes
Servings: 1
Ingredients:
- Chickpeas: 1 cup can drain and rinsed
- Tomato: 1 small sliced
- Cucumber: 1 sliced
- Avocado: 1 sliced

cake and cook the other side until set and golden brown too.
4. Plate the cake and make three more with the remaining oil and batter.
5. Top the cakes with some tofu mayonnaise before serving.

Nutrition:
Calories: 896 Fat: 50.7g Carbohydrates: 91.6g Proteins: 17.3g

- Hummus: 4 tbsp.
- Blueberries: 1 cup
- Ripe avocado: 1 medium
- Fresh chopped parsley
- Hemp seeds: 2 tbsp.

Directions:
1. Take a large skillet and apply gentle heat
2. Add sweet potatoes, coat them with salt and pepper and pour some oil
3. Cook till sweet potatoes turns browns
4. Take a bowl and mix lemon juice, salt, and pepper
5. Add salad, sweet potatoes, and the serving together
6. Mix well, dress and serve

Nutrition:
Calories: 523 Carbohydrates: 57.6g Proteins: 7.5g Fat: 37.6g

Directions:
1. Add oats, nutmeg, vanilla extract, almond milk, and chia seeds to a bowl and mix well
2. Add in cubed plums and cover and place in the fridge for a night
3. Mix the oats well next morning and add into the serving bowl
4. Serve with your favorite toppings

Nutrition:
Calories: 248 Carbohydrates: 24.7g Proteins: 9.5g Fat: 10.8g

- Rye bread: 4 slices toasted

Directions:
1. In a bowl add sesame oil, white beans, miso, cashew cream, and lemon juice and mash using a potato masher
2. Make a spread
3. Spread it on a toast and top with spring onions and sesame seeds
4. Serve with lemon wedges

Nutrition:
Calories: 332 Carbohydrates: 44.5g Proteins: 14.5g Fat: 9.25g

- Cumin: 1 tsp.
- Carrot: 1 cup diced
- Maple syrup: 1 tsp.
- Tahini: 3 tbsp.
- Garlic: 1 clove
- Lemon: 2 tbsp.
- Extra-virgin olive oil: 2 tbsp.
- Salt: as per your need

- Bread slices: 4

Directions:
1. Add carrot to the boiling hot water and boil for 15 minutes
2. Blend boiled carrots, maple syrup, cumin, chickpeas, tahini, olive oil, salt, and garlic together in a blender
3. Add in lemon juice and mix

125. Avocado Miso Chickpeas Toast

Preparation time: 30 Minutes
Cooking time: 15 Minutes
Servings: 1
Ingredients:
- Chickpeas: 400g drained and rinsed
- Avocado: 1 medium
- Toasted sesame oil: 1 tsp.
- White miso paste: 1 1/2 tbsp.
- Sesame seeds: 1 tbsp.
- Spring onion: 1 finely sliced
- Lemon: 1 half for the juice and half wedged to serve
- Rye bread: 4 slices toasted

126. Banana Malt Bread

Preparation time: 30 Minutes
Cooking time: 1 Hour and 20 Minutes
Servings: 1
Ingredients:
- Hot strong black tea: 120ml
- Malt extract: 150g plus extra for brushing
- Bananas: 2 ripe mashed
- Sultanas: 100g
- Pitted dates: 120g chopped
- Plain flour: 250g
- Soft dark brown sugar: 50g
- Baking powder: 2 tsp.

Directions:
1. Preheat the oven to 140C
2. Line the loaf tin with the baking paper

127. Banana Vegan Bread

Preparation time: 30 Minutes
Cooking time: 1 Hour and 15 Minutes
Servings: 1
Ingredients:
- Overripe banana:
- 3 larges mashed
- All-purpose flour: 200 g
- Unsweetened non-dairy milk: 50 ml
- White vinegar: 1/2 tsp.
- Ground flaxseed: 10 g
- Ground cinnamon: 1/4 tsp.
- Granulated sugar: 140 g
- Vanilla: 1/4 tsp.
- Baking powder: 1/4 tsp.
- Baking soda: 1/4 tsp.
- Salt: 1/4 tsp.

128. Berry Compote Pancakes

Preparation time: 30 Minutes
Cooking time: 30 Minutes
Servings: 1

4. Add to the serving bowl and you can refrigerate for up to 5 days
5. In between two bread slices, spread hummus and place 2-3 slices of cucumber, avocado, and tomato and serve

Nutrition:
Calories: 490 Carbohydrates: 53.15g Proteins: 14.1g Fat: 27g

Directions:
1. In a bowl add sesame oil, chickpeas, miso, and lemon juice and mash using a potato masher
2. Roughly crushed avocado in another bowl using a fork
3. Add the avocado to the chickpeas and make a spread
4. Spread it on a toast and top with spring onion and sesame seeds
5. Serve with lemon wedges

Nutrition:
Calories: 456 Carbohydrates: 13.3g Proteins: 14.6g Fat: 26.6g

3. Brew tea and include sultanas and dates to it
4. Take a small pan and heat the malt extract and gradually add sugar to it
5. Stir continuously and let it cook
6. In a bowl, attach flour, salt, and baking powder and now top with sugar extract, fruits, bananas, and tea
7. Mix the batter well and add to the loaf tin
8. Bake the mixture for an hour
9. Brush the bread with extra malt extract and let it cool down before removing from the tin
10. When done, wrap in a foil; it can be consumed for a week

Nutrition:
Calories: 194 Carbohydrates: 43.3g Proteins: 3.4g Fat: 0.3g

- Canola oil: 3 tbsp.
- Chopped walnuts: 1/2 cup

Directions:
1. Warmth the oven to 350F and line the loaf pan with parchment paper
2. Mash bananas using a fork
3. Take a large bowl, and add in mash bananas, canola oil, oat milk, sugar, vinegar, vanilla, and ground flax seed
4. Also whisk in baking powder, cinnamon, flour, and salt
5. Attach batter to the loaf pan and bake for 50 minutes
6. Remove from pan and let it sit for 10 minutes
7. Slice when completely cooled down

Nutrition:
Calories: 240 Carbohydrates: 40.3g Proteins: 2.8g Fat: 8.2g

Ingredients:
- Mixed frozen berries: 200g
- Plain flour: 140 g

- Unsweetened almond milk: 140ml
- Icing sugar: 1 tbsp.
- Lemon juice: 1 tbsp.
- Baking powder: 2 tsp.
- Vanilla extract: a dash
- Salt: a pinch
- Caster sugar: 2 tbsp.
- Vegetable oil: 1/2 tbsp.

Directions:

1. Take a small pan and add berries, lemon juice, and icing sugar

129. Southwest Breakfast Bowl

Preparation time: 30 Minutes
Cooking time: 15 Minutes
Servings: 1
Ingredients:

- Mushrooms: 1 cup sliced
- Chopped cilantro: 1/2 cup
- Chili powder: 1 tsp.
- Red pepper: 1/2 diced
- Zucchini: 1 cup diced
- Green onion: 1/2 cup chopped
- Onion: 1/2 cup
- Vegan sausage: 1 sliced

130. Buckwheat Crepes

Preparation time: 30 Minutes
Cooking time: 25 Minutes
Servings: 1
Ingredients:

- Raw buckwheat flour: 1 cup
- Light coconut milk: 1 and 3/4 cups
- Ground cinnamon: 1/8 tsp.
- Flaxseeds: 3/4 tbsp.
- Melted coconut oil: 1 tbsp.
- Sea salt: a pinch
- Any sweetener: as per your taste

Directions:

131. Chickpeas Spread Sourdough Toast

Preparation time: 30 Minutes
Cooking time: 15 Minutes
Servings: 1
Ingredients:

- Chickpeas: 1 cup rinsed and drained
- Pumpkin puree: 1 cup
- Vegan yogurt: 1/2 cup
- Salt: as per your need

132. Chickpeas with Harissa

Preparation time: 30 Minutes
Cooking time: 20 Minutes
Servings: 1
Ingredients:

- Chickpeas: 1 cup can rinse and drained well
- Onion: 1 small diced
- Cucumber: 1 cup diced
- Tomato: 1 cup diced
- Salt: as per your taste
- Lemon juice: 2 tbsp.

2. Cook the mixture for 10 minutes to give it a saucy texture and set aside
3. Take a bowl and add caster sugar, flour, baking powder, and salt and mix well
4. Add in almond milk and vanilla and combine well to make a batter
5. Take a non-stick pan, and heat 2 teaspoons oil in it and spread it over the whole surface
6. Attach 1/4 cup of the batter to the pan and cook each side for 3-4 minutes
7. Serve with compote

Nutrition:
Calories: 463 Carbohydrates: 92g Proteins: 9.4g Fat: 5.2g

- Garlic powder: 1 tsp.
- Paprika: 1 tsp.
- Cumin: 1/2 tsp.
- Salt and pepper: as per your taste
- Avocado: for topping

Directions:

1. Put everything in a bowl and apply gentle heat until vegetables turn brown
2. Pour some pepper and salt as you like and serve with your favorite toppings

Nutrition:
Calories: 361 Carbohydrates: 31.6g Proteins: 33.8g Fat: 12.2g

1. Take a bowl and add flaxseed, coconut milk, salt, avocado, and cinnamon
2. Mix them all well and fold in the flour
3. Now take a nonstick pan and pour oil and provide gentle heat
4. Add a big spoon of a mixture
5. Cook till it appears bubbly, and then change side
6. Perform the task until all crepes are prepared
7. For enhancing the taste, add the sweetener of your liking

Nutrition:
Calories: 71 Carbohydrates: 8g Proteins: 1g Fat: 3g

- Sourdough: 2 slices toasted

Directions:

1. In a bowl add chickpeas and pumpkin puree and mash using a potato masher
2. Add in salt and yogurt and mix
3. Spread it on a toast and serve

Nutrition:
Calories: 187 Carbohydrates: 33.7g Proteins: 8.45g Fat: 2.5g

- Harissa: 2 tsp.
- Olive oil: 1 tbsp.
- Flat-leaf parsley
- 2 tbsp. chopped

Directions:

1. Add lemon juice, harissa, and olive oil in a bowl and whisk
2. Take a serving bowl and add onion, cucumber, chickpeas, salt and the sauce you made
3. Add parsley from the top and serve

Nutrition:

Calories: 398 Carbohydrates: 55.6g Proteins: 17.8g Fat: 11.8g

133. Quinoa Quiche Cups

Preparation time: 5 minutes
Cooking time: 20 minutes
Servings: 6
Ingredients:

- 1 (10-ounce) bag frozen mixed vegetables, thawed
- 3/4 cup quinoa flour
- 3/4 cup water
- 2 tablespoons freshly squeezed lemon juice
- 1/4 cup nutritional yeast
- 1/4 teaspoon granulated garlic
- 1/4 teaspoon sea salt
- Freshly ground black pepper

Directions:

1. In a medium bowl, mix the vegetables, quinoa flour, water, lemon juice, nutritional yeast, granulated garlic, salt, and pepper to taste until well combined.
2. Spoon the mixture into 6 cupcake molds, dividing it evenly.
3. Place the filled molds into the air fryer and bake at 340F for 20 minutes. Let cool slightly before enjoying.

Nutrition:
Calories: 239 Fat: 2g Carbohydrates: 39g Fiber: 8g Proteins: 16g

134. French toast

Preparation time: 5 minutes
Cooking time: 10 minutes
Servings: 4
Ingredients:

- 1 ripe banana, mashed
- 1/4 cup protein powder
- 1/2 cup plant-based milk
- 2 tablespoons ground flaxseed
- 4 slices whole-grain bread
- Nonstick cooking spray

Directions:

1. In a shallow bowl, mix the banana, protein powder, plant-based milk, and flaxseed until well combined.
2. Set both sides of each slice of bread into the mixture. Lightly spray your pan or air fryer basket with oil and place the slices on it in a single layer. Pour any remaining mixture evenly over the bread.
3. Bring the pan in the air fryer and fry at 370F for 10 minutes, or until golden brown and crispy. Be sure to flip the toast over halfway through. Enjoy warm.

Nutrition:
Calories: 365 Fat: 11g Carbohydrates: 48g Fiber: 9g Proteins: 22g

135. Blueberry-Banana Muffins

Preparation time: 16 minutes
Cooking time: 5 minutes
Servings: 6
Ingredients:

- 1 ripe banana
- 1/2 cup unsweetened plant-based milk
- 1 teaspoon apple cider vinegar
- 1 teaspoon vanilla extract
- 2 tablespoons ground flaxseed
- 2 tablespoons coconut sugar
- 3/4 cup all-purpose flour
- 1 teaspoon baking powder
- 1/2 teaspoon baking soda
- 3/4 cup blueberries

Directions:

1. In a medium bowl, press the banana with a fork. Add the plant-based milk, apple cider vinegar, vanilla, flaxseed, and coconut sugar and mix until well combined. Set aside.
2. In a small bowl set together the flour, baking powder, and baking soda. Add this mixture to the medium bowl and mix until just combined. (Over mixing will make the muffins tough.)
3. Pour the batter into 6 cupcake molds, dividing it evenly. Then divide the blueberries evenly among the muffins and lightly press them into the batter so that they are at least partially submerged.
4. Place the molds in the air fryer and bake at 350°F for 16 minutes. Let cool before enjoying.

Nutrition:
Calories: 248 Fat: 3g Carbohydrates: 50g Fiber: 4g Proteins: 6g

136. Apple Pie Oat Bowls

Preparation time: 12 minutes
Cooking time: 5 minutes
Servings: 2
Ingredients:

- 2/3 cup rolled oats
- 1 apple, cored and diced
- 4 dates, pitted and diced
- 1/2 teaspoon ground cinnamon
- 3/4 cup unsweetened plant-based milk

Directions:

1. In a heatproof cake pan or bowl, combine the oats, apple, dates, and cinnamon. Pour the plant-based milk over the top.
2. Bring the pan in the air fryer and bake at 350F for 6 minutes. Remove the pan and stir until well mixed. Bake for another 6 minutes until the apples are soft.
3. Stir again and let cool slightly before enjoying.

Nutrition:
Calories: 222 Fat: 3g Carbohydrates: 44g Fiber: 7g Proteins: 7g

137. Hash Browns

Preparation time: 12 minutes
Cooking time: 5 minutes
Servings: 4
Ingredients:

- 3 cups frozen shredded potatoes, thawed
- 2 tablespoons nutritional yeast
- 1 teaspoon No-Salt Spice Blend
- 1 tablespoon Aquafina
- 1 Cut 4 pieces of parchment paper, each about 12 inches long.

Directions:

1. In a medium bowl, mix the potatoes, nutritional yeast, spice blend, and Aquafina until well combined. Divide the mixture into 4 equal portions.

2. Place 1 portion onto the middle of a piece of parchment paper. Fold the sides of the paper together and then the top and bottom to create a rectangle about 3 by 5 inches. With the use of your hand, push down on the hash brown to flatten and spread it.

3. Unwrap the parchment paper and use a spatula to carefully transfer the hash brown to the air fryer basket or rack. Repeat step 3 with the remaining portions.

4. Fry the hash browns at 400F for 12 minutes, or until they are lightly browned and crispy. Be sure to flip the hash browns halfway through cooking. Enjoy warm.

Nutrition:
Calories: 92 Fat: 0g Carbohydrates: 20g Fiber: 3g Proteins: 3g

138. Apple-Cinnamon Breakfast Cookies

Preparation time: 5 Minutes
Cooking time: 9 Minutes
Servings: 15
Ingredients:

- 1 medium apple
- 1 cup oat flour
- 2 tablespoons pure maple syrup
- 1/4 cup natural peanut butter
- 1/3 cup raisins
- 1/2 teaspoon ground cinnamon

Directions:

1. Using a grater or a julienne mandolin, carefully grate each side of the apple down to the core.

   Bring the grated apple in a medium bowl along with the oat flour, maple syrup, peanut butter, raisins and cinnamon. Mix until well combined.

2. Scoop out 2-tablespoon balls of dough onto parchment paper. Wet your hand to avoid sticking and flatten each cookie.

3. Bring the cookies from the parchment paper to the air fryer basket or rack and bake at 350F for 9 minutes, or until the edges of the cookies start to brown. Enjoy warm.

Nutrition:
Calories: 384 Fat: 14g Carbohydrates: 58g fiber: 6g Proteins: 11g

139. Cinnamon Rolls

Preparation time: 10 minutes
Cooking time: 8 minutes
Servings: 8
Ingredients:

- 1/2 (16-ounce) frozen pizza dough, thawed
- 1/3 cup Date Paste
- 1/4 cup natural peanut butter
- 1/2 teaspoon ground cinnamon
- Nonstick cooking spray

Directions:

1. With a sheet of parchment paper, set out the pizza dough to about a 6-by-9-inch rectangle.

2. Spread the date paste and peanut butter evenly over the dough, covering it all the way to the edges. Then sprinkle the cinnamon evenly on top.

3. Roll the dough into a log. Set the log into 8 equal pieces, being careful not to compress the dough too much.

4. Place the pieces, spiral-side up, in your air fryer basket or on a flat tray. Let the dough rest and rise.

5. Lightly spray the rolls with cooking spray. Bake at 360F for 8 minutes, or until lightly browned. Serve warm.

Nutrition:
Calories: 270 Fat: 10g Carbohydrates: 39g Fiber: 3g Proteins: 9g

140. Tofu Scramble Brunch Bowls

Preparation time: 10 minutes
Cooking time: 15 minutes
Servings: 2
Ingredients:

- 1 medium russet potato, cut into fries or 1-inch cubes
- 1 bell pepper, seedless and cut into 1-inch strips
- 1/2 (14-ounce) block medium-firm tofu, drained and cubed
- 1 tablespoon nutritional yeast
- 1/2 teaspoon granulated garlic
- 1/2 teaspoon granulated onion
- 1/4 teaspoon ground turmeric
- 1 tablespoon apple cider vinegar

Directions:

1. Place the potato and pepper strips in the air fryer basket or on the rack and fry at 400°F for 10 minutes.

2. Meanwhile, in a small pan, place the tofu, nutritional yeast, granulated garlic, granulated onion, turmeric and apple cider vinegar and stir gently to combine.

3. Add the pan to the air fryer, on a rack above the potatoes and peppers. Continue to fry at 400F for an additional 5 minutes, or until the potatoes are crispy and the tofu is heated through.

4. Detach the food from the air fryer and stir the tofu in the pan. Divide the potatoes and peppers evenly

between 2 bowls. Then spoon half the tofu over each bowl. Serve warm.

Nutrition:

141. PB and J Power Tarts

Preparation time: 15 minutes
Cooking time: 8 minutes
Servings: 2
Ingredients:

- 1/4 cup natural peanut butter
- 1 tablespoon coconut sugar
- 2 tablespoons unsweetened coconut yogurt
- 1/2 cup oat flour
- 2 tablespoons Blueberry Fruit Spread

Directions:

1. Cut 2 pieces of parchment paper, each 8 inches long. On one of the pieces of parchment paper, measure out and draw a 5-by-12-inch rectangle.
2. In a medium bowl, merge the peanut butter, coconut sugar, and coconut yogurt. Once they are combined, mix in the oat flour to form dough.

142. Avocado Bagels

Preparation time: 25 minutes
Cooking time: 10 minutes
Servings: 2
Ingredients:

- 2/3 cup all-purpose flour
- 1/2 teaspoon active dry yeast
- 1/3 cup unsweetened coconut yogurt
- 8 cherry or grape tomatoes
- 1 ripe avocado
- 1 tablespoon freshly squeezed lemon juice
- 2 tablespoons finely chopped red onion
- Freshly ground black pepper

Directions:

1. In a bowl, merge the flour, yeast, and coconut yogurt. Knead into smooth dough.
2. Divide the dough into 2 equal balls. Roll each ball into a 9-inch-long rope. Then form a ring with each rope and press the ends together to connect them, creating 2 bagels.

143. Samosa Rolls

Preparation time: 15 minutes
Cooking time: 15 minutes
Servings: 8
Ingredients:

- 2/3 cup frozen peas, thawed
- 4 scallions, both white and green parts
- 2 cups grated sweet potato
- 2 tablespoons freshly squeezed lemon juice
- 1 teaspoon ground ginger
- 1 teaspoon curry powder
- 1/4 cup chickpea flour
- 1 tablespoon tahini
- 1/3 cup water
- 8 (6-inch) rice paper wrappers

Directions:

Calories: 267 Fat: 6g Carbohydrates: 42g Fiber: 4g Proteins: 15g

3. Place the dough on the blank piece of parchment paper and cover it with the other piece, with the rectangle facing you. Use a rolling pin to evenly set out the dough to fit in the rectangle. Carefully peel off the top piece of parchment paper.
4. Set the dough into 4 equal rectangles, each 3 by 5 inches. Place 1 tablespoon of the fruit spread on 2 of the rectangles and spread it out evenly. Carefully place the remaining 2 rectangles on top of the fruit spread and gently press on the edges with a fork.
5. Place the tarts in the air fryer basket or on the rack and bake at 350F for 8 minutes. Enjoy warm.

Nutrition:
Calories: 358 Fat: 19g Carbohydrates: 38g Fiber: 4g Proteins: 12g

3. Fill a medium bowl with hot (but not boiling) water. Soak the bagels in the water for 1 minute. Then shake off the excess water and move them to the air fryer basket or rack to rise for 15 minutes.
4. Bake at 400F for 5 minutes. Then flip the bagels over and add the tomatoes to the air fryer basket. Bake for an additional 5 minutes.
5. 5 Meanwhile, cut the avocado in half and carefully remove the pit. Scoop the avocado out into a small bowl and mash it with a fork. Mix in the lemon juice and red onion.
6. Let the bagels cool slightly before cutting them in half. Divide the avocado mixture among the 4 bagel halves. Top each bagel half with 2 baked tomatoes and season with pepper.

Nutrition:
Calories: 375 Fat: 16g Carbohydrates: 52g Fiber: 9g Proteins: 9g

1. In a medium bowl, combine the peas, scallions, sweet potato, lemon juice, ginger, curry powder, and chickpea flour. Set aside.
2. In a small bowl, merge the tahini and water until well combined. Pour the mixture onto a plate.
3. Dip both sides of a rice paper wrapper into the tahini mixture. When the wrapper starts to soften up, transfer it to another plate.
4. Spoon one-eighth of the filling (about 1/3 cups) onto the wrapper and wrap it up tightly, burrito style. Place the roll, seam-side down, in the air fryer basket or on the rack, and redo this process.
5. Bake at 350F for 15 minutes until the wrappers are lightly browned and crispy. Flip the rolls over halfway through cooking. Serve warm.

Nutrition:
Calories: 222 Fat: 6g Carbohydrates: 43g Fiber: 5g Proteins: 3g

144. Tofu-Spinach Scramble

Preparation time: 15 minutes
Cooking time: 20 minutes
Servings: 5
Ingredients:

- 1(14-ounce) package water-packed extra-firm tofu
- 1 tsp. extra-virgin olive oil
- 1 small yellow onion, diced
- 3 teaspoons minced garlic (about 3 cloves)
- 3 large celery stalks, chopped
- 2 large carrots, peeled (optional) and chopped
- 1 teaspoon chili powder
- 1/2 teaspoon ground cumin
- 1/2 teaspoon ground turmeric
- 1/2 teaspoon salt (optional)
- 1/4 teaspoon freshly ground black pepper
- 5 cups loosely packed spinach

Directions:

1. Drain the tofu by placing it, wrapped in a paper towel on a plate in the sink. Place a cutting board over the tofu, then set a heavy pot, can, or cookbook on the cutting board. Remove after 10 minutes. (Alternatively, use a tofu press).
2. In a medium bowl, crumble the tofu with your hands or a potato masher.
3. Heat the olive oil. Add the onion, garlic, celery, and carrots, and sauté for 5 minutes until the onion is softened.
4. Add the crumbled tofu, chili powder, cumin, turmeric, salt (if using), and pepper, and continue cooking for 7 to 8 more minutes, stirring frequently, until the tofu begins to brown.
5. Add the spinach and mix well. Cover and reduce the heat to medium. Steam the spinach for 3 minutes.
6. Divide evenly among 5 single-serving containers. Let cool before sealing the lids.

Nutrition:
Calories: 122 Fat: 15g Proteins: 14g Carbohydrates: 54g Fiber: 8g

145. Savory Pancakes

Preparation time: 10 minutes
Cooking time: 15 minutes
Servings: 4
Ingredients:

- 1 cup whole-wheat flour
- 1 teaspoon garlic salt
- 1 teaspoon onion powder
- 1/2 teaspoon baking soda
- 1/4 teaspoon salt
- 1 cup lightly pressed, crumbled soft or firm tofu
- 1/2 cup unsweetened plant-based milk
- 1/4 cup lemon juice
- 2 tablespoons extra-virgin olive oil
- 1/2 cup finely chopped mushrooms
- 1/2 cup finely chopped onion
- 2 cups tightly packed greens (arugula, spinach, or baby kale work great)

Directions:

1. Attach the flour, garlic salt, onion powder, baking soda, and salt. Mix well. In a blender, combine the tofu, plant-based milk, lemon juice, and olive oil. Purée at high speed for 30 seconds.
2. Spill the contents of the blender into the bowl of the dry ingredients and whisk until combined well. Fold in the mushrooms, onion, and greens.

Nutrition:
Calories: 132 Fat: 10g Proteins: 12g Carbohydrates: 44g Fiber: 9g

146. English Muffins with Tofu

Preparation time: 10 minutes
Cooking time: 15 minutes
Servings: 4
Ingredients:

- 2 tablespoons olive oil
- 16 ounces extra-firm tofu
- 1 tablespoon nutritional yeast
- 1/4 teaspoon turmeric powder
- 2 handfuls fresh kale, chopped
- Kosher salt and ground black pepper, to flavor
- 4 English muffins, cut in half
- 4 tablespoons ketchup
- 4 slices vegan cheese

Directions:

1. Warmth the olive oil in a frying skillet over medium heat. When it's hot, add the tofu and sauté for 8 minutes, stirring occasionally to promote even cooking.
2. Add in the nutritional yeast, turmeric and kale and continue sautéing an additional 2 minutes or until the kale wilts. Season with salt and pepper to taste.
3. Meanwhile, toast the English muffins until crisp.
4. To assemble the sandwiches, spread the bottom halves of the English muffins with ketchup; top them with the tofu mixture and vegan cheese; place the bun topper on, close the sandwiches and serve warm.
5. Bon appétit!

Nutrition:
Calories: 150 Fat: 7.3g Fiber: 6.1g Carbohydrates: 18g Proteins: 3.7g

147. Multigrain Hot Cereal with Apricots

Preparation time: 30 minutes
Cooking time: 30 minutes
Servings: 2
Ingredients:

- 1/4 cup long-grain brown rice
- 2 tablespoons rye
- 2 tablespoons millet
- 2 tablespoons wheat berries
- 2 tablespoons barley
- 6 dried apricots, chopped
- 2 cups water

Directions:

1. Clean the grains and soak them in water for 30 minutes until softened and drain.
2. In a saucepan, add the soaked grains, apricots, and 2 cups of water and stir to combine.

148. Cinnamon Pear Oatmeal

Preparation time: 10 minutes
Cooking time: 15 minutes
Servings: 22
Ingredients:

- 3 cups water
- 1 cup steel-cut oats
- 1 tbsp. cinnamon powder
- 1 cup pear, cored and peeled, cubed

149. Hearty Pineapple Oatmeal

Preparation time: 10 minutes
Cooking time: 4-8 hours
Servings: 4
Ingredients:

- 1 cup steel-cut oats
- 4 cups unsweetened almond milk
- 2 medium apples, sliced
- 1 teaspoon coconut oil
- 1 teaspoon cinnamon
- 1/4 teaspoon nutmeg

150. Cool Mushroom Munchies

Preparation time: 5 minutes.
Cooking time: 10 minutes.
Servings: 2
Ingredients:

- 4 Portobello mushroom caps
- 3 tablespoons coconut amines
- 2 tbsp. sesame oil
- 1 tbsp. fresh ginger, minced
- 1 small garlic clove, minced

Directions:

151. Delightful Berry Quinoa Bowl

Preparation time: 5 minutes.
Cooking time: 15 minutes.
Servings: 4
Ingredients:

- 1 cup quinoa
- 2 cups of water
- 1 piece, 2-inch sized cinnamon stick
- 2-3 tablespoons of maple syrup

Flavorful Toppings

- 1/2 cup blueberries, raspberries or strawberries
- 2 tablespoons raisins
- 1 teaspoon lime
- 1/4 teaspoon nutmeg, grated
- 3 tablespoons whipped coconut cream
- 2 tablespoon cashew nuts, chopped

Directions:

152. Cinnamon-Banana French Toast

Preparation time: 5 minutes.
Cooking time: 25 minutes.
Servings: 3

---

3. Cook for about 17 minutes over low heat, or until the liquid is absorbed, stirring periodically.
4. Allow to cool before serving.

Nutrition:
Calories: 242 Fat: 1.6g Carbohydrates: 50.5g Proteins: 6.5g Fiber: 6.1g

Directions:

1. Take a pot and attach the water, oats, cinnamon, and pear and toss well. Bring it to parboil over medium heat.
2. Let it cook for 15 minutes and set into two bowls.
3. Enjoy!

Nutrition:
Calories: 365 Fat: 11g Carbohydrates: 48g Fiber: 9g

- 2 tablespoons maple syrup, unsweetened
- A drizzle of lemon juice

Directions:

1. Attach listed ingredients to a cooking pan and mix well. Cook on very low flame for 8 hours/or on high flame for 4 hours.
2. Gently stir. Attach your desired toppings.
3. Serve and enjoy!

Nutrition:
Calories: 332 Carbohydrates: 44.5g Proteins: 14.5g Fat: 9.25g

1. Set your broiler to low, keeping the rack 6 inches from the heating source. Rinse mushrooms under cold water and transfer them to a baking sheet (top side down).
2. Take a bowl and merge in sesame oil, garlic, coconut aminos, ginger and pour the mixture over the mushrooms tops,
3. Cook for 10 minutes. Serve and enjoy!

Nutrition:
Calories: 248 Fat: 3g Carbohydrates: 50g Fiber: 4g

1. Take a metal strainer and pass your grain through them to strain them well. Rinse the grains under cold water thoroughly.
2. Take a medium-sized saucepan and pour in the water.
3. Add the strained grains and bring the whole mixture to a boil.
4. Add cinnamon sticks and cover the saucepan.
5. Lower the heat and let the mixture parboil for 15 minutes to allow the grain to absorb the liquid. Remove the heat and fluff up the mixture using a fork.
6. Add maple syrup if you want additional flavor. Also, if you are looking to make things a bit more interesting, just add any of the above-mentioned ingredients.

Nutrition:
Calories: 187 Carbohydrates: 33.7g Proteins: 8.45g Fat: 2.5g

Ingredients:

- 1/3 cup coconut milk
- 1/2 cup banana, mashed

- 2 tablespoons bean (chickpea flour)
- 1/2 teaspoon baking powder
- 1/2 teaspoon vanilla paste
- A pinch of sea salt
- 1 tablespoon agave syrup
- 1/2 teaspoon ground allspice
- A pinch of grated nutmeg
- 6 slices day-old sourdough bread
- 2 bananas, sliced
- 2 tablespoons brown sugar
- 1 teaspoon ground cinnamon

Directions:

1. To make the batter, thoroughly combine the coconut milk, mashed banana, bean, baking powder, vanilla, salt, agave syrup, allspice and nutmeg.
2. Set each slice of bread into the batter until well coated on all sides.
3. Preheat an electric griddle to medium heat and lightly oil it with a nonstick cooking spray.
4. Cook each slice of bread on the preheated griddle for about 3 minutes per side until golden brown.
5. Garnish the French toast with the bananas, brown sugar and cinnamon. Bon appétit!

Nutrition:
Calories: 222 Fat: 6g Carbohydrates: 43g Fiber: 5g Proteins: 3g

153. Frosty Hemp and Blackberry Smoothie Bowl

Preparation time: 5 minutes.
Cooking time: 25 minutes.
Servings: 2
Ingredients:
- 2 tablespoons hemp seeds
- 1/2 cup coconut milk
- 1 cup coconut yogurt
- 1 cup blackberries, frozen
- 2 small-sized bananas, frozen
- 4 tablespoons granola

Directions:

1. In your blender, mix all ingredients, trying to keep the liquids at the bottom of the blender to help it break up the fruits.
2. Divide your smoothie between serving bowls.
3. Garnish each bowl with granola and some extra frozen berries, if desired. Serve immediately!

Nutrition:
Calories: 219 Fat: 4.9g Carbohydrates: 38.0g Proteins: 7.2g Fiber: 6.0g

154. Chocolate and Walnut Steel-Cut Oats

Preparation time: 5 minutes
Cooking time: 25 minutes
Servings: 3
Ingredients:
- 2 cups oat milk
- 1/3 cup steel-cut oats
- 1 tablespoon coconut oil
- 1/4 cup coconut sugar
- A pinch of grated nutmeg
- A pinch of flaky sea salt
- 1/4 teaspoon cinnamon powder
- 1/4 teaspoon vanilla extract
- 4 tablespoons cocoa powder
- 1/3 cup English walnut halves

- 4 tablespoons chocolate chips

Directions:

1. Bring the oat milk and oats to a boil over a moderately high heat. Then, turn the heat to low and add in the coconut oil, sugar and spices; let it simmer for about 25 minutes, stirring periodically.
2. Add in the cocoa powder and continue simmering an additional 3 minutes.
3. Spoon the oatmeal into serving bowls. Top each bowl with the walnut halves and chocolate chips.
4. Bon appétit!

Nutrition:
Calories: 660 Fat: 19g Carbohydrates: 110g Fiber: 10g Proteins: 15g

155. Traditional Indian Roti

Preparation time: 5 minutes.
Cooking time: 25 minutes.
Servings: 5
Ingredients:
- 2 cups bread flour
- 1 teaspoon baking powder
- 1/2 teaspoon salt
- 3/4 warm water
- 1 cup vegetable oil, for frying

Directions:

1. Thoroughly merge the flour, baking powder and salt in a mixing bowl. Gradually add in the water until the dough comes together.
2. Divide the dough into five balls; flatten each ball to create circles.
3. Heat the olive oil in a frying pan over a moderately high flame. Fry the first bread, turning it over to promote even cooking; fry it for about 10 minutes or until golden brown.
4. Repeat with the remaining dough. Transfer each roti to a paper towel-lined plate to drain the excess oil.
5. Bon appétit!

Nutrition:
Calories: 339.8 Fat: 19g Carbohydrates: 39g Proteins: 4.3g Fiber: 1g

156. Chocolate Chia Pudding

Preparation time: 5 minutes
Cooking time: 10minutes
Servings: 4
Ingredients:

- 4 tablespoons unsweetened cocoa powder
- 4 tablespoons maple syrup
- 1 2/3 cups coconut milk

- A pinch of grated nutmeg
- A pinch of ground cloves
- 1/2 teaspoon ground cinnamon
- 1/2 cup chia seeds

Directions:
1. Add the cocoa powder, maple syrup, milk and spices to a bowl and stir until everything is well incorporated.

157. Easy Morning Polenta

Preparation time: 5 minutes
Cooking time: 10minutes
Servings: 2
Ingredients:
- 2 cups vegetable broth
- 1/2 cup cornmeal
- 1/2 teaspoon sea salt
- 1/4 tsp. ground black pepper, to taste
- 1/4 teaspoon red pepper flakes, crushed
- 2 tablespoons olive oil

Directions:

158. Mixed Berry and Almond Butter Swirl Bowl

Preparation time: 5 minutes
Cooking time: 10minutes
Servings: 3
Ingredients:
- 1 1/2 cups almond milk
- 2 small bananas
- 2 cups mixed berries, fresh or frozen
- 3 dates, pitted
- 3 scoops hemp protein powder
- 3 tablespoons smooth almond butter
- 2 tablespoons pepitas

Directions:

159. Everyday Oats with Coconut and Strawberries

Preparation time: 5 minutes
Cooking time: 10minutes
Servings: 2
Ingredients:
- 1/2 tablespoon coconut oil
- 1 cup rolled oats
- A pinch of flaky sea salt
- 1/8 teaspoon grated nutmeg
- 1/4 teaspoon cardamom
- 1 tablespoon coconut sugar
- 1 cup coconut milk, sweetened
- 1 cup water
- 2 tablespoons coconut flakes

160. The Best Chocolate Granola Ever

Preparation time: 5 minutes
Cooking time: 60 minutes
Servings: 10
Ingredients:
- 1/2 cup coconut oil
- 1/2 cup agave syrup
- 1 teaspoon vanilla paste
- 3 cups rolled oats
- 1/2 cup hazelnuts, chopped
- 1/2 cup pumpkin seeds

2. Add in the chia seeds and stir again to combine well. Spoon the mixture into four jars, cover and place in your refrigerator overnight.
3. On the actual day, stir with a spoon and serve. Bon appétit!

Nutrition:
Calories: 222 Fat: 3g Carbohydrates: 44g Fiber: 7g

1. In a medium saucepan, set the vegetable broth to boil over medium-high heat. Now, add in the cornmeal, whisking continuously to prevent lumps.
2. Set with salt, black pepper and red pepper.
3. Reduce the heat to a simmer. Continue to simmer, whisking periodically, for about 18 minutes, until the mixture has thickened.
4. Now, spill the olive oil into a saucepan and stir to combine well. Bon appétit!

Nutrition:
Calories: 365 Fat: 11g Carbohydrates: 48g Fiber: 9g

1. In your blender or food processor, mix the almond milk with the bananas, berries and dates.
2. Process until everything is well combined. Divide the smoothie between three bowls.
3. Top each smoothie bowl with almond butter and use a butter knife to swirl the almond butter into the top of each smoothie bowl.
4. Afterwards, garnish each smoothie bowl with pepitas, serve well-chilled and enjoy!

Nutrition:
Calories: 248 Fat: 3g Carbohydrates: 50g Fiber: 4g

- 4 tablespoons fresh strawberries

Directions:
1. In a saucepan, dissolve the coconut oil over a moderate flame. Then, toast the oats for about 3 minutes, stirring continuously.
2. Add in the salt, nutmeg, cardamom, coconut sugar, milk and water; continue to cook for 12 minutes more or until cooked through.
3. Set the mixture into serving bowls, top with coconut flakes and fresh strawberries. Bon appétit!

Nutrition:
Calories: 466 Fat: 27g Carbohydrates: 29.4g Proteins: 26.6g

- 1/2 teaspoon ground cardamom
- 1 teaspoon ground cinnamon
- 1/4 teaspoon ground cloves
- 1 teaspoon Himalayan salt
- 1/2 cup dark chocolate, cut into cubes

Directions:
1. Begin by preheating your oven to 260 F: line two rimmed baking sheets with a piece parchment paper.
2. Then, thoroughly combine the coconut oil, agave syrup and vanilla in a mixing bowl.

3. Gradually add in the oats, hazelnuts, pumpkin seeds and spices; toss to coat well. Set the mixture out onto the prepared baking sheets.
4. Bake in the middle of the oven, stirring halfway through the cooking time, for about 1 hour or until golden brown.

161. Autumn Pumpkin Griddle Cakes

Preparation time: 5 minutes
Cooking time: 30 minutes
Servings: 4
Ingredients:

- 1/2 cup oat flour
- 1/2 cup whole-wheat white flour
- 1 teaspoon baking powder
- 1/4 teaspoon Himalayan salt
- 1 teaspoon sugar
- 1/2 teaspoon ground allspice
- 1/2 teaspoon ground cinnamon
- 1/2 teaspoon crystalized ginger
- 1 teaspoon lemon juice, freshly squeezed
- 1/2 cup almond milk
- 1/2 cup pumpkin puree

162. Cinnamon Semolina Porridge

Preparation time: 5 minutes
Cooking time: 30 minutes
Servings: 3
Ingredients:

- 3 cups almond milk
- 3 tablespoons maple syrup
- 3 teaspoons coconut oil
- 1/4 teaspoon kosher salt
- 1/2 teaspoon ground cinnamon
- 1 1/4 cups semolina

Directions:

163. Decadent Applesauce French Toast

Preparation time: 5 minutes
Cooking time: 15 minutes
Servings: 1
Ingredients:

- 1/4 cup almond milk, sweetened
- 2 tablespoons applesauce, sweetened
- 1/2 teaspoon vanilla paste
- A pinch of salt
- A pinch of grated nutmeg
- 1/4 teaspoon ground cloves
- 1/4 teaspoon ground cinnamon
- 2 slices rustic day-old bread slices
- 1 tablespoon coconut oil
- 1 tablespoon maple syrup

164. Nutty Morning Bread Pudding

Preparation time: 5 minutes
Cooking time: 2 hours 30 minutes
Servings: 6
Ingredients:

- 1 1/2 cups almond milk
- 1/2 cup maple syrup
- 2 tablespoons almond butter
- 1/2 teaspoon vanilla extract
- 1/2 teaspoon almond extract

5. Stir in the dark chocolate and let your granola cool completely before storing. Store in an airtight container.
6. Bon appétit!

Nutrition:
Calories: 194 Carbohydrates: 43.3g Proteins: 3.4g Fat: 0.3g

- 2 tablespoons coconut oil

Directions:

1. In a mixing bowl, thoroughly merge the flour, baking powder, salt, sugar and spices. Gradually add in the lemon juice, milk and pumpkin puree.
2. Heat an electric griddle on medium and lightly slick it with the coconut oil.
3. Cook your cake for approximately 3 minutes until the bubbles form; flip it and cook on the other side for 3 minutes longer until browned on the underside.
4. Repeat with the remaining oil and batter. Serve dusted with cinnamon sugar, if desired. Bon appétit!

Nutrition:
Calories: 365 Fat: 11g Carbohydrates: 48g Fiber: 9g

1. In a saucepan, heat the almond milk, maple syrup, coconut oil, salt and cinnamon over a moderate flame.
2. Once hot, gradually stir in the semolina flour. Turn the heat to a simmer and continue cooking until the porridge reaches your preferred consistency.
3. Brush with your favorite toppings and serve warm. Bon appétit!

Nutrition:
Calories: 122 Fat: 15g Proteins: 14g Carbohydrates: 54g Fiber: 8g

Directions:

1. In a mixing bowl, thoroughly combine the almond milk, applesauce, vanilla, salt, nutmeg, cloves and cinnamon.
2. Set each slice of bread into the custard mixture until well coated on all sides.
3. Preheat the coconut oil in a frying pan over medium-high heat. Cook on each side, until golden brown.
4. Set the French toast with maple syrup and serve immediately. Bon appétit!

Nutrition:
Calories: 122 Fat: 15g Proteins: 14g Carbohydrates: 54g Fiber: 8g

- 1/2 teaspoon ground cinnamon
- 1/2 teaspoon ground cloves
- 1/3 teaspoon kosher salt
- 1/2 cup almonds, roughly chopped
- 4 cups day-old white bread, cubed

Directions:

1. In a mixing bowl, merge the almond milk, maple syrup, almond butter, vanilla extract, almond extract and spices.

2. Add the bread cubes to the custard mixture and stir to combine well. Fold in the almonds and allow it to rest for about 1 hour.
3. Then, spoon the mixture into a lightly oiled casserole dish.
4. Bake in the preheated oven at 350 F for about 1 hour or until the top is golden brown.

165. Moroccan Lentil and Raisin Salad

Preparation time: 5 minutes
Cooking time: 20 minutes
Servings: 4
Ingredients:

- 1 cup red lentils, rinsed
- 1 large carrot, julienned
- 1 Persian cucumber, thinly sliced
- 1 sweet onion, chopped
- 1/2 cup golden raisins
- 1/4 cup fresh mint, snipped
- 1/4 cup fresh basil, snipped
- 1/4 cup extra-virgin olive oil
- 1/4 cup lemon juice, freshly squeezed
- 1 teaspoon grated lemon peel
- 1/2 tsp. fresh ginger root, peeled and minced
- 1/2 teaspoon granulated garlic
- 1 teaspoon ground allspice

166. Pumpkin Oatmeal

Preparation time: 15 minutes
Cooking time: 45 minutes
Servings: 4
Ingredients:

- 2 1/2 cups rolled oats
- 3 tablespoons chia seeds
- 1 teaspoon baking powder
- 1 teaspoon cinnamon
- 1/2 teaspoon cardamom
- 1/2 teaspoon salt
- 1 3/4 cups almond milk
- 1 (15-ounce) can pumpkin
- 1/3 cup maple syrup

167. Cauliflower Oatmeal

Preparation time: 5 minutes
Cooking time: 20 minutes
Servings: 2
Ingredients:

- 1 cup cauliflower rice
- 1/2 cup unsweetened almond milk
- 1/2 teaspoon cinnamon
- 1 tablespoon maple syrup
- 1/2 tablespoon peanut butter
- 1 strawberry, sliced

Directions:

168. Hemp Breakfast Cookies

Preparation time: 15 minutes
Cooking time: 15 minutes
Servings: 6
Ingredients:

- 3 cups almond flour
- 1 cup dried dates, pitted
- 1/2 cup hemp seeds

5. Place the bread pudding on a wire rack for 10 minutes before slicing and serving. Bon appétit!

Nutrition:
Calories: 278 Fat: 8.9g Carbohydrates: 41.9g Proteins: 12.0g Fiber: 11.4g

- Sea salt and ground black pepper

Directions:
1. In a large-sized saucepan, bring 3 cups of the water and 1 cup of the lentils to a boil.
2. Immediately turn the heat to a parboil and continue to cook your lentils for a further 15 to 17 minutes or until they've softened but are not mushy yet. Drain and let it cool completely.
3. Transfer the lentils to a salad bowl; add in the carrot, cucumber and sweet onion. Then, add the raisins, mint and basil to your salad.
4. In a small mixing dish, whisk the olive oil, lemon juice, lemon peel, ginger, granulated garlic, allspice, salt and black pepper.
5. Dress your salad and serve well-chilled. Bon appétit!

Nutrition:
Calories: 523 Carbohydrates: 57.6g Proteins: 7.5g Fat: 37.6g

- 1 tablespoon pure vanilla extract

Directions:
1. Preheat your oven to 350F.
2. Layer an 8x8-inch baking dish with wax paper.
3. Mix oats with salt, cardamom, cinnamon, baking powder, and chia seeds in a bowl.
4. Now, stir the rest of the oatmeal ingredients and mix it well until smooth.
5. Spread this batter in the baking dish and bake for 45 minutes.
6. Allow the oatmeal to cool and serve.

Nutrition:
Calories: 284 Fat: 7.9g Carbohydrates: 31g Fiber: 3.6g

1. Mix milk with cauliflower rice, honey and cinnamon in a saucepan.
2. Cook the rice mixture to a boil then reduce the heat to low.
3. Now cook the mixture for 10 minutes on a simmer.
4. Allow the oatmeal to cool, then garnish it with a strawberry.
5. Serve.

Nutrition:
Calories: 332 Carbohydrates: 44.5g Proteins: 14.5g Fat: 9.25g

- 1 cup almond milk

Directions:
1. Mix almond milk with hemp seeds and dates in a bowl and leave for 1 hour.
2. Blend almond flour with the rest of the ingredients and milk mixture in a mixer until it makes a smooth dough.

3. Preheat your oven to 350F.
4. Set the dough into 9 portions and shape each into a cookie.
5. Place these cookies in a baking sheet, lined with wax paper.

169. Zucchini Oatmeal

Preparation time: 5 minutes
Cooking time: 4 minutes
Servings: 4
Ingredients:

- 2 cups rolled oats
- 6 tablespoons pea protein
- 2 teaspoons cinnamon
- 1 teaspoon nutmeg
- 2 1/4 cups almond milk
- 1 cup zucchini, grated
- 1/4 cup maple syrup
- 1 teaspoon vanilla extract

Toppings

- Banana
- Nuts
- Seeds

170. Peanut Butter Muffins

Preparation time: 15 minutes
Cooking time: 27 minutes
Servings: 6
Ingredients:

- 3/4 cup oat flour
- 1/4 cup coconut sugar
- 2 tablespoons pea protein powder
- 1 tablespoon baking powder
- 2 teaspoons baking soda
- 3 large bananas, mashed
- 1/2 cup peanut butter
- 2 tablespoons flaxseed
- 1/2 cup water
- 1/2 cup almond milk

171. Chocolate Zucchini Bread

Preparation time: 15 minutes
Cooking time: 55 minutes
Servings: 6
Ingredients:

- 11/4 cup whole wheat flour
- 3/4 cup coconut sugar
- 1/2 cup raw cacao powder
- 3 teaspoons baking powder
- 2 teaspoons baking soda
- 1 cup zucchini, shredded
- 1/2 cup almond milk
- 1/3 cup unsweetened applesauce
- 1/3 cup coconut oil, melted
- 2 teaspoons vanilla extract
- 2/3 cup sugar-free chocolate chip

Directions:

6. Bake the cookies for 15 minutes in the oven and flip them once cooked halfway through.
7. Serve.

Nutrition:
Calories: 92 Fat: 0g Carbohydrates: 20g

- Sugar-free chocolate chips
- 1 teaspoon coconut oil

Directions:

1. Sauté oats with coconut oil in an Instant Pot for 2 minutes on Sauté mode.
2. Set in the rest of the ingredients, cover and seal its lid.
3. Cook for 2 minutes on high pressure.
4. When done, release all the pressure and remove the lid.
5. Allow the oatmeal to cool and garnish with desired toppings.
6. Serve.

Nutrition:
Calories: 150 Fat: 7.3g Fiber: 6.1g Carbohydrates: 18g
Proteins: 3.7g

- 1 teaspoon vanilla extract

Directions:

1. Preheat the oven to 350F and layer two muffin trays with cupcake liners.
2. Soak flaxseed with 1/2 cup water in a bowl for 5 minutes.
3. Mix mashed banana with milk, peanut butter and flaxseed mixture in a large bowl.
4. Now, stir it with the rest of the muffin ingredients and mix well evenly.
5. Divide the prepared batter into the muffin tray and bake for 27 minutes.
6. Allow the muffins to cool and serve.

Nutrition:
Calories: 395 Fat: 9.5g Carbohydrates: 34g Fiber: 0.4g

1. Preheat your oven to 350F and layer a 9-inch loaf pan with wax paper.
2. Dry the shredded zucchini and keep it aside.
3. Mix flour with baking soda, baking powder, cacao powder, coconut sugar and flour in a bowl.
4. Stir it with vanilla, applesauce, milk, and peanut butter, then mix until smooth.
5. Fold in sugar-free chocolate chips and zucchini shreds.
6. Spread this batter in the prepared loaf pan.
7. Bake this bread for 55 minutes in the oven.
8. Allow the bread to cool, then slice.
9. Serve.

Nutrition:
Calories: 375 Fat: 16g Carbohydrates: 52g Fiber: 9g Proteins: 9g

172. Roasted Tomatoes

Preparation time: 5 minutes
Cooking time: 25 minutes
Servings: 3
Ingredients:

- 3 1/2 cups halved cherry tomatoes
- 3 teaspoons minced garlic
- 1/2 teaspoon salt
- 1 tablespoon minced basil
- 1/4 teaspoon red chili flakes
- 1/2 teaspoon balsamic vinegar
- 1 tablespoon olive oil
- 1 tablespoon minced parsley

Directions:
1. Switch on the oven, then set it to 375F and let it preheat.
2. Take a large bowl, place all the ingredients in it and then toss until mixed.
3. Take a baking sheet, line it with a parchment sheet, spread tomato mixture, and then bake for 25 minutes until roasted.
4. Serve straight away.

Nutrition:
Calories: 202 Fat: 22g Carbohydrates: 5g Proteins: 34g

173. Vegan Mushroom Pho

Preparation time: 10 minutes
Cooking time: 30 minutes
Servings: 3
Ingredients:

- 14-oz. block firm tofu, drained
- 6 cups vegetable broth
- 3 green onions, thinly sliced
- 1 tsp. minced ginger
- 1 tbsp. olive oil
- 3 cups mushrooms, sliced
- 2 tbsp. hoisin sauce
- 1 tbsp. sesame oil
- 2 cups gluten-free rice noodles
- 1 cup raw bean sprouts
- 1 cup matchstick carrots
- 1 cup bok choy, chopped
- 1 cup cabbage, chopped
- ¼ tsp Salt
- ¼ tsp pepper

Directions:
1. Cut the tofu into ¼-inch cubes and set it aside.
2. Take a deep saucepan and heat the vegetable broth, green onions, and ginger over medium high heat.
3. Boil for 1 minute before reducing the heat to low; then cover the saucepan with a lid and let it simmer for 20 minutes.
4. Take another frying pan and heat the olive oil in it over medium-high heat.
5. Add the cut-up mushrooms to the frying pan and cook until they are tender, for about 5 minutes.
6. Add the tofu, hoisin sauce, and sesame oil to the mushrooms.
7. Heat until the sauce thickens (around 5 minutes) and remove the frying pan from the heat.

8 Prepare the gluten-free rice noodles according to the package instructions.

9 Top the rice noodles with a scoop of the tofu mushroom mixture, a generous amount of broth, and the bean sprouts.

174. Ruby Red Root Beet Burger

Preparation time: 20 minutes
Cooking time: 21 minutes
Servings: 6
Ingredients:
- 1 cup dry chickpeas
- ½ cup dry quinoa
- 2 large beets
- 2 tbsp. olive oil
- 2 tbsp. garlic powder
- 1 tbsp. balsamic vinegar
- 2 tsp. onion powder
- 1 tsp. fresh parsley, chopped
- ¼ tsp Salt
- ¼ tsp pepper
- 2 cups spinach, fresh or frozen, washed and dried
- 6 buns or wraps of choice

Directions:
1 Preheat the oven to 400°F.
2 Peel and dice the beets into ¼-inch or smaller cubes, put them in a bowl, and coat the cubes with 1 tablespoon of olive oil and the onion powder.
3 Spread the beet cubes out across a baking pan and put the pan in the oven.

175. Creamy Squash Pizza

Preparation time: 25 minutes
Cooking time: 21 minutes
Servings: 4
Ingredients:
- 3 cups butternut squash, fresh or frozen, cubed
- 2 tbsp. minced garlic
- 1 tbsp. olive oil
- 1 tsp. red pepper flakes
- 1 tsp. cumin
- 1 tsp. paprika
- 1 tsp. oregano

Crust:
- 2 cups dry French green lentils
- 2 cups water
- 2 tbsp. minced garlic
- 1 tbsp. Italian seasoning
- 1 tsp. onion powder

Toppings:
- 1 tbsp. olive oil
- 1 medium green bell pepper, pitted, diced
- 1 cup chopped broccoli
- 1 small purple onion, diced

Directions:
1 Preheat the oven to 350°F.

176. Lasagna Fungo

Preparation time: 20 minutes
Cooking time: 40 minutes
Servings: 8

10 Add the carrots, and optional cabbage and bok choy (if desired), right before serving.

11 Top with salt and pepper to taste and enjoy or store ingredients separately!

Nutrition:
Calories: 610 Fat: 18.9g Carbohydrates: 83g Proteins: 29.6g

4 Roast the beets until they have softened, approximately 10-15 minutes. Take them out and set aside so the beets can cool down.
5 After the beets have cooled down, transfer them into a food processor and add the cooked chickpeas and quinoa, vinegar, garlic, parsley, and a pinch of pepper and salt.
6 Pulse the ingredients until everything is crumbly, around 30 seconds.
7 Use your palms to form the mixture into 6 equal-sized patties and place them in a small pan.
8 Put them in a freezer, up to 1 hour, until the patties feel firm to the touch.
9 Heat the remaining 1 tablespoon of olive oil in a skillet over medium-high heat and add the patties.
10 Cook them until they're browned on each side, about 4-6 minutes per side.
11 Store or serve the burgers with a handful of spinach, and if desired, on the bottom of the optional bun.
12 Top the burger with your sauce of choice.

Nutrition:
Calories: 353 Fat: 9.2g Carbohydrates: 57.8g Proteins: 13.9g

2 Prepare the French green lentils according to the method.
3 Add all the sauce ingredients to a food processor or blender, and blend on low until everything has mixed and the sauce looks creamy. Set the sauce aside in a small bowl.
4 Clean the food processor or blender; then add all the ingredients for the crust and pulse on high speed until a dough-like batter has formed.
5 Heat a large deep-dish pan over medium-low heat and lightly grease it with 1 tablespoon of olive oil.
6 Press the crust dough into the skillet until it resembles a round pizza crust and cook until the crust is golden brown—about 5-6 minutes on each side.
7 Put the crust on a baking tray covered with parchment paper.
8 Coat the topside of the crust with the sauce using a spoon, and evenly distribute the toppings across the pizza.
9 Bake the pizza in the oven
10 Slice into 4 equal pieces and serve, or store.

Nutrition:
Calories: 258 Fat: 9.2g Carbohydrates: 38.3g Proteins: 9g

Ingredients:
- 10 lasagna sheets
- 2 cups matchstick carrots

- 1 cup mushrooms, sliced
- 2 cups raw kale
- 1 14-oz. package extra firm tofu, drained
- 1 cup hummus
- ½ cup nutritional yeast
- 2 tbsp. Italian seasoning
- 1 tbsp. garlic powder
- 1 tbsp. olive oil
- 4 cups marinara sauce
- 1 tsp. salt

Directions:
1. Preheat the oven to 400°F.
2. Cook the lasagna noodles or sheets according to method.
3. Take a large frying pan, put it over medium heat, and add the olive oil.
4. Throw in the carrots, mushrooms, and half a teaspoon of salt; cook for 5 minutes.
5. Add the kale, sauté for another 3 minutes, and remove the pan from the heat.

177. Sweet and Sour Tofu
Preparation time: 40 minutes
Cooking time: 21 minutes
Servings: 4
Ingredients:
- 14-oz. package extra firm tofu, drained
- 2 tbsp. olive oil
- 1 large red bell pepper, pitted, chopped
- 1 medium white onion, diced
- 2 tbsp. minced garlic
- ½-inch minced ginger
- 1 cup pineapple chunks
- 1 tbsp. tomato paste
- 2 tbsp. rice vinegar
- 2 tbsp. low sodium soy sauce
- 1 tsp. cornstarch
- 1 tbsp. cane sugar
- ¼ tsp Salt
- ¼ tsp pepper

Directions:
1. whisk together the tomato paste, vinegar, soy sauce, cornstarch, and sugar in a bowl.
2. Cut the tofu into ¼-inch cubes, place in a medium bowl, and marinate in the soy sauce mixture until the tofu has absorbed the flavors (up to 3 hours).

178. Stuffed Sweet Potatoes
Preparation time: 30 minutes
Cooking time: 21 minutes
Servings: 3
Ingredients:
- ½ cup dry black beans
- 3 small or medium sweet potatoes
- 2 tbsp. olive oil
- 1 large red bell pepper, pitted, chopped
- 1 small sweet yellow onion, chopped
- 2 tbsp. garlic, minced or powdered
- 1 8-oz. package tempeh, diced into ¼" cubes
- ½ cup marinara sauce

6. Take a large bowl, crumble in the tofu, and set the bowl aside for now.
7. Take another bowl and add the hummus, nutritional yeast, Italian seasoning, garlic, and ½ teaspoon salt; mix everything.
8. Coat the bottom of an 8x8 baking dish with 1 cup of the marinara sauce.
9. Cover the sauce with a couple of the noodles or sheets, and top these with the tofu crumbles.
10. Add a layer of the vegetables on top of the tofu.
11. Continue to build up the lasagna by stacking layers of marinara sauce, noodles or sheets, tofu, and vegetables, and top it off with a cup of marinara sauce.
12. Cover the lasagna with aluminum foil and bake in the oven for 20-25 minutes.
13. Take away the foil and put back in the oven for an additional 5 minutes.
14. Allow the lasagna to sit for 10 minutes before serving, or store for another day!

Nutrition:
Calories: 491 Fat: 13.1g Carbohydrates: 73.5g Proteins: 23.3g

3. Heat 1 tablespoon of the olive oil in a frying pan over medium-high heat.
4. Add the tofu chunks and half of the remaining marinade to the pan, leaving the rest for later.
5. Stir frequently until the tofu is cooked golden brown, approximately 10-12 minutes. Remove the tofu from the heat and set aside in a medium-sized bowl.
6. Add the other tablespoon of olive oil to the same pan, then the garlic and ginger; heat for about 1 minute.
7. Add in the peppers and onions. Mix until the vegetables have softened, about 5 minutes.
8. Pour the leftover marinade into the pan with the vegetables and heat until the sauce thickens while continuously stirring, around 4 minutes.
9. Add the pineapple chunks and tofu cubes to the pan while stirring and cook for 3 minutes.
10. Serve and enjoy right away, or, let the sweet and sour tofu cool down and store for later!

Nutrition:
Calories: 290 Fat: 16.9g Carbohydrates: 19.5g Proteins: 15.9g

- ½ cup water
- 1 tbsp. chili powder
- 1 tsp. parsley
- ½ tsp. cayenne
- ¼ tsp Salt
- ¼ tsp pepper

Directions:
1. Preheat the oven to 400°F.
2. Using a fork, stab several holes in the skins of the sweet potatoes.
3. Wrap the sweet potatoes tightly with aluminum foil and place them in the oven until soft and tender, or for approximately 45 minutes.

4   While sweet potatoes are cooking, heat the olive oil in a deep pan over medium-high heat. Add the onions, bell peppers, and garlic; cook until the onions are tender, for about 10 minutes.

5   Add the water, together with the cooked beans, marinara sauce, chili powder, parsley, and cayenne. Bring the mixture to a boil and then lower the heat to medium or low. Allow the mixture to simmer until the liquid has thickened, for about 15 minutes.

6   Add the diced tempeh cubes and heat until warmed, around 1 minute.

179. Sweet Potato Quesadillas

Preparation time: 30 minutes
Cooking time: 21 minutes
Servings: 3
Ingredients:

- 1 cup dry black beans
- ½ cup dry rice of choice
- 1 large sweet potato, peeled and diced
- ½ cup salsa
- 4 tortilla wraps
- 1 tbsp. olive oil
- ½ tsp. garlic powder
- ½ tsp. onion powder
- ½ tsp. paprika

Directions:

1   Preheat the oven to 350°F.
2   Line a baking pan with parchment paper.
3   Cut the sweet potato into ½-inch cubes and drizzle these with olive oil. Transfer the cubes to the baking pan.

180. Satay Tempeh with Cauliflower Rice

Preparation time: 60 minutes
Cooking time: 15 minutes
Servings: 4
Ingredients:

- ¼ cup water
- 4 tbsp. peanut butter
- 3 tbsp. low sodium soy sauce
- 2 tbsp. coconut sugar
- 1 garlic clove, minced
- 1 tbsp ginger, minced
- 2 tsp. rice vinegar
- 1 tsp. red pepper flakes
- 4 tbsp. olive oil
- 2 8-oz. packages tempeh, drained
- 2 cups cauliflower rice
- 1 cup purple cabbage, diced
- 1 tbsp. sesame oil
- 1 tsp. agave nectar

Directions:

1   Take a large bowl, combine all the ingredients for the sauce, and then whisk until the mixture is smooth and any lumps have dissolved.

181. Teriyaki Tofu Wraps

Preparation time: 30 minutes
Cooking time: 15 minutes
Servings: 3

7   Blend in salt and pepper to taste.
8   When the potatoes are done baking, get rid of them from the oven. Cut a slit across the top of each one, but do not split the potatoes in half.
9   Top each potato with a scoop of the beans, vegetables, and tempeh mixture. Place the filled potatoes back in the hot oven for about 5 minutes.
10   Serve after cooling for a few minutes, or store for another day!

Nutrition:
Calories: 548 Fat: 19.7g Carbohydrates: 76g Proteins: 25.3g

4   Put the pan in the oven and bake the potatoes until tender, for around 1 hour.
5   Allow the potatoes to cool for 5 minutes and then add them to a large mixing bowl with the salsa and cooked rice. Use a fork to smash the ingredients together into a thoroughly combined mixture.
6   Heat a saucepan over medium-high heat and add the potato/rice mixture, cooked black beans, and spices to the pan.
7   Cook everything for about 5 minutes or until it is heated through.
8   Take another frying pan and put it over medium-low heat. Place a tortilla in the pan and fill half of it with a heaping scoop of the potato, bean, and rice mixture.
9   Fold the tortilla in half to cover the filling and cook the tortilla until both sides are browned—about 4 minutes per side.
10   Serve the tortillas with some additional salsa on the side.

Nutrition:
Calories: 683 Fat: 12.7g Carbohydrates: 121g Proteins: 24.9g

2   Cut the tempeh into ½-inch cubes and put them into the sauce, stirring to make sure the cubes get coated thoroughly.
3   Place the bowl in the refrigerator to marinate the tempeh for up to 3 hours.
4   Before the tempeh is done marinating, preheat the oven to 400°F.
5   Spread the tempeh out in a single layer on a baking sheet lined with parchment paper or lightly greased with olive oil.
6   Bake the marinated cubes until browned and crisp—about 15 minutes.
7   Heat the cauliflower rice in a saucepan with 2 tablespoons of olive oil over medium heat until it is warm.
8   Rinse the large bowl with water, and then mix the cabbage, sesame oil, and agave.
9   Serve a scoop of the cauliflower rice topped with the marinated cabbage and cooked tempeh on a plate or in a bowl and enjoy. Or store for later.

Nutrition:
Calories: 554 Fat: 38.8g Carbohydrates: 32.3g Proteins: 28.1g

Ingredients:

- 1 14-oz. drained, package extra firm tofu
- 1 small white onion, diced

- 1 cup chopped pineapple
- ¼ cup soy sauce
- 2 tbsp. sesame oil
- 1 garlic clove, minced
- 1 tsp. coconut sugar
- 4 large lettuce leaves
- 1 tbsp. roasted sesame seeds
- ¼ tsp Salt
- ¼ tsp pepper

Directions:
1. Take a medium-sized bowl and mix the soy sauce, sesame oil, coconut sugar, and garlic.
2. Cut the tofu into ½-inch cubes, place them in the bowl, and transfer the bowl to the refrigerator to marinate, up to 3 hours.
3. Meanwhile, cut the pineapple into rings or cubes.

182. Tex-Mex Tofu & Beans

Preparation time: 25 minutes
Cooking time: 12 minutes
Servings: 2
Ingredients:
- 1 cup dry black beans
- 1 cup dry brown rice
- 1 14-oz. package firm tofu, drained
- 2 tbsp. olive oil
- 1 small purple onion, diced
- 1 medium avocado, pitted, peeled
- 1 garlic clove, minced
- 1 tbsp. lime juice
- 2 tsp. cumin
- 2 tsp. paprika
- 1 tsp. chili powder
- ¼ tsp Salt
- ¼ tsp pepper

Directions:
1. Cut the tofu into ½-inch cubes.

183. Vegan Friendly Fajitas

Preparation time: 30 minutes
Cooking time: 19 minutes
Servings: 6
Ingredients:
- 1 cup dry black beans
- 1 large green bell pepper, seeded, diced
- 1 poblano pepper, seeded, thinly sliced
- 1 large avocado, peeled, pitted, mashed
- 1 medium sweet onion, chopped
- 3 large portobello mushrooms
- 2 tbsp. olive oil
- 6 tortilla wraps
- 1 tsp. lime juice
- 1 tsp. chili powder
- 1 tsp. garlic powder
- ¼ tsp. cayenne pepper
- ¼ tsp Salt

Directions:
1. Prepare the black beans according to the method.
2. Heat 1 tablespoon of olive oil in a large frying pan over high heat.

4. After the tofu is adequately marinated, place a large skillet over medium heat, and pour in the tofu with the remaining marinade, pineapple cubes, and diced onions; stir.
5. Add salt and pepper to taste, making sure to stir the ingredients frequently, and cook until the onions are soft and translucent—about 15 minutes.
6. Divide the mixture between the lettuce leaves and top with a sprinkle of roasted sesame seeds.
7. Serve right away, or store the mixture and lettuce leaves separately.

Nutrition:
Calories: 247 Fat: 16.2g Carbohydrates: 16.1g Proteins: 13.4g

2. Warmth the olive oil in a large skillet over high heat. Add the diced onions and cook until soft, for about 5 minutes.
3. Add the tofu and cook an additional 2 minutes, flipping the cubes frequently.
4. Meanwhile, cut the avocado into thin slices and set aside.
5. Lower the heat to medium and mix in the garlic, cumin, and cooked black beans.
6. Stir until everything is incorporated thoroughly, and then cook for an additional 5 minutes.
7. Add the remaining spices and lime juice to the mixture in the skillet. Mix thoroughly and remove the skillet from the heat.
8. Serve the Tex-Mex tofu and beans with a scoop of rice and garnish with the fresh avocado.
9. Enjoy immediately, or store the rice, avocado, and tofu mixture separately.

Nutrition:
Calories: 1175 Fat: 46.8g Carbohydrates: 152.1g Proteins: 47.6g

3. Add the bell peppers, poblano peppers, and half of the onions.
4. Mix in the chili powder, garlic powder, and cayenne pepper; add salt to taste.
5. Cook the vegetables until tender and browned, around 10 minutes.
6. Add the black beans, continue cooking for an additional 2 minutes; then remove the frying pan from the stove.
7. Add the portobello mushrooms to the skillet and turn heat down to low. Sprinkle the mushrooms with salt.
8. Stir/flip the ingredients often and cook until the mushrooms have shrunken down to half their size, around 7 minutes. Remove the frying pan from the heat.
9. Mix the avocado, remaining 1 tablespoon of olive oil, and the remaining onions together in a small bowl to make a simple guacamole. Mix in the lime juice and add salt and pepper to taste.
10. Spread the guacamole on a tortilla with a spoon and then top with a generous scoop of the mushroom mixture.

11   Serve and enjoy right away or allow the prepared tortillas to cool down and wrap them in paper towels to store!

184. Tofu Cacciatore

Preparation time: 45 minutes
Cooking time: 35 minutes
Servings: 3
Ingredients:

- 1 14-oz. package extra firm tofu, drained
- 1 tbsp. olive oil
- 1 cup matchstick carrots
- 1 medium sweet onion, diced
- 1 medium green bell pepper, seeded, diced
- 1 28-oz. can have diced tomatoes
- 1 4-oz. can tomato paste
- ½ tbsp. balsamic vinegar
- 1 tbsp. soy sauce
- 1 tbsp. maple syrup
- 1 tbsp. garlic powder
- 1 tbsp. Italian seasoning
- ¼ tsp Salt
- ¼ tsp pepper

Directions:

185. Portobello Burritos

Preparation time: 50 minutes
Cooking time: 40 minutes
Servings: 4
Ingredients:

- 3 large portobello mushrooms
- 2 medium potatoes
- 4 tortilla wraps
- 1 medium avocado, pitted, peeled, diced
- ¾ cup salsa
- 1 tbsp. cilantro
- ½ tsp salt
- 1/3 cup water
- 1 tbsp. lime juice
- 1 tbsp. minced garlic
- ¼ cup vegan teriyaki sauce

Directions:

1   Preheat the oven to 400°F.
2   Lightly oil a sheet pan with olive oil (or line with parchment paper) and set it aside.
3   Combine the water, lime juice, teriyaki, and garlic in a small bowl.

186. Mushroom Madness Stroganoff

Preparation time: 30 minutes
Cooking time: 25 minutes
Servings: 4
Ingredients:

- 2 cups gluten-free noodles
- 1 small onion, chopped
- 2 cups vegetable broth
- 2 tbsp. almond flour
- 1 tbsp. tamari
- 1 tsp. tomato paste
- 1 tsp. lemon juice
- 3 cups mushrooms, chopped

Nutrition:
Calories: 429 Fat: 3.2g Carbohydrates: 59.2g Proteins: 14.8g

1   Chop the tofu into ¼- to ½-inch cubes.
2   Warmth the olive oil in a large skillet over medium-high heat.
3   Add the onions, garlic, bell peppers, and carrots; sauté until the onions turn translucent, around 10 minutes. Make sure to stir frequently to prevent burning.
4   Now add the balsamic vinegar, soy sauce
5   , maple syrup, garlic powder and Italian seasoning.
6   Stir well while pouring in the diced tomatoes and tomato paste; mix until all ingredients are thoroughly combined.
7   Add the cubed tofu and stir one more time.
8   Cover the pot, turn the heat to medium-low, and allow the mixture to simmer until the sauce has thickened, for around 20-25 minutes.
9   Serve the tofu cacciatore in bowls and top with salt and pepper to taste, or store for another meal!

Nutrition:
Calories: 319 Fat: 12g Carbohydrates: 43.1g Proteins: 17.6g

4   Slice the portobello mushrooms into thin slices and add these to the bowl. Allow the mushrooms to marinate thoroughly, for up to three hours.
5   Cut the potatoes into large matchsticks, like French fries. Sprinkle the fries with salt and then transfer them to the sheet pan. Place the fries in the oven and bake them until crisped and golden, around 30 minutes. Flip once halfway through for even cooking.
6   Heat a large frying pan over medium heat. Add the marinated mushroom slices with the remaining marinade to the pan. Cook until the liquid has absorbed, around 10 minutes. Remove from heat.
7   Fill the tortillas with a heaping scoop of the mushrooms and a handful of the potato sticks. Top with salsa, sliced avocados, and cilantro before serving.
8   Serve right away, enjoy, or store the tortillas, avocado, and mushrooms separately for later!

Nutrition:
Calories: 391 Fat: 14.9g Carbohydrates: 57g Proteins: 11.2g

- 1 tsp. thyme
- 3 cups raw spinach
- 1 tbsp. apple cider vinegar
- 1 tbsp. olive oil
- ¼ tsp Salt
- ¼ tsp pepper
- 2 tbsp. fresh parsley

Directions:

1   Organize the noodles according to the package instructions.
2   Warmth the olive oil in a large skillet over medium heat.

3 Add the chopped onion and sauté until soft—for about 5 minutes.

4 Stir in the flour, vegetable broth, tamari, tomato paste, and lemon juice; cook for an additional 3 minutes.

5 Blend in the mushrooms, thyme, and salt to taste, then cover the skillet.

6 Cook until the mushrooms are tender, for about 7 minutes, and turn the heat down to low.

187. Moroccan Eggplant Stew

Preparation time: 45 minutes
Cooking time: 32 minutes
Servings: 4
Ingredients:

- 1 cup dry green lentils
- 1 cup dry chickpeas
- 1 tsp. olive oil
- 1 large sweet onion, chopped
- 1 medium green bell pepper, seeded, diced
- 1 large eggplant
- 1 cup vegetable broth
- ¾ cup tomato sauce
- ½ cup golden raisins
- 2 tbsp. turmeric
- 1 garlic clove, minced
- 1 tsp. cumin
- ½ tsp. allspice
- ¼ tsp. chili powder
- ¼ tsp Salt
- ¼ tsp pepper

Directions:

188. Barbecued Greens & Grits

Preparation time: 60 minutes
Cooking time: 35 minutes
Servings: 4
Ingredients:

- 1 14-oz. package tempeh
- 3 cups vegetable broth
- 3 cups collard greens, chopped
- ½ cup vegan BBQ sauce
- 1 cup gluten-free grits
- ¼ cup white onion, diced
- 2 tbsp. olive oil
- 2 garlic cloves, minced
- 1 tsp. salt

Directions:

1 Preheat the oven to 400°F.

2 Sliced the tempeh into thin slices and combine it with the vegan BBQ sauce in a shallow baking dish. Set aside and let marinate for up to 3 hours.

3 Heat 1 tablespoon of olive oil in a frying pan over medium heat and then add the garlic and sauté until it is fragrant.

189. Refined Ratatouille

Preparation time: 90 minutes
Cooking time: 1 hour
Servings: 2

7 Add the cooked noodles, spinach, and vinegar to the pan and top the ingredients with salt and pepper to taste.

8 Cover the skillet again and let the flavors combine for another 8-10 minutes.

9 Serve immediately, topped with the optional parsley if desired, or store and enjoy the stroganoff another day of the week!

Nutrition:
Calories: 240 Fat: 11.9g Carbohydrates: 26.1g Proteins: 9.9g

1 Warmth the olive oil in a medium-sized skillet over medium high heat.

2 Add the onions and cook until they begin to caramelize and soften, in 5-8 minutes.

3 Cut the eggplant into ½-inch eggplant cubes and add it to the skillet along with the bell pepper, cumin, allspice, garlic, and turmeric.

4 Stir the ingredients to combine everything evenly and heat for about 4 minutes; then add the vegetable broth and tomato sauce.

5 Cover the skillet, turn the heat down to low, and simmer the ingredients until the eggplant feels tender, or for about 20 minutes. You should be able to insert a fork into the cubes easily.

6 Uncover and mix in the cooked chickpeas and green lentils, as well as the raisins and chili powder. Simmer the ingredients until all the flavors have melded together, or for about 3 minutes.

7 Store the stew for later, or serve in a bowl, top with salt and pepper to taste, and enjoy!

Nutrition:
Calories: 506 Fat: 6g Carbohydrates: 91.7g Proteins: 26.7g

4 Add the collard greens and ½ teaspoon of salt and cook until the collards are wilted and dark. Remove the pan from the heat and set aside.

5 Cover the tempeh and vegan BBQ sauce mixture with aluminum foil. Put the baking dish into the oven and bake the ingredients for 15 minutes. Reveal and continue to bake for another 10 minutes, until the tempeh is browned and crispy.

6 While the tempeh cooks, heat the remaining tablespoon of olive oil in the previously used frying pan over medium heat.

7 Cook the onions until brown and fragrant, around 10 minutes.

8 Pour in the vegetable broth, bring it to a boil; then turn the heat down to low.

9 Slowly whisk the grits into the simmering broth. Add the remaining ½ teaspoon of salt before covering the pan with a lid.

10 Let the ingredients simmer for about 8 minutes, until the grits are soft and creamy.

11 Serve the tempeh and collard greens on top of a bowl of grits and enjoy, or store for later!

Nutrition:
Calories: 374 Fat: 19.1g Carbohydrate: 31.1g Proteins: 23.7g

Ingredients:

- 1 14-oz. block extra firm tofu, drained
- 2 large heirloom tomatoes

- 1 large eggplant
- 1 large zucchini
- 1 large sweet yellow onion, diced
- 1 cup chopped kale
- 1 cup tomato sauce
- 2 tbsp. olive oil
- 1 tbsp. minced garlic
- ¼ tsp. chili powder
- ¼ tsp. apple cider vinegar
- 1/8 tsp. fennel seeds
- ¼ tsp Salt
- ¼ tsp pepper
- 5 large basil leaves, finely chopped

Directions:

1. Preheat the oven to 350°F.
2. Lightly grease an 8x8" square dish with 1 tablespoon of olive oil and set it aside.
3. Combine the tomato sauce, vinegar, remaining 1 tablespoon of olive oil, garlic, fennel seeds, and chili powder in a large mixing bowl.
4. Pour the mixture into the baking dish and use a spoon to smear the ingredients out evenly across the dish's bottom.

190. Stuffed Indian Eggplant

Preparation time: 90 minutes
Cooking time: 21 minutes
Servings: 5
Ingredients:

- ½ cup dry black beans
- 6 medium eggplants, peeled
- 3 large roma tomatoes, diced
- 1 large purple onion, chopped
- 1 large yellow bell pepper, chopped
- 2 cups raw spinach
- 2 tbsp. olive oil
- 2 cloves garlic, minced
- 1 tbsp. tomato paste
- 1 tsp. coconut sugar
- 1 tsp. cumin
- 1 tsp. turmeric
- Salt and pepper to taste
- 2 tbsp. thyme, chopped

Directions:

1. Preheat the oven to 400°F.
2. Line a baking sheet or pan with parchment paper and set it aside.
3. Cut the peeled eggplants open across the top from one side to the other, being careful not to slice all the way through.
4. Sprinkle the inside of the cut eggplants with salt and wrap them in a paper towel to drain the excess water. This could take up to 30 minutes.

191. Sweet Potato Sushi

Preparation time: 90 minutes
Cooking time: 35 minutes
Servings: 3
Ingredients:

- 1 14-oz. package silken tofu, drained
- 3 nori sheets

5. Lay out the kale in one even layer on top of the mixture.
6. Vertically slice the tomatoes, eggplant, zucchini, and onion into thick, round discs; they should look like small plates or saucers.
7. Cut the tofu into thin slices, each similar in size to the vegetable discs for even cooking.
8. Layer the vegetable discs and tofu slices on top of the kale in the baking dish with an alternating pattern. For instance: tomato, eggplant, tofu, zucchini, squash, onion, repeat.
9. Fill up every inch of the pan with all the slices and stack them against the edge.
10. Put the baking dish into the oven and bake until the tomato sauce has thickened and the vegetable slices have softened, around 50 minutes to an hour.
11. Scoop the ratatouille into a bowl and garnish it with the chopped basil.
12. Serve and enjoy or store for another day!

Nutrition:
Calories: 493 Fat: 27g Carbohydrates: 47g Proteins: 29.1g

5. Place the eggplants on the baking sheet and bake in the oven for 15 minutes. Remove the baking sheet from the oven and set it aside.
6. Heat 1 tablespoon of olive oil in a large skillet over medium-high heat. Add the chopped onions and sauté until soft, around 5 minutes.
7. Stir frequently, adding in the bell peppers and garlic. Cook the ingredients until the onions are translucent and peppers are tender, for about 15 minutes.
8. Season the spinach with sugar, cumin, turmeric, salt, and pepper.
9. Stir everything well to coat the ingredients evenly; then mix in the tomatoes, black beans, spinach, and tomato paste.
10. Heat everything for about 5 minutes, and then remove the skillet from the heat and set aside.
11. Stuff the eggplants with heaping scoops of the vegetable mixture. Sprinkle more salt and pepper to taste on top.
12. Drizzle the remaining 1 tablespoon of olive oil across the eggplants, return them to the oven, and bake until they shrivel and flatten—for 20-30 minutes.
13. Serve the eggplants, and if desired, garnish with the optional fresh thyme.
14. Enjoy right away, or store to enjoy later!

Nutrition:
Calories: 308 Fat: 7.5g Carbohydrates: 57g Proteins: 11.9g

- 1 large sweet potato, peeled
- 1 medium avocado, pitted, peeled, sliced
- 1 cup water
- ¾ cup dry sushi rice
- 1 tbsp. rice vinegar
- 1 tbsp. agave nectar

- 1 tbsp. amino acids

Directions:
1. Preheat the oven to 400°F / 200°C.
2. Stir the amino acids (or tamari) and agave nectar together in a small bowl until it is well combined and set aside.
3. Cut the sweet potato into large sticks, around ½-inch thick. Place them on a baking sheet lined with parchment and coat them with the tamari/agave mixture.
4. Bake the sweet potatoes in the oven until softened—for about 25 minutes—and make sure to flip them halfway so the sides cook evenly.
5. Meanwhile, bring the sushi rice, water, and vinegar to a boil in a medium-sized pot over medium heat, and cook until liquid has evaporated, for about 10 minutes.
6. While cooking the rice, cut the block of tofu into long sticks. The sticks should look like long, thin fries. Set aside.

192. Brown Basmati Rice Pilaf
Preparation time: 10 minutes
Cooking time: 3 minutes
Servings: 2
Ingredients:
- ½ tablespoon vegan butter
- ½ cup mushrooms, chopped
- ½ cup brown basmati rice
- 3 tablespoons water
- 1/8 teaspoon dried thyme
- Ground pepper to taste
- ½ tablespoon olive oil
- ¼ cup green onion, chopped
- 1 cup vegetable broth
- ¼ teaspoon salt
- ¼ cup chopped, toasted pecans

193. Mediterranean Vegetable Mix
Preparation time: 15 minutes
Cooking time: 7 hours
Servings: 8
Ingredients:
- 1 zucchini
- 2 eggplants
- 2 red onions
- 4 potatoes
- 4 oz. asparagus
- 2 tablespoons olive oil
- 1 teaspoon ground black pepper
- 1 teaspoon paprika
- 1 teaspoon salt
- 1 tablespoon Mediterranean seasoning
- 1 teaspoon minced garlic

Directions:

194. Fresh Dal
Preparation time: 15 minutes
Cooking time: 5 hours
Servings: 11
Ingredients:
- 1 teaspoon cumin

7. Remove the pot from heat and let the rice sit for 10-15 minutes.
8. Cover your work area with a piece of parchment paper, clean your hands, wet your fingers, and lay out a sheet of nori on the parchment paper.
9. Cover the nori sheet with a thin layer of sushi rice, while wetting the hands frequently. Leave sufficient space for rolling up the sheet.
10. Place the roasted sweet potato strips in a straight line across the width of the sheet, about an inch away from the edge closest to you.
11. Lay out the tofu and avocado slices right beside the potato sticks and use the parchment paper as an aid to roll up the nori sheet into a tight cylinder.
12. Slice the cylinder into 8 equal pieces and refrigerate. Repeat the process for the remaining nori sheets and fillings.
13. Serve chilled, or store to enjoy this delicious sushi later!

Nutrition:
Calories: 567 Fat: 17.1g Carbohydrates: 64g Proteins: 15.4g

Directions:
1. Place a saucepan over medium-low heat. Add butter and oil.
2. When it melts, add mushrooms and cook until slightly tender.
3. Stir in the green onion and brown rice. Cook for 3 minutes. Stir constantly.
4. Stir in the broth, water, salt and thyme.
5. When it begins to boil, lower heat and cover with a lid. Simmer until rice is cooked. Add more water or broth if required.
6. Stir in the pecans and pepper.
7. Serve.

Nutrition:
Calories: 256 Fat: 8.8g Carbohydrates: 39.8g Proteins: 4.5g

1. Combine the olive oil, Mediterranean seasoning, salt, paprika, ground black pepper, and minced garlic.
2. Whisk the mixture well. Wash all the vegetables carefully.
3. Cut the zucchini, eggplants, and potatoes into the medium cubes. Cut the asparagus into 2 parts.
4. Then peel the onions and cut them into 4 parts. Toss all the vegetables in the slow cooker and sprinkle them with the spice mixture.
5. Close the slow cooker lid and cook the vegetable mix for 7 hours on LOW.
6. Serve the prepared vegetable mix hot. Enjoy!

Nutrition:
Calories: 227 Fat: 3.9g Fiber: 9g Carbohydrates: 44.88g Proteins: 6g

- 1 oz. mustard seeds
- 10 oz. lentils
- 1 teaspoon fennel seeds
- 7 cups water

- 6 oz. tomato, canned
- 4 oz. onion
- ½ teaspoon fresh ginger, grated
- 1 oz. bay leaf
- 1 teaspoon turmeric
- 1 teaspoon salt
- 2 cups rice

Directions:
1. Peel the onion. Chop the onion and tomatoes and place them in a slow cooker.
2. Combine the cumin, mustard seeds, and fennel seeds in a shallow bowl.

195. Chickpeas Soup

Preparation time: 10 minutes
Cooking time: 4 hours
Servings: 6
Ingredients:

- 30 ounces canned chickpeas, drained
- 2 tablespoons mild curry powder
- 1 cup lentils, dry
- 1 sweet potato, cubed
- 15 ounces canned coconut milk
- 1 teaspoon ginger powder
- 1 teaspoon turmeric, ground
- A pinch of salt

196. Hot and Delicious Soup

Preparation time: 10 minutes
Cooking time: 8 hours
Servings: 4
Ingredients:

- 8 ounces canned bamboo shoots, drained and chopped
- 10 ounces' mushrooms, sliced
- 8 shiitake mushrooms, sliced
- 4 garlic cloves, minced
- 2 tablespoons ginger, grated
- 15 ounces extra firm tofu, pressed and cubed
- 2 tablespoons vegan bouillon
- 4 cups water
- 1 teaspoon sesame oil
- 2 tablespoons coconut aminos

197. Delicious Eggplant Salad

Preparation time: 10 minutes
Cooking time: 8 hours
Servings: 4
Ingredients:

- 1 big eggplant, cut into quarters and then sliced
- 25 ounces canned plum tomatoes
- 2 red bell peppers, chopped
- 1 red onion, sliced
- 2 teaspoons cumin, ground
- A pinch of sea salt
- Black pepper to the taste
- 1 teaspoon smoked paprika

198. Tasty Black Beans Soup

Preparation time: 10 minutes
Cooking time: 6 hours
Servings: 6

---

3. Add the bay leaf and mix. Sprinkle the vegetables in the slow cooker with the spice mixture.
4. Add salt, turmeric, and grated fresh ginger. Add rice and mix.
5. Add the lentils and water. Stir gently.
6. Then close the slow cooker lid and cook Dal for 5 hours on LOW.
7. When the dish is done, stir and transfer to serving plates. Enjoy!

Nutrition:
Calories: 102 Fat: 22g Carbohydrates: 5g Proteins: 34g

- 6 cups veggie stock
- Black pepper to the taste

Directions:
1. Put chickpeas in your slow cooker.
2. Add lentils, sweet potato cubes, curry powder, ginger, turmeric, salt, pepper and stock.
3. Stir and then mix with coconut milk.
4. Stir again, cover and cook on High for 4 hours.
5. Ladle chickpeas soup into bowls and serve.
6. Enjoy!

Nutrition:
Calories: 302 Fat: 22g Carbohydrates: 5g Proteins: 34g

- 1 teaspoon chili paste
- 1 and ½ cups peas
- 2 tablespoons rice wine vinegar

Directions:
1. Put the water in your slow cooker.
2. Add bamboo shoot, mushrooms, shiitake mushrooms, garlic, 1 tablespoon ginger, tofu, vegan bouillon, oil, aminos, chili paste, peas and vinegar.
3. Stir, cover and cook on Low for 8 hours.
4. Add the rest of the ginger, stir soup again, ladle into bowls and serve right away.
5. Enjoy!

Nutrition:
Calories: 102 Fat: 22g Carbohydrates: 5g Proteins: 34g

- Juice of 1 lemon

Directions:
1. In your slow cooker, mix eggplant pieces with tomatoes, bell peppers, onion, cumin, salt, pepper, paprika and lemon juice, stir, cover and cook on Low for 8 hours.
2. Stir again, divide into bowls and serve cold.
3. Enjoy!

Nutrition:
Calories: 302
Fat: 22g
Carbohydrates: 5g
Proteins: 34g

Ingredients:
- 4 cups veggie stock

- 1 pound black beans, soaked overnight and drained
- 1 yellow onion, chopped
- 2 jalapenos, chopped
- 1 red bell pepper, chopped
- 1 cup tomatoes, chopped
- 4 garlic cloves, minced
- 1 tablespoon chili powder
- Black pepper to the taste
- 2 teaspoons cumin, ground
- A pinch of sea salt
- ½ teaspoon cayenne pepper

199. Rich Sweet Potato Soup

Preparation time: 10 minutes
Cooking time: 8 hours
Servings: 5
Ingredients:

- 5 cups veggie stock
- 2 celery stalks, chopped
- 3 sweet potatoes, chopped
- 1 cup yellow onion, chopped
- 2 garlic cloves, minced
- 1 cup rice milk
- 1 teaspoon tarragon, dried
- 2 cups baby spinach
- 8 tablespoons almonds, sliced
- A pinch of salt

200. Pumpkin Chili

Preparation time: 10 minutes
Cooking time: 8 hours
Servings: 6
Ingredients:

- 1 cup pumpkin, pureed
- 45 ounces canned black beans, drained
- 30 ounces canned tomatoes, chopped
- 1 yellow bell pepper, chopped
- 1 yellow onion, chopped
- ¼ teaspoon nutmeg, ground
- 1 teaspoon cinnamon powder
- 1 tablespoon chili powder
- 1 teaspoon cumin, ground

201. Crazy Cauliflower and Zucchini Surprise

Preparation time: 10 minutes
Cooking time: 3 hours and 30 minutes
Servings: 4
Ingredients:

- 1 cauliflower head, florets separated
- 2 garlic cloves, minced
- ¾ cup red onion, chopped
- 1 teaspoon basil, dried
- 2 teaspoons oregano flakes
- 28 ounces canned tomatoes, chopped
- ¼ teaspoon red pepper flakes
- ½ cup veggie stock
- 5 zucchinis, cut with a spiralizer

- 1 avocado, pitted, peeled and chopped
- ½ teaspoon sweet paprika

Directions:
1. Put the stock in your slow cooker.
2. Add beans, onion, jalapenos, bell pepper, tomatoes, garlic, chili powder, black pepper, salt, cumin, cayenne and paprika.
3. Stir, cover and cook on Low for 6 hours.
4. Blend soup using an immersion blender, ladle into bowls and serve with chopped avocado on top.
5. Enjoy!

Nutrition:
Calories: 202 Fat: 22g Carbohydrates: 5g Proteins: 34g

- Black pepper to the taste

Directions:
1. Put the stock in your slow cooker.
2. Add celery, potatoes, onion, garlic, salt, pepper and tarragon.
3. Stir, cover and cook on Low for 8 hours.
4. Add rice milk and blend using an immersion blender.
5. Add almonds and spinach, stir, cover and leave aside for 20 minutes.
6. Ladle into bowls and serve.
7. Enjoy!

Nutrition:
Calories: 302 Fat: 22g Carbohydrates: 5g Proteins: 34g

- 1/8 teaspoon cloves, ground
- A pinch of sea salt
- Black pepper to the taste

Directions:
1. Put pumpkin puree in your slow cooker.
2. Add black beans, tomatoes, onion, bell pepper, cumin, nutmeg, cinnamon, chili powder, cloves, salt and pepper, stir, cover and cook on Low for 8 hours.
3. Stir your chili again, divide into bowls and serve.
4. Enjoy!

Nutrition:
Calories: 242 Fat: 22g Carbohydrates: 5g Proteins: 34g

- A pinch of salt
- Black pepper to the taste

Directions:
1. Put cauliflower florets in your slow cooker.
2. Add garlic, onion, basil, oregano, tomatoes, stock, pepper flakes, salt and pepper, stir, cover and cook on High for 3 hours and 30 minutes.
3. Mash cauliflower mix a bit using a potato masher.
4. Divide zucchini noodles in bowls, top each with cauliflower mix and serve.
5. Enjoy!

Nutrition:
Calories: 302 Fat: 22g Carbohydrates: 5g Proteins: 34g

202. Quinoa and Veggies

Preparation time: 10 minutes
Cooking time: 4 hours
Servings: 4
Ingredients:

- 1 tablespoon olive oil
- 1 and ½ cups quinoa
- 3 cups veggie stock
- 1 yellow onion, chopped
- 1 carrot, chopped
- 1 sweet red pepper, chopped
- 1 cup green beans, chopped
- 2 garlic cloves, minced

203. Iron Abs Tabbouleh

Preparation time: 15 minutes
Cooking time: 10 minutes
Servings: 4
Ingredients:

- 1 cup whole-wheat couscous
- 1 cup boiling water
- Zest and juice of 1 lemon
- 1 garlic clove, pressed
- Pinch of sea salt
- 1 tablespoon olive oil
- 2 cups canned chickpeas
- ½ cucumber
- 1 tomato
- 1 cup fresh parsley
- ¼ cup fresh mint

204. Mushroom Cream

Preparation time: 10 minutes
Cooking time: 20 minutes
Servings: 2
Ingredients:

- 2 teaspoons olive oil
- 1 onion
- 2 garlic cloves
- 2 cups chopped mushrooms
- 2 tablespoons whole-grain flour
- 1 teaspoon dried herbs
- 4 cups Economical Vegetable Broth
- 1½ cups nondairy milk

Directions:

205. Fast Twitch Quinoa

Preparation time: 5 minutes
Cooking time: 0 minute
Servings: 7
Ingredients:

- 3 tablespoons olive oil
- Juice of 1½ lemons
- 1 teaspoon garlic powder
- ½ teaspoon dried oregano
- 1 bunch curly kale
- 2 cups cooked tricolor quinoa
- 1 cup canned mandarin oranges in juice
- 1 cup diced yellow summer squash
- 1 red bell pepper
- ½ red onion

- 1 teaspoon cilantro, chopped
- A pinch of salt
- Black pepper to the taste

Directions:

1. Put the stock in your slow cooker.
2. Add oil, quinoa, onion, carrot, sweet pepper, beans, cloves, salt and pepper, stir, cover and cook on Low for 4 hours.
3. Add cilantro, stir again, divide on plates and serve.
4. Enjoy!

Nutrition:
Calories: 302 Fat: 22g Carbohydrates: 5g Proteins: 34g

- 2 scallions
- 4 tablespoons sunflower seeds

Directions:

1. Soak couscous with boiling water until all the grains are submerged. Cover. Set aside.
2. Put the lemon zest and juice in a large salad bowl, then stir in the garlic, salt, and the olive oil
3. Put the cucumber, chickpeas, tomato, parsley, mint, and scallions in the bowl, and toss them to coat with the dressing. Stir with fork
4. Stir in cooked couscous to the vegetables and toss to combine.
5. Serve topped with the sunflower seeds

Nutrition:
Calories: 304 Fat: 11g Proteins: 10g

1. Preheat oil over medium-high heat.
2. Add the onion, garlic, mushrooms, and salt. Sauté for about 5 minutes, until softened. Throw flour over the ingredients in the pot and mix.
3. Cook for 1 to 2 minutes more to toast the flour.
4. Add the dried herbs, vegetable broth, milk, and pepper.
5. Set heat to low, and let the broth come to a simmer.
6. Cook for 10 minutes, until slightly thickened.

Nutrition:
Calories: 102 Proteins: 10g Fiber: 3g

- ½ cup dried cranberries
- ½ cup slivered almonds

Directions:

1. Scourge the oil, lemon juice, garlic powder, and oregano.
2. Mix the kale with the oil-lemon mixture until well coated. Add the quinoa, oranges, squash, bell pepper, and red onion and toss until all the ingredients are well combined. Divide among bowls or transfer to a large serving platter. Top with the cranberries and almonds.

Nutrition:
Calories: 343 Proteins: 24g Fiber: 11g

206. Eggplant Parmesan

Preparation time: 10 minutes
Cooking time: 15 minutes
Servings: 1
Ingredients:

- ¼ cup nondairy milk
- ¼ cup breadcrumbs or panko
- 2 tablespoons nutritional yeast
- ¼ teaspoon salt
- 4 (¼-inch-thick) eggplant slices
- 1 tablespoon olive oil
- 4 tablespoons Simple Homemade Tomato Sauce
- 4 teaspoons Pram Sprinkle

Directions:

1. Put the milk in a shallow bowl. Blend the breadcrumbs, nutritional yeast and salt.
2. Dip one eggplant slice in the milk, making sure both sides get moistened. Dip it into the breadcrumbs, flipping to coat both sides. Transfer to a plate and repeat to coat the remaining slices. Preheat oil over medium heat and add the breaded eggplant slices.
3. Cook for 6 minutes. Flip, adding more oil as needed. Top each slice with 1 tablespoon tomato sauce and 1 teaspoon Pram Sprinkle. Cook for 5 to 7 minutes more.

Nutrition:
Calories: 460 Proteins: 9g Fiber: 13g

207. Pepper & Kale

Preparation time: 5 minutes
Cooking time: 15 minutes
Servings: 4
Ingredients:

- 2 cans chickpeas
- 4 cloves garlic
- 1 large sweet onion
- 4 tbsp olive oil
- 2 red peppers
- 6 cups kale

Directions:

1. Heat BBQ and prepare a greased BBQ basket or pan.
2. Meanwhile, mix chickpeas, garlic, onion, red peppers and olive oil in a bowl and add to the BBQ basket and place on the grill. Stir regularly.
3. When almost ready to serve add kale and stir constantly until the kale is slightly wilted. Serve with garlic toast, pita bread or rice.

Nutrition:
Calories: 520 Fiber: 16g Proteins: 18g

208. Caesar Pasta

Preparation time: 10 minutes
Cooking time: 0 minute
Servings: 1
Ingredients:

- 2 cups chopped romaine lettuce
- 2 tablespoons Vegan Caesar Dressing
- ½ cup cooked pasta
- ½ cup canned chickpeas
- 2 additional tablespoons Caesar Dressing

Directions:

1. Blend the lettuce, dressing, (if using).
2. Add the pasta, chickpeas, and additional dressing. Toss to coat.

Nutrition:
Calories: 415 Proteins: 9g Fiber: 13g

209. Quinn-Otto with Dried Tomatoes

Preparation time: 10 minutes
Cooking time: 30 min
Servings: 2
Ingredients:

- 3 cups vegetable broth
- 2 cloves garlic, minced
- ½ cup quinoa
- ¼ cup sun-dried tomatoes in oil
- 1 teaspoon parsley
- 1 small onion, minced
- 1 ½ tablespoons olive oil
- 2 tablespoons basil

Directions:

1. Place a saucepan over medium heat. Add oil. Once heated, sauté onion and garlic.
2. Cook the quinoa: Cook 2/3 cup uncooked quinoa in water, according to package directions.
3. Add a cup of broth and mix well. Season.
4. Add some more broth, tomatoes and herbs. Mix well. Cook until nearly dry.
5. Repeat adding the broth, a little at a time and cook until nearly dry each time, add cooked quinoa. Stir often.

Nutrition:
Calories: 402 Fat: 13g Proteins: 11g

210. Steamed Eggplants with Peanut Dressing

Preparation time: 10 minutes
Cooking time: 20 minutes
Servings: 2
Ingredients:

- 6 ounces baby eggplants
- ½ tablespoon soy sauce
- ½ teaspoon sugar
- 1 teaspoon toasted sesame seeds
- 1 tablespoon cilantro leaves, to garnish
- 1 tablespoon peanut butter
- ½ tablespoon rice vinegar
- ½ tablespoon chili oil + extra to serve
- 1 spring onion, thinly sliced
- 1 tablespoon boiling water

Directions:

1. Steam the eggplants in the steaming equipment you possess for about 15 minutes or until soft.
2. Place peanut butter in a bowl. Add boiling water into it and whisk well.
3. Add soy sauce, sugar, rice vinegar and chili oil and whisk well.

211. Cauliflower Rice Wok

Preparation time: 10 minutes
Cooking time: 20 minutes
Servings: 4
Ingredients:

- 1 lb. (450 g) tofu
- 1/2 cup (150 g) peas
- 1 tablespoon ginger
- 3 garlic cloves, minced
- 1/4 cup (30 g) green onions
- 1 cauliflower head, riced
- 2 carrots, diced
- 2 tablespoons sesame oil
- 3 tablespoons cashews
- 3 tablespoons soy sauce

212. Spicy Root and Lentil Casserole

Preparation time: 10 minutes
Cooking time: 35 minutes
Servings: 4
Ingredients:

- 2 tbsp vegetable oil
- 1 onion, chopped
- 2 garlic cloves, crushed
- 700g potatoes, peeled and cut into chunks
- 4 carrots, thickly sliced
- 2 parsnips, thickly sliced
- 2 tbsp curry paste or powder
- 1 liter/1¾ pints vegetable stock
- 100g red lentils

213. Seitan

Preparation time: 25 minutes
Cooking time: 20 minutes
Servings: 5
Ingredients:

- Firm Tofu, 250 grams
- Unsweetened soy milk, 150ml
- Miso paste 2 tsp
- Marmite 2 tsp
- Onion powder 1 tsp
- Garlic powder 2 tsp
- Wheat gluten 160g
- Pea protein or vegan protein powder, 40g
- Vegetable stock 1 ½ liters

214. Gear Up Lentils

Preparation time: 5 minutes
Cooking time: 40 minutes
Servings: 6
Ingredients:

- 5 cups water
- 2¼ cups brown lentils
- 3 teaspoons minced garlic
- 1 bay leaf

4. Place the eggplants on a serving platter. Trickle the sauce mixture over the eggplants.
5. Sprinkle sesame seeds, cilantro, spring onion on top. Drizzle some chili oil on top and serve.

Nutrition:
Calories: 87 Proteins: 3.8g Fiber: 2.9g

Directions:
1. Press and drain the tofu. Then crumble it slightly in a bowl. Set aside.
2. Add oil to a wok pan and place over medium heat. Cook garlic and ginger. Add the tofu and stir for about 6 minutes, until golden and well cooked. Set the tofu aside.
3. Fill more oil to the pan and cook the carrots.
4. Mix peas along with the cauliflower rice. Cook for 7 minutes. Add the green onions, cooked tofu, cashews and soy sauce.
5. Serve the cauliflower fried rice and garnish with the sesame seeds. Enjoy!

Nutrition:
Calories: 47 Proteins: 2.14g Fiber: 3.2g

Directions:
1. Cook oil in a large pan, cook the onion and garlic over a medium heat for 3 minutes. Continue stirring in between to cook them well. Add potatoes, carrots and parsnips, turn up the heat and cook for 6 to 7 minutes. Stir well
2. Stir in the curry paste or powder, fill in the stock, and bring to a boil. Reduce the heat, add the lentils. Cover and simmer for 18 minutes.
3. Once done, season with coriander and heat for a minute. Serve with yogurt and the rest of the coriander.

Nutrition:
Calories: 378 Proteins: 14g Fiber: 10g

Directions:
1. Blitz the tofu, soy milk, miso, marmite, onion powder, garlic powder, 1 tsp salt and ½ tsp white pepper in a food processor. Blend until smooth.
2. Mix them all to form a dough. Knead the dough well, stretching and tearing for 10-15 minutes.
3. Fill vegetable stock into a pan and let it simmer. Flatten out the seitan to a thickness of 1 cm and chop into chunks. Simmer it in the stock for 20 minutes covering with a lid. Once it's done, allow it to cool down. Chop or tear it into smaller pieces before cooking as per your choice.

Nutrition:
Calories: 211 Proteins: 35g Fiber: 2g

- ½ teaspoon dried basil
- ½ teaspoon dried oregano
- ½ teaspoon dried rosemary
- ½ teaspoon dried thyme

Directions:
1. Boil water, lentils, garlic, bay leaf, basil, oregano, rosemary, and thyme. Decrease heat to low, and simmer for 35 minutes. Drain any excess cooking liquid.

2   Transfer to a container, or scoop 1 cup of lentils into each of 6 storage containers. Let cool before sealing the lids.

215. Boulders Bean Burgers

Preparation time: 10 minutes
Cooking time: 10 minutes
Servings: 4
Ingredients:

- 1 tablespoon olive oil
- ¼ cup couscous
- ¼ cup boiling water
- 1 (15-ounce) can white beans
- 2 tablespoons balsamic vinegar
- 2 tablespoons chopped sun-dried tomatoes or olives
- ½ teaspoon garlic powder
- ½ teaspoon salt
- 4 burger buns

Directions:

1   Preheat the oven to 350°F.

216. Black Bean Pizza Plate

Preparation time: 10 minutes
Cooking time: 20 minutes
Servings: 2
Ingredients:

- 2 prebaked pizza crusts
- ½ cup Spicy Black Bean Dip
- 1 tomato, thinly sliced
- 1 carrot, grated
- 1 red onion
- 1 avocado

Directions:

1   Preheat the oven to 400°F.
2   Lay the two crusts out on a large baking sheet. Spread half the Spicy Black Bean Dip on each pizza crust.

217. Instant Peas Risotto

Preparation time: 10 min.
Cooking time: 10 min.
Servings: 3
Ingredients:

- 1 cup baby green peas
- 1 cup Arborio rice
- 2 cloves garlic, diced
- 3 tablespoons olive oil
- 1 brown onion, diced
- ½ teaspoon salt
- 2 celery sticks, make small cubes
- ½ teaspoon pepper
- 2 tablespoons lemon juice
- 2 cups vegetable stock

Directions:

1   Take your Instant Pot and place it on a clean kitchen platform. Turn it on after plugging it into a power socket.

218. Pumpkin Bean Stew

Preparation time: 8-10 min.
Cooking time: 20-22 min.
Servings: 4

Nutrition:
Calories: 257 Fat: 1g Proteins: 19g

2   Grease rimmed baking sheet with olive oil or line it with parchment paper. Mix couscous and boiling water.
3   Cover and set aside for about 5 minutes. Once the couscous is soft and the water is absorbed, fluff it with a fork. Add the beans, and mash them to a chunky texture. Add the vinegar, olive oil, sun-dried tomatoes, garlic powder, and salt; stir until combined but still a bit chunky.
4   Portion mixture into 4, and shape each into a patty. Put the patties on the prepared baking sheet and bake for 25 to 30 minutes. Alternatively, heat some olive oil in a large skillet over medium heat, then add the patties, making sure each has oil under it.
5   Fry for about 5 minutes. Flip, adding more oil as needed, and fry for about 5 minutes more. Serve.

Nutrition:
Calories: 315 Fiber: 12g Proteins: 16g

3   Then layer on the tomato slices with a pinch pepper if you like. Sprinkle the grated carrot with the sea salt and lightly massage it in with your hands.
4   Spread the carrot on top of the tomato, then add the onion.
5   Pop the pizzas in the oven for 10 to 20 minutes, or until they're done to your taste. Top the cooked pizzas with sliced avocado and another sprinkle of pepper.

Nutrition:
Calories: 379 Fiber: 15g Proteins: 13g

2   Put the pot on "Sauté" mode. In the pot, add the oil, celery, onions, pepper, and salt; cook for 4-5 minutes until the ingredients become soft.
3   Mix in the zest, stock, garlic, peas, and rice. Stir the ingredients.
4   Close the lid and lock. Ensure that you have sealed the valve to avoid leakage.
5   Press "Manual" mode and set timer for 5 minutes. It will take a few minutes for the pot to build inside pressure and start cooking.
6   After the timer reads zero, press "Cancel" and quick release pressure.
7   Carefully remove the lid, add the lemon juice and serve warm!

Nutrition:
Calories: 362 Fat: 13g Carbohydrates: 52.5g Fiber: 3g
Proteins: 8g

Ingredients:

- 2 cloves garlic, minced

- 3 cups water
- 2 medium tomatoes, chopped
- 1/2 cup dried chickpeas (soaked for 12 hours and drained)
- 3 small onions, chopped
- 1 cup raw pumpkin, peeled, cubed
- 1/2 cup dried navy beans (soaked for 12 hours and drained)
- Pepper and salt as needed
- 2 teaspoon harissa
- 2 tablespoons parsley, chopped

Directions:

1. Take your Instant Pot and place it on a clean kitchen platform. Turn it on after plugging it into a power socket.
2. Put the pot on "Sauté" mode. In the pot, add the oil, garlic, and onions; cook for 2-3 minutes until the ingredients become soft.

219. Mushroom Bean Farro

Preparation time: 8-10 min.
Cooking time: 30 min.
Servings: 3-4
Ingredients:

- 3 cups mushrooms, chopped
- 1 seeded jalapeno pepper, chopped
- 1 tablespoon shallot powder
- 2 tablespoons barley
- 1 tablespoon red curry paste
- ½ cup farro
- 1 cup navy beans, dried
- 2 tablespoons onion powder
- 9 garlic cloves, minced
- 2 tomatoes, diced
- Pepper and salt as needed

Directions:

1. Take your Instant Pot and place it on a clean kitchen platform. Turn it on after plugging it into a power socket.

220. Sorghum Raisin Meal

Preparation time: 8-10 min.
Cooking time: 60 min.
Servings: 4
Ingredients:

- 3 cups water
- 1 cup coconut milk
- 3 tablespoons rice wine vinegar
- 1 cup sorghum
- ½ teaspoon chili powder
- 1 tablespoon curry powder
- 2 cups chopped carrots
- ½ cup raisins, golden
- ¼ cup green onion, finely chopped
- 2 teaspoons palm sugar
- Salt as needed

Directions:

1. Take your Instant Pot and place it on a clean kitchen platform. Turn it on after plugging it into a power socket.

3. Add other ingredients to the pot. Stir gently.
4. Close the lid and lock. Ensure that you have sealed the valve to avoid leakage.
5. Press "Bean/Chili" mode and set the timer for 6 minutes. It will take a few minutes for the pot to build inside pressure and start cooking.
6. After the timer reads zero, press "Cancel" and naturally release pressure. It takes about 8-10 minutes to naturally release pressure.
7. Carefully remove the lid.
8. Check if the beans are tender, if not add some more water; cook on "Manual" mode for 8-10 minutes.
9. Top with parsley and serve.

Nutrition:
Calories: 166 Fat: 8g Carbohydrates: 24g Fiber: 6.5g Proteins: 9g

2. Open the lid from the top and put it aside; start adding the beans, faro, barley, mushrooms, garlic, jalapeno, curry paste, shallot and onion powder, pepper and salt.
3. Add water to cover all the ingredients; gently stir them.
4. Close the lid and lock. Ensure that you have sealed the valve to avoid leakage.
5. Press "Manual" mode and set timer for 30 minutes. It will take a few minutes for the pot to build inside pressure and start cooking.
6. After the timer reads zero, press "Cancel" and naturally release pressure. It takes about 8-10 minutes to naturally release pressure.
7. Carefully remove the lid and add the tomatoes.
8. Sprinkle cilantro and scallions; serve warm!

Nutrition:
Calories: 238 Fat: 6.5g Carbohydrates: 38g Fiber: 1.5g Proteins: 11g

2. Open the lid from the top and put it aside; start adding the sorghum, salt and water. Gently stir them.
3. Close the lid and lock. Ensure that you have sealed the valve to avoid leakage.
4. Press "Manual" mode and set timer for 55-60 minutes. It will take a few minutes for the pot to build inside pressure and start cooking.
5. After the timer reads zero, press "Cancel" and naturally release pressure. It takes about 8-10 minutes to naturally release pressure.
6. Carefully remove the lid; drain the sorghum.
7. In a medium-size bowl, mix the palm sugar, coconut milk, vinegar, salt, curry powder and chili powder.
8. In the bowl, add the sorghum, carrots, and onions. Serve!

Nutrition:
Calories: 294 Fat: 6g Carbohydrates: 19.5g Fiber: 12g Proteins: 22.5g

221. Squash Eggplant Mania

Preparation time: 8-10 min.
Cooking time: 20 min.
Servings: 4
Ingredients:

- 14 ounces eggplant, chopped
- 2 yellow onions, chopped
- 14 ounces squash, chopped
- 4 tomatoes, chopped
- 1 tablespoon olive oil, extra virgin
- 3 garlic cloves, finely minced
- ½ teaspoon thyme, dried
- 1 red capsicum, chopped
- 1 green capsicum, chopped
- 2 teaspoons dried basil
- Black pepper and salt as needed

Directions:

1. Take your Instant Pot and place it on a clean kitchen platform. Turn it on after plugging it into a power socket.
2. Put the pot on "Sauté" mode. In the pot, add the oil, garlic, and onion; cook for 3-4 minutes until the ingredients become soft.
3. Add the squash, eggplant, both capsicum, tomatoes, thyme, salt, pepper and basil; stir well.
4. Close the lid and lock. Ensure that you have sealed the valve to avoid leakage.
5. Press "Manual" mode and set timer for 10 minutes. It will take a few minutes for the pot to build inside pressure and start cooking.
6. After the timer reads zero, press "Cancel" and naturally release pressure. It takes about 8-10 minutes to naturally release pressure.
7. Carefully remove the lid and serve warm!

Nutrition:
Calories: 152 Fat: 10g Carbohydrates: 11.5g Fiber: 3g Proteins: 2g

222. Tofu Veggie Treat

Preparation time: 5-8 min.
Cooking time: 5 min.
Servings: 4
Ingredients:

- 3 teaspoons tamari
- 8 ounces soft tofu, make small cubes
- ½ cup red bell pepper
- 1 yellow onion, thinly sliced
- 6 large mushrooms, sliced
- ½ cup green beans
- ¼ cup vegetable stock
- Cooking oil as needed
- Salt and white pepper to the taste

Directions:

1. Take your Instant Pot and place it on a clean kitchen platform. Turn it on after plugging it into a power socket.
2. Put the pot on "Sauté" mode. In the pot, add the oil, mushrooms, and onions; cook for 2-3 minutes until the ingredients become soft.
3. Add the tamari and tofu; cook for 2 more minutes. Mix in the stock and stir gently.
4. Close the lid and lock. Ensure that you have sealed the valve to avoid leakage.
5. Press "Manual" mode and set timer for 3 minutes. It will take a few minutes for the pot to build inside pressure and start cooking.
6. After the timer reads zero, press "Cancel" and quick release pressure.
7. Add the green beans and bell pepper. Press "Manual" mode and set timer to 1 minutes. After the timer reads zero, press "Cancel" and quick release pressure.
8. Carefully remove the lid; add the pepper and salt. Serve warm!

Nutrition:
Calories: 112 Fat: 6g Carbohydrates: 9g Fiber: 1.5g Proteins: 7g

223. Mushroom Zucchini Pasta

Preparation time: 8 min.
Cooking time: 20 min.
Servings: 5-6
Ingredients:

- 12 mushrooms, thinly sliced
- 1 zucchini, thinly sliced
- A few drops of sherry wine
- 1 shallot, finely chopped
- 15 ounces penne pasta
- 5 ounces tomato paste
- 2 tablespoons soy sauce
- 1 yellow onion, thinly sliced
- 2 garlic cloves, minced
- 1 tablespoon olive oil
- 1 cup vegetable stock
- 2 cups water
- A pinch of basil, dried
- A pinch of oregano, dried
- Black pepper and salt as needed

Directions:

1. Take your Instant Pot and place it on a clean kitchen platform. Turn it on after plugging it into a power socket.
2. Put the pot on "Sauté" mode. In the pot, add the oil, onion, shallot, pepper and salt; cook for 2-3 minutes until the ingredients become soft.
3. Add the garlic, stir and cook for 1 minute more. Mix in the mushrooms, zucchini, basil, and oregano, stir and cook 1 more minute.
4. Mix in the wine, stock, water and soy sauce; stir well and then add the pasta and tomato sauce. Add more pepper and salt, if needed.
5. Close the lid and lock. Ensure that you have sealed the valve to avoid leakage.

6. Press "Manual" mode and set timer for 5 minutes. It will take a few minutes for the pot to build inside pressure and start cooking.
7. After the timer reads zero, press "Cancel" and quick release pressure.

224. Potato Mustard Salad

Preparation time: 8-10 min.
Cooking time: 10 min.
Servings: 6
Ingredients:

- 1 celery stalk, chopped
- 1 cup water
- 3 teaspoons dill, finely chopped
- 1 small yellow onion, chopped
- 1 teaspoon cider vinegar
- 3 ounces vegan mayo
- 6 red potatoes
- 1 teaspoon mustard
- Black pepper and salt as needed

Directions:

1. Take your Instant Pot and place it on a clean kitchen platform. Turn it on after plugging it into a power socket.

225. Chickpea Burger

Preparation time: 8-10 min.
Cooking time: 20 min.
Servings: 5-6
Ingredients:

- 1 teaspoon cumin
- 2 bay leaves
- 1 cup chickpeas (dried), soaked for 4 hours
- 1 teaspoon thyme, dried
- 3 tablespoons tomato paste
- ½ cup whole wheat flour
- 1 teaspoon salt
- 1 teaspoon garlic powder
- Pepper as needed

Directions:

1. Take your Instant Pot and place it on a clean kitchen platform. Turn it on after plugging it into a power socket.
2. Open the lid from the top and put it aside; add the chickpeas and enough water to cover them.

226. Spinach Pasta Treat

Preparation time: 5 min.
Cooking time: 15 min.
Servings: 4
Ingredients:

- 2 garlic cloves, crushed
- 2 garlic cloves, chopped
- 1 pound spinach
- 1 pound fusilli pasta
- A drizzle of olive oil
- ¼ cup pine nuts, chopped
- Black pepper and salt to taste

Directions:

1. Take your Instant Pot and place it on a clean kitchen platform. Turn it on after plugging it into a power socket.

8. Carefully remove the lid and serve warm!

Nutrition:
Calories: 248 Fat: 12.5g Carbohydrates: 12g Fiber: 1g Proteins: 3.5g

2. Open the lid from the top and put it aside; add the potatoes and water.
3. Close the lid and lock. Ensure that you have sealed the valve to avoid leakage.
4. Press "Manual" mode and set timer for 3 minutes. It will take a few minutes for the pot to build inside pressure and start cooking.
5. After the timer reads zero, press "Cancel" and quick release pressure.
6. Carefully remove the lid and chop the potatoes.
7. In a bowl of medium size, thoroughly mix the onion, potatoes, celery, salt, pepper, and dill.
8. Add the vegan mayo, vinegar, and mustard; stir well. Serve warm!

Nutrition:
Calories: 141 Fat: 2g Carbohydrates: 22.5g Fiber: 2g Proteins: 4g

3. Add the cumin powder, bay leaves, garlic powder, thyme, onion salt and pepper. Gently stir them.
4. Close the lid and lock. Ensure that you have sealed the valve to avoid leakage.
5. Press "Manual" mode and set timer for 15 minutes. It will take a few minutes for the pot to build inside pressure and start cooking.
6. After the timer reads zero, press "Cancel" and quick release pressure.
7. Carefully remove the lid. Discard bay leaves and drain water.
8. Transfer the mixture in a blender; blend to make it smooth. Add the flour and tomato paste, blend again.
9. Make 5 burger patties from the mix and grill them until turn golden on both sides.
10. Add them to the burger buns and add your favorite veggies and vegan mayo. Enjoy!

Nutrition:
Calories: 109 Fat: 2g Carbohydrates: 20g Fiber: 4.5g Proteins: 5g

2. Put the pot on "Sauté" mode. In the pot, add the oil, garlic, and spinach; cook for 6-7 minutes until the ingredients become soft.
3. Add the pasta, salt, and pepper; add water to cover the pasta.
4. Close the lid and lock. Ensure that you have sealed the valve to avoid leakage.
5. Press "Manual" mode and set timer for 6 minutes. It will take a few minutes for the pot to build inside pressure and start cooking.
6. After the timer reads zero, press "Cancel" and quick release pressure.
7. Carefully remove the lid; mix the chopped garlic and pine nuts.
8. Serve warm!

Nutrition:

Calories: 198 Fat: 1g Carbohydrates: 6.5g Fiber: 1g Proteins: 7g

227. Mexican Style Vegan Rice

Preparation time: 5 min.
Cooking time: 8-10 min.
Servings: 5-6
Ingredients:

- ½ piece chopped white onion
- 2 cups water
- 2 cups white rice, long-grain
- 3 cloves minced garlic
- 1 jalapeño, optional
- ½ cup tomato paste
- 2 teaspoon salts

Directions:

1. Take your Instant Pot and place it on a clean kitchen platform. Turn it on after plugging it into a power socket.

2. Put the pot on "Sauté" mode. In the pot, add the oil, garlic, onion, rice, and salt; cook for 3-4 minutes until the ingredients become soft.
3. Mix the tomato paste, pepper and water; stir well.
4. Close the lid and lock. Ensure that you have sealed the valve to avoid leakage.
5. Press "Manual" mode and set timer for 4 minutes. It will take a few minutes for the pot to build inside pressure and start cooking.
6. After the timer reads zero, press "Cancel" and naturally release pressure. It takes about 8-10 minutes to naturally release pressure.
7. Carefully remove the lid, fluff the mix and serve warm!

Nutrition:
Calories: 521 Fat: 1.5g Carbohydrates: 39g Fiber: 3g Proteins: 6g

228. Wholesome Lentil Tacos

Preparation time: 5 min.
Cooking time: 15 min.
Servings: 6-8
Ingredients:

- 1 teaspoon onion powder
- 2 cups lentils, dry
- 1 teaspoon chili powder
- 4 cups water
- 4-ounce tomato sauce
- 1 teaspoon garlic powder
- ½ teaspoon cumin
- 1 teaspoon salt

Directions:

1. Take your Instant Pot and place it on a clean kitchen platform. Turn it on after plugging it into a power socket.

2. Open the lid from the top and put it aside; start adding the mentioned ingredients inside and gently stir them.
3. Close the lid and lock. Ensure that you have sealed the valve to avoid leakage.
4. Press "Manual" mode and set timer for 15 minutes. It will take a few minutes for the pot to build inside pressure and start cooking.
5. After the timer reads zero, press "Cancel" and naturally release pressure. It takes about 8-10 minutes to naturally release pressure.
6. Carefully remove the lid.
7. Take your choice of tacos and add the cooked mixture; enjoy the vegan tacos!

Nutrition:
Calories: 174 Fat: 0.5g Carbohydrates: 30.5g Fiber: 15g Proteins: 13g

229. Green Beans Gremolata

Preparation time: 15 minutes
Cooking time: 5 minutes
Servings: 6
Ingredients:

- 1-pound fresh green beans
- 3 garlic cloves, minced
- Zest of 2 oranges
- 3 tablespoons minced fresh parsley
- 2 tablespoons pine nuts
- 3 tablespoons olive oil
- Sea salt
- Freshly ground black pepper

Directions:

1. 1. Boil water over high heat. Cook green beans for 3 minutes. Drain r and rinse with cold water to stop the cooking.
2. 2. Blend garlic, orange zest, and parsley.
3. 3. In a huge sauté pan over medium-high heat, toast the pine nuts in the dry, hot pan for 3 minutes. Remove from the pan and set aside.
4. 4. Cook olive oil in the same pan until it shimmers. Add the beans and cook, -stirring frequently, until heated through, about 2 minutes. Take pan away from the heat and add the parsley mixture and pine nuts. Season with salt and pepper. Serve immediately.

Nutrition:
Calories: 98 Fiber: 2g Proteins: 3g

230. Minted Peas

Preparation time: 5 minutes
Cooking time: 5 minutes
Servings: 4
Ingredients:

- 1 tablespoon olive oil
- 4 cups peas, fresh or frozen (not canned)
- ½ teaspoon sea salt
- Freshly ground black pepper
- 3 tablespoons chopped fresh mint

Directions:

1. In a large sauté pan, cook olive oil over medium-high heat until hot. Add the peas and cook, about 5 minutes. Remove the pan from heat. Stir in the salt, season with pepper, and stir in the mint. Serve hot.

Nutrition:
Calories: 90 Fiber: 5g Proteins: 8g

231. Sweet and Spicy Brussels Sprout Hash

Preparation time: 10 minutes
Cooking time: 15 minutes
Servings: 4
Ingredients:

- 3 tablespoons olive oil
- 2 shallots, thinly sliced
- 1½ pounds Brussel sprouts
- 3 tablespoons apple cider vinegar
- 1 tablespoon pure maple syrup
- ½ teaspoon sriracha sauce (or to taste)
- Sea salt
- Freshly ground black pepper

Directions:

1. In pan, cook olive oil over medium-high heat until it shimmers. Mix the shallots and Brussels sprouts and cook, stirring frequently, until the -vegetables soften and begin to turn golden brown, about 10 minutes. Stir in the vinegar, using a spoon to scrape any browned bits from the pan's bottom. Stir in the maple syrup and Sriracha.
2. Simmer, stirring frequently, until the liquid reduces, 3 to 5 minutes. Season and serve immediately.

Nutrition:
Calories: 97 Fiber: 4g Proteins: 7g

232. Glazed Curried Carrots

Preparation time: 5 minutes
Cooking time: 15 minutes
Servings: 6
Ingredients:

- 1-pound carrots
- 2 tablespoons olive oil
- 2 tablespoons curry powder
- 2 tablespoons pure maple syrup
- Juice of ½ lemon

Directions:

1. Cook carrots with water over medium-high heat for 10 minutes. Drain and return them to the pan over medium-low heat.
2. Stir in the olive oil, curry powder, maple syrup, and lemon juice. Cook, stirring constantly, until the liquid reduces, about 5 minutes. Season well and serve immediately.

Nutrition:
Calories: 91 Fiber: 5g Proteins: 9g

233. Pepper Medley

Preparation time: 10 minutes
Cooking time: 15 minutes
Servings: 4
Ingredients:

- 3 tablespoons olive oil
- 1 red bell pepper, sliced
- 1 orange bell pepper, sliced
- 1 yellow bell pepper, sliced
- 1 green bell pepper, sliced
- 2 garlic cloves, minced
- 3 tablespoons red wine vinegar
- 2 tablespoons chopped fresh basil

Directions:

1. Warm up olive oil over medium-high heat. Stir in the bell peppers and cook, stir, for 7 to 10 minutes. Cook garlic for 30 seconds. Add the vinegar, using a spoon to scrape any browned bits off the bottom of the pan.
2. Simmer until the vinegar reduces, 2 to 3 minutes. Season. Stir in the basil and serve immediately.

Nutrition:
Calories: 96 Fiber: 3g Proteins: 5g

234. Garlicky Red Wine Mushrooms

Preparation time: 10 minutes
Cooking time: 15 minutes
Servings: 4
Ingredients:

- 3 tablespoons olive oil
- 2 cups sliced mushrooms
- 3 garlic cloves, minced
- ½ cup red wine
- 1 tablespoon dried thyme

Directions:

1. Cook olive oil over medium-high heat until it shimmers. Mix in the mushrooms and sit, untouched, until they release their liquid and begin to brown, about 5 minutes. Stir the mushrooms occasionally, cooking until softened and golden brown, about 5 minutes more. Cook garlic. Add the red wine and thyme, using a wooden spoon to scrape any browned bits off the pan's bottom.
2. Adjust heat to medium. Cook for 5 minutes. Season well and serve.

Nutrition:
Calories: 98 Fiber: 4g Proteins: 6g

235. Sautéed Citrus Spinach

Preparation time: 10 minutes
Cooking time: 10 minutes
Servings: 4
Ingredients:

- 2 tablespoons olive oil
- 1 shallot, chopped
- 2 garlic cloves, minced
- 10 ounces' baby spinach
- Zest and juice of 1 orange

Directions:

1. Cook olive oil over medium-high heat. Cook the shallot for 3 minutes. Cook garlic for 30 seconds.
2. Add the spinach, orange juice, and orange zest. Cook for 2 minutes. Season with salt and pepper. Serve warm.

Nutrition:
Calories: 91 Fiber: 4g Proteins: 7g

236. Waffles with Almond Flour

Preparation time: 15 minutes
Cooking time: 15 minutes
Servings: 4
Ingredients:

- 1 cup almond milk
- 2 tbsps. chia seeds
- 2 tsp. lemon juice
- 4 tbsps. coconut oil
- 1/2 cup almond flour
- 2 tbsps. maple syrup
- Cooking spray or cooking oil

Directions:

1. Mix coconut milk with lemon juice in a mixing bowl.

237. Cantaloupe Smoothie Bowl

Preparation time: 5 minutes
Cooking time: 0 minutes
Servings: 2
Ingredients:

- 3/4 Cup carrot Juice
- 4 Cps Cantaloupe, Frozen and Cubed

238. Double Chocolate Hazelnut Espresso Shake

Preparation time: 5 minutes
Cooking time: 0 minute
Servings: 1
Ingredients:

- 1 frozen banana, sliced
- 1/4 cup roasted hazelnuts
- 4 Medrol dates, pitted, soaked
- 2 tablespoons cacao nibs, unsweetened
- 1 1/2 tablespoons cacao powder, unsweetened
- 1/8 teaspoon sea salt
- 1 teaspoon vanilla extract, unsweetened

239. Banana Bread Shake with Walnut Milk

Preparation time: 5 minutes
Cooking time: 0 minute
Servings: 2
Ingredients:

- 2 cups sliced frozen bananas
- 3 cups walnut milk
- 1/8 teaspoon grated nutmeg
- 1 tablespoon maple syrup
- 1 teaspoon ground cinnamon
- 1/2 teaspoon vanilla extract, unsweetened

240. Creamy Pumpkin Pie Oatmeal

Preparation time: 5 minutes
Cooking time: 35 minutes
Servings: 4
Ingredients:

- 3 cups plant-based milk
- 1 cup unsweetened pumpkin purée
- 1 cup steel-cut oats
- 2 tablespoons maple syrup (optional)
- 1 teaspoon ground cinnamon
- 1/8 Teaspoon ground nutmeg
- 1/8 Teaspoon ground cloves

2. Leave it for 5-8 minutes on room temperature to turn it into butter milk.
3. Once coconut milk is turned into butter milk, add chai seeds into milk and whisk together.
4. Add other ingredients in milk mixture and mix well.
5. Preheat a waffle iron and spray it with coconut oil spray.
6. Pour 2 tbsp. of waffle mixture into the waffle machine and cook until golden.
7. Top with some berries and serve hot.

Nutrition:
Calories: 194 Carbohydrates: 43.3g Proteins: 3.4g Fat: 0.3g

- Mellon Balls or Berries to Serve
- Pinch Sea Salt

Directions:

1. Blend everything together until smooth.

Nutrition:
Calories: 399 Fat: 29.4g Carbohydrates: 17.3g Proteins: 23.3g

- 1 cup almond milk, unsweetened
- 1/2 cup ice
- 4 ounces espresso, chilled

Directions:

1. Set all the ingredients in the order in a food processor or blender and then pulse for 2 to 3 minutes at high speed until smooth.
2. Pour the smoothie into a glass and then serve.

Nutrition:
Calories: 210 Fat: 5g Carbohydrates: 27g Proteins: 16.8g
Fiber: 0.2g

- 2 tablespoons cacao nibs

Directions:

1. Set all the ingredients in the order in a food processor or blender and then pulse for 2 to 3 minutes at high speed until smooth.
2. Pour the smoothie into two glasses and then serve.

Nutrition:
Calories: 339.8 Fat: 19g Carbohydrates: 39g Proteins: 4.3g
Fiber: 1g

Directions:

1. Set the milk to a boil in a medium saucepan over medium-high heat.
2. Once it starts to boil stir in the remaining ingredients.
3. Cover and cook for 30 minutes, stirring frequently, and serve.

Nutrition:
Calories: 219 Fat: 4.9g Carbohydrates: 38.0g Proteins: 7.2g
Fiber: 6.0g

241. Spinach and Orange Salad

Preparation time: 5 minutes
Cooking time: 0 minutes
Servings: 6
Ingredients:

- 10 ounces fresh spinach
- 1 teaspoon Brazil nuts
- 10 strawberries, sliced
- 1 teaspoon sunflower seeds
- 10 ounces canned clementine oranges

242. Red Beans with Cauliflower Rice

Preparation time: 15 minutes
Cooking time: 17 minutes
Servings: 4
Ingredients:

- 1 large head cauliflower
- 2 tablespoons avocado oil (optional)
- 1/2 cup diced celery ribs
- 1/2 cup chopped green bell pepper
- 1/2 cup chopped sweet onion
- 11/2 cups cooked red beans
- 1 cup cooked brown rice
- 2 teaspoons cumin
- 1 tablespoon minced garlic
- 1 teaspoon chili powder
- 1/2 teaspoon basil
- 1/2 teaspoon chopped fresh parsley

243. Mushroom Cream

Preparation time: 10 minutes
Cooking time: 20 minutes
Servings: 2
Ingredients:

- 2 teaspoons olive oil
- 1 onion
- 2 garlic cloves
- 2 cups chopped mushrooms
- 2 tablespoons whole-grain flour
- 1 teaspoon dried herbs
- 4 cups Economical Vegetable Broth
- 11/2 cups nondairy milk

Directions:

244. Pepper and Kale

Preparation time: 5 minutes
Cooking time: 15 minutes
Servings: 4
Ingredients:

- 2 cans chickpeas
- 4 cloves garlic
- 1 large sweet onion
- 4 tbsp. olive oil
- 2 red peppers
- 6 cups kale

Directions:

245. Caesar Pasta

Preparation time: 10 minutes
Cooking time: 0 minute
Servings: 1
Ingredients:

- 1/4 cup raspberry vinaigrette

Directions:

1. Take a medium bowl, set all the ingredients in it and then toss until coated.
2. Serve straight away.

Nutrition:
Calories: 109 Fat: 2g Proteins: 3g Carbohydrates: 18g Fiber: 4g

- 1 teaspoon paprika
- 1/2 teaspoon ground black pepper
- 2 cups water

Directions:

1. Smash the cauliflower in a food processor to make the cauliflower rice. Set aside.
2. Heat the avocado oil (if desired) in a skillet over medium-high heat.
3. Attach the celery, green pepper, and onion to the skillet and sauté for 7 minutes or until tender.
4. Attach the remaining ingredients to the skillet and sauté for 10 minutes until well combined and the cauliflower rice is soft.
5. Serve immediately.

Nutrition:
Calories: 278 Fat: 8.9g Carbohydrates: 41.9g Proteins: 12.0g Fiber: 11.4g

1. Preheat oil over medium-high heat.
2. Add the onion, garlic, mushrooms, and salt. Sauté for about 5 minutes, until softened. Throw flour over the ingredients in the pot and mix.
3. Cook for 1 to 2 minutes more to toast the flour.
4. Add the dried herbs, vegetable broth, milk, and pepper.
5. Set heat to low, and let the broth come to a simmer.
6. Cook for 10 minutes, until slightly thickened.

Nutrition:
Calories: 267 Fat: 6g Carbohydrates: 42g Fiber: 4g Proteins: 15g

1. Warmth BBQ and prepare a greased BBQ basket or pan.
2. Meanwhile, merge together chickpeas, garlic, onion, red peppers and olive oil in a bowl and add to the BBQ basket and place on the grill. Stir regularly.
3. When almost ready to serve attach kale and stir constantly until the kale is slightly wilted. Serve with garlic toast, pita bread or rice.

Nutrition:
Calories: 393 Fat: 15g Proteins: 10g Carbohydrates: 52g Fiber: 9g

- 2 cups chopped romaine lettuce
- 2 tablespoons Vegan Caesar Dressing
- 1/2 cup cooked pasta
- 1/2 cup canned chickpeas

- 2 additional tablespoons Caesar Dressing

Directions:
1. Blend the lettuce, dressing, (if using).

246. Gingery Carrot Mash

Preparation time: 5 minutes
Cooking time: 15 minutes
Servings: 4
Ingredients:
- 2 pounds carrots, cut into rounds
- 2 tablespoons olive oil
- 1 teaspoon ground cumin
- Salt ground black pepper, to taste
- 1/2 teaspoon cayenne pepper
- 1/2 teaspoon ginger, peeled and minced
- 1/2 cup whole milk

Directions:

247. Silky Kohlrabi Puree

Preparation time: 10 minutes
Cooking time: 30 minutes
Servings: 4
Ingredients:
- 1 1/4 pounds kohlrabi, peeled and cut into pieces
- 4 tablespoons vegan butter
- salt and ground black pepper, to taste
- 1/2 teaspoon cumin seeds
- 1/2 teaspoon coriander seeds
- 1/2 cup soy milk
- 1 teaspoon fresh dill

248. Aromatic Sautéed Kohlrabi

Preparation time: 5 minutes
Cooking time: 15 minutes
Servings: 4
Ingredients:
- 3 tablespoons sesame oil
- 1 1/2 pounds kohlrabi, peeled and cubed
- 1 teaspoon garlic, minced
- 1/2 teaspoon dried basil
- 1/2 teaspoon dried oregano
- salt and ground black pepper, to season

249. Classic Braised Cabbage

Preparation time: 5 minutes
Cooking time: 15 minutes
Servings: 4
Ingredients:
- 4 tablespoons sesame oil
- 1 shallot, chopped
- 2 garlic cloves, minced
- 2 bay leaves
- 1 cup vegetable broth
- 1 1/2 pounds purple cabbage, cut into wedges
- 1 teaspoon red pepper flakes
- Sea salt and black pepper, to taste

Directions:

250. Seitan

Preparation time: 25 minutes
Cooking time: 20 minutes
Servings: 5

2. Add the pasta, chickpeas, and additional dressing. Toss to coat.

Nutrition:
Calories: 166 Proteins: 9g Carbohydrates: 2.4g Fat: 13.5g Fiber: 0.3g

1. Warmth your oven to 400 degrees F.
2. Set the carrots with the olive oil, cumin, salt, black pepper and cayenne pepper. Set them in a single layer on a parchment-lined roasting sheet.
3. Roast the carrots in the warmth oven for about 20 minutes, until crisp-tender.
4. Add the roasted carrots, ginger and milk to your food processor; puree the ingredients until everything is well blended.
5. Bon appétit!

Nutrition:
Calories: 202 Fat: 22g Carbohydrates: 5g Proteins: 34g

- 1 teaspoon fresh parsley

Directions:
1. Set the kohlrabi in boiling salted water until soft, about 30 minutes; drain.
2. Puree the kohlrabi with the vegan butter, salt, black pepper, cumin seeds and coriander seeds.
3. Puree the ingredients with an immersion blender, gradually adding the milk. Top with fresh dill and parsley. Bon appétit!

Nutrition:
Calories: 92 Fat: 0g Carbohydrates: 20g

Directions:
1. In a nonstick skillet, heat the sesame oil. Once hot, sauté the kohlrabi for about 6 minutes.
2. Add in the garlic, basil, oregano, salt and black pepper. Continue to cook.
3. Serve warm. Bon appétit!

Nutrition:
Calories: 141 Fat: 2g Carbohydrates: 22.5g Fiber: 2g Proteins: 4g

1. Warmth the sesame oil in a saucepan over medium flame. Once hot, fry the shallot for 3 to 4 minutes, stirring periodically to promote even cooking.
2. Add in the garlic and bay laurel and continue sautéing an additional 1 minute or until fragrant.
3. Add in the broth, cabbage red pepper flakes, salt and black pepper and continue to parboil, secured, for about 12 minutes or until the cabbage has softened.
4. Taste and adjust the seasonings and serve hot. Bon appétit!

Nutrition:
Calories: 248 Fat: 3g Carbohydrates: 50g Fiber: 4g

Ingredients:
- Firm Tofu, 250 grams
- Unsweetened soy milk, 150ml

- Miso paste 2 tsp.
- Marmite 2 tsp.
- Onion powder 1 tsp.
- Garlic powder 2 tsp.
- Wheat gluten 160g.
- Pea protein or vegan protein powder, 40g.
- Vegetable stock 1 1/2 liters

Directions:
1. Blitz the tofu, soy milk, miso, marmite, onion powder, garlic powder, 1 tsp. salt and 1/2 tsp.

251. Sautéed Carrots with Sesame Seeds

Preparation time: 25 minutes
Cooking time: 10 minutes
Servings: 4
Ingredients:
- 1/3 cup vegetable broth
- 2 pounds carrots, trimmed and cut into sticks
- 4 tablespoons sesame oil
- 1 teaspoon garlic, chopped
- Himalayan salt and ground black pepper
- 1 teaspoon cayenne pepper
- 2 tablespoons fresh parsley, chopped
- 2 tablespoons sesame seeds

Directions:

252. Roasted Carrots with Tahini Sauce

Preparation time: 5 minutes
Cooking time: 25 minutes
Servings: 4
Ingredients:
- 2 1/2 pounds carrots washed, trimmed and halved lengthwise
- 4 tablespoons olive oil
- salt and ground black pepper, to taste

Sauce:
- 4 tablespoons tahini
- 1 teaspoon garlic, pressed
- 2 tablespoons white vinegar
- 2 tablespoons soy sauce
- 1 teaspoon deli mustard
- 1 teaspoon agave syrup

253. Roasted Cauliflower with Herbs

Preparation time: 5 minutes
Cooking time: 25 minutes
Servings: 4
Ingredients:
- 1 1/2 pounds cauliflower florets
- 1/4 cup olive oil
- 4 cloves garlic, whole
- 1 tablespoon fresh basil
- 1 tablespoon fresh coriander
- 1 tablespoon fresh oregano
- 1 tablespoon fresh rosemary
- 1 tablespoon fresh parsley

254. Creamy Rosemary Broccoli Mash

Preparation time: 5 minutes
Cooking time: 15 minutes
Servings: 4

white pepper in a food processor. Blend until smooth.
2. Mix them all to form dough. Knead the dough well, stretching and tearing for 10-15 minutes.
3. Fill vegetable stock into a pan and let it simmer. Flatten out the seitan to a thickness of 1 cm and chop into chunks. Simmer it in the stock for 20 minutes covering with a lid. Once it's done, allow it to cool down. Chop or tear it into smaller pieces before cooking as per your choice.

Nutrition:
Calories: 420 Fat: 15.2g Carbohydrates: 64.3g Proteins: 11.6g

1. In a large saucepan, set the vegetable broth to a boil. Turn the heat to medium-low. Attach in the carrots and continue to cook, covered, for about 8 minutes, until the carrots are crisp-tender.
2. Heat the sesame oil over medium-high heat; now, sauté the garlic for 30 seconds or until aromatic. Add in the salt, black pepper and cayenne pepper.
3. In a skillet, roast the sesame seeds for 1 minute or until just fragrant and golden.
4. To serve, garnish the sautéed carrots with parsley and toasted sesame seeds. Bon appétit!

Nutrition:
Calories: 278 Fat: 8.9g Carbohydrates: 41.9g Proteins: 12.0g
Fiber: 11.4g

- 1/2 teaspoon cumin seed
- 1/2 teaspoon dried dill weed

Directions:
1. Warmth your oven to 400 degrees F.
2. Set the carrots with the olive oil, salt and black pepper. Set them in a single layer on a parchment-lined roasting sheet. Roast the carrots in the warmth oven for about 20 minutes, until crisp-tender.
3. Meanwhile, whisk all the sauce ingredients until well combined.
4. Serve the carrots with the sauce for dipping. Bon appétit!

Nutrition:
Calories: 141 Fat: 2g Carbohydrates: 22.5g Fiber: 2g Proteins: 4g

- salt and ground black pepper, to taste
- 1 teaspoon red pepper flakes

Directions:
1. Warmth the oven to 425 degrees F. Toss the cauliflower with the olive oil and arrange them on a parchment-lined roasting pan.
2. Then, roast the cauliflower florets for about 20 minutes; toss them with the garlic and spices and continue cooking an additional 10 minutes.
3. Serve warm. Bon appétit!

Nutrition:
Calories: 523 Carbohydrates: 57.6g Proteins: 7.5g Fat: 37.6g

Ingredients:
- 1 1/2 pounds broccoli florets
- 3 tablespoons vegan butter

- 4 cloves garlic, chopped
- 2 sprigs fresh rosemary, leaves picked and sliced
- Sea salt and red pepper, to taste
- 1/4 cup soy milk, unsweetened

Directions:
1. Boil the broccoli florets for about 10 minutes; set it aside to cool.
2. In a saucepan, melt the vegan butter over a moderately high heat; now, sauté the garlic and rosemary until they are fragrant.

255. Classic Tomato Bruschetta

Preparation time: 5 minutes
Cooking time: 15 minutes
Servings: 4
Ingredients:
- 4 slices bread
- 2 tablespoons extra-virgin olive oil
- 1 clove garlic, halved
- 2 tomatoes, diced
- 1 teaspoon dried oregano
- 1 teaspoon dried basil
- salt and ground black pepper

256. Sweet Potato Chili with Kale

Preparation time: 15 minutes
Cooking time: 43 minutes
Servings: 6
Ingredients:
- 2 medium sweet potatoes, diced
- 1 large red onion, chopped
- 2 (15-ounce) cans kidney beans
- 2 red bell peppers, seeded and diced
- 2 pounds fresh tomatoes, diced
- 1 tablespoon chili powder
- 2 teaspoons smoked paprika
- 1/4 teaspoon chipotle powder

257. Potato Cauliflower Curry

Preparation time: 15 minutes
Cooking time: 38 minutes
Servings: 4
Ingredients:
- 4 cups cauliflower florets
- 2 cups potato pieces, cubed
- 1 cup onion wedges
- 1/4 cup tomato paste
- 1 tablespoon mild curry powder
- 11/2 teaspoon fresh ginger, grated
- 1 teaspoon cumin seeds
- 1 garlic clove, minced
- 11/2 cups fresh peas
- 1/4 cup raw cashews, ground
- 2 tablespoons lime juice
- Cayenne pepper, to taste
- Sea salt, to taste
- 4 cups cooked brown rice
- 1 tablespoon fresh cilantro, snipped

Directions:

3. Attach the broccoli florets to your food processor followed by the sautéed garlic/rosemary mixture, salt, pepper and milk. Puree until everything is well incorporated.
4. Garnish with some extra fresh herbs, if desired and serve hot. Bon appétit!

Nutrition:
Calories: 92 Fat: 0g Carbohydrates: 20g

Directions:
1. Garnish the bread slices with the olive oil and toast them in a skillet.
2. Now, rub the toasted bread on one side with halved garlic cloves.
3. Top with the tomatoes; sprinkle oregano, basil, salt and black pepper over everything. Bon appétit!

Nutrition:
Calories: 150 Fat: 7.3g Fiber: 6.1g Carbohydrates: 18g
Proteins: 3.7g

- 2 cups Lacinato kale, shredded
- 3 cups of orange, juiced

Directions:
1. Sauté onion with bell pepper and orange juice in a skillet for 10 minutes.
2. Swirl in the rest of the ingredients, reserving the kale and cook for 30 minutes on medium heat.
3. Mash the cooked mixture a little then add kale.
4. Cook for 3 minutes then serve warm.

Nutrition:
Calories: 457 Fat: 19g Carbohydrates: 29g Fiber: 1.8g
Proteins: 32.5g

1. Add cauliflower to a steamer basket, cover and cook for 5 minutes.
2. Transfer the cauliflower to a bowl.
3. Add potato pieces to the steamer and cook for 10 minutes.
4. Transfer these potatoes to the cauliflower then mix well.
5. Blend onion wedges with garlic, cumin seeds, ginger, curry powder, and tomato paste in a blender. Pour this mixture into a skillet along with 1 cup water and cook for 7 minutes.
6. Reduce its heat to medium-low heat and cook for 10 minutes until the sauce thickens.
7. Add potatoes, cauliflower and the rest of the ingredients.
8. Mix well and cook for 7 minutes. Garnish with cilantro and serve warm.

Nutrition:
Calories: 392 Fat: 16g Carbohydrates: 39g Fiber: 0.9g
Proteins: 48g

258. Zucchini and Chickpea Sauté

Preparation time: 15 minutes
Cooking time: 25 minutes
Servings: 6
Ingredients:

- 1 onion, chopped
- 1 large red bell pepper, chopped
- 6 garlic cloves, minced
- 1 teaspoon dried oregano
- 1/2 teaspoon dried thyme
- 1 cup oil-free marinara sauce
- 1 tablespoon white wine vinegar
- Salt and black pepper, to taste
- 3 medium zucchinis, halved lengthwise and sliced
- 1 15-ounce can chickpeas, rinsed and drained
- 10 fresh basil leaves, chopped

Directions:

1. Sauté onion, bell pepper, garlic, oregano, and thyme in a greased skillet for 10 minutes.
2. Stir in zucchini and cook for 10 minutes.
3. Stir in vinegar, marinara sauce, black pepper, salt and chickpeas.
4. Cook the mixture for 5 minutes then garnish with basil.
5. Serve warm.

Nutrition:
Calories: 321 Fat: 7.4g Carbohydrates: 23g Fiber: 2.4g Proteins: 37.2g

259. Raw Collard Wraps

Preparation time: 15 minutes
Cooking time: 0 minutes
Servings: 3
Ingredients:

- 4 large collard leaves
- 1 red bell pepper, julienned
- 1 avocado
- 3 ounces alfalfa sprouts
- 1/2 lime, juiced
- 1 cup raw pecans, chopped
- 1 tablespoon tamari
- 1/2 teaspoon garlic, minced
- 1/2 teaspoon ginger, grated
- 1 teaspoon olive oil

Directions:

1. Soak the leaves in warm water for 10 minutes then drain.
2. Puree cumin with olive oil, tamari and pecans in a blender.
3. Spread the collard leaf on the working surface and top them with the pecan's mixture.
4. Divide the avocado slices, red pepper slices and alfalfa sprouts on top.
5. Drizzle the lime juice on top and roll the leaves.
6. Cut the roll in half and serve.

Nutrition:
Calories: 332 Fat: 10g Carbohydrates: 21g Fiber: 0.4g Proteins: 8g

260. Avocado Chickpea Lettuce Cups

Preparation time: 10 minutes
Cooking time: 0 minutes
Servings: 5
Ingredients:

- 1 tablespoon Dijon mustard
- 1 tablespoon shallots, minced
- 1 lime, juiced
- 2 tablespoons fresh cilantro, chopped
- 1 tablespoon apple cider vinegar
- 2 1/2 tablespoons olive oil
- 1 can chickpeas, drained
- 8 ounces jarred hearts of palm, drained
- 1/2 cup fresh cucumber, diced
- 2 small avocados, peeled, seeded and diced
- 4 handfuls of mixed greens
- Salt and black pepper to taste

Directions:

1. Mix shallots with apple cider vinegar, cilantro, lime zest and juice in a bowl.
2. Stir in oil, black pepper and salt then mix well.
3. Add cucumber, heart of palm and chickpeas then mix well.
4. Fold in avocados and greens then mix again.
5. Serve.

Nutrition:
Calories: 285 Fat: 8g Carbohydrates: 35g Fiber: 0.1g Proteins: 1g

261. Coconut Green Soup

Preparation time: 15 minutes
Cooking time: 17 minutes
Servings: 4
Ingredients:

- 1 teaspoon whole cumin seeds
- 1 teaspoon whole coriander seeds
- 2 teaspoons coconut oil
- 1 large shallot, chopped
- 1 medium zucchini, chopped
- 1 small bunch celery, chopped
- 1 medium apple, peeled, cored and chopped
- 3-inch ginger, peeled and chopped
- 6 cups vegetable stock
- Salt and black pepper, to taste
- 4 cups greens, chopped
- 1 (14-ounce) can full fat coconut milk
- 2 tablespoons lime juice
- Garnishing
- Cooked brown rice
- Cooked lentils or chickpeas
- Sliced ripe avocado
- Coconut milk
- Chili-infused olive oil
- Chopped basil

Directions:

1. Roast coriander seeds and cumin in a skillet for 1 minute then transfer to a grinder and grind.
2. Sauté shallots with coconut oil in a saucepan for 3 minutes.
3. Stir in apple, celery, zucchini, ginger, coriander powder and cumin powder.
4. Sauté for 3 minutes, then add vegetable stock, black pepper and salt.
5. Boil and reduce its heat and cook for 10 minutes.

262. Roasted Cauliflower Soup

Preparation time: 15 minutes
Cooking time: 1 hour 15 minutes
Servings: 4
Ingredients:

- 1 cauliflower head, cut into florets
- 1 lb. Yukon gold potatoes, scrubbed
- 2 yellow onions, skin removed
- 2 tablespoons rosemary leaves
- 2 tablespoons olive oil
- Salt and black pepper, to taste
- 1 tablespoon fresh lemon juice
- 6 cups vegetable stock
- Olive oil
- Croutons
- Nuts, toasted and chopped
- Leafy herbs, chopped
- Balsamic reduction
- Squeezes of lemon

263. Squash and Chestnut Soup

Preparation time: 15 minutes
Cooking time: 55 minutes
Servings: 4
Ingredients:

- 1 lb. chestnuts
- 2 tablespoons olive oil
- 1 onion, chopped
- 4 garlic cloves, chopped
- 1 teaspoon salt
- 7 cups water
- 1 large sage sprig
- 3 bay leaves
- 2 teaspoons tamari soy sauce
- 1 kabocha squash, peeled, seeded and diced
- Black pepper, to taste
- Kale Sesame Crisps
- 1 bunch Lacinato kale, leaves separated
- 2 teaspoons olive oil
- 1 teaspoon maple syrup
- Salt and black pepper, to taste
- 2 tablespoons sesame seeds

Directions:

264. Shiitake Tortilla Soup

Preparation time: 15 minutes
Cooking time: 30 minutes
Servings: 4
Ingredients:

- 6 (6-inch) corn tortillas
- 2 tablespoons avocado oil

6. Stir in coconut milk, and chopped greens, and then cook for 3 minutes.
7. Puree this soup with a hand blender until smooth.
8. Add lime juice and mix well.
9. Serve warm with favorite garnishes on top.

Nutrition:
Calories: 361 Fat: 16g Carbohydrates: 18g Fiber: 0.1g
Proteins: 33.3g

- Black pepper

Directions:
1. Preheat your oven to 400F.
2. Spread the cauliflower florets, onion and potatoes in a baking sheet.
3. Sprinkle oil, black pepper, salt and rosemary on top, then toss well.
4. Roast these veggies for 1 hour and toss them after every 10 minutes.
5. Puree veggies with lemon juice and vegetable stock in a blender.
6. Transfer this blend to a saucepan and cook to a boil.
7. Add more stock or water if needed.
8. Serve warm.

Nutrition:
Calories: 405 Fat: 22.7g Carbohydrates: 36g Fiber: 1.4g
Proteins: 45.2g

1. Preheat your oven to 425F.
2. Make a slit on top of each chestnut and add them to a saucepan.
3. Pour enough water to cover them and cook to a boil then drain. Spread these chestnuts in a baking sheet and roast for 20 minutes. Allow them to cool then peel off their shells. Reduce the oven's heat to 400F.
4. Toss kale leaves with black pepper, salt, 2 teaspoons olive oil and maple syrup in a baking sheet. Drizzle sesame seeds on top and bake for 8 minutes.
5. Sauté onion with olive oil in a soup pan over medium heat for 6 minutes. Add garlic and sauté for 30 seconds. Stir in bay leaves, sage, water, chestnuts, squash, and salt then cook to a boil. Reduce its heat and cook for 20 minutes.
6. Puree this soup with a blender in batches then return to the pot. Stir in black pepper, salt and tamari and boil again. Garnish with kale chips.
7. Serve warm.

Nutrition:
Calories: 345 Fat: 36g Carbohydrates: 41g Fiber: 0.2g
Proteins: 22.5g

- 1 (15-ounce) can crushed tomatoes
- 4 cups vegetable stock
- 1 small white onion, diced
- 4 garlic cloves, minced
- 1 jalapeño, minced
- 1/2 teaspoon dried Mexican oregano

- 1 teaspoon cumin
- 1 teaspoon chipotle powder
- 3/4 lb. shiitake mushrooms, sliced
- 1 (15-ounce) can black beans, drained
- 1 cup corn kernels
- Salt and black pepper, to taste

Serve:
- Ripe avocado, diced
- Cilantro, chopped
- Lime wedges

Directions:
1. Cut each tortilla into thin strips and spread them in a greased baking sheet.
2. Bake these tortillas strips for 12 minutes in the oven at 350 degrees.

265. Mushroom Bean Faro

Preparation time: 8-10 minutes
Cooking time: 30 minutes
Servings: 3-4
Ingredients:
- 3 cups mushrooms, chopped
- 1 seeded jalapeno pepper, chopped
- 1 tablespoon shallot powder
- 2 tablespoons barley
- 1 tablespoon red curry paste
- 1/2 cup faro
- 1 cup navy beans, dried
- 2 tablespoons onion powder
- 9 garlic cloves, minced
- 2 tomatoes, diced
- Pepper and salt as needed

Directions:
1. Take your Instant Pot and place it on a clean kitchen platform. Turn it on after plugging it into a power socket.

266. Collard Green Pasta

Preparation time: 15 minutes
Cooking time: 30 minutes
Servings: 4
Ingredients:
- 2 Tablespoons Olive Oil
- 4 Cloves Garlic, Minced
- 8 Ounces Whole Wheat Pasta
- 1/2 Cup Panko Breadcrumbs
- 1 Tablespoon Nutritional Yeast
- 1 Teaspoon Red Pepper Flakes
- 1 Large Lemon, Juiced and Zested
- 1 Bunch Collard Greens, Large

Directions:
1. Set a pot with water and salt it. Bring it to a boil using high heat. Add in the pasta and cool al dente before rinsing under cold water to stop the cooking.

3. Toss them once cooked halfway and then allow them to cool when cooked. Blend crushed tomatoes with half of the tortilla strips, and 1 cup stock until smooth.
4. Sauté onion with oil in a cooking pot over medium heat for 3 minutes. Stir in chipotle powder, cumin, oregano, jalapeño, and garlic then cook for 30 seconds.
5. Stir in mushrooms and cook. Add vegetable stock, corn, black beans, black pepper and salt. Stir in blended tomato mixture then cook to a boil.
6. Now, reduce its heat and cook for 10 minutes. Garnish with remaining tortillas strips, cilantro, lime wedges, and avocado.
7. Serve warm.

Nutrition:
Calories: 395 Fat: 9.5g Carbohydrates: 34g Fiber: 0.4g
Proteins: 28.3g

2. Open the lid from the top and put it aside; start adding the beans, faro, barley, mushrooms, garlic, jalapeno, curry paste, shallot and onion powder, pepper and salt.
3. Add water to cover all the ingredients; gently stir them.
4. Close the lid and lock. Ensure that you have sealed the valve to avoid leakage.
5. Press "Manual" mode and set timer for 30 minutes.
6. After the timer reads zero, press "Cancel" and naturally release pressure. It takes about 8-10 minutes to naturally release pressure.
7. Carefully remove the lid and add the tomatoes.
8. Sprinkle cilantro and scallions; serve warm!

Nutrition:
Calories: 238 Fat: 6.5g Carbohydrates: 38g Fiber: 1.5g
Proteins: 11g

2. Set half a cup of the cooking liquid from the pasta and set it to the side.
3. Set it over medium heat and add in a tablespoon of olive oil. Stir in half of your garlic, sautéing for a half a minute.
4. Add in the breadcrumbs and then sauté, cooking for five more minutes.
5. Toss in the red pepper flakes and nutritional yeast, mixing well.
6. Transfer the breadcrumbs in the pan.
7. Add the remaining olive oil and then stir in your salt, pepper, garlic clove, and greens.
8. Cook for five minutes. Cook until wilted.
9. Add in the pasta, mix in the reserved pasta liquid, and then mix well. Add in the lemon juice, zest, and garlic crumbs. Toss before serving.

Nutrition:
Calories: 231 Proteins: 14.9g Carbohydrates: 3.2g Fat: 18g
Fiber: 1.1g

267. Plant Pad Thai

Preparation time: 10 minutes
Cooking time: 25 minutes
Servings: 4
Ingredients:

- 2 Teaspoons Coconut Oil
- 1 Red Pepper, Sliced
- 2 Carrots, Sliced
- 1/2 White Onion, Sliced
- 1 Thai Chili, Chopped
- 8 Ounces Brown Rice Noodles
- 1/2 Cup Peanuts, Chopped
- 1/2 Cup Cilantro, Chopped

Sauce:

- 3 Tablespoons Soy Sauce
- 3 Tablespoons Lime Juice, Fresh
- 3 Tablespoons Brown Sugar
- 1 Tablespoon Sriracha
- 3 Tablespoons Vegetable Broth
- 1 Teaspoon Chili Garlic Paste
- 2 Cloves Garlic, Minced

Tofu:

- 1 lb. Extra Firm Tofu, Sliced
- 1 Tablespoon Peanut Butter
- 2 Tablespoons Sriracha

268. Quinoa Cranberry Salad

Preparation time: 10 minutes
Cooking time: 30 minutes
Servings: 4
Ingredients:

- 1 Cup Dry Quinoa
- 1 1/2 Cups Water
- 1/2 cup Cranberries, Dried
- 4 Tablespoon Cilantro, Fresh and Chopped
- 1 Lime, Juiced
- 1 1/2 Teaspoon Curry Powder
- 1/8 Teaspoon Cumin
- 1/4 Cup Green Onion, Chopped
- 1/2 Cup Bell Pepper, Diced
- 1/3 Cup Toasted Almonds, Sliced
- 1/2 Carrots, Shredded

269. Eggplant Pasta

Preparation time: 10 minutes
Cooking time: 30 minutes
Servings: 4
Ingredients:

- 12 Ounces Dry Pasta
- 2 Cups Cremini Mushrooms, Sliced
- 1/2 Eggplant, Small and Cubed
- 1 1/2 Cups Marinara Sauce, Preferably Vegan
- 2 Cups Water
- Sea Salt and Black Pepper to Taste
- 3 Tablespoons Olive Oil
- Basil, Fresh to Garnish

Directions:

- 3 Tablespoons Soy Sauce
- 2 Tablespoons Rice Vinegar
- 2 Teaspoons Sesame Oil
- 2 Teaspoons Ginger, Grated

Directions:

1. Get out a large pot of water and soak the rice noodles in it. Press your tofu to get out the excess liquid. Get out a nonstick pan and heat it over medium-high heat. Add in the tofu, searing for three minutes per side.
2. Whisk all ingredients for the tofu in a bowl, stirring in the tofu, and mixing well to marinate.
3. Separately mix your Thai sauce in a bowl, adding the tofu in.
4. Get a wok and put it over medium heat, adding in a teaspoon of oil.
5. Toss in the carrots, onion, red pepper, and chili. Cook for three minutes.
6. Transfer the vegetables to the tofu bowl and add in more oil. Stir the drained noodles in, and then cook for an additional minute.
7. Transfer the noodles to your tofu and toss before serving warm. Garnish with cilantro and peanuts.

Nutrition:
Calories: 398 Carbohydrates: 55.6g Proteins: 17.8g Fat: 11.8g

- 4 Tablespoons Pepitas
- Sea Salt and Black Pepper to Taste
- Olive Oil for Drizzling
- Lime Wedges to Garnish

Directions:

1. Rinse your quinoa and then throw it in a saucepan over medium heat. Cook for five minutes before adding the water.
2. Bring it to a boil before reducing your pot to a simmer. Cover and cook for thirteen minutes.
3. Toss all remaining ingredients into a salad bowl and mix with quinoa. Serve fresh.

Nutrition:
Calories: 132 Fat: 10g Proteins: 34g Carbohydrates: 54g Fiber: 9g

1. Put your eggplant in a colander before sprinkling with salt. They will drain as it rests for half an hour. Rinse thoroughly after the thirty-minute mark.
2. Put a saucepan over medium-high heat with your eggplant, olive oil, 1/2 teaspoon of salt, and a third of your minced garlic. Stir and then cook for an additional six minutes. It should be golden brown and then add n the mushrooms. Sauté for two minutes before putting it in a bowl.
3. Cook your pasta and drain. Add in the marinara sauce and garlic into the saucepan with your pasta. Season with salt and pepper as necessary.
4. Toss in the eggplant and garnish with basil.

Nutrition:
Calories: 302 Fat: 22g Carbohydrates: 5g Proteins: 34g

270. Cream of Broccoli Soup

Preparation time: 10 minutes
Cooking time: 25 minutes
Servings: 6
Ingredients:

- 2 Celery Stalks, Diced
- 1/4 Teaspoon Thyme
- 1 Carrot, Peeled and Diced
- 2 Broccoli Heads, Chopped
- 2 Bay Leaves
- 1 Can Cannellini Beans
- 4 Cups Vegetable Broth
- 2 Cups Water
- 2 Tablespoons Nutritional Yeast
- 1 Packet Vegetable Powder

Directions:

271. Red Lentil Pasta

Preparation time: 10 minutes
Cooking time: 30 minutes
Servings: 6
Ingredients:

- 1 Tablespoon Oregano
- 1 Tablespoon Basil
- 6 Cloves Garlic, Minced
- 1 Sweet Onion, Chopped
- 1/4 Cup Olive Oil
- 2 Teaspoons Turmeric
- Salt and Pepper to Taste
- 28 Ounces Fire Roasted Tomatoes
- 1/2 Cup Sundried Tomatoes, Oil Packed and Chopped
- 8 Ounces Red Lentil Pasta

272. Tart Cabbage Soup

Preparation time: 10 minutes
Cooking time: 1 hour 15 minutes
Servings: 4
Ingredients:
Marinade:

- 1 Tablespoon Tamari, Low Salt
- 1/4 Teaspoon Liquid Smoke
- 1/2 Block Tofu, Firm, Diced and Drained

Soup:

- 2 Tablespoons Balsamic Vinegar
- 2 Teaspoons Garlic, Minced
- 1 Cup Leek, Chopped
- 6 Baby Bella Mushrooms, Fresh and Sliced
- 3 Cups Purple Cabbage, Chopped
- 1/2 Cup Bell Pepper, Chopped
- 1/2 Cup Sauerkraut
- 1 Teaspoon Caraway Seeds
- 2 Teaspoons Tamari, Low Salt
- 7 Cups Vegetable Broth
- 1 Tablespoon Sriracha Sauce
- 1 Tablespoon Lime Juice, Fresh

273. Parsnip and Matzo Soup

Preparation time: 10 minutes
Cooking time: 1 hour and 25 minutes
Servings: 4

1. Get out a pot and add the carrot, celery, and thyme.
2. Cover and cook for five minutes using medium heat.
3. Pour in a dash of water, and then take it off the heat. Chop the florets and stalks again after peeling. Add the stock, water, bay leaf, beans, broccoli to your carrot mixture.
4. Cover the soup and bring it all to a boil.
5. Allow it to simmer for ten minutes, and then discard the bay leaf before taking it from the heat.
6. Stir in the vegetable powder and nutritional powder. Blend using an immersion blender before serving.

Nutrition:
Calories: 463 Carbohydrates: 92g Proteins: 9.4g Fat: 5.2g

- 1 Tablespoon Apple Cider Vinegar
- 2 Handfuls Baby Spinach, Large

Directions:

1. Set out a large pot and heat the oil over medium heat. Add your onion and cook for ten minutes.
2. Stir in the turmeric, oregano, salt, pepper, basil, and garlic, cooking for another minute. Add in the tomatoes with the juices, sundried tomatoes, and vinegar. Cook for fifteen minutes, and then use an immersion blender. Toss the spinach into your sauce and cook for another five minutes. Boil your pasta according to the box and serve with the spinach mixture and garnish as desired.

Nutrition:
Calories: 523 Carbohydrates: 57.6g Proteins: 7.5g Fat: 37.6g

Directions:

1. Start by turning the oven to 400. Prepare your marinade and then marinate the tofu. Allow the tofu to marinate for fifteen minutes.
2. Place this tofu on a baking tray afterward and bake for twelve minutes.
3. Get out a large pot and put it over medium heat. Add your leeks and a tablespoon of water. Stir well before cooking for five minutes. Toss in your chopped mushrooms before adding your garlic.
4. Stir well before cooking for another five minutes. Add in the vinegar. Use this to deglaze your pot.
5. Toss the sauerkraut with the juice it comes in. Add the cabbage, broth, bell pepper, hot sauce, lime juice, tamari, and caraway seeds.
6. Set it all to a boil and then reduce it to a simmer.
7. Cook for twenty-five minutes. During this time, you'll need to stir occasionally. Stir in your tofu and adjust seasonings if needed.

Nutrition:
Calories: 151 Fat: 3.9g Fiber: 3.3g Carbohydrates: 23.6g
Proteins: 4.9g

Ingredients:
Balls:

- 1 Teaspoon Garlic Powder

- 2 Teaspoons Onion Powder
- 1 1/2 Cups Flour
- 1 1/2 Cups Quinoa Flakes
- 1/4 Teaspoon Sea Salt
- 2 Cups Water, Boiling
- 6 Tablespoons Pumpkin Puree

Soup:

- 1/4 Cup Coconut Aminos
- 1 Yellow Onion, Chopped
- Black Pepper to Taste
- 5 Carrots, Peeled and Sliced
- 3 Celery Stalks, Diced
- 2 Parsnips, Sliced and Peeled
- 8 Cups Vegetable Broth
- 1 Cup Parsley, Fresh and Chopped
- 3 Tablespoons Dill, Fresh and Chopped to Garnish

274. Pesto Quinoa

Preparation time: 10 minutes
Cooking time: 25 minutes
Servings: 1
Ingredients:

- 1 Teaspoon Olive Oil
- 1 Cup Onion, Chopped
- 1 Clove Garlic, Minced
- 1 Cup Zucchini, Chopped
- Pinch Sea Salt
- 1 Tomato, Chopped
- 2 Tablespoons Sun-Dried Tomatoes, Chopped
- 3 Tablespoons Basil Pesto
- 2 Cups Quinoa, Cooked

275. Walnut and Orange Pasta

Preparation time: 10 minutes
Cooking time: 40 minutes
Servings: 3
Ingredients:

- 1/2 Spaghetti Squash (or 7 Ounces Whole Grain Pasta
- 1 Orange, Juiced and Zested
- 2 Tablespoons Olive Oil
- 1 Clove Garlic, Pressed
- Sea Salt to Taste
- 3 Tablespoons Parsley, Fresh and Chopped Fine
- 10 Olives, Pitted and Chopped
- 1/4 Cup Walnuts, Chopped
- 3 Tablespoons Nutritional Yeast

Directions:

276. Kale and Quinoa Salad

Preparation time: 10 minutes
Cooking time: 45 minutes
Servings: 4
Ingredients:
Vegetables:

- 4 Carrots, Chopped and Large
- 1 Beet, Sliced Thin
- 2 Tablespoons Water
- Dash Sea Salt
- 1/2 Teaspoon Curry Powder

Quinoa:

Directions:

1. Heat the oven to 300, and then get a fifteen by thirteen tray. Line it with parchment paper.
2. Prepare your balls by mixing all its ingredients in a bowl and roll into balls. Arrange them on your baking sheet. This should bake about thirty balls.
3. Bake for twenty minutes but flip at the ten-minute mark. Allow the dish to cool for an additional ten minutes.
4. Make your soup by adding in your ingredients and bringing it to a boil in a large pot. Simmer for twenty minutes. Add in the balls and cook for another thirty-five minutes. Garnish with dill before serving.

Nutrition:
Calories: 294 Fat: 6g Carbohydrates: 19.5g Fiber: 12g
Proteins: 22.5g

- 1 Tablespoon Nutritional Yeast

Directions:

1. Warmth the oil in a skillet. Sauté the onion and cook for five minutes.
2. Add the garlic and cook until your onion has softened. Add in the salt and zucchini.
3. Add five minutes and then turn off the heat. Add in your sun-dried tomatoes and mix to combine. Toss in your pesto and then toss the vegetables to coat. Layer your spinach in a bowl and then quinoa. Top with your zucchini mixture, and sprinkle with nutritional yeast.

Nutrition:
Calories: 242 Fat: 22g Carbohydrates: 5g Proteins: 34g

1. To cook your spaghetti squash boil until soft, which will take about fifteen to twenty minutes. Set the flesh out of the skin, and then drain it. If using whole grain pasta, cook according to package instructions and drain well.
2. Get out a large bowl and mix your orange juice, orange zest, and a little olive oil. You'll want a ratio of half of your orange juice. Add in the pressed garlic and a dash of salt. Stir well. Add in your noodles and dress well.
3. Serve topped with parsley, chopped olives, nutritional yeast, and walnuts.

Nutrition:
Calories: 166 Proteins: 9g Carbohydrates: 2.4g Fat: 13.5g
Fiber: 0.3g

- 1 1/2 Cups Water
- 3/4 Cup Quinoa, Rinsed Well

Dressing:

- 1/3 Cup Tahini
- 3 Tablespoons Lemon Juice, Fresh
- 2 Tablespoons Maple Syrup
- Pinch Sea Salt
- 1/4 Cup Water

Salad:

- 8 Cups Kale, Chopped

- 1/2 Cup Cherry Tomatoes, Chopped
- 1 Avocado, Cubed
- 1/2 Cup Sprouts
- 1/4 Cup Hemp Seeds

Directions:
1. Add your quinoa to a pot after it's been rinsed and then place it over medium heat. Stir and cook before adding your water. Set it to a boil, and then set it to a simmer.
2. Cook for an additional 20 minutes more.

277. Quinoa and Parsley Salad

Preparation time: 15 minutes.
Cooking time: 0 minutes.
Servings: 2
Ingredients:
- 1/2 cup quinoa, uncooked
- 1 cup water
- 3/4 cup parsley leaves
- 1/2 cup celery, sliced
- 1/2 cup green onions, sliced
- 3 tablespoons fresh lemon juice
- 1/2 cup dried apricots, chopped
- 1 tablespoon agave syrup
- 1 tablespoon olive oil

278. Broccoli and Mushroom Stir-Fry

Preparation time: 15 minutes.
Cooking time: 20 minutes.
Servings: 4
Ingredients:
- 2 cups broccoli, cut into small florets
- 1/4cup red onion, chopped small
- 3 cloves garlic, minced
- 2 cups mushrooms, sliced
- 1/4teaspoon crushed red pepper
- 2 teaspoons fresh ginger, grated
- 1 tablespoon olive oil
- 1/4 cup water or broth
- 1/2 cup carrot, shredded
- 1/4 cup cashews

279. Lentil Vegetable Loaf

Preparation time: 15 minutes.
Cooking time: 55 minutes.
Servings: 4
Ingredients:
- 2 cups cooked lentils, drained well
- 1 tablespoon olive oil
- 1 small onion, diced
- 1 carrot, finely diced
- 1 stalk celery, diced
- 1 x 8 ounces package white or button mushrooms, cleaned and diced
- 3 tablespoons tomato paste
- 2 tablespoons soy sauce
- 1 tablespoon balsamic vinegar
- 1 cup old-fashioned oats, uncooked
- 1/2 cup almond meal
- 1(1/2) teaspoon dried oregano
- 1/3 cup ketchup

3. Preheat your oven to 375F. Put your carrots and beats spread out on a baking sheet. Drizzle your oil over them and then season. Toss to coat. Roast for an additional twenty minutes.
4. Prepare your dressing by mixing all ingredients.
5. Put your kale on a serving platter, topping with tomatoes, avocado, vegetables, quinoa, and additional toppings.

Nutrition:
Calories: 222 Fat: 6g Carbohydrates: 43g Fiber: 5g Proteins: 3g

- 1/4 cup unsalted pumpkinseed kernels, toasted
- 1/4 teaspoon salt
- 1/4 teaspoon black pepper

Directions:
1. Attach quinoa and water to a pan and bring to a boil. Cover to reduce the heat, and simmer for 20 minutes. Attach to a bowl and fluff with a fork. Add celery, parsley, onions, and apricots.
2. Whisk olive oil, lemon juice, syrup, salt, and black pepper. Add to quinoa mixture and toss well. Top with seeds and serve.

Nutrition:
Calories: 238 Fat: 8.6g Carbohydrates: 35g Proteins: 6g

- 2 tablespoons of rice wine vinegar
- 2 tablespoons soy sauce
- 1 tablespoon coconut sugar
- 1 tablespoon sesame seeds

Directions:
1. Pop a large skillet over medium heat and add the olive oil. Add the broccoli, onion, garlic, mushrooms, red pepper, ginger, and water.
2. Cook until the veggies are soft. Add the carrots, cashews, vinegar, soy, and coconut sugar. Stir well and cook for 2 minutes. Drizzle with sesame seeds, then serve and enjoy.

Nutrition:
Calories: 133 Carbohydrates: 9g Fat: 8g Proteins: 6g

- 1 teaspoon balsamic vinegar
- 1 teaspoon Dijon mustard

Directions:
1. Warm your oven to 400F and grease a 5" x 7" loaf tin, and then pop to one side. Add olive oil to a skillet and pop over medium heat.
2. Add the onion and cook for five minutes until soft. Attach the carrots, celery, and mushrooms and cook until soft.
3. Grab your food processor and add the lentils, tomato paste, soy sauce, vinegar, oats, almond, and oregano. Whizz well until combined, and then transfer to a medium bowl.
4. Pop the veggies into the food processor and pulse until combined. Transfer to the bowl. Stir everything together.
5. Move the mixture into the loaf pan, press down, and pop into the oven. Cook for 35 minutes, add the topping and then bake again for 15 minutes.

Remove from the oven and allow about10 minutes to cool.

280. Maple Glazed Tempeh with Quinoa and Kale

Preparation time: 15 minutes.
Cooking time: 30 minutes.
Servings: 5
Ingredients:

- 1 cup quinoa
- 1(1/2) cup vegetable stock
- 8 ounces tempeh, cubed
- 2 tablespoons pure maple syrup
- 3 tablespoons dried cranberries
- 1 tablespoon fresh chopped thyme
- 1 tablespoon fresh chopped rosemary
- 1 tablespoon olive oil
- Juice of 1 orange
- 1 clove garlic, minced
- 4 ounces baby kale, chopped

Directions:

281. Slow Cooker Chili

Preparation time: 15 minutes.
Cooking time: 9 hours.
Servings: 12
Ingredients:

- 3 cups dry pinto beans
- 1 large onion, chopped
- 3 bell peppers, chopped
- 8 large green jalapeno peppers, dice after removing seeds by scraping out
- 2 x 14.5 ounces cans of diced tomatoes, or equivalent
- 1 tablespoon chili powder
- 2 tablespoons oregano flakes
- 1 tablespoon cumin powder
- 1 tablespoon garlic powder

282. Spicy Hummus Quesadillas

Preparation time: 5 minutes.
Cooking time: 15 minutes.
Servings: 4
Ingredients:

- 4 x 8" whole grain tortilla
- 1 cup hummus
- Your choice of fillings: spinach, sundried tomatoes, olives, etc.
- Extra-virgin olive oil for brushing

To serve:

- Extra hummus
- Hot sauce

283. Quinoa Lentil Burger

Preparation time: 5 minutes
Cooking time: 25 minutes
Servings: 4
Ingredients:

- 1 tablespoon + 2 teaspoons of olive oil
- 1/4 cup red onion, diced
- 1 cup quinoa, cooked
- 1 cup cooked, drained brown lentils
- 1 x 4 ounces green chilies, diced
- 1/3 cup oats, rolled

Nutrition:
Calories: 226 Carbohydrates: 25g Fat: 6g Proteins: 12g

1. Preheat the oven to 400F and use parchment to line on a paper baking sheet. Add the stock to a saucepan and pop over medium heat. Bring to the boil and add the quinoa.
2. Lower the heat, cover, and allow 15 minutes to simmer until cooked. Take a medium bowl, add the tempeh and pour the maple syrup and stir well until combined.
3. Set the tempeh onto the baking sheet and pop it into the oven for 15 minutes until brown. Meanwhile, grab a large bowl and attach the rest of the ingredients. Stir well to combine.
4. Add the quinoa and cooked tempeh, season well with salt and pepper. Serve and enjoy.

Nutrition:
Calories: 321 Carbohydrates: 35g Fat: 12g Proteins: 16g

- 3 bay leaves, freshly ground
- 1 teaspoon ground black pepper
- 1 tablespoon sea salt (or to taste)

Directions:

1. Put the beans into your large pan, filled with water, and leave to soak overnight. The next morning, drain and transfer to a 6-quart slow cooker.
2. Cover with salt and two inches of water. Cook on high for 6 hours until soft. Drain the beans and add the other ingredients. Stir well to combine. Cover and cook again within 3 hours on high. Serve and enjoy.

Nutrition:
Calories: 216 Carbohydrates: 30g Fat: 1g Proteins: 12g

- Pesto

Directions:

1. Put your tortillas on a flat surface and cover each with hummus. Add the fillings, and then fold over to form a half-moon shape.
2. Pop a skillet over medium heat and add a drop of oil. Add the quesadillas and flip when browned. Repeat with the remaining quesadillas, then serve and enjoy.

Nutrition:
Calories: 256 Carbohydrates: 25g Fat: 12g Proteins: 7g

- 1/4 cup flour
- 2 teaspoons corn starch
- 1/4 cup panko breadcrumbs, whole-wheat
- 1/4 teaspoon garlic powder
- 1/2 teaspoon cumin
- 1 teaspoon paprika
- Salt and pepper
- 2 tablespoons Dijon mustard
- 3 teaspoons maple syrup

Directions:

1. Put 2 teaspoons olive oil into your skillet over medium heat. Add the onion and cook for five minutes until soft. Grab a small bowl and add the maple syrup and Dijon mustard.
2. Grab a large bowl and add the burger ingredients; stir well. Form into 4 patties with your hands. Put a

284. Spanish Vegetable Paella

Preparation time: 15 minutes
Cooking time: 1 hour and 30 minutes
Servings: 6
Ingredients:

- 3 tablespoons virgin olive oil, divided
- 1 medium chopped fine yellow onion
- 1(1/2) tsp. fine sea salt, divided
- 6 garlic cloves, minced or pressed
- 2 teaspoons smoked paprika
- 15 ounces can dice tomatoes, drained
- 2 cups short-grain brown rice
- 15 ounces can garbanzo beans, clean and drained
- 3 cups vegetable broth
- 1/3 cup dry white wine/vegetable broth
- 1/2 teaspoon saffron threads, crumbled (optional)
- 14 ounces can quarter artichokes
- 2 red bell peppers, sliced into long, 1/2"-wide strips
- 1/2 cup Kalamata olives
- 1/4 teaspoons ground black pepper
- 1/4 cup chopped fresh parsley, + about 1 tablespoon more for garnish
- 2 tablespoons lemon juice
- Lemon wedges for garnish
- 1/2 cup frozen peas

285. Tex-Mex Tofu and Beans

Preparation time: 25 minutes
Cooking time: 12 minutes
Servings: 2
Ingredients:

- 1 cup dry black beans
- 1 cup dry brown rice
- 1(14-ounces) package firm tofu, drained
- 2 tablespoons olive oil
- 1 small purple onion, diced
- 1 medium avocado, pitted, peeled
- 1 garlic clove, minced
- 1 tablespoon lime juice
- 2 teaspoons cumin
- 2 teaspoons paprika
- 1 teaspoon chili powder
- Salt and pepper to taste

Directions:

286. No-Egg Salad

Preparation time: 15 minutes
Cooking time: 0 minutes
Servings: 6
Ingredients:

- 1(13-ounce) package firm tofu
- 1 celery stalk, finely chopped

tablespoon of oil into your skillet over medium heat.

3. Add the patties and cook for 10 minutes on each side. Serve with the honey mustard and enjoy!

Nutrition:
Calories: 268 Carbohydrates: 33g Fat: 8g Proteins: 10g

Directions:

1. Preheat the oven to 350F. Put 2 tablespoons of oil into your skillet and pop over medium heat. Add the onion and cook for five minutes until soft.
2. Add salt, garlic, and paprika—Cook for 30 seconds. Attach the tomatoes, stir through and cook for 2 minutes. Add the rice, stir through, and cook again for a minute.
3. Add the garbanzo beans, broth, wine or stock, saffron, and salt, and bring to a boil. Cover and pop into the oven within 40 minutes until the rice has been absorbed. Line a baking sheet with parchment paper.
4. Grab a large bowl and add the artichoke, peppers, olives, 1 tablespoon olive oil, 1/2 tsp. of salt, and black pepper to flavor. Toss to combine, and then dust over the prepared baking sheet.
5. Pop into the oven and cook within 30 minutes. Detach from the oven and leave to cool slightly. Add the parsley, lemon juice, and seasoning as required. Toss.
6. Pop the rice onto a stove, turn up the heat and bake the rice for five minutes. Garnish and serve with the veggies.

Nutrition:
Calories: 437 Carbohydrates: 60g Fat: 16g Proteins: 10g

1. Cut the tofu into 1/2-inch cubes. Heat the olive oil in a skillet. Put the diced onions and cook until soft, for about 5 minutes.
2. Add the tofu and cook an additional 2 minutes, flipping the cubes frequently. Meanwhile, cut the avocado into thin slices and set aside.
3. Lower the heat and add in the garlic, cumin, and cooked black beans. Stir until everything is incorporated thoroughly and then cook for an additional 5 minutes.
4. Add the remaining spices and lime juice to the mixture in the skillet. Mix thoroughly and remove the skillet from the heat.
5. Serve the Tex-Mex tofu and beans with a scoop of rice and garnish with the fresh avocado. Enjoy immediately, or store the rice, avocado, and tofu mixture separately.

Nutrition:
Calories: 315 Carbohydrates: 27.8g Fat: 17g Proteins: 12.7g

- 1/4 cup chives, finely chopped
- 1 tablespoon nutritional yeast
- 1 teaspoon turmeric
- 1/4 teaspoon garlic powder
- 1/4 teaspoon celery seed (optional)
- 1/2 teaspoon black salt (Kala namak)

- 2 tablespoons vegan mayonnaise
- 2 tablespoons dill pickle relish
- 1 tablespoon Dijon mustard
- 1 tablespoon fresh lemon juice
- Salt to taste
- Freshly ground black pepper to taste

Directions:
1. Crumble the tofu into a medium bowl with your hands. Then add the celery, chives, nutritional

287. Chickpea No Tuna Salad

Preparation time: 5 minutes
Cooking time: 0 minutes
Servings: 3
Ingredients:
- 1(14-ounce) can chickpeas, drained and rinsed
- 2 celery stalks, finely chopped
- 2 scallions, coarsely chopped
- 2 tablespoons vegan mayonnaise
- Juice of 1/2 lemon
- 2 heaping teaspoons capers and brine
- 1 teaspoon dried dill or 1 handful fresh dill, chopped
- 1/2 teaspoon Dijon mustard

288. Crunchy Rainbow Salad

Preparation time: 15 minutes
Cooking time: 0 minutes
Servings: 6
Ingredients:
- 4 cups shredded cabbage, red or green, or bagged slaw mix
- 2 cups cooked edamame
- 1 cup grated or shredded carrots
- 1/2 bunch cilantro, coarsely chopped
- 2 scallions, thinly sliced
- 1/2 cup dry roasted peanuts, chopped

289. Three-Bean Salad

Preparation time: 15 minutes
Cooking time: 0 minutes
Servings: 6
Ingredients:
- 1(14-ounce) can kidney beans
- 1(14-ounce) can chickpeas, drained and rinsed
- 1(14-ounce) can white navy or cannellini beans, drained and rinsed
- 1/2 bunch parsley, coarsely chopped
- 2 celery stalks, finely chopped
- 1 red bell pepper, finely chopped
- 1 jalapeno pepper, minced (optional)
- 1 garlic clove, diced (optional)
- 1/4 cup apple cider vinegar
- 1/4 cup extra-virgin olive oil
- 1 tablespoon Dijon mustard

290. Greek Salad with Tofu Feta

Preparation time: 15 minutes
Cooking time: 0 minutes
Servings: 6
Ingredients:
- 1 green bell pepper, coarsely chopped

yeast, turmeric, garlic powder, celery seed (if using), and black salt and mix well.
2. In a small measuring cup or bowl, merge the vegan mayo, relish, mustard, and lemon juice to make a dressing. Put the dressing over the tofu batter and stir until everything is well combined.
3. Taste and season with salt and pepper. Enjoy.

Nutrition:
Calories: 87 Fat: 5g Carbohydrate: 5g Proteins: 7g

- 1/4 teaspoon kelp flakes
- 1/4 to 1/2 teaspoon salt
- Freshly ground black pepper to taste

Directions:
1. In a medium bowl, merge the chickpeas, celery, scallions, mayo, lemon juice, capers, dill, mustard, kelp flakes, salt, and pepper.
2. Mix and mash everything together using a potato masher. Taste then flavors with additional salt, pepper, or lemon, if desired. Enjoy on its own, on top of a romaine or endive leaf, or with rice cakes.

Nutrition:
Calories: 193 Fat: 4g Carbohydrate: 33g Proteins: 7g

- 3/4 cup Sweet Peanut Dressing
- Salt

Directions:
1. Combine the cabbage, edamame, carrots, cilantro, scallions, and dry roasted peanuts in a medium bowl and mix well.
2. Add the peanut dressing and mix again, ensuring the dressing is evenly distributed—season with salt to taste.

Nutrition:
Calories: 276 Fat: 16g Carbohydrate: 21g Proteins: 20g

- 1 tablespoon maple syrup
- 1/2 teaspoon salt
- Freshly ground black pepper to taste

Directions:
1. Combine the kidney beans, chickpeas, navy beans, parsley, celery, bell pepper, jalapeno pepper, and garlic (if used) in a medium bowl. Mix until evenly combined.
2. Put the apple cider vinegar, olive oil, mustard, maple syrup, and salt into the mixture and attach as much black pepper as you'd like. Mix everything thoroughly, taste it, and adjust the seasoning with extra salt, if needed.

Nutrition:
Calories: 284 Fat: 10g Carbohydrate: 40g Proteins: 11g

- 1-pint cherry or grape tomatoes halved
- 1 small red onion, chopped
- 1 cucumber, chopped
- 1(14-ounce) can butter beans
- 1/2 bunch parsley, coarsely chopped

- 1/2 cup pitted kalamata olives
- 1 garlic clove, minced
- Juice of 1 lemon
- 3 tablespoons red wine vinegar
- 3 tablespoons olive oil
- 1 big Tofu feta
- 1 teaspoon salt
- Freshly ground black pepper

Directions:

291. Mushroom Lentil Soup

Preparation time: 15 minutes
Cooking time: 40 minutes
Servings: 6
Ingredients:

- 1 tablespoon olive oil
- 1 yellow onion, chopped
- 2 celery stalks, chopped
- 2 carrots, cut into thin rounds
- Pinch + 1/2 teaspoon salt, divided
- 3 garlic cloves, minced
- 2 cups Cremini mushrooms, chopped
- 1 tablespoon dried rosemary
- 6 cups vegetable broth
- 1 cup brown lentils
- 4 cups chopped kale
- 3 tablespoons apple cider vinegar
- Freshly ground black pepper to taste

292. Spicy Peanut Bowl

Preparation time: 25 minutes
Cooking time: 0 minutes
Servings: 4
Ingredients:

- 1(8-ounce) package black bean noodles, cooked
- 2 cups cooked edamame beans
- 1 cup red cabbage, thinly sliced
- 1 cup carrots, grated or shredded
- 1 cup red peppers, finely chopped
- 1 cup mug bean or soybean sprouts
- 1/4 cup dry roasted peanuts
- 1/4 cup cilantro, coarsely chopped
- 4 scallions, coarsely chopped
- Sweet peanut dressing for serving

293. Plant-Strong Power Bowl

Preparation time: 25 minutes
Cooking time: 0 minutes
Servings: 4
Ingredients:

- 2 cups white or brown rice, cooked
- 1 can of black beans, drained and clean
- 1(14-ounce) can chickpeas, drained and rinsed
- 4 cups spinach, chopped
- 1 cucumber, chopped
- Micro greens for garnish

294. Burrito Bowl

Preparation time: 15 minutes
Cooking time: 20 minutes
Servings: 4
Ingredients:

1. In a medium bowl, merge the bell pepper, tomatoes, onion, cucumber, beans, parsley, olives, and garlic. Next, add the lemon juice, vinegar, and oil. Mix well.
2. Add the tofu feta (and any of the tofu marinade) to the salad. Season with salt and as much pepper as you would like and then mix again.

Nutrition:
Calories: 142 Fat: 8g Carbohydrate: 14g Proteins: 4g

Directions:

1. In a large stockpot, warm the oil over medium heat. Add the onion, celery, carrots, and a pinch of salt. Cook until the onions are slightly translucent, within 5 minutes.
2. Add the garlic and cook within 1 minute more; then add the mushrooms and rosemary. Set everything together and cook for 5 minutes more or until the mushrooms have started to release liquid.
3. Add the vegetable broth and lentils. Boil: then reduce the heat to simmer. Cook within 30 minutes or until the lentils have softened. Stir in the kale and allow it to wilt for 1 or 2 minutes more.
4. Add the vinegar, the remaining salt, and as much pepper as you'd like.

Nutrition:
Calories: 205 Fat: 4g Carbohydrate: 27g Proteins: 14g

- Hot sauce or red chili flakes (optional)

Directions:

1. Divide the noodles evenly among 4 food storage containers. Top each container of noodles with 1/2 cup of edamame, 1/4 cup of cabbage, 1/4 cup of peppers, 1/4 cup of carrots, 1/4 cup of sprouts, and 1 tablespoon of peanuts.
2. Garnish each container with cilantro and scallions. Top it with 3 tablespoons of peanut dressing and hot sauce or chili flakes (if using). Cover the remaining containers with airtight lids and store them in the refrigerator.

Nutrition:
Calories: 417 Fat: 11g Carbohydrate: 69g Proteins: 14g

- Lemon Parsley Dressing

Directions:

1. Divide the rice evenly among 4 food storage containers, and then add to each container 1/4 cup of chickpeas, 1/4 cup of black beans, 1 cup of spinach, and 1/4 of the chopped cucumber.
2. Garnish each container with a small handful of micro greens. Serve.

Nutrition:
Calories: 514 Fat: 22g Carbohydrate: 70g Proteins: 14g

- 1 tablespoon olive oil
- 1 red onion, thinly sliced
- 1 bell pepper, thinly sliced

- Pinch salt
- 1 garlic clove, minced
- 1/2 teaspoon cumin
- 2 cups white or brown rice, cooked
- 1(14-ounce) can pinto beans, drained and clean
- 4 cups spinach or arugula, chopped
- 1 avocado, chopped
- 4 scallions, coarsely chopped
- Hot sauce or salsa for serving
- Cilantro lime dressing for serving

Directions:

1. In a small skillet, warm the oil over medium-high heat. Add the onion, bell pepper, and a big pinch of salt. Sauté for 15 minutes or until the onions begin to caramelize slightly. Add the garlic and cumin and cook for 3 more minutes. Set aside.
2. Set out 4 food storage containers. To each container, attach 1/2 cup of rice, 1/4 of the bell pepper mixture, 1/4 cup of beans, 1 cup of greens, and 1/4 of the avocado.
3. Garnish each container with scallions and a hot sauce or salsa of your choice.

Nutrition:
Calories: 483 Fat: 31g Carbohydrate: 50g Proteins: 10g

295. Harvest Bowl

Preparation time: 15 minutes.
Cooking time: 35 minutes.
Servings: 4
Ingredients:
- 1 tablespoon olive oil
- 2 small sweet potatoes, chopped (about 2 cups)
- 1/2 teaspoon cinnamon
- 1/4 teaspoon salt
- 2 cups wild rice, cooked
- 1 (14-ounce) can lentils, drained and rinsed
- 1 (14-ounce) can chickpeas, drained and rinsed
- 4 cups kale, thinly sliced and gently massaged
- 1 cup grated or shredded carrots
- 1/4 cup hemp hearts
- 1/4 cup raw sauerkraut (optional)
- Tahini apple cider vinaigrette for serving

Directions:

1. Warm oven to 400F and line a baking sheet with parchment paper. In a small bowl, mix the oil, potatoes, cinnamon, and salt.
2. Bring the potatoes on the baking sheet and bake for 35 minutes or until the potatoes are nice and soft.
3. In each of the 4 food storage containers, put 1/2 cup of rice, 1/4 cup of lentils, 1/4 cup of chickpeas, 1/4 of the sweet potatoes, 1 cup of kale, and 1/4 cup of carrots.
4. Garnish it with 1 tablespoon of hemp hearts and 1 tablespoon of sauerkraut (if using).
5. Finally, top it with 3 tablespoons of tahini vinaigrette. Cover the remaining containers with airtight lids and store them in the refrigerator.

Nutrition:
Calories: 563 Fat: 19g Carbohydrate: 75g Proteins: 24g

296. Cauliflower Fried Rice

Preparation time: 15 minutes
Cooking time: 15 minutes
Servings: 6
Ingredients:
- 1 head cauliflower
- 1 tablespoon sesame oil
- 1 white onion, finely chopped
- 1 large carrot, finely chopped
- 4 garlic cloves, minced
- 2 cups frozen edamame or peas
- 3 scallions, sliced
- 3 tablespoons Bragg liquid aminos or tamari
- Salt to taste
- Freshly ground black pepper to taste

Directions:

1. Divide the cauliflower into florets and transfer them to a food processor. Process the cauliflower using the chopping blade and pulsing until the cauliflower is the consistency of rice. Set aside.
2. Warmth a large skillet. Drizzle in the sesame oil and then add the onion and carrot, cooking until the carrots begin to soften about 5 minutes. Stir in the garlic and cook within another minute.
3. Add the cauliflower and edamame or peas. Heat until the cauliflower softens and the edamame or peas cook for about 5 minutes. Then add the scallions and liquid aminos or tamari. Mix well. Add in black pepper if desired.

Nutrition:
Calories: 117 Fat: 3g Carbohydrate: 19g Proteins: 7g

297. Curried Quinoa Salad

Preparation time: 15 minutes
Cooking time: 15 minutes
Servings: 6
Ingredients:
- 1 tablespoon olive oil
- 1 garlic clove, minced
- 1 teaspoon-sized piece of ginger, minced
- 2 teaspoons curry powder
- 1 cup quinoa, rinsed under cold water using a fine-mesh strainer
- 1(1/2) cup vegetable broth
- 1(14-ounce) can chickpeas, drained and rinsed
- 2 celery stalks, finely chopped
- 1 cup carrots, shredded
- 3/4 cup raisins
- 1 cup cilantro, chopped
- 3 tablespoons olive oil
- 3 tablespoons apple cider vinegar
- 1/2 teaspoon salt
- Freshly ground black pepper to taste

Directions:

1. Warm-up oil over medium heat in a small saucepan. Attach the garlic and ginger and cook for 1 minute. Add the curry powder and stir it.
2. Next, add the quinoa and toast it for about 5 minutes, stirring regularly. Then pour in the broth, turn the heat to high, and boil.
3. Adjust your heat to simmer, cover the saucepan, and cook for about 15 minutes or until the quinoa is light and fluffy.

298. Lettuce Wraps with Smoked Tofu

Preparation time: 15 minutes.
Cooking time: 25 minutes.
Servings: 4
Ingredients:

- 1(13-ounce) package organic, extra-firm smoked tofu, drained and cubed
- 1 tablespoon coconut oil
- 1/2 cup yellow onion, finely chopped
- 3 celery stalks, finely chopped
- 1 red bell pepper, chopped
- Pinch salt
- 1 cup Cremini mushrooms, finely chopped
- 1 garlic clove, minced
- 1/2 teaspoon ginger, minced
- 3 tablespoons Bragg Liquid Aminos, coconut aminos, or tamari
- 1/2 teaspoon red pepper flakes
- Freshly ground black pepper to taste
- 8 to 10 large romaine leaves, washed and patted dry

Directions:

299. Quinoa Avocado Salad

Preparation time: 15 minutes.
Cooking time: 4 minutes.
Servings: 4
Ingredients:

- 2 tablespoons balsamic vinegar
- 1/4 cup coconut yogurt
- 1/4 cup vegetable cream
- 5 tablespoons freshly squeezed lemon juice, divided
- 1 clove garlic, grated
- 2 tablespoons shallot, minced
- Salt and pepper to taste
- 2 tablespoons avocado oil, divided
- 1(1/4) cup quinoa, cooked
- 2 heads endive, sliced

300. Chilled Cucumber Soup

Preparation time: 15 minutes.
Cooking time: 30 minutes.
Servings: 4
Ingredients:

- 3 large English cucumbers
- 1 cup unsweetened plant-based milk
- 1 cup unsweetened applesauce
- 1 teaspoon garlic powder
- 1 red bell pepper, diced

Directions:

4. In a medium bowl, merge the chickpeas, celery, carrots, raisins, and cilantro. Once the quinoa is processed, add it to the bowl as well. Then dress it with olive oil, vinegar, salt, and as much pepper as you'd like. Mix until well combined.

Nutrition:
Calories: 327 Fat: 12g Carbohydrate: 50g Proteins: 8g

1. Preheat the oven to 350F. Prepare a baking sheet lined using parchment paper or a silicone liner; then place the tofu cubes in a single layer. Bake the tofu cubes for 25 minutes, flipping them after 10 to 15 minutes. Set aside.
2. Meanwhile, warm the coconut oil in a nonstick sauté pan over medium-high heat. Add the onion, celery, bell pepper, and salt and cook for about 5 minutes or until the onions are slightly translucent.
3. Add the mushrooms, garlic, and ginger and sauté for about 5 minutes more or until the mushrooms begin to release water. Adjust the heat to medium, and then put the aminos or tamari and the red pepper flakes.
4. Add the baked tofu cubes to the pan and sprinkle with pepper. Sauté for a few minutes more, until the tofu is coated with sauce and the veggies are tender.
5. To serve, scoop as much of the veggie and tofu mixture into each romaine leaf as you'd like.

Nutrition:
Calories: 160 Fat: 8g Carbohydrate: 6g Proteins: 14g

- 2 firm pears, sliced thinly
- 2 avocados, sliced
- 1/4 cup fresh dill, chopped

Directions:
1. Merge the vinegar, cream, milk, 1 tbsp. garlic, lemon juice, shallot, salt, and pepper in a bowl. Spill 1 tbsp. oil into a pan over medium heat. Heat the quinoa for 4 minutes.
2. Set quinoa to a plate. Whisk the endive and pears in a mixture of the remaining oil, the remaining lemon juice, salt, and pepper. Transfer to a plate.
3. Toss the avocado in the reserved dressing. Add to the plate. Top with the dill and quinoa.

Nutrition:
Calories: 431 Fat: 28.5g Carbohydrates: 42.7g Proteins: 6.6g

1. Peel, slice, and seed 21/2 cucumbers. Set aside the unsliced cucumber half for later.
2. Combine the chopped cucumber, plant-based milk, applesauce, and garlic powder in a blender and blend for 60 seconds until it reaches your desired consistency.
3. Chill the soup in the refrigerator.
4. Slice the remaining half cucumber. Add the slices to the chilled soup.
5. Serve the soup cold, topped with the bell pepper.

Nutrition:
Calories: 68 Fat: 1g Proteins: 3g Carbohydrates: 15g Fiber: 4g

301. Edamame Miso Soup

Preparation time: 10 minutes.
Cooking time: 10 minutes.
Servings: 5
Ingredients:

- 2 cups vegetable stock
- 1/2 cup cooked edamame beans
- 11/2 cups mushrooms, sliced
- 3 medium scallions, diced
- 3 tablespoons white or yellow miso paste

Directions:

1. In a medium pot, set the stock and 3 cups of water to a boil.

302. Ginger and Bok Choy Soup

Preparation time: 10 minutes.
Cooking time: 20 minutes.
Servings: 5
Ingredients:

- 2 cups vegetable stock
- 4 tablespoons peeled and grated fresh ginger
- 3 medium carrots, cut into coins
- 2 tablespoons Savory Spice
- 4 baby bok choy

Directions:

303. Chick and Noodle Soup

Preparation time: 5 minutes.
Cooking time: 15 minutes.
Servings: 5
Ingredients:

- 2 cups vegetable stock
- 3 tablespoons Savory Spice
- 1 cup broken (1 inch) whole-grain linguine noodles
- 3/4 cup cooked chickpeas
- 11/2 cups mixed frozen vegetables

Directions:

1. Combine the stock, savory spice, and 5 cups of water in a large pot. Bring to a boil over high heat.

304. Tomato-Carrot Bisque

Preparation time: 10 minutes.
Cooking time: 40 minutes.
Servings: 4
Ingredients:

- 1/2 cup sliced carrots (1/4-inch coins)
- 1/2 cup sun-dried or dehydrated tomatoes
- 1 (19-ounce) can diced tomatoes, with their liquid
- 2 tablespoons Savory Spice
- 1 cup unsweetened plant-based milk

Directions:

305. French Onion Soup

Preparation time: 10 minutes.
Cooking time: 50 minutes.
Servings: 4
Ingredients:

- 4 medium onions, yellow or red, thinly sliced
- 3 tablespoons balsamic vinegar
- 3 cups vegetable stock
- 1 tablespoon dried thyme
- 3 dried bay leaves

2. Add the beans and mushrooms. Set the heat to low and stew for 10 minutes, until the mushrooms soften.
3. Detach the pot from the heat and add the scallions.
4. In a bowl, merge the miso paste with 1/4 cup of the warmed soup stock to dissolve, and then stir the mixture into the soup. (The miso won't incorporate easily into the soup without first being thinned.)
5. Serve immediately.

Nutrition:
Calories: 67 Fat: 1g Proteins: 6g Carbohydrates: 10g Fiber: 4g

1. In a large stockpot, bring the stock, 3 cups of water, the ginger, carrots, and savory spice to a boil. Cover and reduce the heat to medium. Cook for 15 minutes, stirring occasionally.
2. Chop the white bottoms off the bok choy, about 1 inch of the base. Cut the leaves lengthwise in half. After the soup has cooked, add the bok choy to the soup and bring to a boil once more. Boil for 1 to 2 minutes until steamy hot.
3. Serve warm.

Nutrition:
Calories: 54 Fat: 1g Proteins: 3g Carbohydrates: 11g Fiber: 3g

2. Once boiling, add the linguine noodles. Stir occasionally.
3. After 7 minutes of boiling, or once the noodles are al dente, reduce the heat to low. Add the chickpeas and mixed vegetables.
4. Parboil for an additional 5 minutes until the noodles are soft.
5. Serve warm.

Nutrition:
Calories: 204 Fat: 2g Proteins: 10g Carbohydrates: 40g Fiber: 7g

1. In a deep nonstick saucepan, bring 3 cups of water to a boil. Add the carrots and boil for 10 minutes.
2. Attach the sun-dried and canned tomatoes and the savory spice. Lower the heat and cook, stir occasionally to prevent sticking.
3. Transfer the soup to a high-speed blender. Add the plant-based milk and blend until smooth.
4. Serve warm.

Nutrition:
Calories: 91 Fat: 1g Proteins: 4g Carbohydrates: 17g Fiber: 5g

Directions:

1. In a large nonstick saucepan, sauté the onions, stirring occasionally and adding 1 tablespoon of water at a time to prevent sticking, for about 25 minutes or until the onions are translucent and caramelized.
2. Add the vinegar and sauté for 5 more minutes, until the onions darken in color.

3. Attach the stock, 2 cups of water, the thyme, and bay leaves.
4. Cover and simmer for 20 minutes, until thickened.
5. Remove from the heat and discard the bay leaves.
6. Serve hot.

306. Lasagna Soup
Preparation time: 10 minutes.
Cooking time: 15 minutes.
Servings: 4
Ingredients:
- 2 cups mini whole-grain lasagna noodles
- 1 (26-ounce) can diced tomatoes
- 2 cups Mushroom Crumble
- 2 1/2 tablespoons Italian seasoning
- 1 tablespoon garlic powder

Directions:

307. Black Bean and Mushroom Stew
Preparation time: 10 minutes.
Cooking time: 20 minutes.
Servings: 5
Ingredients:
- 7 cups sliced mushrooms (about 1 pound)
- 3 cups vegetable stock
- 1 (19-ounce) can black beans (about 2 cups cooked), rinsed and drained
- 3 tablespoons tomato paste
- 3 tablespoons Savory Spice

Directions:

308. Spicy Peanut Ramen
Preparation time: 5 minutes.
Cooking time: 10 minutes.
Servings: 4
Ingredients:
- 4 servings brown rice ramen noodles
- 1/2 cup Peanut Sauce
- 1 tablespoon Shichimi Togarashi Spice Mix
- 1 cup cooked edamame beans
- 1/2 cup chopped scallions

Directions:
1. Cook the noodles.

309. Creamy Mushroom Soup
Preparation time: 10 minutes.
Cooking time: 20 minutes.
Servings: 4
Ingredients:
- 5 cups sliced mushrooms
- 5 garlic cloves, minced
- 1 1/2 cups vegetable stock
- 1 1/2 cups unsweetened plant-based milk
- 1 tablespoon dried thyme

Directions:

310. Potato Harvest Stew
Preparation time: 10 minutes.
Cooking time: 15 minutes.
Servings: 5
Ingredients:

Serving Tip: For an authentic presentation, you can make bread tops for this soup. Use slices of a whole-grain baguette, top with a dollop of my Cheesy Sauce, and broil on high for 4 minutes.
Nutrition:
Calories: 68 Fat: 1g Proteins: 1g Carbohydrates: 15g Fiber: 2g

1. Set 5 cups of water to a boil and attach the pasta noodles. Boil for 6 minutes.
2. Set the heat to medium and attach the tomatoes, mushroom crumble, Italian seasoning, and garlic powder. Stir to combine.
3. Simmer for 5 minutes, until fragrant.
4. Detach from the heat and serve warm or allow cooling and refrigerating in an airtight container for up to 3 days.
Nutrition:
Calories: 244 Fat: 2g Proteins: 11g Carbohydrates: 50g Fiber: 10g

1. In a nonstick saucepan over medium-high heat, sauté the mushrooms for 10 minutes, until soft and brown. Stir often to avoid sticking. Attach the stock, 1 tablespoon at a time, if needed to prevent sticking.
2. Attach the beans to the pan, along with the tomato paste and savory spice. Stir to combine.
3. Set to a boil over high heat, set the heat to low, cover, and simmer for 8 minutes. Stir occasionally.
4. Serve hot.
Nutrition:
Calories: 181 Fat: 1g Proteins: 14g Carbohydrates: 32g Fiber: 10g

2. Meanwhile, in a nonstick pan, combine the peanut sauce, spice mix, beans, and 1/2 cup of water. Set the heat to medium and stew for 5 minutes, stirring occasionally, until warmed.
3. Drain the noodles and divide among 4 bowls.
4. Top with the warmed peanut sauce and edamame. Garnish with the scallions.
5. Serve immediately.
Nutrition:
Calories: 333 Fat: 9g Proteins: 13g Carbohydrates: 53g Fiber: 5g

1. Warmth a deep nonstick pan over medium-high heat and sauté the mushrooms and garlic for 10 minutes or until the mushrooms are soft. Attach 1/4 cup of water if the pan gets too dry.
2. Mix in the stock, plant-based milk, and thyme.
3. Set the heat to low and stew for 8 minutes, stirring occasionally, until the soup thickens.
4. Serve warm.
Nutrition:
Calories: 46 Fat: 1g Proteins: 3g Carbohydrates: 7g Fiber: 1g

- 3 cups chopped, unpeeled yellow potatoes
- 1 cup sliced carrots
- 1 small yellow onion, diced
- 3 tablespoons tomato paste

- 11/2 tablespoons poultry seasoning

Directions:
1. In a large stockpot, bring the potatoes and carrots to boil in 6 cups of water. Boil for 8 minutes.
2. Meanwhile, in a nonstick pan, sauté the onion.
3. Reserving 3 cups of the boiling water drain the potatoes and carrots.
4. In the stockpot, combine the reserved cooking water, tomato paste, and poultry seasoning. Stir to combine. Set to a boil over high heat and then reduce the heat to low.
5. Add the potatoes, carrots, and onion. Remove from the heat.
6. Serve warm.

Nutrition:
Calories: 114 Fat: 1g Proteins: 3g Carbohydrates: 26g Fiber: 4g

311. Quick Black Bean Chili

Preparation time: 5 minutes.
Cooking time: 20 minutes.
Servings: 5
Ingredients:
- 1 (15-ounce) can diced tomatoes
- 1 (19-ounce) can black beans, rinsed and washed
- 11/2 cups tomato sauce
- 2 cups Mushroom Crumble
- 3 tablespoons Chipotle Spice

Directions:
1. In a pot with a lid, combine the tomatoes, black beans, tomato sauce, mushroom crumble, and chipotle spice. Stir.
2. Set to a boil over high heat and then set the heat to low. Cover and simmer, stirring occasionally, until fragrant, about 20 minutes.
3. Serve warm or allow cooling.

Nutrition:
Calories: 199 Fat: 1g Proteins: 13g Carbohydrates: 37g Fiber: 13g

312. Sweet Potato and Peanut Stew

Preparation time: 15 minutes.
Cooking time: 30 minutes.
Servings: 4
Ingredients:
- 2 onions, diced
- 2 tablespoons extra-virgin olive oil or coconut oil
- 2 large sweet potatoes, peeled and chopped
- 1/3 cup chunky peanut butter
- 1 teaspoon smoked paprika
- 1/4 tsp. red pepper flakes
- 2 cups water or unsalted vegetable broth
- 1/4 teaspoon salt
- 2 cups finely chopped fresh spinach or kale
- Freshly ground black pepper

Directions:
1. On your electric pressure cooker, select Sauté. Add the onions and olive oil, and then cook for 4-5 minutes, stirring occasionally, until the onion has softened. Stir in the sweet potatoes, peanut butter, paprika, chili flakes, water and salt. Stir to mix the peanut butter with the water a little, but don't worry too much as it will melt when heated. Cancel Sauté.
2. High pressure for 6 minutes close and lock the lid and make sure the pressure valve is sealed and set the time to 6 minutes.
3. Releasing the pressure. At the end of the cooking time, quickly release the pressure. Once all pressure has been released, carefully unlock and remove the lid. Incorporate the spinach to wilt. Set and season with more salt and pepper.

Nutrition:
Calories: 350 Proteins: 10g Fat: 18g Carbohydrates: 16g Fiber: 8g

313. Split Pea Soup

Preparation time: 10 minutes.
Cooking time: 30 minutes.
Servings: 6
Ingredients:
- 3 or 4 carrots, scrubbed or peeled and chopped
- 1 large yellow onion, chopped
- 1 cup dried split green peas
- 3 cups water or unsalted vegetable broth
- 1 tablespoon tamari or soy sauce
- 2 to 3 teaspoons dried thyme or 1 teaspoon ground thyme
- 1 teaspoon onion powder
- 1/2 teaspoon garlic powder
- Pinch freshly ground black pepper
- 1/4 cup chopped sun-dried tomatoes or chopped pitted black olives
- Salt

Directions:
1. 1. In the electric pressure cooker, combine the carrots, onion, split peas, water, tamari, thyme, onion powder, garlic powder and pepper.
2. High pressure for 10 minutes. Secure and lock the lid and make sure the pressure valve is sealed, then select High pressure and set the time to 10 minutes.
3. Relief of pressure. Once the cooking time is done, let the pressure naturally release for about 20 minutes. Once all pressure is released, carefully unlock and remove the lid. Let it cool then blend the soup: use an immersion blender directly into the pot.

Nutrition:
Calories: 182 Proteins: 12g Fat: 1g Carbohydrates: 26g Fiber: 12g

314. Sour Soup

Preparation time: 5 minutes
Cooking time: 20 minutes
Servings: 4
Ingredients:

- 2 tablespoons dried wood ears
- 3.5ounces bamboo shoots, sliced into thin strips
- 1 medium carrot, peeled, sliced into thin strips
- 5 dried shiitake mushrooms
- 1 tablespoon grated ginger
- 1 teaspoon minced garlic
- 1 teaspoon ground black pepper
- 1 teaspoon salt
- 1/4 cup soy sauce
- 1 teaspoon sugar
- 1/2 cup rice vinegar
- 4 cups vegetable stock
- 1 1/2 cup water, boiling
- 7.5ounces tofu, extra-firm, drained
- 1 tablespoon green onion tops, chopped
- 1/4 cup water, at room temperature
- 2 tablespoons cornstarch
- 1 teaspoon sesame oil

Directions:

1. Take a small bowl, put some wooden ears in it, then pour the boiling water until it is covered and let it rest for 30 minutes.
2. In the meantime, take another bowl, put the mushrooms in it, pour 1 1/2 cups of water and let the mushrooms rest for 30 minutes.
3. After 30 minutes, drain the ears of wood, rinse them well and cut them into slices, remove and discard the hard pieces.
4. Similarly, drain the mushrooms, reserving their soaking liquid and slice the mushrooms, removing and discarding their stems.
5. Take a large pot, put it on medium-high heat, adds the whole Shopping List: including the reserved mushroom liquid, leave the last five Shopping List: mix well and bring to a boil.
6. Then bring the heat to medium and simmer the soup for 10 minutes until cooked.
7. Meanwhile, put the cornstarch in a bowl, add the room temperature water and mix well until smooth.
8. Cut the tofu into 1-inch pieces, add it to the hot soup along with the cornstarch mixture, and continue to simmer the soup until it reaches the desired thickness.
9. Drizzle with sesame oil, spread soup into bowls, garnish with green onions and serve.

Nutrition:
Calories: 152 Fat: 2g Carbohydrates: 35g Proteins: 4g Fiber: 8g

315. Roasted Tomato Soup

Preparation time: 10 minutes.
Cooking time: 50 minutes.
Servings: 4
Ingredients:

- 2 pounds ripe tomatoes, cored and halved
- 2 large garlic cloves, crushed
- 3 tablespoons extra-virgin olive oil
- 1 tablespoon balsamic vinegar
- Salt and freshly ground black pepper
- 1/2 cup chopped red onion
- 2 cups light vegetable broth or store-bought, or water
- 1/2 cup lightly packed fresh basil leaves

Directions:

1. Preheat the oven to 450F. In a large bowl, merge the tomatoes, garlic, 2 tablespoons of oil, vinegar, salt and pepper. Spread the tomato mixture into a 9 x 13-inch pan and roast until the tomatoes begin to brown for about 30 minutes. Remove from the oven and set aside.
2. In a large saucepan, warmth the remaining tablespoon of oil over medium heat. Attach the onion, cover and cook until very soft for about 10 minutes, stirring occasionally. Add the roasted tomatoes and stock, and then bring to a boil. Set the heat and simmer, uncovered, for 10 minutes. Remove from the heat, add the basil and season with salt and pepper. Merge the soup in the pot with an immersion blender or in a blender or food processor, as much as needed, and return to the pot. Reheat over medium heat if needed. To serve this cold soup, refrigerate it for at least 1 hour before serving.

Nutrition:
Calories: 222 Fat: 6g Carbohydrates: 43g Fiber: 5g Proteins: 3g

316. Butternut Squash

Preparation time: 10 minutes
Cooking time: 35 minutes
Servings: 6
Ingredients:

- 1 cup diced parsnips
- 2 cups diced sweet potato
- 1 large sweet onion, peeled, diced
- 1 1/2 cups diced carrots
- 4 cups diced butternut squash
- 2 teaspoons minced garlic
- 1/4 teaspoon ground ginger
- 1/4 teaspoon ground black pepper
- 1/2 teaspoon of sea salt
- 1/4 teaspoon ground allspice
- 1 teaspoon poultry seasoning
- 1 teaspoon pumpkin pie spice
- 1/4 teaspoon ground cinnamon
- 32 ounces vegetable stock
- 14 ounces coconut milk, unsweetened

Directions:

1. Take a large Dutch oven, put it over medium heat, add the onions, and drizzle with 2 tablespoons of

water and cook for 5 minutes until softened, sprinkling with more 2 tablespoons at a time as needed.
2. Then attach the garlic, cook for another minute, bring the heat to high, add the remaining shopping list: set aside milk, salt and black pepper and bring the soup to a boil.
3. Then change the heat to medium-low and simmer for 20 minutes until the vegetables are tender.

317. Wonton Soup
Preparation time: 15 minutes
Cooking time: 10 minutes
Servings: 4
Ingredients:
For the Soup:
- 4 cups vegetable broth
- 2 green onions, chopped

For the Wontons Filling:
- 1 cup chopped mushrooms
- 1/4 cup walnuts, chopped
- 1 green onion, chopped
- 1/2 inch of ginger, grated
- 1/2 teaspoon minced garlic
- 1 tablespoon rice vinegar
- 2 teaspoons soy sauce
- 1 teaspoon brown sugar
- 20 Vegan Wonton Wrappers

318. Potato and Kale Soup
Preparation time: 5 minutes
Cooking time: 15 minutes
Servings: 2
Ingredients:
- 1 small white onion, peeled, chopped
- 2 1/2 cups cubed potatoes
- 2 cups leek, cut into rings
- 1/2 cup chopped carrots
- 1/2 cup chopped celery
- 1/2 teaspoon minced garlic
- 2/3 teaspoon salt
- 1/3 teaspoon ground black pepper
- 1 tablespoon olive oil
- 3 1/2 cups vegetable broth
- 1 cup kale, cut into stripes

319. Ramen Soup
Preparation time: 10 minutes
Cooking time: 20 minutes
Servings: 2
Ingredients:
For the Mushrooms and Tofu:
- 2 cups sliced shiitake mushrooms
- 6 ounces tofu, extra-firm, drained, sliced
- 1 tablespoon olive oil
- 1 tablespoon soy sauce

For the Noodle Soup:
- 2 packs of dried ramen noodles
- 1 medium carrot, peeled, grated
- 1 inch of ginger, grated
- 1 teaspoon minced garlic
- 3/4 cup baby spinach leaves

4. When done, blend the soup using a hand blender, then stir in the coconut milk, set with salt and pepper and cook.
5. Serve immediately.

Nutrition:
Calories: 188.4 Fat: 7.7g Carbohydrates: 29.3g Proteins: 3.7g Fiber: 8.2g

Directions:
1. Prepare the filling of the wontons and for this, take a bowl, and put the whole shopping list: in it, except the paper, and mix until well blended.
2. Place a wonton wrapper on the workspace, place 1 teaspoon of the prepared filling in the center, then brush some water around the edges, fold into a crescent shape, and seal the wraps by pinching the edges.
3. Take a large pot, put it on medium-high heat, add the broth and bring it to a boil.
4. Then pour in the prepared wontons, one at a time, and boil for 5 minutes.
5. When cooked, garnish the soup with green onions and serve.

Nutrition:
Calories: 196.9 Fat: 4g Carbohydrates: 31g Proteins: 6.6g Fiber: 2.4g

- Croutons, for serving

Directions:
1. Take a large pot, put it on medium heat, add the oil and, when it is hot, attach the onion and cook for 2 minutes until it is sautéed.
2. Set the garlic, cook for another minute, then add all the vegetables and continue cooking for 3 minutes.
3. Pour in the broth, cook for 15 minutes, then add the kale and cook for 2 minutes until tender.
4. Flavor the soup with salt and black pepper, blend using a hand blender until smooth, then top with croutons and serve.

Nutrition:
Calories: 337 Fat: 7g Carbohydrates: 62g Proteins: 10g Fiber: 8g

- 1 tablespoon olive oil
- 6 cups vegetable broth

For Garnish:
- Sesame seeds as needed
- Soy sauce as needed
- Sriracha sauce as needed

Directions:
1. Prepare the mushrooms and tofu and for this, put the tofu pieces in a plastic bag, add the soy sauce, seal the bag and turn it upside down until the tofu is coated.
2. Take a skillet, set it over medium heat, add the oil and, when hot, add the tofu slices and cook for 5-10 minutes until crisp and golden on all sides,

turning often and when cooked., set aside until needed.

3. Attach the mushrooms to the pan, cook for 8 minutes until golden brown, pour the soy sauce from the tofu pieces and stir until coated.

4. In the meantime, prepare the noodle soup and for this, take a pot, put it on medium-high heat, attach the oil and when it is hot adding the garlic and ginger and cook for 1 minute until not it is fragrant.

320. Vegetable and Barley Stew

Preparation time: 15 minutes
Cooking time: 20 minutes
Servings: 6
Ingredients:

- 2 or 3 parsnips, peeled and chopped
- 2 cups chopped peeled sweet potato, russet potato, winter squash, or pumpkin
- 1 large yellow onion, chopped
- 1 cup pearl barley
- 1 (28-ounce) can diced tomatoes
- 4 cups water or unsalted vegetable broth
- 2 to 3 teaspoons dried mixed herbs or 1 teaspoon dried basil plus 1 teaspoon dried oregano
- Salt

321. Vegan Pho

Preparation time: 5 minutes
Cooking time: 15 minutes
Servings: 6
Ingredients:

- 1 package of wide rice noodles, cooked
- 1 medium white onion, peeled, quartered
- 2 teaspoons minced garlic
- 1 inch of ginger, sliced into coins
- 8 cups vegetable broth
- 3 whole cloves
- 2 tablespoons soy sauce
- 3 whole star anise
- 1 cinnamon stick
- 3 cups of water

For Toppings:

322. Garden Vegetable Stew

Preparation time: 6 minutes
Cooking time: 60 minutes
Servings: 4
Ingredients:

- 2 tablespoons extra-virgin olive oil
- 1 medium red onion, chopped
- 1 medium carrot
- 1/2 cup dry white wine
- 3 medium new potatoes, unpeeled and cut into 1-inch pieces
- 1 medium red bell pepper
- 11/2 cups vegetable broth
- 2 medium zucchinis, trimmed, halved lengthwise, and cut into 1/2-inch slices
- 1 medium yellow summer squash, trimmed, halved lengthwise, and cut into 1/2-inch slices
- 1 pound ripe plum tomatoes, chopped

5. Then spill in the broth, bring the mixture to a boil, add the noodles and cook until tender.

6. Then mix the spinach into the noodle soup, remove the pot from the heat and distribute evenly between bowls.

7. Add the mushrooms and tofu along with the garnish and then serve.

Nutrition:
Calories: 647 Fat: 12g Carbohydrates: 106g Proteins: 28g Fiber: 6g

- Freshly ground black pepper

Directions:

1. In your electric pressure cooker, combine the parsnips, sweet potato, onion, and barley, tomatoes with their juice, water, and herbs.

2. High pressure for 20 minutes. Secure the lid, then select High pressure and set the time to 20 minutes.

3. Pressure release. Once the cooking time is finished, quickly release the pressure. Once all pressure has been released, carefully unlock and remove the lid. Taste and season with salt and pepper.

Nutrition:
Calories: 300 Proteins: 9g Fat: 2g Carbohydrates: 16g Fiber: 14g

- Basil as needed for topping
- Chopped green onions as needed for topping
- Ming beans as needed for topping
- Hot sauce as needed for topping
- Lime wedges for serving

Directions:

1. Take a large pot, put it on medium-high heat, add the whole Shopping List: for the soup, except the soy sauce and broth, and bring to a boil.

2. Then change the heat to medium-low, simmer the soup for 30 minutes and then add the soy sauce.

3. When finished, spread the cooked noodles into bowls, add the soup, then garnish and serve.

Nutrition:
Calories: 31 Fat: 0g Carbohydrates: 7g Proteins: 0g Fiber: 2g

- Salt and freshly ground black pepper
- 2 cups fresh corn kernels
- 1 cup fresh peas
- 1/4 cup fresh basil
- 1/4 cup chopped fresh parsley
- 1 tbsp. minced fresh savory or 1 teaspoon dried

Directions:

1. In a large saucepan, warmth the oil over medium heat. Attach the onion and carrot, cover and cook until softened for 7 minutes. Attach the wine and cook, uncovered, for 5 minutes. Stir in the potatoes, pepper and broth, then bring to a boil. Lower the heat to medium and stew for 15 minutes.

2. Add the courgette, yellow squash and tomatoes. Flavor with salt and black pepper, cover and simmer until vegetables are tender for 20-30 minutes.

3. Finish and serve
4. Mix the corn, peas, basil, parsley and savory. Taste, adjusting the seasonings if necessary. Stew to mix the flavors for about 10 more minutes. Serve immediately.

323. Moroccan Vegetable Stew

Preparation time: 5 minutes
Cooking time: 35 minutes
Servings: 4
Ingredients:

- 1 tablespoon extra-virgin olive oil
- 2 medium yellow onions, chopped
- 2 medium carrots
- 1/2 teaspoon ground cumin
- 1/2 teaspoon ground cinnamon or allspice
- 1/2 teaspoon ground ginger
- 1/2 teaspoon sweet or smoked paprika
- 1/2 teaspoon saffron or turmeric
- 1 (14.5-ounce) can diced tomatoes, undrained
- 8 ounces green beans
- 2 cups peeled, seeded, and diced winter squash
- 1 large russet or other baking potato, peeled and cut into 1/2-inch dice
- 11/2 cups vegetable broth
- 11/2 cups cooked or 1 can chickpeas, drained and rinsed
- 3/4 cup frozen peas
- 1/2 cup pitted dried plums (prunes)
- 1 teaspoon lemon zest

324. Matzo Ball Soup

Preparation time: 5 minutes
Cooking time: 45 minutes
Servings: 4
Ingredients:

- 1 tablespoon extra-virgin olive oil
- 1 small onion, finely chopped
- 1 medium carrot, chopped
- 1 celery rib, chopped
- 3 green onions, chopped
- 6 cups vegetable broth, homemade or store-bought, or water
- 2 tablespoons minced fresh parsley
- 1 teaspoon fresh or dried dill weed
- 1/2 teaspoon salt, or more if needed
- 1/4 teaspoon freshly ground black pepper

325. White Bean and Broccoli Salad

Preparation time: 10 minutes
Cooking time: 15 minutes
Servings: 4-6
Ingredients:

- 1 pound Yukon Gold potatoes, peel off and cut into 1-inch chunks
- 3 cups broccoli florets
- 11/2 cups cooked or15.5-ounce can cannellini or other white beans, drained and rinsed
- 1/4 cup kalamata olives
- 1/2 cup walnut pieces
- 2 garlic cloves, finely minced

Nutrition:
Calories: 166 Fat: 8g Carbohydrates: 24g Fiber: 6.5g Proteins: 9g

- Salt and freshly ground black pepper
- 1/2 cup pitted green olives
- 1 tablespoon minced fresh cilantro or parsley, for garnish
- 1/2 cup toasted slivered almonds, for garnish

Directions:

1. In a large saucepan, warmth the oil over medium heat. Attach the onions and carrots, cover and cook for 5 minutes. Incorporate the cumin, cinnamon, ginger, paprika and saffron. Cook uncovered and mix for 30 seconds. Add the tomatoes, green beans, squash, potato and broth and bring to a boil. Lower the heat, secure and simmer until the vegetables are tender for about 20 minutes.
2. Finish and serve
3. Add the chickpeas, peas, prunes and lemon zest. Season with salt and pepper. Incorporate the olives and simmer, uncovered, until the flavors have blended for about 10 minutes. Sprinkle with cilantro and almonds, and then serve immediately.

Nutrition:
Calories: 139 Fat: 1.4g Carbohydrates: 28g Fiber: 11g Proteins: 5g

- Matzo Balls (recipe follows)

Directions:

1. In a large saucepan, set the oil over medium heat. Add the onion, carrot and celery. Secure and cook until softened for about 5 minutes. Add the green onions and cook 3 minutes more. Incorporate the broth, parsley, dill, salt and pepper. Set to a boil, and then lower the heat to low and simmer, uncovered, until the vegetables are tender for about 30 minutes.
2. Finish and serve
3. When ready to serve, place three matzo balls in each bowl and pour the soup over them. Serve immediately.

Nutrition:
Calories: 420 Fat: 15.2g Carbohydrates: 64.3g Proteins: 11.6g

- 1/2 cup chopped fresh parsley
- 1/4 cup walnut oil
- 1/4 cup extra-virgin olive oil
- 1/4 cup white wine vinegar
- 1/2 teaspoon salt (optional)
- 1/4 teaspoon crushed red pepper

Directions:

1. Steam the potatoes until almost tender for about 10 minutes. Steam the broccoli until tender for about 5 minutes. Drain the potatoes and broccoli and put them in a large bowl. Add the beans, olives and 1/4 cup of walnuts and set aside.

2. In a blender or food processor, merge the remaining 1/4 cup of walnuts with the garlic and blend until well-chopped. Add the parsley, walnut oil, olive oil, vinegar, salt, sugar and chopped chili

326. Chinese Black Bean Chili
Preparation time: 15 minutes
Cooking time: 0 minutes
Servings: 4
Ingredients:
- 1 tablespoon extra-virgin olive oil
- 1 medium yellow onion, finely chopped
- 2 medium carrots, finely chopped
- 1 teaspoon grated fresh ginger
- 2 tablespoons chili powder
- 1 teaspoon brown sugar
- 1 (28-ounce) can diced tomatoes, undrained
- 1/2 cup Chinese black bean sauce
- 3/4 cup water
- 1/2 cans black beans, drained and rinsed
- Salt and freshly ground black pepper

327. Coconut Rice
Preparation time: 10 minutes
Cooking time: 25 minutes
Servings: 7
Ingredients:
- 2 1/2 cups white rice
- 1/8 teaspoon salt
- 40 ounces coconut milk, unsweetened

Directions:

328. Baked Beans
Preparation time: 5 minutes
Cooking time: 45 minutes
Servings: 4
Ingredients:
- 1 tablespoon extra-virgin olive oil
- 1 medium yellow onion, minced
- 3 garlic cloves, minced
- 1 (14.5-ounce) can crushed tomatoes
- 1/2 cup pure maple syrup
- 2 tablespoons blackstrap molasses
- 1 tablespoon soy sauce
- 11/2 teaspoons dry mustard
- 1/4 teaspoon ground cayenne
- Salt and freshly ground black pepper
- 3 cups cooked Great Northern beans

Directions:

329. Lemony Quinoa
Preparation time: 10 minutes
Cooking time: 0 minute
Servings: 6
Ingredients:
- 1 cup quinoa, cooked
- 1/4 of medium red onion, peeled, chopped
- 1 bunch of parsley, chopped
- 2 stalks of celery, chopped
- 1/4 teaspoon of sea salt

and blend until smooth. Spill the dressing over the salad, stirring gently to combine, and then serve.
Nutrition:
Calories: 294 Fat: 6g Carbohydrates: 19.5g Fiber: 12g Proteins: 22.5g

- 2 tablespoons minced green onion, for garnish

Directions:
1. In a large saucepan, set the oil over medium heat. Add the onion and carrot. Cover and cook until softened for about 10 minutes.
2. Stir in the ginger, chili powder and sugar. Add the tomatoes, black bean sauce and water. Incorporate the black beans and season with salt and pepper.
3. Set to a boil, and then lower the heat to medium and simmer, covered, until the vegetables are tender for about 30 minutes.
4. Simmer for about 10 minutes more. Serve immediately garnished with green onion.

Nutrition:
Calories: 302 Fat: 22g Carbohydrates: 5g Proteins: 34g

1. Take a large saucepan; put it on medium heat, add the whole Shopping List: inside and mix until combined.
2. Set the mixture to a boil, then bring the heat to medium-low and simmer the rice for 25 minutes until tender and all liquid is absorbed.
3. Serve immediately.

Nutrition:
Calories: 535 Fat: 33.2g Carbohydrates: 57g Proteins: 8.1g Fiber: 2.1g

1. Preheat the oven to 350F.
2. Lightly grease a 2-quart saucepan and set aside.
3. In a large saucepan, warmth the oil over medium heat. Add the onion and garlic. Secure and cook until softened for about 5 minutes.
4. Stir in the tomatoes, maple syrup, molasses, soy sauce, mustard, and cayenne pepper and set to a boil.
5. Set the heat to low and stew, unsealed, until slightly reduced for about 10 minutes. Season with salt and pepper.
6. Put the beans in the prepared saucepan. Add the sauce, stirring to mix and coat the beans. Cover and cook until hot and bubbly for about 30 minutes. Serve immediately

Nutrition:
Calories: 398 Carbohydrates: 55.6g Proteins: 17.8g Fat: 11.8g

- 1/4 teaspoon cayenne pepper
- 1/2 teaspoon ground cumin
- 1/4 cup lemon juice
- 1/4 cup pine nuts, toasted

Directions:
1. Take a large bowl, place all the Shopping List: in it, and stir until combined.
2. Serve straight away.

Nutrition:

Calories: 147 Fat: 4.8g Carbohydrates: 21.4g Proteins: 6g

330. Vegan Curried Rice

Preparation time: 5 minutes
Cooking time: 25 minutes
Servings: 4
Ingredients:

- 1 cup white rice
- 1 tablespoon minced garlic
- 1 tablespoon ground curry powder
- 1/3 teaspoon ground black pepper
- 1 tablespoon red chili powder
- 1 tablespoon ground cumin
- 2 tablespoons olive oil
- 1 tablespoon soy sauce
- 1 cup vegetable broth

Directions:

331. Spicy Cabbage Salad

Preparation time: 5 minutes
Cooking time: 5 minutes
Servings: 4
Ingredients:

- 1 head Napa cabbage
- 1 cup carrots
- 1/2 cup green onions
- 1 bell pepper
- 1/2 cup cilantro
- 1 jalapeño chili pepper
- 1/2 cup sunflower seeds
- 1/2 cup almond butter
- 1/4 cup canned coconut milk
- 1/4 cup apple cider vinegar
- 1/4 cup onion
- 2 tbsp. white miso paste
- 2 tbsp. maple syrup

332. Wholesome Farm Salad

Preparation time: 15 minutes
Cooking time: 4 hours
Servings: 5
Ingredients:

- 1/2 cup hulled barley
- 2 beetroots
- 2 tbsp. sunflower seeds
- 6 cups romaine lettuce
- 1/2 cup scallions
- 1/2 cup coriander
- 2 tbsp. raisins
- 1/2 cup orange juice
- 1 tbsp. lemon juice
- Black pepper
- Himalayan pink salt

Directions:

1. In a large bowl, cover barley with water, then leave to soak for at least 3 hours.
2. Drain the barley water and add barley to a pot over high heat. Attach 2 cups water and boil for 5 to 7 minutes, then turn heat to low and cover pot.

Fiber: 3g

1. Take a saucepan, put it on low heat, add the oil and when it is hot attach the garlic and cook for 3 minutes.
2. Then add all the spices, cook for 1 minute until fragrant, pour in the broth and bring the heat to a high level.
3. Stir in the soy sauce, bring the mixture to a boil, add the rice, stir until combined, then turn the heat to low and simmer for 20 minutes until the rice is tender and all the liquid is absorbed.
4. Serve immediately.

Nutrition:
Calories: 262 Fat: 8g Carbohydrates: 43g Proteins: 5g Fiber: 2g

- 1 tbsp. red curry paste
- 3 garlic cloves
- 1/2-inch piece ginger

Directions:

1. Cut the end of the cabbage, halve and core it, then cut thinly. Shred carrots thinly slice green onions and pepper, chop cilantro and jalapeño. Combine all in a large bowl with sunflower seeds. Set aside.
2. Roughly chop onion.
3. Make the sauce by blending the almond butter, coconut milk, vinegar, onion, miso, maple syrup, curry paste, garlic, and ginger. Blend until smooth and mixed. If needed, attach water to thin it out.
4. Pour the dressing over the veggie mix and toss to coat.

Nutrition:
Calories: 301 Carbohydrates: 21g Fat: 17g Proteins: 8g

Simmer 25 minutes or until the barley is tender but not soft. Drain and set aside to cool to room temperature.

3. Scrub the outside of the beets then cut each into quarters.
4. Put beets in a medium pan and add water until it covers the beets. Set to a boil, then simmer partially covered. Stew for 30 minutes or until the beets are tender. Drain. Peel off the beets while they are still warm and cut them into bite-size pieces. Set aside.
5. Toast the sunflower seeds over medium high heat, stirring every so often, for 5 minutes or until barely toasted. Let cool on a plate.
6. Chop romaine, green onion, and cilantro.
7. In a large bowl, attach the barley and beets. Add romaine, green onions, cilantro, raisins, orange juice, lemon juice, a sprinkle of pepper, and a pinch of salt. Toss gently then sprinkle the toasted sunflower seeds over the salad.

Nutrition:
Calories: 245 Fat: 18.9g Carbohydrate: 15.9g Proteins: 6.4g

333. Spicy Chickpea Crunch

Preparation time: 5 minutes
Cooking time: 5 minutes
Servings: 2
Ingredients:

- 1 garlic clove
- 1 tbsp. sesame oil
- 2 tbsp. rice vinegar
- 1/2 tsp. hot sauce
- 2 tbsp. tamari
- 1 tsp. maple syrup
- 2 tsp. sesame seeds
- 2 cups spinach
- 1 can chickpeas
- 2 stalks celery
- 2 carrots
- 1/2 cucumber
- 2 green onions
- 1 ripe avocado
- 4 tbsp. walnuts

Directions:

1. Mince garlic and whisk with the oil, vinegar, hot sauce, tamari, maple syrup, and sesame seeds until combined. Refrigerate until ready to serve.
2. Evenly divide the spinach between two serving bowls.
3. Drain and rinse the chickpeas, then half it between the bowls.
4. Thinly slice the celery, carrots, cucumber, green onions, and chop the avocado. Divide evenly between each bowl.
5. Thinly slice or chop walnuts and sprinkle half over each bowl. Use a measuring spoon to pour 1 tbsp. of the previously prepared dressing into each bowl and serve promptly.

Nutrition:
Calories: 384 Fat: 14g Carbohydrates: 58g Fiber: 6g Proteins: 11g

334. Easy Italian Bowl

Preparation time: 15 minutes
Cooking time: 15 minutes
Servings: 5
Ingredients:

- 1 red onion
- 1 cup basil
- 12 ounces wheat spiral pasta
- 1 bag assorted frozen vegetables
- 1 cup balsamic vinaigrette
- Salt
- Pepper

Directions:

1. Finely dice onion and basil.
2. Boil water and cook the pasta. During the last 5 minutes of cooking, attach frozen vegetables to the pot. Drain the pasta and vegetables. Rinse under cold water until cool.
3. Move mixture to a large bowl. Add the onion, vinaigrette, and basil. Gently mix to coat. Add a pinch of salt and pepper. Can be served cold or room-temperature.

Nutrition:
Calories: 150 Fat: 7.3g Fiber: 6.1g Carbohydrates: 18g Proteins: 3.7g

335. Light Lemon Salad

Preparation time: 15 minutes
Cooking time: 20 minutes
Servings: 4
Ingredients:

- 1 bunch kale
- 1 bunch parsley
- 4 garlic cloves
- 2 tsp. avocado oil
- 1/4 cup pitted Kalamata olives
- Grated zest and juice of 1 lemon
- Salt
- Pepper

Directions:

1. Esteem the kale, and chop finely. Roughly chop parsley and garlic.
2. Set a pot with water and heat to medium heat. Place a steamer tray over the pot and fill it with kale, parsley, and garlic. Cover and leave for 15 minutes.
3. Attach the oil to a pan over medium heat. Once the oil is hot, add the steamed greens. Cook and stir for 5 minutes.
4. Chop olives, then transfer with the greens to a bowl and add lemon zest and juice. Serve on toast with hummus and season with salt and pepper for the best experience!

Nutrition:
Calories: 141 Fat: 2g Carbohydrates: 22.5g Fiber: 2g Proteins: 4g

336. Cooked Cauliflower Bowl

Preparation time: 15 minutes
Cooking time: 20 minutes
Servings: 4
Ingredients:

- 1 head cauliflower
- 1/2 cup avocado oil
- 11/4 tsp. salt
- 1 tsp. pepper
- 1 green onion
- 1/3 cup raisins
- 1 tsp. lemon zest
- 1 tbsp. lemon juice
- 1 tsp. coriander powder
- 1 cup parsley
- 1/2 cup mint
- 1/4 cup almond

Directions:

1. Set oven rack to lowest position and pre-heat to 475°F. Degrees.
2. Cut the cauliflower into small florets. Chop and save the core of the cauliflower.
3. Add cauliflower florets, 1 tablespoon oil, 1 teaspoon salt, and 1/2 teaspoon pepper to a bowl. Toss to coat.
4. Transfer to baking pan and roast for 15 minutes or until florets are soft and browned on bottoms. Set aside and let cool.
5. While florets are roasting, finely chop green onion and combine with raisins, lemon zest and juice, coriander, remaining 1/4 cup oil, remaining 1/4

337. Seasoned Tofu Potato Salad

Preparation time: 15 minutes
Cooking time: 1 hour and 20 minutes
Servings: 8
Ingredients:

- 8 potatoes
- 1 package firm tofu
- 2 tbsp. yellow mustard
- 1 tbsp. Dijon mustard
- 4 cloves garlic
- 1 tbsp. fresh lime juice
- 1/2 tsp. salt
- 1/4 cup pickle relish
- 4 large stalks celery
- 1 onion
- Pepper

Directions:

338. Classic Potato Comfort

Preparation time: 10 minutes
Cooking time: 60 minutes
Servings: 4
Ingredients:

- 1 1/2 cups long-grain rice
- 1/4 cup roasted cashews
- 4 large potatoes
- 4 cups white mushrooms
- 1 clove garlic
- 4 cups vegetable broth
- 1/2 tsp. dried sage
- 1/2 tsp. dried marjoram
- 1/2 tsp. dried thyme
- 2 tbsp. fresh lemon juice
- 1/2 tsp. pepper
- Salt

Directions:

1. Cook the rice.
2. Set the cashews in a small bowl and cover with 1 cup water. Set aside to soak for 30 minutes.
3. Scrub the outside of the potatoes then chop into inch pieces. Slice the mushrooms, and finely chop garlic.

339. Fried Zucchini

Preparation time: 10 minutes
Cooking time: 40 minutes
Servings: 4
Ingredients:

teaspoon salt, and remaining 1/2 teaspoon pepper in large bowl. Mix thoroughly and set aside.

6. Add cauliflower core to blender and until finely chopped. Add to the bowl with dressing.
7. Add parsley and mint to the blender and pulse until coarsely chopped. Add to bowl with dressing.
8. Finely slice almonds.
9. Add cooked cauliflower and almonds to bowl with dressing mixture and gently mix. Season with salt and pepper to taste. Serve.

Nutrition:
Calories: 231 Proteins: 14.9g Carbohydrates: 3.2g Fat: 18g Fiber: 1.1g

1. Roughly chop potatoes into chunks, then put in a large pot and add cold water to cover.
2. Set to a boil then lower heat to simmer the potatoes until just tender, 8 to 10 minutes. Drain potatoes and let cool.
3. Put the tofu, yellow mustard, Dijon mustard, chopped garlic, lime juice, and salt into a food processor and pulse until smooth and creamy.
4. Add the relish to the tofu mix and mix well.
5. Dice the celery, onion and add to the tofu bowl.
6. Chop potatoes into bite-sized pieces. Season with salt and pepper to taste. Gently mix until coated.
7. Secure bowl and refrigerate for at least 1 hour.

Nutrition:
Calories: 222 Fat: 6g Carbohydrates: 43g Fiber: 5g Proteins: 3g

4. Set the potatoes in a pot and secure with water. Place to a boil, then lower the heat and simmer until the potatoes are very tender when skewered, about 20 minutes. Drain and set aside to cool.
5. In a pot, combine the rice, mushrooms, and vegetable broth. Set to a boil then reduce the heat and simmer until the mushrooms are soft, about 10 minutes. Set aside to cool.
6. Using a blender or handheld mixer, blend the mixture until smooth.
7. Put the blended mix back into the pot and add the sage, marjoram, thyme, garlic, lime juice, 1/8 teaspoon of the pepper, and a pinch of salt. Heat over medium heat for 10 minutes and stir occasionally.
8. Spill the cashews and their water into a clean blender. Add a pinch of salt and 1/4 teaspoon pepper. Blend until there are no chunks. Dump the pecan butter in a bowl with the potatoes and mash together until smooth.
9. Serve on a plate with the potatoes and gravy spooned over top.

Nutrition:
Calories: 152 Fat: 10g Carbohydrates: 11.5g Fiber: 3g Proteins: 2g

- 4 zucchinis
- 1/2 cup unsweetened almond milk
- 1 tsp. arrowroot powder
- 1 tsp. lemon juice

- 1/2 tsp. salt
- 1/2 cup panko
- 1/4 cup hemp seeds
- 1/4 cup nutritional yeast
- 1/2 tsp. garlic powder
- 1/4 tsp. pepper
- 1/4 tsp. red pepper flakes

Directions:
1. Slice the zucchini into rounds.
2. Warmth the oven to 375F and grease two large baking pans.

340. Thick Sweet Potato Fries

Preparation time: 10 minutes
Cooking time: 30 minutes
Servings: 2
Ingredients:
- 2 sweet potatoes
- 1 tsp. garlic powder
- 1/2 tsp. cumin powder
- 1/2 tsp. chili powder
- 1/2 tsp. salt
- 1/2 tsp. black pepper

Directions:
1. Preheat the oven to 425F.
2. Peel and quarter sweet potatoes.

341. Hot Wings with Ranch

Preparation time: 10 minutes
Cooking time: 2 hours 30 minute
Servings: 4
Ingredients:
- 1/2 cup chickpea flour
- 1/2 cup water
- 1 tsp. garlic powder
- 1/2 tsp. salt
- 1 head cauliflower, chopped
- 1 tsp. avocado oil
- 2/3 cup hot sauce
- 1/2 cup roasted cashews
- 4 tsp. lime juice
- 1/2 tsp. dill
- 1/4 tsp. garlic powder
- 1/4 tsp. paprika
- Salt
- Pepper

Directions:
1. Set the cashews in a bowl and add 2 tsp. of lime juice. Add enough water to cover cashews and a

342. Breaded Tempeh Bites

Preparation time: 10 minutes
Cooking time: 35 minutes
Servings: 4
- 1/4 cup oat milk
- 1/4 cup nutritional yeast
- 1 tbsp. pre-blended spice mix
- 1 tsp. arrowroot powder
- 1 tsp. fresh lime juice

3. Put the zucchini in a bowl with the milk, arrowroot powder, lemon juice, and 1/4 teaspoon salt. Toss to coat.
4. Mix the panko, hemp seeds, nutritional yeast, garlic powder, pepper, and crushed red pepper in a bowl. Add the zucchini in handfuls and toss to thoroughly coat.
5. Set the zucchini in an even layer on the baking pans. Bake 20 minutes or until the zucchini is toasty.
6. Serve.

Nutrition:
Calories: 91 Fat: 1g Proteins: 4g Carbohydrates: 17g Fiber: 5g

3. Set a pot halfway with water and place over medium heat. Put a steamer tray on top and fill with the potato. Cover and steam for 8 minutes.
4. Spread the potato evenly on a greased baking pan.
5. In a small bowl, whisk the garlic, cumin, chili powder, salt, and pepper. Whisk the spice mixture evenly over the sweet potatoes and toss to coat.
6. Cook for 10 minutes, then flip potatoes and cook for another 10 minutes. Potatoes should be soft and browned.

Nutrition:
Calories: 245 Fat: 18.9g Carbohydrate: 15.9g Proteins: 6.4g

little more. Let soak 2 hours, then drain and wash well.
2. In a strong blender, add cashews, 1/4 cup water, dill, garlic powder, paprika, 2 tsp. lime juice, salt, and pepper to taste. Blend until smooth.
3. Preheat the oven to 450F. Grease a large baking tray.
4. Chop the cauliflower into bite-sized florets.
5. Whisk together the flour, water, garlic powder, and salt.
6. Dip the florets in the batter, coating each piece thoroughly. Place carefully on the baking tray and cook for 8 minutes. Flip florets over and cook another 8 minutes.
7. While the cauliflower is cooking, whisk together the oil and hot sauce.
8. When the cauliflower is done, move the florets to the bowl with the sauce and coat thoroughly. Place the sauce-covered cauliflower back on the baking sheet and cook for 25 minutes or until crispy.
9. Serve the cauliflower with cold sauce.

Nutrition:
Calories: 141 Fat: 2g Carbohydrates: 22.5g Fiber: 2g Proteins: 4g

Ingredients:
- 8 oz. package tempeh

- 1/4 tsp. pepper
- 1/4 tsp. hot sauce
- 1/4 tsp. salt
- 1 cup panko

Directions:

1. Preheat the oven to 400F. Grease a large baking pan.
2. Cut the tempeh in half and cut into 8 pieces. Squish each piece lightly to flatten slightly.
3. In a bowl, combine the milk, nutritional yeast, seasoning blend, arrowroot powder, lime juice, pepper, hot sauce, and salt. Add the tempeh bits

343. Cumin Chili Chickpeas

Preparation time: 10 minutes
Cooking time: 45 minutes
Servings: 6
Ingredients:

- 1 can chickpeas
- 1 tbsp. paprika powder
- 1 tbsp. cumin powder
- 2 tsp. red chili flakes
- 2 tbsp. maple syrup
- 3 tbsp. lemon juice
- 1 tbsp. avocado oil
- Sea salt

344. Summer Sushi

Preparation time: 10 minutes
Cooking time: 10 minutes
Servings: 6
Ingredients:

- 2 cucumbers
- 2 avocados
- 4 tbsp. lime juice
- 2 tbsp. extra-virgin olive oil
- Sea salt
- Black pepper

Directions:

1. Peel the cucumber skin off and throw it away.
2. Peel or slice each cucumber length-wise, going from the bottom to the top. Discard the very

345. Special Cheese Board

Preparation time: 10 minutes
Cooking time: 30 minutes
Servings: 8
Ingredients:

- 2 cups almond flour
- 4 tbsp. onion powder
- Water
- 1 tsp. light soy sauce
- 1 tbsp. poppy seeds
- 5 tsp. agar agar powder
- 1/2 cup bell pepper
- 1/2 cup raw cashews
- 11/3 cup nutritional yeast
- 4 tbsp. lemon juice
- 1/2 tsp. mustard

Directions:

1. Preheat the oven to 350F.
2. To make the crackers, mix the flour, 3 tbsp. onion powder, 3 tbsp. water, soy sauce, and poppy seeds. Form into a ball.
3. Secure a baking tray with parchment paper and place the ball on top. Press it down as flat as

and let soak for 5 minutes. Make sure each piece is evenly coated.

4. Pour the panko on a plate. Dip each piece of tempeh from the batter to roll in the panko. Place on the prepared baking pan.
5. Cook for 15 minutes. Flip all pieces, and then cook for another 15 minutes or until golden brown.

Nutrition:
Calories: 288 Fat: 11.11g Carbohydrates: 45.3g Proteins: 4.4g

- Black pepper

Directions:

1. Preheat oven to 395F.
2. Drain and wash the chickpeas, then spread them on a large oven pan.
3. Mix the paprika, cumin, chili flakes, and a pinch of salt and pepper. Evenly powder over the chickpeas.
4. Merge together the maple syrup, lemon juice, and oil, then pour over the chickpeas. Set the mixture to make sure the chickpeas are fully coated.
5. Cook for 45 minutes, or until browned and crisp.

Nutrition:
Calories: 268 Carbohydrates: 33g Fat: 8g Proteins: 10g

middle of the cucumber, as it is not strong enough to shape.

3. After the cucumbers are sliced, take each slice and tightly roll it from the bottom up.
4. Slice opens the avocado and discards the pit. Cut the avocado flesh into tiny squares and put inside the cucumber circles. Cram as much in as possible for a more stable roll.
5. After you've completed your rolls, lightly cover with lime juice and olive oil. Drizzle a pinch of salt and pepper on top and serve!

Nutrition:
Calories: 523 Carbohydrates: 57.6g Proteins: 7.5g Fat: 37.6g

possible, and then place another piece of parchment sheet on top.

4. On top of the second sheet of parchment, use a rolling pin to roll the cracker mix to about 1/4th inch thick.
5. Remove the second sheet of parchment and cook in oven for about 15 minutes.
6. When the crackers are done baking, let cool and cut into cracker-sized pieces. Store in an airtight container.
7. Put the agar agar and 1 1/2 cups of water into a small pot over high heat. Wait for it to boil and whisk continuously until the mixture becomes thick like custard.
8. Remove from heat and scoop into a blender.
9. Roughly chop pepper and add to the blender along with the cashews, nutritional yeast, lemon juice, 2 tsp. onion powder, and mustard. Pulse until smooth.
10. Pour the blended mix into a bread pan lined with parchment paper and refrigerate for at least 30 minutes before serving.

Nutrition:

Calories: 46 Fat: 1g Proteins: 3g Carbohydrates: 7g Fiber: 1g

346. Three-Ingredient Flatbread

Preparation time: 10 minutes
Cooking time: 25 minutes
Servings: 5
Ingredients:

- 1 cup tri-color quinoa
- 1 1/2 cups water
- 1 tsp. onion powder

Directions:

1. Before starting, preheat the oven to 400F.

347. Spicy Homemade Tortilla Chips

Preparation time: 10 minutes
Cooking time: 16 minutes
Servings: 6
Ingredients:

- 12 corn tortillas
- 1 tsp. olive oil
- 1/4 tsp. chili powder
- 1/4 tsp. cumin powder
- 1/4 tsp. garlic powder
- 1/4 tsp. paprika powder
- Himalayan sea salt

Directions:

1. Before starting, preheat the oven to 425F.

348. Healthy Cereal Bars

Preparation time: 10 minutes
Cooking time: 30 minutes
Servings: 9
Ingredients:

- 1/2 cup toasted almonds
- 1 1/2 cup oats
- 1/2 cup almond flour
- 1/2 cup pure maple syrup
- 1/2 cup raisins
- 1/4 cup almond butter
- 2 tablespoons chia seeds
- 1 tbsp. fractionated coconut oil
- 1 tsp. vanilla extract
- 1/2 tsp. cinnamon powder
- 1/4 tsp. Himalayan pink sea salt

349. Black Bean Taquitos

Preparation time: 10 minutes
Cooking time: 20 minutes
Servings: 12
Ingredients:

- Olive oil
- 1 onion
- 1 poblano chili pepper
- 1 jalapeño Chili pepper
- 4 garlic cloves
- 1 can black beans
- 1/2 cup cilantro leaves
- 1 tsp. chili powder
- 1 tsp. cumin powder
- 1 tsp. sea salt
- 24 corn tortillas

Directions:

2. In a blender, all ingredients. Blend until smooth with no lumps.
3. Set a baking pan with parchment paper (make sure the pan has a small lip).
4. Evenly spread the quinoa blend on the baking sheet and put in the oven for 20-25 minutes.
5. Remove from oven and allow cooling.

Nutrition:

Calories: 188.4 Fat: 7.7g Carbohydrates: 29.3g Proteins: 3.7g Fiber: 8.2g

2. Set 2 large baking pans with parchment paper.
3. Slice each tortilla into 6 triangles, then place on the baking pans, trying not to overlap. Set in oven and cook for 10 minutes.
4. Take the baking pans out of the oven and delicately brush oil over the surface side of the chips (use only a little, otherwise the chips won't be crispy)
5. Mix the spices and salt together and sprinkle over the chips.
6. Put the chips back in the oven for another 6 minutes, or until crispy and golden.

Nutrition:

Calories: 142 Fat: 8g Carbohydrate: 14g Proteins: 4g

- 1/8 tsp. nutmeg powder

Directions:

1. Go ahead and preheat oven to 325F.
2. Use an 8x8 inch baking tin and grease and line with non-stick parchment paper.
3. Slice the almonds and add to a large bowl alongside the oats, almond flour, syrup, raisins, almond butter, chia seeds, oil, vanilla, cinnamon, salt, and nutmeg. Mix until it all sticks together.
4. Pat the almond mix into the pan, making sure the top is even. Put in the oven for 25 to 30 minutes, or until the edges of the pan are golden.
5. Allow to cool.

Nutrition:

Calories: 68 Fat: 1g Proteins: 3g Carbohydrates: 15g Fiber: 4g

1. Preheat your oven to 400F.
2. Set the parchment paper then grease with oil.
3. Chop your onion into quarters. Half both peppers and deseed them before chopping into quarters.
4. Using a food processor, add onion, poblano pepper, jalapeño pepper, and garlic. Use the chopping blade and pulse 3 times before adding the black beans, cilantro, chili powder, cumin, and salt.
5. Pulse another 3 times or until the mixture is finely chopped (you can pulse more if you want a smoother mix).
6. Put the tortillas on a pan and heat them in the oven for about a minute, or until soft and pliable.
7. Smear a large tablespoon of bean mix across each tortilla. Tightly roll like a burrito with open edges and put on a baking pan with the edge facing

down. Leave a smidge of space between each tortilla and cook for 20 minutes or until golden.

Nutrition:

350. Vegetable Tacos

Preparation time: 10 minutes
Cooking time: 35 minutes
Servings: 4
Ingredients:

- 1 head of cauliflower
- 1 sweet potato
- 1 onion
- 2 tbsp. olive oil
- 1/8 tsp. Himalayan salt
- 1/8 tsp. black pepper
- 1 can chickpeas
- 1/2 cup BBQ

Directions:

1. Preheat your oven to 425F and put a sheet of parchment paper on a large baking tray.

351. Tomato Basil Soup

Preparation time: 10 minutes
Cooking time: 60 minutes
Servings: 6
Ingredients:

- 3 pounds of halved tomatoes
- 1 cup of canned crush tomatoes
- 2-3 chopped carrots
- 2 chopped yellow onions
- 5 minced garlic cloves
- 2 ounces of basil leaves
- 2 teaspoons of thyme leaves
- 1 teaspoon of dried oregano
- 1/2 teaspoon of ground cumin
- 1/2 teaspoon of paprika
- 2 1/2 cups of water
- Fresh lime juice, to taste
- Salt, to taste
- Black Pepper, to taste

Directions:

352. Pearl Couscous Salad

Preparation time: 10 minutes
Cooking time: 30 minutes
Servings: 5
Ingredients:

- 3/4 cup of whole-wheat pearl couscous
- 1 1/2 cups of quartered grape tomatoes
- 3/4 pound of thin asparagus spears
- 1/4 cup of chopped red onion
- 1 1/2 juiced lemons
- 2 tablespoons of chopped parsley
- Sea salt, to taste
- Black pepper, to taste

Directions:

353. Vegan Tomato Soup

Preparation time: 10 minutes
Cooking time: 1 hour 30 minutes
Servings: 4
Ingredients:

Calories: 152 Fat: 10g Carbohydrates: 11.5g Fiber: 3g Proteins: 2g

2. Chop the cauliflower into small florets, the sweet potato into inch sized cubes, and dice the onion into small pieces.
3. Evenly place the cauliflower, sweet potato, and onion across the baking tray. Sprinkle oil, salt, and pepper across and mix to coat. Set in the oven for 15 minutes.
4. Set the tray out of the oven and dump the chickpeas on top. Pour 1/2 cup of BBQ sauce on top and stir to coat. Bake for another 8 minutes until the vegetable are soft.

Nutrition:
Calories: 112 Fat: 6g Carbohydrates: 9g Fiber: 1.5g Proteins: 7g

1. Preheat your oven to 450F.
2. Mix carrots with tomatoes in a large bowl. Add salt, black pepper, and toss.
3. Put the vegetable mixture on the baking sheet in a single layer. Roast for 30 minutes, then set aside for 10 minutes.
4. Transfer the roasted vegetables in a food processor or a blender, add just a little water, and blend.
5. Place a large stockpot on medium heat. Add the chopped onions, water and simmer for 3 minutes, then add minced garlic and cook until golden.
6. Pour the blended mixture into the stockpot. Add in 2 1/2 cups of water, the canned tomatoes, thyme, basil, and other seasonings. Set it to a boil, reduce to low heat, and cover. Simmer for about 20 minutes.
7. Serve with a splash of lime juice* and enjoy your Tomato Basil Soup!

Nutrition:
Calories: 104.9 Carbohydrates: 23.4g Proteins: 4.3g Fat: 0.8g

1. Pour water to a large pot, add salt, and bring it to a boil. Attach in asparagus and cook for 3 minutes until tender.
2. Set out asparagus with a slotted spoon and clean it under cold running water.
3. Cook couscous in the boiling water according to package directions.
4. Set the cooked asparagus into 1/2-inch pieces.
5. Drain couscous and wash it under cold running water. Set it in a large bowl.
6. Attach vegetables, lemon juice, parsley, pepper, and salt to the bowl. Toss it.
7. Serve and enjoy your Pearl Couscous Salad!

Nutrition:
Calories: 170 Carbohydrates: 30g Proteins: 6.5g Fat: 4g

- 4 lbs. tomatoes
- 3 shallots, peeled
- 5 garlic cloves, peeled

- 2 teaspoons fresh thyme leaves
- 2 tablespoons olive oil
- Salt and black pepper, to taste
- 1/2 cup raw cashews
- 1 tablespoon tomato paste
- 1/2 cup basil leaves, packed
- 3 cups vegetable stock
- 1 tablespoon balsamic vinegar

Directions:
1. Preheat your oven to 350F. Layer a baking sheet with parchment paper.
2. Spread the tomato pieces in the baking and add garlic cloves on top.

354. Butternut Squash Chickpea Stew

Preparation time: 10 minutes
Cooking time: 30 minutes
Servings: 6
Ingredients://
- 1 tablespoon olive oil
- 1 medium white onion, chopped
- 6 garlic cloves, minced
- 2 teaspoons cumin
- 1 teaspoon cinnamon
- 1 teaspoon ground turmeric
- 1/4 teaspoon cayenne pepper
- 1 (28-ounce) can crushed tomatoes
- 2 1/2 cups vegetable broth
- 1 (15-ounce) can chickpeas, rinsed
- 4 cups butternut squash, cubed
- 1 cup green lentils, rinsed
- 1/2 teaspoon salt

3. Add shallots around the tomato pieces.
4. Set olive oil, black pepper and salt over the veggies.
5. Roast these veggies for 1 hour, then allow them to cool.
6. Blend the roasted tomatoes with cashews, tomato paste, basil, and vegetable stock in a blender until smooth.
7. Transfer this soup to a cooking pan and cook to a boil.
8. Stir in vinegar and garnish with basil and olive oil.
9. Serve warm.

Nutrition:
Calories: 384 Fat: 14g Carbohydrates: 58g Fiber: 6g

- Black pepper, to taste
- fresh juice of 1/2 lemon
- 1/3cup cilantro, chopped
- Basil leaves, chopped

Directions:
1. Sauté garlic and onion with oil in a suitable pot over medium high heat for 5 minutes.
2. Stir in cayenne, turmeric, cinnamon and cumin then sauté for 30 seconds.
3. Add black pepper, salt, lentils. Butternut squash, chickpeas, broth and tomatoes.
4. Cook to a boil, reduce its heat then cover and cook for 20 minutes.
5. Add basil, cilantro and lemon juice.
6. Serve warm.

Nutrition:
Calories: 142 Fat: 8g Carbohydrate: 14g Proteins: 4g

Dinner

355. Mushroom Steak

Preparation time: 30 minutes
Cooking time: 1 hour
Servings: 8
Ingredients:
1 tbsp. of the following:

- fresh lemon juice
- olive oil, extra virgin
- 2 tbsp. coconut oil
- 3 thyme sprigs
- 8 medium Portobello mushrooms

For Sauce:
1 1/2 t. of the following:

- minced garlic
- minced peeled fresh ginger
- 2 tbsp. of the following:
- light brown sugar

- mirin
- 1/2 cup low-sodium soy sauce

Directions:
1. For the sauce, merge all the sauce ingredients, along with 1/4 cup water and simmer to cook.
2. Set the mushroom in the oven to 350F heat setting.
3. Using a skillet, dissolve coconut oil and olive oil, cooking the mushrooms on each side for about 3 minutes.
4. Set the mushrooms in a single layer on a sheet for baking and season with lemon juice, salt, and pepper.
5. Let it rest for 2 minutes. Enjoy.

Nutrition:
Calories: 87 Carbohydrates: 6.2g Proteins: 3g Fat: 6.2g

356. Black Bean Burgers

Preparation time: 5 Minutes
Cooking time: 20 Minutes
Servings: 4
Ingredients:

- 1 Onion, Diced
- 1/2 Cup Corn Nibs
- 2 Cloves Garlic, Minced
- 1/2 Teaspoon Oregano, Dried
- 1/2 Cup Flour
- 1 Jalapeno Pepper, Small

- 2 Cups Black Beans, Mashed & Canned
- 1/4 Cup Breadcrumbs (Vegan)
- 2 Teaspoons Parsley, Minced
- 1/4 Teaspoon Cumin
- 1 Tablespoon Olive Oil
- 2 Teaspoons Chili Powder
- 1/2 Red Pepper, Diced
- Sea Salt to Taste

Directions:

1. Set your flour on a plate, and then get out your garlic, onion, peppers and oregano, throwing it in a pan.
2. Cook over medium-high heat, and then cook until the onions are translucent.
3. Place the peppers in, and sauté until tender.
4. Cook for two minutes, and then set it to the side.

357. Dijon Maple Burgers

Preparation time: 10 Minutes
Cooking time: 40 Minutes
Servings: 12
Ingredients:
- 1 Red Bell Pepper
- 19 Ounces Can Chickpeas, Rinsed & Drained
- 1 Cup Almonds, Ground
- 2 Teaspoons Dijon Mustard
- 1 Teaspoon Oregano
- 1/2 Teaspoon Sage
- 1 Cup Spinach, Fresh
- 1 – 1/2 Cups Rolled Oats
- 1 Clove Garlic, Pressed
- 1/2 Lemon, Juiced
- 2 Teaspoons Maple Syrup, Pure

358. Hearty Black Lentil Curry

Preparation time: 15 Minutes
Cooking time: 6 hours
Servings: 7
Ingredients:
- 1 cup of black lentils, rinsed and soaked overnight
- 14 ounces of chopped tomatoes
- 2 large white onions, peeled and sliced
- 1 1/2 teaspoon of minced garlic
- 1 teaspoon of grated ginger
- 1 red chili
- 1 teaspoon of salt
- 1/4 teaspoon of red chili powder
- 1 teaspoon of paprika
- 1 teaspoon of ground turmeric
- 2 teaspoons of ground cumin
- 2 teaspoons of ground coriander
- 1/2 cup of chopped coriander
- 4-ounce of vegetarian butter
- 4 fluid of ounce water

359. Flavorful Refried Beans

Preparation time: 15 Minutes
Cooking time: 8 hours
Servings: 8
Ingredients:
- 3 cups of pinto beans, rinsed
- 1 small jalapeno pepper, seeded and chopped
- 1 medium-sized white onion, peeled and sliced
- 2 tablespoons of minced garlic
- 5 teaspoons of salt
- 2 teaspoons of ground black pepper
- 1/4 teaspoon of ground cumin
- 9 cups of water

Directions:

5. Use a potato masher to mash your black beans, and then stir in the vegetables, cumin, breadcrumbs, parsley, salt and chili powder, and then divide it into six patties.
6. Coat each side, and then cook until it's fried on each side.

Nutrition:
Calories: 211 Carbohydrates: 12g Fat: 7g Proteins: 12g

Directions:
1. Get out a baking sheet. Line it with parchment paper.
2. Cut your red pepper in half and then take the seeds out. Place it on your baking sheet, and roast in the oven while you prepare your other **Ingredients:**
3. Process your chickpeas, almonds, mustard and maple syrup together in a food processor.
4. Add in your lemon juice, oregano, sage, garlic and spinach, processing again. Make sure it's combined, but don't puree it.
5. Once your red bell pepper is softened, which should roughly take ten minutes, add this to the processor as well. Add in your oats, mixing well.

Nutrition:
Calories: 209 Carbohydrates: 11g Fat: 5g Proteins: 9g

- 2 fluid of ounce vegetarian double cream

Directions:
1. Place a large pan over a moderate heat, add butter and let heat until melt.
2. Add the onion and garlic and ginger and let cook for 10 to 15 minutes or until onions are caramelized.
3. Then stir in salt, red chili powder, paprika, turmeric, cumin, ground coriander, and water.
4. Transfer this mixture to a 6-quarts slow cooker and add tomatoes and red chili.
5. Drain lentils, add to slow cooker and stir until just mix.
6. Plug in slow cooker; adjust cooking time to 6 hours and let cook on low heat setting.
7. When the lentils are done, stir in cream and adjust the seasoning.
8. Serve with boiled rice or whole wheat bread.

Nutrition:
Calories: 171 Carbohydrates: 10g Fat: 7g Proteins: 12g

1. Using a 6-quarts slow cooker, place all the ingredients and stir until it mixes properly.
2. Cover the top, plug in the slow cooker; adjust the cooking time to 6 hours, let it cook on high heat setting and add more water if the beans get too dry.
3. When the beans are done, drain them and reserve the liquid.
4. Mash the beans using a potato masher and pour in the reserved cooking liquid until it reaches your desired mixture.
5. Serve immediately.

Nutrition:
Calories: 198 Carbohydrates: 22g Fat: 7g Proteins: 19g

360. Smoky Red Beans and Rice

Preparation time: 15 Minutes
Cooking time: 5 hours
Servings: 8
Ingredients:

- 30 ounces of cooked red beans
- 1 cup of brown rice, uncooked
- 1 cup of chopped green pepper
- 1 cup of chopped celery
- 1 cup of chopped white onion
- 1 1/2 teaspoon of minced garlic
- 1/2 teaspoon of salt
- 1/4 teaspoon of cayenne pepper
- 1 teaspoon of smoked paprika
- 2 teaspoons of dried thyme

361. Spicy Black-Eyed Peas

Preparation time: 15 Minutes
Cooking time: 60 Minutes
Servings: 8
Ingredients:

- 32-ounce black-eyed peas, uncooked
- 1 cup of chopped orange bell pepper
- 1 cup of chopped celery
- 8-ounce of chipotle peppers, chopped
- 1 cup of chopped carrot
- 1 cup of chopped white onion
- 1 teaspoon of minced garlic
- 3/4 teaspoon of salt
- 1/2 teaspoon of ground black pepper
- 2 teaspoons of liquid smoke flavoring
- 2 teaspoons of ground cumin
- 1 tablespoon of adobo sauce
- 2 tablespoons of olive oil

362. Creamy Artichoke Soup

Preparation time: 5 minutes
Cooking time: 40 minutes
Servings: 4
Ingredients:

- 1 can artichoke hearts, drained
- 3 cups vegetable broth
- 2 tablespoon lemon juice
- 1 small onion, finely cut
- 2 cloves garlic, crushed
- 3 tablespoons olive oil
- 2 tablespoons of flour
- 1/2 cup vegan cream

363. Super Rad-ish Avocado Salad

Preparation time: 10 minutes
Cooking time: 25 minutes
Servings: 2 Salads.
Ingredients:

- 6 shredded carrots
- 6 ounces diced radishes
- 1 diced avocado

364. Beauty School Ginger Cucumbers

Preparation time: 10 minutes
Cooking time: 5 minutes
Servings: 14 slices.

- 1 bay leaf
- 2 1/3 cups of vegetable broth

Directions:

1. Using a 6-quarts slow cooker, all the ingredients are except for the rice, salt, and cayenne pepper.
2. Stir until it mixes appropriately and then cover the top.
3. Plug in the slow cooker; adjust the cooking time to 4 hours, and steam on a low heat setting.
4. Then pour in and stir the rice, salt, cayenne pepper and continue cooking for an additional 2 hours at a high heat setting.

Nutrition:
Calories: 234 Carbohydrates: 13g Fat: 7g Proteins: 19g

- 1 tablespoon of apple cider vinegar
- 4 cups of vegetable broth

Directions:

1. Place a medium-sized non-stick skillet pan over an average temperature of heat; add the bell peppers, carrot, onion, garlic, oil and vinegar.
2. Stir until it mixes properly and let it cook for 5 to 8 minutes or until it gets translucent.
3. Transfer this mixture to a 6-quarts slow cooker and add the peas, chipotle pepper, adobo sauce and the vegetable broth.
4. Stir until mixes properly and cover the top.
5. Plug in the slow cooker; adjust the cooking time to 8 hours and let it cook on the low heat setting or until peas are soft.

Nutrition:
Calories: 211 Carbohydrates: 22g Fat: 7g Proteins: 19g

Directions:

1. Gently sauté the onion and garlic in some olive oil.
2. Add the flour, whisking constantly, and then add the hot vegetable broth slowly, while still whisking. Cook for about 5 minutes.
3. Blend the artichoke, lemon juice, salt and pepper until smooth. Add the puree to the broth mix, stir well, and then stir in the cream.
4. Cook until heated through. Garnish with a swirl of vegan cream or a sliver of artichoke.

Nutrition:
Calories: 211 Carbohydrates: 12g Fat: 7g Proteins: 11g

- 1/3 cup ponzu

Directions:

1. Bring all the above ingredients together in a serving bowl and toss. Enjoy!

Nutrition:
Calories: 211 Carbohydrates: 9g Fat: 7g Proteins: 12g

Ingredients:

- 1 sliced cucumber
- 3 teaspoon rice wine vinegar

- 1 1/2 tablespoon sugar
- 1 teaspoon minced ginger

Directions:

365. Mushroom Salad

Preparation time: 10 minutes
Cooking time: 20 minutes
Servings: 2
Ingredients:

- 1 tablespoon butter
- 1/2 pound cremini mushrooms, chopped
- 2 tablespoons extra-virgin olive oil
- Salt and black pepper to taste
- 2 bunches arugula
- 4 slices prosciutto
- 1 tablespoon apple cider vinegar
- 4 sundried tomatoes in oil, drained and chopped

366. Red Quinoa and Black Bean Soup

Preparation time: 5 minutes
Cooking time: 40 minutes
Servings: 6
Ingredients:

- 1 1/4 cup red quinoa
- 4 minced garlic cloves
- 1/2 tablespoon coconut oil
- 1 diced jalapeno
- 3 cups diced onion
- 2 teaspoon cumin
- 1 chopped sweet potato
- 1 teaspoon coriander
- 1 teaspoon chili powder
- 5 cups vegetable broth
- 15 ounces' black beans
- 1/2 teaspoon cayenne pepper
- 2 cups spinach

367. October Potato Soup

Preparation time: 5 minutes
Cooking time: 20 minutes
Servings: 3
Ingredients:

- 4 minced garlic cloves
- 2 teaspoon coconut oil
- 3 diced celery stalks
- 1 diced onion
- 2 teaspoon yellow mustard seeds
- 5 diced Yukon potatoes
- 6 cups vegetable broth
- 1 teaspoon oregano
- 1 teaspoon paprika
- 1/2 teaspoon cayenne pepper
- 1 teaspoon chili powder

368. Rice with Asparagus and Cauliflower

Preparation time: 5 minutes
Cooking time: 20 minutes
Servings: 2
Ingredients:

- 3 ounces' asparagus
- 3 ounces' cauliflower, chopped

1. Bring all the above ingredients together in a mixing bowl and toss the ingredients well. Enjoy!

Nutrition:
Calories: 210 Carbohydrates: 14g Fat: 7g Proteins: 19g

- Fresh parsley leaves, chopped

Directions:
1. Heat a pan with butter and half of the oil.
2. Add the mushrooms, salt, and pepper. Stir-fry for 3 minutes. Reduce heat. Stir again and cook for 3 minutes more.
3. Add rest of the oil and vinegar. Stir and cook for 1 minute.
4. Place arugula on a platter, add prosciutto on top, add the mushroom mixture, sundried tomatoes, more salt and pepper, parsley, and serve.

Nutrition:
Calories: 191 Carbohydrates: 6g Fat: 7g Proteins: 17g

Directions:
1. Begin by bringing the quinoa into a saucepan to boil with two cups of water. Allow the quinoa to simmer for twenty minutes. Next, remove the quinoa from the heat.
2. To the side, heat the oil, the onion, and the garlic together in a large soup pot.
3. Add the jalapeno and the sweet potato and sauté for an additional seven minutes.
4. Next, add all the spices and the broth and bring the soup to a simmer for twenty-five minutes. The potatoes should be soft.
5. Before serving, add the quinoa, the black beans, and the spinach to the mix. Season, and serve warm. Enjoy.

Nutrition:
Calories: 211 Carbohydrates: 22g Fat: 7g Proteins: 19g

- Salt and pepper to taste

Directions:
1. Begin by sautéing the garlic and the mustard seeds together in the oil in a large soup pot.
2. Next, add the onion and sauté the mixture for another five minutes.
3. Add the celery, the broth, the potatoes, and all the spices, and continue to stir.
4. Allow the soup to simmer for thirty minutes without a cover.
5. Next, Position about three cups of the soup in a blender and puree the soup until you've reached a smooth consistency. Pour this back into the big soup pot, stir, and serve warm. Enjoy.

Nutrition:
Calories: 203 Carbohydrates: 12g Fat: 7g Proteins: 9g

- 2 ounces' tomato sauce
- 1/2 cup of brown rice
- 3/4 cup of water
- 1/3 teaspoon salt
- 1/4 teaspoon ground black pepper
- 1/4 teaspoon garlic powder

- 1 tablespoon olive oil

Directions:
1. Take a medium saucepan, place it over medium heat, add oil, add asparagus and cauliflower and then sauté for 5 to 7 minutes until golden brown.
2. Season with garlic powder, salt, and black pepper, stir in tomato sauce, and then cook for 1 minute.

369. Spaghetti with Tomato Sauce

Preparation time: 5 minutes
Cooking time: 15 minutes
Servings: 2
Ingredients:
- 4 ounces' spaghetti
- 2 green onions, greens, and whites separated
- 1/8 teaspoon coconut sugar
- 3 ounces' tomato sauce
- 1 tablespoon olive oil
- 1/3 teaspoon salt
- 1/4 teaspoon ground black pepper

Directions:
1. Prepare the spaghetti, and for this, cook it according to the **Directions:** on the packet and then set aside.

370. Crispy Cauliflower

Preparation time: 5 minutes
Cooking time: 15 minutes
Servings: 2
Ingredients:
- 6 ounces of cauliflower florets
- 1/2 of zucchini, sliced
- 1/2 teaspoon of sea salt
- 1/2 tablespoon curry powder
- 1/4 teaspoon maple syrup
- 2 tablespoons olive oil

Directions:
1. Switch on the oven, then set it to 450 degrees F and let it preheat.

371. Avocado Toast with Chickpeas

Preparation time: 5 minutes
Cooking time: 5 minutes
Servings: 2
Ingredients:
- 1/2 of avocado, peeled, pitted
- 4 tablespoons canned chickpeas, liquid reserved
- 1 tablespoon lime juice
- 1 teaspoon apple cider vinegar
- 2 slices of bread, toasted
- 1/4 teaspoon salt
- 1/4 teaspoon paprika
- 1 teaspoon olive oil

Directions:

372. Green Onion Soup

Preparation time: 5 minutes
Cooking time: 12 minutes
Servings: 2
Ingredients:
- 6 green onions, chopped
- 7 ounces diced potatoes

3. Add rice, pour in water, stir until mixed, cover with a lid and cook for 10 to 12 minutes until rice has absorbed all the liquid and become tender.
4. When done, remove the pan from heat, fluff rice with a fork, and then serve.

Nutrition:
Calories: 257 Carbohydrates: 4g Fat: 4g Proteins: 40g

2. Then take a skillet pan, place it over medium heat, add oil and when hot, add white parts of green onions and cook for 2 minutes until tender.
3. Add tomato sauce, season with salt and black pepper and bring it to a boil.
4. Switch heat to medium-low level, simmer sauce for 1 minute, then add the cooked spaghetti and toss until mixed.
5. Divide spaghetti between two plates, and then serve.

Nutrition:
Calories: 265 Carbohydrates: 8g Fat: 2g Proteins: 7g

2. Meanwhile, take a medium bowl, add cauliflower florets and zucchini slices, add remaining ingredients reserving 1 tablespoon oil, and toss until well coated.
3. Take a medium skillet pan, place it over medium-high heat, add remaining oil and wait until it gets hot.
4. Spread cauliflower and zucchini in a single layer and sauté for 5 minutes, tossing frequently.
5. Then transfer the pan into the oven and then bake for 8 to 10 minutes until vegetables have turned golden brown and thoroughly cooked, stirring halfway.

Nutrition:
Calories: 161 Carbohydrates: 2g Fat: 2g Proteins: 7g

1. Take a medium skillet pan, place it over medium heat, add oil and when hot, add chickpeas and cook for 2 minutes.
2. Sprinkle 1/8 teaspoon each salt and paprika over chickpeas, toss to coat, and then remove the pan from heat.
3. Place avocado in a bowl, mash by using a fork, drizzle with lime juice and vinegar and stir until well mixed.
4. Spread mashed avocado over bread slices, scatter chickpeas on top and then serve.

Nutrition:
Calories: 235 Carbohydrates: 5g Fat: 5g Proteins: 31g

- 1/3 teaspoon salt
- 2 tablespoons olive oil
- 1 1/4 cup vegetable broth
- 1/4 teaspoon ground white pepper
- 1/4 teaspoon ground coriander

Directions:

1. Take a small pan, place potato in it, cover with water, and then place the pan over medium heat.
2. Boil the potato until cooked and tender, and when done, drain the potatoes and set aside until required.
3. Return saucepan over low heat, add oil and add green onions and cook for 5 minutes until cooked.
4. Season with salt, pepper, and coriander, add potatoes, pour in vegetable broth, stir until mixed and bring it to simmer.

373. Potato Soup

Preparation time: 5 minutes
Cooking time: 12 minutes
Servings: 2
Ingredients:

- 2 potatoes, peeled, cubed
- 1/3 teaspoon salt
- 1 1/2 cup vegetable broth
- 3/4 cup of water
- 1/8 teaspoon ground black pepper
- 1 tablespoon Cajun seasoning

Directions:
1. Take a small pan, place potato cubes in it, cover with water and vegetable broth, and then place the pan over medium heat.

374. Teriyaki Eggplant

Preparation time: 5 minutes
Cooking time: 15 minutes
Servings: 2
Ingredients:

- 1/2-pound eggplant
- 1 green onion, chopped
- 1/2 teaspoon grated ginger
- 1/2 teaspoon minced garlic
- 1/3 cup soy sauce
- 1 tablespoon coconut sugar
- 1/2 tablespoon apple cider vinegar
- 1 tablespoon olive oil

Directions:
1. Prepare vegan teriyaki sauce and for this, take a medium bowl, add ginger, garlic, soy sauce, vinegar,

375. Broccoli Stir-Fry with Sesame Seeds

Preparation time: 10 Minutes
Cooking time: 8 Minutes
Servings: 4
Ingredients:

- Two tablespoons extra-virgin olive oil (optional)
- One tablespoon grated fresh ginger
- cups broccoli florets
- ¼teaspoon sea salt (optional)
- Two garlic cloves, minced
- Two tablespoons toasted sesame seeds

Directions:

376. Bok Choy Stir-Fry

Preparation time: 12 Minutes
Cooking time: 10 to 13 Minutes
Servings: 4 to 6
Ingredients:

- Two tablespoons coconut oil (optional)
- One large onion, finely diced

5. Then remove the pan from heat and blend the mixture by using an immersion blender until creamy.
6. Taste to adjust seasoning, then ladle soup into bowls and then serve.

Nutrition:
Calories: 191 Carbohydrates: 1g Fat: 1g Proteins: 15g

2. Boil the potato until cooked and tender, and when done, remove the pan from heat and blend the mixture by using an immersion blender until creamy.
3. Return pan over medium-low heat, add remaining ingredients stir until mixed and bring it to a simmer.
4. Taste to adjust seasoning, then ladle soup into bowls and then serve.

Nutrition:
Calories: 203 Carbohydrates: 5g Fat: 6g Proteins: 37g

and sugar in it and then whisk until sugar has dissolved completely.
2. Cut eggplant into cubes, add them into vegan teriyaki sauce, toss until well coated and marinate for 10 minutes.
3. When ready to cook, take a grill pan, place it over medium-high heat, grease it with oil, and when hot, add marinated eggplant.
4. Cook for 3 to 4 minutes per side until nicely browned and beginning to be charred, drizzling with excess marinade frequently and transfer to a plate.
5. Sprinkle green onion on top of the eggplant and then serve.

Nutrition:
Calories: 132 Carbohydrates: 4g Fat: 4g Proteins: 13g

1. Heat the olive oil (if desired) in a large nonstick skillet over medium-high heat until shimmering.
2. Fold in the ginger, broccoli, and sea salt (if desired) and stir-fry for 5 to 7 minutes, or until the broccoli is browned.
3. Cook the garlic until tender, about 30 seconds.
4. Sprinkle with the sesame seeds and serve warm.

Nutrition:
Calories: 135 Fat: 10.9g Carbohydrates: 9.7g Proteins: 4.1g Fiber: 3.3g

- Two teaspoons ground cumin
- 1-inch piece fresh ginger, grated
- One teaspoon ground turmeric
- ½ teaspoon salt (optional)

- 12 baby bok choy heads, ends trimmed and sliced lengthwise
- Water, as needed
- cups cooked brown rice

Directions:
1. Heat the coconut oil (if desired) in a large pan over medium heat.
2. Sauté with onion for 5 minutes until translucent.

377. Spicy Grilled Tofu Steak

Preparation time: 30 minutes
Cooking time: 20 minutes
Servings: 4
Ingredients:
- 1 tbsp. chopped scallion
- 1 tbsp. chopped cilantro
- 1 tbsp. soy sauce
- 1 tbsp. hoisin sauce
- 2 tbsp. oil
- 1/4 tsp. salt
- 1/4 tsp. garlic powder
- 1/4 tsp. red chili pepper powder
- 1/4 tsp. ground Sichuan peppercorn powder
- 1/2 tsp. cumin
- 1 pound firm tofu

378. Piquillo Salsa Verde Steak

Preparation time: 30 minutes
Cooking time: 25 minutes
Servings: 8
Ingredients:
- 4-1/2 inch thick slices of ciabatta
- 18 oz. firm tofu, drained
- 5 tbsp. olive oil, extra virgin
- Pinch of cayenne
- 1/2 t. cumin, ground
- 1 1/2 tbsp. sherry vinegar
- 1 shallot, diced
- 8 piquillo peppers and cut to 1/2 inch strips
- 3 tbsp. parsley, finely chopped
- 3 tbsp. capers, drained and chopped

Directions:

379. Butternut Squash Steak

Preparation time: 30 minutes
Cooking time: 50 minutes
Servings: 4
Ingredients:
- 2 tbsp. coconut yogurt
- 1/2 t. sweet paprika
- 1 1/4 cup low-sodium vegetable broth
- 1 sprig thyme
- 1 finely chopped garlic
- 1 big thinly sliced shallot
- 1 tbsp. margarine
- 2 tbsp. olive oil
- Salt and pepper

Directions:

3. Stir in the cumin, ginger, turmeric, and salt (if desired). Combine the bok choy and stir-fry for 5 to 8 minutes or until the bok choy is tender but still crisp.
4. Pour water 1 to 2 tablespoons at a time to keep from sticking to the pan.
5. Serve over the brown rice.

Nutrition:
Calories: 447 Fat: 8.9g Carbohydrates: 75.6g Proteins: 29.7g Fiber: 19.1g

Directions:
1. Set the tofu on a plate and drain the excess liquid for about 10 minutes.
2. Slice drained tofu into 3/4 thick stakes.
3. Set the cumin, Sichuan peppercorn, chili powder, garlic powder, and salt in a mixing bowl until merged.
4. Merge soy sauce, hoisin, and 1 teaspoon of oil.
5. Warmth a skillet to medium temperature with oil, then carefully set the tofu in the skillet.
6. Whisk the spices over the tofu. Cook for 3-5 minutes, flip, and set spice on the other side.
7. Garnish with sauce and plate.
8. Sprinkle some scallion and cilantro and enjoy.

Nutrition:
Calories: 155 Carbohydrates: 7.6g Proteins: 9.9g Fat: 11.8g

1. Set the tofu and drain the excess liquid, and then divide into 8 rectangle pieces.
2. You can either set your grill.
3. Merge 3 tbsp. of olive oil, cayenne, cumin, shallot, parsley, capers, vinegar and piquillo peppers in a bowl to make our salsa verde. Season with salt and pepper.
4. Dry the tofu slices.
5. Garnish olive oil on each side, seasoning with salt and pepper lightly.
6. Set the bread on the grill and toast for about 2 minutes using medium-high heat.
7. Grill the tofu.
8. Set the toasted bread on the plate then the tofu on top of the bread.
9. Serve

Nutrition:
Calories: 427 Carbohydrates: 67.5g Proteins: 14.2g Fat: 14.6g

1. Warmth the oven to 37F.
2. Divide the squash, lengthwise, into 4 steaks.
3. Carefully core one side of each squash in a crosshatch pattern.
4. Garnish with olive oil each side of the steak then season with salt and pepper.
5. In an oven-safe, non-stick skillet, bring 2 tbsp. of olive oil to a warm temperature.
6. Set the steaks on the skillet and cook at medium temperature until browned, approximately 5 minutes. Bend and repeat on the other side for about 3 minutes.
7. Set the skillet into the oven to roast the squash.
8. Take out from the oven, set on a plate and covering with aluminum foil to keep warm.

9. Using the previously used skillet, attach thyme, garlic, and shallot, cooking at medium heat. Stir frequently for about 2 minutes. Attach brandy and cook for an additional minute.
10. Attach paprika and whisk the mixture together for 3 minutes.

380. Cauliflower Steak Kicking Corn

Preparation time: 30 minutes
Cooking time: 60 minutes
Servings: 6
Ingredients:
- 2 tsp. capers, drained
- 4 scallions, chopped
- 1 red chili, minced
- 1/4 c. vegetable oil
- 2 ears of corn, shucked
- 2 big cauliflower heads
- Salt and pepper to taste

Directions:
1. Heat the oven to 375F.
2. Boil 4 cups of water
3. Attach corn in the saucepan, cooking approximately 3 minutes or until tender.
4. Drain and allow the corn to cool, and then divide the kernels away from the cob.

381. Pistachio Watermelon Steak

Preparation time: 5 minutes
Cooking time: 10 minutes
Servings: 4
Ingredients:
- Micro greens
- Pistachios chopped
- Malden sea salt
- 1 tbsp. olive oil
- 1 watermelon
- Salt

Directions:
1. Cut the ends of the watermelon.

382. Spicy Veggie Steaks with Veggies

Preparation time: 30 minutes
Cooking time: 45 minutes
Servings: 4
Ingredients:
- 1 3/4 cup vital wheat gluten
- 1/2 cup vegetable stock
- 1/4 tsp. liquid smoke
- 1 tbsp. Dijon mustard
- 1 t. paprika
- 1/2 c. tomato paste
- 2 tbsp. soy sauce
- 1/2 tsp. oregano
- 1/4 tsp. of the following:
- coriander powder
- cumin
- 1 tsp. of the following:
- onion powder
- garlic powder
- 1/4 cup nutritional yeast
- 3/4 cup canned chickpeas

11. Attach in the yogurt seasoning with salt and pepper.
12. Garnish with parsley and enjoy!

Nutrition:
Calories: 300 Carbohydrates: 46g Proteins: 5.3g Fat: 10.6g

5. Warm 2 tbsp. of vegetable oil in a skillet.
6. Merge the chili pepper with the oil, cooking for approximately 30 seconds.
7. Attach the scallions, sautéing with the chili pepper until soft.
8. Merge in the corn and capers in the skillet and cook for approximately 1 minute to blend the flavors. Then remove from heat.
9. Warm 1 tbsp. of vegetable oil in a skillet and attach the cauliflower steaks to the pan.
10. Once processed, slide onto the cookie sheet and redo with the remaining cauliflower.
11. Set the corn mixture and press into the spaces between the florets of the cauliflower. Bake for 25 minutes.
12. Serve warm and enjoy!

Nutrition:
Calories: 153 Carbohydrates: 15g Proteins: 4g Fat: 10g

2. Peel off the skin from the watermelon along the white outer edge.
3. Set the watermelon into 4 slices, approximately 2 inches thick.
4. Warmth a skillet to medium heat and add 1 tablespoon of olive oil.
5. Attach watermelon steaks and cook until the edges begin to caramelize.
6. Plate and top with pistachios and micro greens.
7. Sprinkle with Malden salt.
8. Serve warm and enjoy!

Nutrition:
Calories: 67 Carbohydrates: 3.8g Proteins: 1.6g Fat: 5.9g

Marinade:
- 1/2 tsp. red pepper flakes
- 2 cloves garlic, minced
- 2 tbsp. soy sauce
- 1 tbsp. lemon juice, freshly squeezed
- 1/4 cup maple syrup

For skewers:
- 15 skewers, soaked in water
- 3/4 tsp. salt
- 8 oz. zucchini or yellow summer squash
- 1/4 tsp. black pepper
- 1 tbsp. olive oil
- 1 red onion

Directions:
1. In a food processor, attach chickpeas, liquid smoke, Dijon mustard, pepper, paprika, tomato paste, soy sauce, oregano, coriander, cumin, vegetable stock onion powder, garlic, and natural yeast.
2. Attach the vital wheat gluten to a big mixing bowl and pour the contents from the food processor

into the center. Merge with a spoon until soft dough is formed.
3. Knead the dough for approximately 2 minutes.
4. Once the dough is processed, flatten it to divide 4 equal-sized steaks.
5. Roll the steaks in tin foil; be sure not to wrap the steaks too tightly, as they will expand when steaming.
6. Steam for 20 minutes.
7. In a bowl, set the red pepper, soy sauce, lemon juice, garlic and syrup. Reserve half of the sauce for garnish during grilling.
8. Divide the onion and zucchini or yellow squash into 1/2-inch chunks.

383. Beans with Sesame Hummus
Preparation time: 10 minutes
Cooking time: 0 minutes
Servings: 6
Ingredients:
- 4 Tbsp. sesame oil
- 2 cloves garlic finely sliced
- 1 can cannellini beans
- 4 Tbsp. sesame paste
- 2 Tbsp. lemon juice
- 1/4 tsp. red pepper flakes
- 2 Tbsp. fresh basil finely

384. Candied Maple syrup -Coconut Peanuts
Preparation time: 15 minutes
Cooking time: 10 minutes
Servings: 8
Ingredients:
- 1/2 cup maple syrup
- 4 Tbsp. coconut butter
- 1 tsp. ground cinnamon
- 4 cups roasted, salted peanuts

Directions:

385. Choco Walnuts Fat Bombs
Preparation time: 15 minutes
Cooking time: 0 minutes
Servings: 6
Ingredients:
- 1/2 cup coconut butter
- 1/2 cup coconut oil softened
- 4 Tbsp. cocoa powder, unsweetened
- 4 Tbsp. brown sugar firmly packed
- 1/3 cup silken tofu mashed
- 1 cup walnuts, roughly chopped

Directions:

386. Crispy Honey Pecans
Preparation time: 2 hours and 15 minutes
Cooking time: 3 hours
Servings: 4
Ingredients:
- 16 oz. pecan halves
- 4 Tbsp. coconut butter melted
- 4 to 5 Tbsp. maple syrup

9. In a glass bowl, attach the red onion, zucchini, and yellow squash then coat with olive oil, pepper, and salt to taste. Bring the vegetables on the skewers.
10. Unwrap and set on a cookie sheet. Spill the marinade over the steaks, fully covering them.
11. Set your skewers, steaks, and glaze to the grill. Set the skewers on the grill over direct heat. Garnish skewers with glaze. Grill for approximately 3 minutes then flip.
12. Set the steaks directly on the grill, glaze side down, and brush the top with additional glaze. Cook to your desired doneness.
13. Enjoy!!

Nutrition:
Calories: 458 Carbohydrates: 65.5g Proteins: 39.1g Fat: 7.6g

- 2 Tbsp. fresh parsley finely
- Sea salt to taste

Directions:
1. Attach all ingredients in your food processor.
2. Set until all ingredients are combined well and smooth.
3. Transfer mixture into a bowl and refrigerate until servings.

Nutrition:
Calories: 231 Proteins: 14.9g Carbohydrates: 3.2g Fat: 18g Fiber: 1.1g

1. Attach maple syrup, coconut butter, and cinnamon in a microwave-safe bowl.
2. Set at HIGH for about 4 to 5 minutes.
3. Stir in nuts, merge thoroughly to coat.
4. Set the oven at HIGH 5 to 6 minutes until foamy; stir.
5. Scatter in a single layer on a greased tray. Break into small pieces and serve.

Nutrition:
Calories: 109 Fat: 2g Carbohydrates: 20g Fiber: 4.5g Proteins: 5g

1. Attach coconut butter and coconut oil into a microwave dish; melt it for 10-15 seconds.
2. Attach in cocoa powder and whisk well. Spill mixture into a blender with brown sugar and silken tofu cream; blend for 3-4 minutes.
3. Set silicone molds onto a sheet pan and fill halfway with chopped walnuts.
4. Spill the mixture over the walnuts and place it in the freezer for 6 hours.
5. Ready! Serve!

Nutrition:
Calories: 239 Fat: 2g Carbohydrates: 39g Fiber: 8g Proteins: 16g

- 1/4 tsp. chopped ginger
- 1/4 tsp. allspice
- 1 1/2 tsp. cinnamon

Directions:
1. Attach pecans and melted coconut butter into your 4-quart Slow Cooker. Stir until combined well.
2. Add in maple syrup and stir well.

3. In a bowl, merge spices and sprinkle over nuts; stir lightly.
4. Cook on LOW unsealed for about 2 to 3 hours until nuts are crispy.

387. Crunchy Fried Pickles

Preparation time: 10 minutes
Cooking time: 5 minutes
Servings: 6
Ingredients:

- 1/2 cup Vegetable oil
- 1 cup all-purpose flour
- 1 cup breadcrumbs
- salt and pepper
- 30 pickle chips (cucumber, dill)

Directions:

388. Granola bars with Maple Syrup

Preparation time: 20 minutes
Cooking time: 0 minutes
Servings: 12
Ingredients:

- 3/4 cup dates
- 2tablespoon chia seeds
- 3/4 cup rolled oats
- 4 Tbsp. Chopped nuts such Macadamia, almond, Brazilian,
- 2 Tbsp. shredded coconut
- 2 Tbsp. pumpkin seeds
- 2 Tbsp. sesame seeds
- 2 Tbsp. hemp seeds
- 1/2 cup maple syrup
- 1/4 cup peanut butter

389. Green Soybeans Hummus

Preparation time: 15 minutes
Cooking time: 0 minutes
Servings: 6
Ingredients:

- 1 1/2 cups frozen green soybeans
- 4 cups of water
- coarse salt to taste
- 1/4 cup sesame paste
- 1/2 tsp. grated lemon peel
- 3 Tbsp. fresh lemon juice
- 2 cloves of garlic crushed
- 1/2 tsp. ground cumin
- 1/4 tsp. ground coriander
- 4 Tbsp. extra virgin olive oil
- 1 Tbsp. fresh parsley leaves chopped

390. High Protein Avocado Guacamole

Preparation time: 15 minutes
Cooking time: 0 minutes
Servings: 4
Ingredients:

- 1/2 cup of onion, finely chopped
- 1 chili pepper (peeled and finely chopped)
- 1 cup tomato, finely chopped
- Cilantro leaves, fresh
- 2 avocados
- 2 Tbsp. linseed oil

5. Serve cold.

Nutrition:
Calories: 398 Carbohydrates: 55.6 g Proteins: 17.8g Fat: 11.8g

1. Warmth oil in a large frying skillet over medium-high heat.
2. Beat the flour, breadcrumbs, and the salt and pepper in a bowl.
3. Set the pickles in the flour/breadcrumbs mixture to coat completely.
4. Cook in batches until golden brown on all sides.
5. Serve.

Nutrition:
Calories: 199 Fat: 1g Proteins: 13g Carbohydrates: 37g Fiber: 13g

Directions:
1. Attach all ingredients (except maple syrup and peanut butter) into a food processor and pulse just until roughly merged.
2. Attach maple syrup and peanut butter and process until all ingredients are combined well.
3. Set baking paper onto a medium baking dish and spread the mixture.
4. Secure with a plastic wrap and press down to make it flat.
5. Chill granola in the fridge. Divide it into 12 bars and serve.

Nutrition:
Calories: 302 Fat: 22g Carbohydrates: 5g Proteins: 34g

Serving options:

- sliced cucumber, celery, olives

Directions:
1. In a saucepan, set to boil 4 cups of water with 2 to 3 pinches of coarse salt.
2. Attach in frozen soybeans and cook for 5 minutes or until tender.
3. Rinse and drain soybeans into a colander.
4. Attach soybeans and all remaining ingredients into a food processor.
5. Pulse until smooth and creamy.
6. Taste and adjust salt to taste.
7. Serve with sliced cucumber, celery, olives, bread.

Nutrition:
Calories: 215 Proteins: 8.7g Carbohydrates: 18g Fat: 11.5g Fiber: 2.3g

- 1/2 cup ground walnuts
- 1/2 lemon (or lime)
- Salt

Directions:
1. Chop the onion, chili pepper, cilantro, and tomato, place in a large bowl.
2. Slice avocado, open vertically, and remove the pit.
3. Using the spoon take out the avocado flesh.
4. Mash the avocados with a fork and attach into the bowl with onion mixture.

5. Add all remaining ingredients and stir well until ingredients combine well.
6. Set and adjust salt and lemon/lime juice.
7. Keep refrigerated into covered glass bowl up to 5 days.

391. Homemade Energy Nut Bars

Preparation time: 15 minutes
Cooking time: 0 minutes
Servings: 4
Ingredients:
- 1/2 cup peanuts
- 1 cup almonds
- 1/2 cup hazelnut, chopped
- 1 cup shredded coconut
- 1 cup almond butter
- 2 tsp. sesame seeds toasted
- 1/2 cup coconut oil, freshly melted
- 2 Tbsp. maple syrup
- 1/4 tsp. cinnamon

392. Honey Peanut Butter

Preparation time: 10 minutes
Cooking time: 0 minutes
Servings: 6
Ingredients:
- 1 cup peanut butter
- 3/4 cup maple syrup
- 1/2 cup ground peanuts

393. Mediterranean Marinated Olives

Preparation time: 10 minutes
Cooking time: 0 minutes
Servings: 2
Ingredients:
- 24 large olives, black, green, Kalamata
- 1/2 cup extra-virgin olive oil
- 4 cloves garlic, thinly sliced
- 2 Tbsp. fresh lemon juice
- 2 tsp. coriander seeds, crushed
- 1/2 tsp. crushed red pepper
- 1 tsp. dried thyme

394. Nut Butter and Dates Granola

Preparation time: 1 hour
Cooking time: 55 minutes
Servings: 8
Ingredients:
- 3 cups rolled oats
- 2 cups dates, pitted and chopped
- 1 cup flaked or shredded coconut
- 1/2 cup wheat germ
- 1/4 cup soymilk powder
- 1/2 cup almonds chopped
- 3/4 cup maple syrup
- 1/2 cup almond butter (plain, unsalted) softened
- 1/4 cup peanut butter softened

395. Oven-baked Caramelize Plantains

Preparation time: 30 minutes
Cooking time: 17 minutes
Servings: 4
Ingredients:
- 4 medium plantains, peeled and sliced

Nutrition:
Calories: 153 Proteins: 6.2g Carbohydrates: 19.2g Fat: 5g Fiber: 2.6g

Directions:
1. Add all nuts into a food processor and pulse for 1-2 minutes.
2. Add in shredded coconut, almond butter, sesame seeds, melted coconut oil, cinnamon, and maple syrup; process only for one minute.
3. Cover a square plate/tray with parchment paper and apply the nut mixture.
4. Spread mixture vigorously with a spatula.
5. Set in the freezer for. Ready! Enjoy!

Nutrition:
Calories: 222 Fat: 6g Fiber: 4.4g Carbohydrates: 36.5g Proteins: 7.1g

- 1 tsp. ground cinnamon

Directions:
1. Add all ingredients into your fast-speed blender, and blend until smooth.
2. Keep refrigerated.

Nutrition:
Calories: 254 Fat: 13.1g Carbohydrates: 34g Proteins: 3.4g

- 1 tsp. dried rosemary, crushed
- Salt and ground pepper to taste

Directions:
1. Place olives and all remaining ingredients in a large container or bag and shake to combine well.
2. Cover and refrigerate to marinate overnight.
3. Serve.
4. Keep refrigerated.

Nutrition:
Calories: 420 Fat: 15.2g Carbohydrates: 64.3g Proteins: 11.6g

Directions:
1. Preheat oven to 300F.
2. Set all ingredients into a food processor and pulse until roughly combined.
3. Spread mixture evenly into greased 10 x 15-inch baking pan.
4. Bake for 45 to 55 minutes.
5. Stir mixture several times during baking.
6. Remove from the oven and cool completely.
7. Store in a covered glass jar.

Nutrition:
Calories: 393 Fat: 15g Proteins: 10g Carbohydrates: 52g Fiber: 9g

- 2 Tbsp. fresh orange juice
- 4 Tbsp. brown sugar or to taste
- 1 Tbsp. grated orange zest
- 4 Tbsp. coconut butter, melted

Directions:

1. Preheat oven to 360 F/180 C.
2. Place plantain slices in a heatproof dish.
3. Pour the orange juice over plantains, and then sprinkle with brown sugar and grated orange zest.

396. Powerful Peas and Lentils Dip

Preparation time: 10 minutes
Cooking time: 0 minutes
Servings: 4
Ingredients:

- 4 cups frozen peas
- 2 cup green lentils cooked
- 1 piece of grated ginger
- 1/2 cup fresh basil chopped
- 1 cup ground almonds
- Juice of 1/2 lime
- Pinch of salt

397. Protein "Raffaello" Candies

Preparation time: 15 minutes
Cooking time: 0 minutes
Servings: 12
Ingredients:

- 1 1/2 cups desiccated coconut flakes
- 1/2 cup coconut butter softened
- 4 Tbsp. coconut milk canned
- 4 Tbsp. coconut palm sugar (or granulated sugar)
- 1 tsp. pure vanilla extract
- 1 Tbsp. vegan protein powder (pea or soy)
- 15 whole almonds

Directions:

398. Protein-Rich Pumpkin Bowl

Preparation time: 10 minutes
Cooking time: 0 minutes
Servings: 2
Ingredients:

- 1 1/2 cups almond milk (depending on desired consistency)
- 1 cup pumpkin puree canned, with salt
- 1/2 cup chopped walnuts
- 1 scoop vegan soy protein powder

399. Savory Red Potato-Garlic Balls

Preparation time: 40 minutes
Cooking time: 25 minutes
Servings: 4
Ingredients:

- 1 1/2 lbs. of red potatoes
- 3 cloves of garlic finely chopped
- 1 Tbsp. of fresh finely chopped parsley
- 1/4 tsp. ground turmeric
- Salt and ground pepper to taste

Directions:

1. Rinse potatoes and place unpeeled into a large pot.
2. Pour water to cover potatoes and bring to boil.

400. Spicy Smooth Red Lentil Dip

Preparation time: 35 minutes
Cooking time: 20 minutes
Servings: 4
Ingredients:

4. Melt coconut butter and pour evenly over plantains.
5. Cover with foil and bake for 15 to 17 minutes.
6. Serve warm or cold with honey or maple syrup.

Nutrition:
Calories: 288 Fat: 11.11g Carbohydrates: 45.3g Proteins: 4.4g

- 4 Tbsp. sesame oil
- 1/4 cup Sesame seeds

Directions:

1. Set all ingredients in a food processor or in a blender.
2. Blend until all ingredients combined well.
3. Keep refrigerated in an airtight bag up to 4 days.

Nutrition:
Calories: 248 Carbohydrates: 24.7g Proteins: 9.5g Fat: 10.8g

1. Put 1 cup of desiccated coconut flakes, and all remaining ingredients in the blender (except almonds), and blend until soft.
2. If your dough is too thick, attach some coconut milk.
3. In a bowl, add remaining coconut flakes.
4. Coat every almond in one tablespoon of mixture and roll into a ball.
5. Roll each ball in coconut flakes.
6. Chill in the fridge for several hours.

Nutrition:
Calories: 320 Fat: 7 g   Carbohydrates: 64g Proteins: 10g Fiber: 12g

- 1 tsp. pure vanilla extract
- A handful of cacao nibs

Directions:

1. Add all ingredients in a blender apart from the cacao nibs.
2. Blend until smooth.
3. Serve in bowls and sprinkle with cacao nibs.

Nutrition:
Calories: 458 Carbohydrates: 65.5g Proteins: 39.1g Fat: 7.6g

3. Cook for about 20 to 25 minutes on medium heat.
4. Rinse potatoes and let them cool down.
5. Peel potatoes and mash them; add finely chopped garlic, and the salt and pepper.
6. Form the potato mixture into small balls.
7. Sprinkle with chopped parsley and refrigerate for several hours.
8. Serve.

Nutrition:
Calories: 348 Fat: 20.8g Fiber: 12.3g Carbohydrates: 38.7g Proteins: 7.1g

- 1 cup red lentils
- 1 bay leaf
- Sea salt to taste
- 2 garlic cloves, finely chopped

- 2 Tbsp. chopped cilantro leaves
- 1 Tbsp. tomato paste
- Lemon juice from 2 lemons, freshly squeezed
- 2 tsp. ground cumin
- 4 Tbsp. extra-virgin olive oil

Directions:
1. Rinse lentils and drain.
2. Combine lentils and bay leaf in a medium saucepan.
3. Pour enough water to cover lentils completely and bring to boil.
4. Cover tightly, set heat to medium, and simmer for about 20 minutes.
5. Season salt to taste and stir well. Note: Always season with the salt after cooking – if salt is added before, the lentils will become tough.
6. Drain the lentils in a colander. Detach the bay leaf and let the lentils cool for 10 minutes.
7. Set the lentils to a food processor and add all remaining ingredients.
8. Pulse until all ingredients combined well.
9. Taste and adjust seasonings if needed.
10. Transfer a lentil dip into a glass container and refrigerate at least 2 hours before serving.

Nutrition:
Calories: 168 Fat: 10.1 g Fiber: 6g Carbohydrates: 21g Proteins: 2.1g

401. Steamed Broccoli with Sesame

Preparation time: 15 minutes
Cooking time: 5 minutes
Servings: 2
Ingredients:
- 1 1/2 lb. fresh broccoli florets
- 1/2 cup sesame oil
- 4 Tbsp. sesame seeds
- Salt and ground pepper to taste

Directions:

1. Set broccoli florets in a steamer basket above boiling water.
2. Cover and steam for about 4 to 5 minutes.
3. Remove from steam and place broccoli in serving the dish.
4. Set with the salt and pepper, and drizzle with sesame oil; toss to coat.
5. Sprinkle with sesame seeds and serve immediately.

Nutrition:
Calories: 248 Fat: 12.5g Carbohydrates: 12g Fiber: 1g Proteins: 3.5g

402. Vegan Eggplant Patties

Preparation time: 30 minutes
Cooking time: 15 minutes
Servings: 6
Ingredients:
- 2 big eggplants
- 1 onion finely diced
- 1 Tbsp. garlic cloves
- 1 bunch raw parsley, cut
- 1/2 cup almond meal
- 4 Tbsp. Kalamata olives, pitted and cut
- 1 Tbsp. baking soda
- Salt and ground pepper
- Olive oil or avocado oil

Directions:
1. Peel off eggplants, wash, and cut in half.
2. Sauté eggplant cubes in a non-stick skillet - occasionally stirring - about 10 minutes.
3. Set to a large bowl and mash with an immersion blender.
4. Attach eggplant puree into a bowl and add in all remaining ingredients (except oil).
5. Set a mixture using your hands until the dough is smooth, sticky, and easy to shape. Shape mixture into 6 patties.
6. Warmth the olive oil in a frying skillet on medium-high heat.
7. Fry patties for about 3 to 4 minutes per side.
8. Detach patties on a platter lined with kitchen paper towel to drain.
9. Serve warm.

Nutrition:
Calories: 105 Proteins: 6g Carbohydrates: 3.3g Fat: 7.9g Fiber: 0.6g

403. Chickpea and Mushroom Burger

Preparation time: 20minutes
Cooking time: 16 minutes
Servings: 4
Ingredients:
- 240g chickpeas
- 1/2 tsp. sea salt
- 2 level tsp. gram flour
- 1 medium sized apple
- 1 tsp. dried onion
- parsley
- 2 large cloves
- 1 tsp. fresh garlic
- 75g tasty rosemary
- 1 medium-sized mushrooms
- tomato
- 1 tsp. tahini

Directions:
1. Set garlic, diced onion and slash the mushrooms into little pieces, sauté together in a search for a gold couple of moments.
2. Set chickpeas in an enormous blending bowl in with a potato masher or fork.
3. Mesh the half apple.
4. Include the gram flour, tahini, salt, and apple and combine all utilizing the rear of a metal spoon
5. Finely slice the rosemary and slash the tomato into little pieces.
6. Include the sautéed things alongside every single residual ingredient into a bowl, pressing down and blending completely with a metal spoon.
7. Set into 4 and solidly shape and form into patties.

8.   Spot onto a barbecue plate and warmth under a medium flame broil on each side.
Nutrition:

404. Carrot Cake Oatmeal

Preparation time: 10
Cooking time: 15 minutes
Servings: 2
Ingredients:

- 1/4 cup pecans
- 1 cup finely shredded carrot
- 1/2 cup rolled oats
- 11/4 cups unsweetened plant-based milk
- 1 tablespoon pure maple syrup
- 1 teaspoon ground cinnamon
- 1 teaspoon ground ginger
- 1/4 teaspoon ground nutmeg
- 2 tablespoons chia seeds

Directions:

405. Plant-Powered Pancakes

Preparation time: 5
Cooking time: 15 minutes
Servings: 4
Ingredients:

- 1 cup whole-wheat flour
- 1/2 teaspoon ground cinnamon
- 1 teaspoon baking powder
- 1 cup unsweetened plant-based milk
- 1/2 cup unsweetened applesauce
- 1/4 cup pure maple syrup
- 1 teaspoon vanilla extract

Directions:

406. Cauliflower Scramble

Preparation time: 15 minutes
Cooking time: 13 minutes
Servings: 4
Ingredients:

- 1 onion, diced
- 3 garlic cloves, minced
- 1 green bell pepper, coarsely chopped
- 1 red bell pepper, coarsely chopped
- 1 large head cauliflower, cored and chopped into 1/2-inch florets
- 1 teaspoon ground turmeric
- 1/4 cup nutritional yeast
- 1/4 teaspoon ground nutmeg
- 1/4 teaspoon cayenne pepper
- 1/4 teaspoon freshly ground black pepper
- 1 tablespoon coconut aminos
- 1 (15-ounce) can chickpeas, drained and rinsed

407. Tofu Chilaquiles

Preparation time: 5 minutes
Cooking time: 10 minutes
Servings: 4
Ingredients:

- 1 (14-ounce) firm tofu, drained and crumbled
- 1 tablespoon onion powder
- 1/2 teaspoon ground cumin
- 1/4 teaspoon salt

Calories: 150 Fat: 7.3g Fiber: 6.1g Carbohydrates: 18g Proteins: 3.7g

1.   In a skillet, toast the pecans for 3 to 4 minutes, stirring, until browned and fragrant (watch closely, as they can burn quickly). Pour the pecans onto a cutting board and roughly chop them. Set aside.
2.   In an 8-quart pot over medium-high heat, combine the carrot, oats, milk, maple syrup, cinnamon, ginger, and nutmeg. Set to a boil, and then reduce the heat to medium-low. Cook, uncovered, for 10 minutes, stirring occasionally.
3.   Stir in the chopped pecans and chia seeds. Serve immediately.

Nutrition:
Calories: 388 Fat: 19g Carbohydrates: 45g Fiber: 12g Proteins: 13g

1.   In a large bowl, merge the flour, cinnamon, and baking powder.
2.   Stir in the milk, applesauce, maple syrup, and vanilla until no dry flour is left and the batter is smooth.
3.   Warmth a large nonstick skillet or griddle over medium heat. For each pancake, pour 1/4 cup of batter onto the hot skillet. Cook for 1 to 2 minutes. Bend and cook for 1 to 2 minutes, until browned.
4.   Repeat until all the batter is used, then serve.

Nutrition:
Calories: 204 Fat: 2g Carbohydrates: 42g Fiber: 5g Proteins: 6g

Directions:
1.   In a nonstick skillet over medium heat, merge the onion, garlic, and green and red bell peppers. Cook, stirring, until the onion is processed. Attach 1 to 2 tablespoons of water as needed to prevent burning.
2.   Add the cauliflower and toss to combine. Secure the skillet and cook for 5 to 6 minutes, or until the cauliflower is fork-tender.
3.   While the cauliflower is processed, in a bowl, stir together the turmeric, nutritional yeast, nutmeg, cayenne, and black pepper. Set aside.
4.   Evenly sprinkle the coconut aminos over the cauliflower mixture and stir to combine. Stir in the spice mixture. Set in the chickpeas and cook, uncovered, for 5 minutes to warm. Serve.

Nutrition:
Calories: 166 Fat: 2g Carbohydrates: 31g Fiber: 10g Proteins: 9g

- 1/4 teaspoon garlic powder
- 1/4 teaspoon turmeric
- 1 (15-ounce) can black beans
- 1 (16-ounce) jar salsa
- 4 baked tostadas, roughly broken
- 2 tablespoons chopped fresh cilantro
- 1/4 cup sliced onion, rinsed
- 2 to 4 lime wedges

- 1 avocado, pitted, peeled, and chopped

Directions:

1. In a large nonstick sauté pan or skillet over medium heat, combine the tofu, onion powder, cumin, salt, garlic powder, and turmeric. Cook; stir frequently, for 3 to 5 minutes, until heated through. Attach 1 to 2 tablespoons of water as needed to prevent burning.

408. Vegan "Toona" Salad

Preparation time: 15 minutes
Cooking time: 10 minutes
Servings: 4
Ingredients:

- 2 (15-ounce) cans chickpeas, drained and rinsed
- 1 avocado, pitted and peeled
- 1/2 cup chopped red onion
- 1/4 cup chopped celery
- 2 tablespoons Dijon mustard
- 11/2 tablespoons freshly squeezed lemon juice
- 1/2 tablespoon pure maple syrup
- 1 teaspoon garlic powder

Directions:

409. Lentil Potato Soup

Preparation time: 5 minutes
Cooking time: 20 minutes
Servings: 4
Ingredients:

- 4 cups vegetable broth
- 3 cups diced potatoes
- 1 cup dried brown lentils, rinsed
- 1 tablespoon onion powder
- 1 tablespoon nutritional yeast
- 1/2 teaspoon smoked paprika
- 1/4 teaspoon garlic powder
- 1/4 teaspoon salt
- 1/4 teaspoon freshly ground black pepper
- 1/8 teaspoon celery seed

410. Cheesy Broccoli Soup

Preparation time: 10 minutes
Cooking time: 10 minutes
Servings: 4-6
Ingredients:

- 1 (9-ounce) bag frozen squash
- 4 cups vegetable broth, divided
- 1/4 cup nutritional yeast
- 1 tablespoon onion powder
- 1/4 teaspoon smoked paprika
- 1/4 teaspoon garlic powder
- 1/4 teaspoon freshly ground black pepper
- 1/4 cup raw cashews
- 1 (10.5-ounce) bag frozen broccoli
- 1 teaspoon red miso paste

Directions:

411. Coconut Curry Soup

Preparation time: 5 minutes
Cooking time: 15 minutes
Servings: 4

2. Add the beans, salsa, and tostadas, carefully submerging the tostadas in the liquid. Reduce the heat to medium-low. Simmer for about 5 minutes, until the tostadas soften. Detach from the heat and stir in the cilantro.
3. Serve warm with the onion, lime, and avocado. Garnish with cilantro.

Nutrition:
Calories: 343 Fat: 15g Total Carbohydrates: 41g Fiber: 13g Proteins: 18g

1. In a large bowl, merge the chickpeas and the avocado. Mash them down until most of the chickpeas have been broken apart. (You don't want to purée the chickpeas; just smash them enough so they're able to absorb the rest of the flavors of the dish.)
2. Stir in the onion, celery, mustard, lemon juice, maple syrup, and garlic powder, making sure everything is thoroughly combined, and serve.

Nutrition:
Calories: 276 Fat: 10g Carbohydrates: 40g Fiber: 11g Proteins: 12g

- 1/8 teaspoon red pepper flakes
- 1 bay leaf

Directions:

1. In a large saucepan over high heat, merge the broth, potatoes, lentils, onion powder, nutritional yeast, smoked paprika, garlic powder, salt, pepper, celery seed, red pepper flakes, and bay leaf. Bring to a boil.
2. Reduce the heat to medium-low. Secure and simmer for 18 to 20 minutes, until the potatoes are knife-tender. Remove and discard the bay leaf. Serve warm.

Nutrition:
Calories: 164 Fat: 0g Carbohydrates: 35g Fiber: 7g Proteins: 7g

1. In a large saucepan over high heat, merge the squash, 2 cups of broth, the nutritional yeast, onion powder, smoked paprika, garlic powder, and pepper. Set to a boil, and then cook for 3 to 5 minutes, until the squash is tender.
2. Transfer the solids and at least 1 cup of broth to a high-speed blender. Attach the cashews and blend until smooth and creamy.
3. Transfer the blended soup mixture back to the pan. Add the 2 remaining cups of broth and return to a boil. Add the broccoli and miso paste, and simmer for 7 to 10 minutes, until the broccoli is crisp-tender. Serve warm.

Nutrition:
Calories: 120 Fat: 5g Carbohydrates: 18g Fiber: 4g Proteins: 5g

Ingredients:

- 11/2 cups vegetable broth
- 1 (15-ounce) can chickpeas, drained and rinsed

- 1 (13.5-ounce) can lite coconut milk
- 1 large carrot, coarsely chopped
- 1 small red onion, quartered
- 1/2 teaspoon tandoori seasoning
- 1/2 teaspoon curry powder
- 1/4 tsp. salt
- 1/4 tsp. white pepper

Directions:
1. In a blender or food processor, merge the broth, chickpeas, coconut milk, carrot, onion, tandoori

412. Hot and Sour Tofu Soup

Preparation time: 5 minutes
Cooking time: 15 minutes
Servings: 2
Ingredients:
- 1/4 cup gluten-free tamari or low-sodium soy sauce
- 2 teaspoons red or yellow miso paste
- 2 teaspoons red chili paste
- 1 teaspoon minced garlic
- 2 teaspoons minced fresh ginger
- 1 cup sliced mushrooms
- 3 cups water
- 1 (12-ounce) package silken tofu
- 1/4 cup crushed unsalted peanuts (optional)
- 1/4 cup chopped scallions, green parts only

413. Vegetable and Avocado Quesadillas

Preparation time: 5 minutes
Cooking time: 10 minutes
Servings: 2
Ingredients:
- 4 oil-free whole-grain tortillas
- 2 avocados, pitted, peeled, and mashed
- 1/2 cup shredded baby spinach
- 1/2 cup broccoli slaw
- 1/2 cup thinly cut red bell pepper
- 2 tablespoons thinly sliced scallion, green and white parts
- 2 tablespoons sliced olives
- 1/2 cup salsa
- 1/2 cup Green Goddess Dressing and Dipping Sauce

Directions:

414. Beet Reuben Sandwiches

Preparation time: 5 minutes
Cooking time: 10 minutes
Servings: 4
Ingredients:
For the Reuben sauce
- 1/4 block firm tofu, drained
- 3 tablespoons ketchup
- 11/2 tablespoons apple cider vinegar
- 2 teaspoon Dijon mustard
- 1 teaspoon water, plus more as needed
- 1/8 teaspoon garlic powder
- 1/4 cup diced pickles

For the sandwiches:
- 8 whole-grain bread slices, lightly toasted

seasoning, curry powder, and salt and blend until smooth.
2. Transfer the soup mixture to a large saucepan or Dutch oven. Bring to a simmer over medium-high heat (constant small bubbles will form), then reduce the heat to low. Gently simmer for 10 minutes, until the flavors meld. Stir in the pepper just before serving.

Nutrition:
Calories: 292 Fat: 21g Carbohydrates: 19g Fiber: 5g Proteins: 6g

Directions:
1. In a saucepan, set the tamari until it just begins to bubble. Add the miso and mash it with a fork to create thick slurry. Attach the chili paste, garlic, and ginger and cook, stirring frequently, for 3 minutes.
2. Attach the mushrooms and water and bring to a boil, then reduce the heat to medium-low. Attach the tofu, crumbling it with your fingers and dropping it into the pan. Cover and simmer for 10 minutes.
3. Divide the peanuts (if using) and scallions between two large bowls. Set half the soup into each bowl and serve.

Nutrition:
Calories: 149 Fat: 7g Carbohydrates: 10g Fiber: 2g Proteins: 16g

1. On each tortilla, evenly spread half of the mashed avocado.
2. Divide the spinach, broccoli slaw, bell pepper, scallion, and olives between the tortillas and fold them in half.
3. Warmth a large nonstick skillet over medium heat. Gently place the tortillas in the pan and cook for 3 to 5 minutes per side, until tortillas are lightly browned and crisped.
4. Serve with salsa and green goddess dressing.

Nutrition:
Calories: 394 Fat: 25g Carbohydrates: 37g Fiber: 14g Proteins: 11g

- 2 cups cooked beets, warmed and sliced
- 1 cup sauerkraut
- 1 teaspoon Salt-Free Spice Blend

Directions:
1. Make the Reuben sauce: Combine the tofu, ketchup, vinegar, mustard, water, and garlic powder in a blender. Blend until smooth, adding water 1 teaspoon at a time if the texture is too thick. Bring the sauce to a bowl and stir in the diced pickles. You should have about 1 cup of sauce.
2. Make the sandwiches: On one piece of bread, layer 1/2 cup of beets, 1/4 cup of sauerkraut, 1/4 teaspoon of salt-free spice blend, and 1/4 cup of Reuben sauce. Repeat with three more bread slices,

then top the four sandwiches with the remaining bread slices and serve.

Nutrition:

415. Vegetable Pita Pizzas

Preparation time: 5 minutes
Cooking time: 15 minutes
Servings: 2
Ingredients:

- 4 whole-grain pitas
- 1 cup Weeknight Tomato Sauce
- Pinch red pepper flakes (optional)
- 1/4 cup 1/2-inch broccoli florets
- 1/4 cup shredded spinach
- 1/4 cup chopped asparagus
- 1/4 cup sliced grape tomatoes
- 1/4 cup sliced red onion
- 1/4 cup sliced red bell pepper
- 1/4 cup sliced olives
- 1/4 cup sliced mushrooms
- 1 avocado, pitted, peeled, and diced

Directions:

416. Black Bean and Sweet Potato Tacos

Preparation time: 10 minutes
Cooking time: 15 minutes
Servings: 4
Ingredients:

- 2 teaspoons minced garlic (about 2 cloves)
- 1 tablespoon water
- 1 pound sweet potatoes, unpeeled and cut into 1/2-inch cubes
- 1 small jalapeño pepper
- 1 (15-ounce) can black beans, drew (off) and washed
- 1/2 teaspoon salt
- 1/4 teaspoon freshly ground black pepper
- 8 oil-free corn tortillas, warmed according to package instructions
- Pumpkin seeds and/or pomegranate seeds, for garnish (optional)

417. Veg Inspired Plant-Based Bowl Formula

Preparation time: 10 minutes
Cooking time: 15 minutes
Servings: 2
Ingredients:

- 2 cups cooked grains, such as rice, quinoa, faro, or freekeh
- 1 cup protein, such as beans, tofu, or tempeh
- 1 cup chopped greens, such as baby spinach, mixed greens, or massaged kale
- 2 cups raw, roasted, or steamed vegetables of choice
- 1/2 cup sauce, such as Go-To Bowl Sauce

Optional Toppings:

418. Turmeric Tempeh Stir-Fry

Preparation time: 10 minutes
Cooking time: 20 minutes
Servings: 2

Calories: 228 Fat: 3g Carbohydrates: 40g Fiber: 8g Proteins: 12g

1. Place the whole-grain pitas on a baking sheet in a cold oven and preheat to 350°F. The pitas will warm and the top side should get slightly crispy.
2. Remove the pitas from the oven and flip them over onto a plate, crispy-side down.
3. Spread 1/4 cup of tomato sauce on each pita. Add the red pepper flakes (if using).
4. Evenly divide the broccoli, spinach, asparagus, tomatoes, onion, bell pepper, olives, and mushrooms between the pitas.
5. Bake the pizzas for 12 minutes until the pita edges are lightly browned and the vegetables are crisp-tender.
6. Divide the avocado between the pitas and serve.

Nutrition:
Calories: 381 Fat: 19g Carbohydrates: 51g Fiber: 15g Proteins: 11g

Directions:

1. In a large skillet over medium-high heat, merge the garlic and water and cook until the garlic is fragrant. Add the sweet potatoes and jalapeño and cook, stirring frequently, for about 10 minutes, until the sweet potatoes are tender. Attach 1 to 2 tablespoons of water as needed to prevent burning.
2. Add the beans, salt, and pepper and gently stir together. Secure, reduce the heat to medium, and cook for about 3 minutes, until the beans are just heated through.
3. Scoop the potatoes and beans into the tortillas, sprinkle with pumpkin and/or pomegranate seeds (if using) and serve.

Nutrition:
Calories: 311 Fat: 2g Carbohydrates: 64g Fiber: 13g Proteins: 11g

- Nuts, such as raw walnut pieces, raw sliced almonds, or roasted unsalted peanuts
- Seeds; pumpkin seeds, sunflower seeds, hemp hearts, or flaxseed
- Seasoned rice vinegar, balsamic vinegar, or red wine vinegar
- Olives, pickles, or sauerkraut

Directions:

1. Evenly divide the grains, protein, greens, and vegetables between two bowls.
2. Top with the sauce and optional toppings (if using). Serve.

Nutrition:
Calories: 380 Fat: 4g Carbohydrates: 69g Fiber: 17g Proteins: 18g

Ingredients:

- 1 tablespoon minced garlic
- 1 tablespoon unseasoned rice vinegar

- 1 tablespoon tamari or low-sodium soy sauce
- 1 teaspoon ground cinnamon
- 1 teaspoon ground turmeric
- 1 teaspoon ground cumin
- 1 teaspoon chili powder
- 1 (8-ounce) package tempeh, cut into 16 cubes
- 2 large carrots, diced
- 1 large red bell pepper, sliced
- 1 large yellow bell pepper, sliced
- 6 ounces kale, stemmed and chopped
- 2 teaspoons arrowroot powder

Directions:
1. In a medium bowl, merge the garlic, vinegar, tamari, cinnamon, turmeric, cumin, and chili powder and whisk until combined. Add the tempeh and toss to coat. Let sit for 5 minutes.
2. Drain the tempeh, reserving the marinade.
3. In a large skillet, cook the tempeh, stirring, for 4 to 6 minutes, until it begins to brown. Add the carrots, red and yellow bell peppers, and kale and cook, stirring, for 3 to 5 minutes, until the kale has brightened in color and the carrots are tender. Attach 1 to 2 tablespoons of water as needed to prevent burning.
4. Whisk the arrowroot into the reserved marinade until smooth. Spill the mixture into the skillet, stir to combine, and simmer for 3 minutes more, until thickened.
5. Divide the tempeh mixture between two plates, drizzle with the thickened marinade, and serve.

Nutrition:
Calories: 378 Fat: 14g Carbohydrates: 43g Fiber: 10g Proteins: 29g

419. Tofu Pad Thai

Preparation time: 10 minutes
Cooking time: 20 minutes
Servings: 4
Ingredients:
- 1 (16-ounce) package of brown rice noodles
- 1/4 cup freshly squeezed lime juice
- 2 tablespoons low-sodium soy sauce
- 2 tablespoons liquid aminos
- 1 teaspoon molasses
- 1 tablespoon pure maple syrup
- 3/4 cup julienned carrots
- 3/4 cup thinly chopped red bell pepper
- 2 garlic cloves, minced
- 1/2 cup 1-inch sliced scallions, green and white parts
- 1 (14-ounce) package firm tofu, drained
- 1 cup mug bean sprouts, rinsed
- 1/4 cup unsalted peanuts, chopped (optional)
- Chopped fresh cilantro, for garnish (optional)
- 1 lime, cut into wedges (optional)

Directions:
1. Submerge the brown rice noodles in hot water and soak for 8 to 10 minutes. Set aside.
2. Meanwhile, in a small bowl, set together the lime juice, soy sauce, liquid aminos, molasses, and maple syrup. Set aside.
3. In a large nonstick skillet or sauté pan over medium-high heat, combine the carrots and red bell pepper and cook for 4 to 5 minutes, until soft. Attach 1 to 2 tablespoons of water as needed to prevent burning.
4. Attach the garlic and scallions and cook for 1 to 2 minutes, until fragrant.
5. Crumble the tofu into the pan, stir to combine, and cook for about 5 minutes.
6. Add the sauce mixture, the noodles, and the mug beans and stir to combine. Cook until the sauce has thickened slightly. Serve topped with the peanuts (if using), cilantro (if using), and a lime wedge on the side (if using).

Nutrition:
Calories: 536 Fat: 5g Carbohydrates: 105g Fiber: 5g Proteins: 17g

420. Hawaiian-Inspired Luau Burgers

Preparation time: 15 minutes
Cooking time: 10 minutes
Servings: 2
Ingredients:
- 2 (15-ounce) cans black beans
- 2 cups cooked brown rice
- 1 cup quick-cooking oats
- 1/4 cup pineapple juice
- 1/2 cup Barbecue Sauce, divided
- 1 teaspoon garlic powder
- 1 teaspoon onion powder
- 1 pineapple, sliced into 1/4-inch-thick rings
- 8 whole-wheat buns
- Lettuce, tomato, pickles, and onion, for topping (optional)

Directions:
1. Preheat the grill to medium-high heat.
2. In a large bowl, press the black beans.
3. Mix in the rice, oats, and pineapple juice, 1/4 cup of barbecue sauce, the garlic powder, and onion powder. Continue stirring until the mixture begins to hold its shape and can be formed into patties.
4. Set out 1/2 cup of the bean mixture and form it into a patty. Redo until all the bean mixture is used.
5. Set the patties on the hot grill and cook for 4 to 5 minutes on each side, flipping once the burgers easily release from the grill surface.
6. After you flip the burgers, place the pineapple rings on the grill and cook for 1 to 2 minutes on each side.
7. Remove the burgers and pineapple rings from the grill. Place one patty and one pineapple ring on each bun along with a spoonful of the remaining barbecue sauce. Top with your favorite burger fixings (if using) and serve.

Nutrition:
Calories: 422 Fat: 5g Total Carbohydrates: 83g Fiber: 12g Proteins: 15g

421. Cajun-Inspired Red Beans and Rice

Preparation time: 10 minutes
Cooking time: 20 minutes
Servings: 3
Ingredients:

- 1/2 cup diced green bell pepper
- 1 cup diced onion
- 1/2 cup diced celery
- 2 to 3 garlic cloves, minced
- 2 tablespoons water
- 2 (15-ounce) cans red beans
- 1 teaspoon hot sauce
- 1/2 teaspoon smoked paprika
- 1/2 teaspoon salt
- 1/2 teaspoon thyme
- 1/2 teaspoon freshly ground black pepper

422. Creamy Mushrooms and Noodles

Preparation time: 10 minutes
Cooking time: 15 minutes
Servings: 4
Ingredients:

- 1 (16-ounce) box whole-grain rotini pasta
- 8 ounces Cremini mushrooms, sliced
- 1 medium shallot, finely diced
- 1 tablespoon low-sodium soy sauce
- 1 (15-ounce) can lite coconut milk
- 2 tablespoons nutritional yeast
- 1 tablespoon chickpea flour
- 1/4 teaspoon salt
- 1/4 teaspoon freshly ground black pepper

Directions:

423. Spicy Pineapple-Cauliflower Stir-Fry

Preparation time: 15 minutes
Cooking time: 27 minutes
Servings: 2
Ingredients:

- 1/4 cup No-Salt Hot Sauce
- 1/4 cup freshly squeezed lime juice
- 2 teaspoons No-Salt Spice Blend
- 1/2 head cauliflower, cut into bite-size pieces
- 1/2 pineapple, cut into bite-size chunks
- 2 medium carrots, thinly sliced
- 1 cup frozen peas, thawed
- 2 scallions, green parts only, finely chopped

Directions:

1. In a large bowl, mix the hot sauce, lime juice, and spice blend. Add the cauliflower, pineapple, and carrots and toss to coat.

424. Spinach Marguerite Pizza

Preparation time: 15 minutes
Cooking time: 32 minutes
Servings: 4
Ingredients:

- 1/2 cup jarred tomato sauce
- 1 teaspoon dried oregano
- 1 teaspoon granulated garlic
- 1 pound frozen pizza dough, thawed
- 1 cup baby spinach

- 1 bay leaf
- 4 cups cooked rice

Directions:

1. In a large nonstick skillet or sauté pan over medium-low heat, combine the bell pepper, onion, celery, garlic, and water. Sweat, covered, for about 10 minutes, until softened. Stir occasionally to ensure the mixture does not stick.
2. Add the beans and their liquid, hot sauce, paprika, salt, thyme, pepper, and bay leaf. Stir to combine. Simmer vigorously, uncovered, for 10 minutes, until thickened.
3. Remove and discard the bay leaf. Serve over rice.

Nutrition:
Calories: 410 Fat: 3g Carbohydrates: 81g Fiber: 15g

1. Set water to a boil over high heat. Attach the pasta and cook according to package instructions until tender, usually about 10 minutes, and then drain.
2. Meanwhile, in a large sauté pan or skillet over medium heat, add the mushrooms and shallots and cook, stirring until the mushrooms are bright and glistening. Attach 1 to 2 tablespoons of water as needed to prevent burning.
3. Add the soy sauce, coconut milk, nutritional yeast, chickpea flour, salt, and pepper and stir to combine. Simmer until the sauce has thickened.
4. Stir the mushroom mixture into the noodles and serve warm.

Nutrition:
Calories: 514 Fat: 12g Carbohydrates: 90g Fiber: 10g Proteins: 20g

2. Place the vegetable mixture in the air fryer basket or on the rack, leaving behind in the mixing bowl any sauce that wasn't absorbed. Fry at 400°F for 12 minutes. Shake up the air fryer basket or stir the veggies and fry.
3. Meanwhile, put the peas and scallions in the bowl with the remaining sauce. Toss to coat. Set the peas and scallions in a small pan and set aside.
4. Remove the veggies from the air fryer and transfer them to a serving bowl. Fry the peas and scallions for 3 minutes.
5. Add the peas and scallions to the serving bowl and stir. Serve warm.

Nutrition:
Calories: 169 Fat: 1g Carbohydrates: 37g Fiber: 9g Proteins: 8g

- 1/2 cup Cashew Mozzarella

Directions:

1. In a small bowl, merge together the tomato sauce, oregano, and granulated garlic until well combined. Set aside.
2. Divide the pizza dough evenly into 4 balls and roll out each ball into a 6-inch round pizza crust.
3. Place one pizza crust directly in the air fryer basket or on the rack. Spread one-quarter of the sauce

mixture all over the crust, leaving a 1-inch edge all around. Cover the sauce with one-quarter of the baby spinach. Finally, top the pizza with small dollops of the cashew mozzarella and spread it around a little bit.

425. Gluten-Free White Pizza

Preparation time: 15 minutes
Cooking time: 10 minutes
Servings: 2
Ingredients:
- 3/4 cup quinoa flour
- 1/2 teaspoon dried basil
- 1/2 teaspoon dried oregano
- 1 tablespoon apple cider vinegar
- 1/2 cup water
- 1/3 cup Almond Ricotta
- 2/3 cup frozen broccoli, thawed
- 1/2 teaspoon granulated garlic

Directions:
1. In a medium bowl, merge together the quinoa flour, basil, oregano, apple cider vinegar, and water until well combined. Set aside.
2. Set a piece of parchment paper to fit your air fryer basket or rack and transfer the quinoa mixture to

426. Stuffed Roasted Sweet Potatoes

Preparation time: 10 minutes
Cooking time: 30 minutes
Servings: 2
Ingredients:
- 2 medium sweet potatoes
- 1 (15.5-ounce) can black beans
- 2 scallions, both white and green, finely cut
- 1 tablespoon No-Salt Hot Sauce
- 1 teaspoon Mild Taco Seasoning
- 2 tablespoons freshly squeezed lime juice
- 1/4 cup Lemon-Tahini Dressing

Directions:

427. Eggplant Parmigiana

Preparation time: 20 minutes
Cooking time: 20 minutes
Servings: 4
Ingredients:
- 3/4 cup chickpea flour
- 1/2 cup unsweetened plain plant-based milk
- 3 tablespoons freshly squeezed lemon juice
- 1 tablespoon No-Salt Hot Sauce
- 2 teaspoons No-Salt Spice Blend
- 11/2 cups panko breadcrumbs
- 1 medium eggplant
- 2 cups jarred tomato sauce, divided
- 1/2 cup Almond Ricotta
- 1/3 cup Cashew Mozzarella

Directions:
1. In a medium bowl, merge the chickpea flour, plant-based milk, lemon juice, hot sauce, and spice blend until well combined. Set aside. Spill the breadcrumbs onto a plate and set aside.

4. Grill at 400F for 8 minutes, or until the pizza is lightly browned and the crust is crispy. Repeat with each of the remaining pizzas and serve warm.

Nutrition:
Calories: 322 Fat: 5g Carbohydrates: 58g Fiber: 4g Proteins: 12g

the parchment paper. To form the crust, cover the mixture with another piece of parchment and press down on it to flatten it out to the edges of the bottom piece of parchment. Then discard the top layer of parchment.
3. Transfer the crust, along with the bottom piece of parchment, to the air fryer. Bake at 350F for 5 minutes. Then carefully flip the crust over in the air fryer and peel off the parchment paper.
4. Spread the almond ricotta evenly over the crust, leaving a 1/2-inch edge all around. Then place the broccoli over it and sprinkle the granulated garlic on top.
5. Grill at 400F for 5 minutes, or until the toppings are lightly browned. Serve immediately.

Nutrition:
Calories: 256 Fat: 11g Carbohydrates: 33g Fiber: 7g Proteins: 12g

1. Place the whole sweet potatoes in the air fryer basket or on the rack and roast at 400°F for 30 minutes.
2. In a bowl, merge the black beans, scallions, hot sauce, taco seasoning, and lime juice. Set aside.
3. Carefully detach the sweet potatoes from the air fryer and cut each lengthwise, two-thirds of the way through.
4. Fill each sweet potato with half of the bean mixture. Then drizzle half of the lemon-tahini dressing over each. Serve warm.

Nutrition:
Calories: 347 Fat: 5g Carbohydrates: 63g Fiber: 17g Proteins: 15g

2. Trim and discard the ends of the eggplant. Then set the eggplant into 1/2-inch-thick slices. Dip each eggplant slice into the batter, shaking off any excess. Then dip the slices into the breadcrumbs to completely coat them.
3. Set the eggplant slices in the air fryer basket or on the rack in a single layer. Fry at 400F for 10 minutes, flipping over halfway through cooking.
4. Meanwhile, spread 2 tablespoons of the tomato sauce around the bottom of a baking pan.
5. Let the eggplant cool slightly. Set a single layer of the eggplant in the pan with the tomato sauce, spread a thin layer of almond ricotta on top of each slice, and spoon some more tomato sauce over the top. Continue creating these layers of sauce, eggplant, and almond ricotta until all the eggplant is in the pan. Set the remaining tomato sauce over the top. Then place dollops of the cashew mozzarella on top and spread them out a little.

6. Set in the air fryer and bake at 350F for 10 minutes, or until the eggplant is heated through and the cashew mozzarella is lightly browned. Serve warm.

428. Stuffed Bell Peppers

Preparation time: 10 minutes
Cooking time: 30 minutes
Servings: 3
Ingredients:

- 11/2 cups textured vegetable protein
- 1 tablespoon No-Salt Spice Blend
- 3 tablespoons freshly squeezed lemon juice
- 1 cup boiling water
- 3/4 cup No-Cheese Sauce
- 1/2 cup canned diced tomatoes
- 3/4 cup quinoa flour
- 2 tablespoons dried parsley
- 2 tablespoons No-Salt Hot Sauce
- 1/4 teaspoon freshly ground black pepper
- 3 large bell peppers

Directions:

1. In a medium bowl, combine the textured vegetable protein, spice blend, lemon juice, and boiling water. Then add the no-cheese sauce, diced tomatoes with their juices, quinoa flour, parsley, hot sauce, and

429. Baked Mac and Cheese

Preparation time: 10 minutes
Cooking time: 15 minutes
Servings: 3
Ingredients:

- 1 cup No-Cheese Sauce
- 1 cup unsweetened plain plant-based milk
- 1/2 cup Cashew Mozzarella
- 1 tablespoon nutritional yeast
- 1/2 (16-ounce) box uncooked elbow macaroni
- 3 to 4 cups boiling water

Directions:

1. In a small metal baking pan, mix the no-cheese sauce, plant-based milk, cashew mozzarella, and nutritional yeast until well combined. Cover the pan with aluminum foil, place it in the air fryer, and bake at 400F for 6 minutes.

430. Oil-Free Pasta Bake

Preparation time: 10 minutes
Cooking time: 8 minutes
Servings: 3
Ingredients:

- 11/2 cups canned diced tomatoes
- 2 large garlic cloves, minced
- 1 teaspoon granulated onion
- 3/4 teaspoon dried basil
- 3/4 teaspoon dried oregano
- 2 tablespoons freshly squeezed lemon juice
- 1/2 (16-ounce) box uncooked penne pasta
- 3 to 4 cups boiling water

Directions:

1. In a small metal baking pan, mix the diced tomatoes with their juices, garlic, granulated onion, basil, oregano, and lemon juice. Secure tightly with aluminum foil and bake at 400F for 6 minutes.

Nutrition:
Calories: 342 Fat: 13g Carbohydrates: 47g Fiber: 11g Proteins: 16g

black pepper and mix until well combined. Set aside.

2. Using a sharp knife, gently cut all the way around the top of a bell pepper, as if you are cutting out a lid. Do not cut through the core. Twist the top of the pepper and pull out the core and all the seeds without breaking the rest of the pepper. Repeat with the other 2 bell peppers.
3. Divide the stuffing mixture evenly among the 3 bell peppers, filling them all the way to the top.
4. Cover each bell pepper with a 6-inch square of aluminum foil and flip it upside down. Fold the corners of the aluminum foil up against the sides of each pepper.
5. Place the bell peppers in the air fryer basket or on the rack and roast at 375F for 30 minutes, or until the peppers are soft and tender. Let cool slightly before unwrapping and flipping the peppers over. Enjoy warm.

Nutrition:
Calories: 380 Fat: 4g Carbohydrates: 52g Fiber: 16g Proteins: 36g

2. Meanwhile, place the uncooked macaroni in another metal baking pan. Pour just enough boiling water over the macaroni to completely cover it. Then secure the pan tightly with aluminum foil.
3. Place the macaroni pan in the air fryer, on top of the pan with the sauce in it. Bake for 6 minutes.
4. Take both pans out of the air fryer and carefully remove the foil from each. Rinse the macaroni in a colander and return it to the pan. Spill the sauce over the macaroni and stir to coat. Bake, uncovered, for 3 minutes, or until the mac and cheese is heated through and bubbly. Serve immediately.

Nutrition:
Calories: 379 Fat: 5g Carbohydrates: 66g Fiber: 4g Proteins: 17g

2. Meanwhile, place the uncooked pasta in another metal baking pan. Pour just enough boiling water over the pasta to completely cover it. Then secure the pan tightly with aluminum foil.
3. Place the pasta pan in the air fryer, on top of the pan with the sauce in it. Bake for 9 minutes.
4. Take both pans out of the air fryer and carefully remove the foil from each. Drain the pasta in a colander and return it to the pan. Spill the sauce over the pasta and stir to coat. Re-cover the pan with foil and bake for 3 minutes or until the pasta and sauces are heated through and bubbly. Stir thoroughly before serving.

Nutrition:
Calories: 307 Fat: 2g Carbohydrates: 62g Fiber: 5g Proteins: 11g

431. Zucchini Lasagna Roll-Ups

Preparation time: 15 minutes
Cooking time: 25 minutes
Servings: 2
Ingredients:

- 2 medium zucchinis
- 2 tablespoons freshly squeezed lemon juice
- 11/2 cups Almond Ricotta
- 1 tablespoon No-Salt Spice Blend
- 2 cups jarred tomato sauce, divided
- 1/3 cup Cashew Mozzarella

Directions:

1. Cut the ends of the zucchini. Then carefully cut each zucchini lengthwise into about 1/4-inch slices. Set the slices in the air fryer basket or on the rack in a single layer and sprinkle them with the lemon juice. Roast at 400F for 5 minutes, or until the zucchini is pliable.
2. Meanwhile, in a small bowl, merge the almond ricotta and the spice blend together. Set aside.

Then spread 2 tablespoons of the tomato sauce on the bottom of a small baking pan.

3. Let the zucchini cool slightly before spreading 1 to 2 tablespoons of the almond ricotta mixture onto one side of each slice. Roll up each slice tightly and place them, spiral-side up, in the pan with the tomato sauce. Spoon any remaining almond ricotta over the roll-ups. Then spill the remaining tomato sauce over the top.
4. Evenly space out dollops of the cashew mozzarella over the top of the dish and spread them out slightly.
5. Bring the pan in the air fryer and bake at 360°F for 20 minutes, or until the cashew mozzarella is nicely browned. Serve immediately.

Nutrition:
Calories: 685 Fat: 51g Carbohydrates: 44g Fiber: 18g Proteins: 30g

432. Fully Loaded Quesadillas

Preparation time: 10 minutes
Cooking time: 17 minutes
Servings: 4
Ingredients:

- 1 (16-ounce) block super-firm tofu
- 2 tablespoons rice vinegar
- 1 tablespoon Mild Taco Seasoning
- 1 ripe avocado, pitted
- 4 scallions, both white and green parts
- 2 tablespoons freshly squeezed lemon juice
- 4 (10-inch) flour tortillas
- 1/4 cup No-Salt Hot Sauce
- 1/2 cup No-Cheese Sauce
- 11/2 cups cherry or grape tomatoes, halved

Directions:

1. Cut the tofu into 4 equal slabs. Set aside.
2. In a bowl, merge the rice vinegar and taco seasoning. Massage the mixture on both sides of each tofu slab. Set the tofu in the air fryer basket or on the rack and fry at 400F for 12 minutes, or until the tofu is lightly crisped. Be sure to flip the tofu over halfway through cooking.

3. Meanwhile, in a bowl, mash the avocado and mix it with the scallions and lemon juice. Set aside.
4. Let the tofu cool slightly before cutting each slab into 1/2-inch strips.
5. Place a tortilla on a flat surface and make a cut from one edge to the center. Now imagine the circle of the tortilla divided into 4 quadrants. Spread one-quarter of the avocado mixture on one quadrant of the tortilla (next to the cut). Spread 1 tablespoon of the hot sauce on the quadrant next to the avocado, on the other side of the cut. Then spread 2 tablespoons of the no-cheese sauce on the other half of the tortilla. Place one-quarter of the cherry tomatoes and one-quarter of the tofu strips on top of the no-cheese sauce. Starting with the avocado quadrant, fold each quarter over the next one, until you are left with one stacked triangle. Repeat with the rest of the tortillas.
6. Place the quesadillas in the air fryer basket or on the rack and grill at 400F for 5 minutes until the tortillas are crispy. Carefully flip the quesadillas over halfway through cooking. Serve immediately.

Nutrition:
Calories: 439 Fat: 19g Carbohydrates: 50g Fiber: 7g Proteins: 21g

433. Sweet and Spicy Shish Kebabs

Preparation time: 20 minutes
Cooking time: 15 minutes
Servings: 8
Ingredients:

- 1/3 cup natural peanut butter
- 1 (15-ounce) can pineapple rings in 100-percent pineapple juice
- 2 tablespoons apple cider vinegar
- 2 tablespoons No-Salt Hot Sauce
- 1 tablespoon No-Salt Spice Blend
- 1 teaspoon ground ginger
- 1 (16-ounce) block super-firm tofu
- 1 large red bell pepper, stemmed and seedless
- 1 medium red onion, peeled

- 8 whole mushrooms, quartered

Directions:

1. In a large bowl, merge together the peanut butter, pineapple juice from the can, apple cider vinegar, hot sauce, spice blend, and ginger until well combined. Set aside.
2. Cut the tofu into 32 equal cubes. Then cut the bell pepper into 16 even chunks and the red onion into 8 even wedges. Separate each onion wedge into 2 pieces, for 16 chunks of onion. Cut the pineapple rings into quarters. Add the tofu cubes, bell pepper, red onion, mushrooms, and pineapple pieces to the bowl with the peanut butter mixture and toss gently to coat.

3. Thread the tofu, veggies, and fruit onto 8 skewers in an alternating pattern, so that each skewer has 4 cubes of tofu, 4 pieces of mushroom, 4 pieces of pineapple, 2 chunks of bell pepper, and 2 chunks of red onion.
4. Set the skewers in the air fryer basket or on the rack and grill at 400F for 15 minutes until the veggies are thoroughly cooked and browned. Serve immediately.

Nutrition:
Calories: 329 Fat: 18g Carbohydrates: 30g Fiber: 4g Proteins: 18g

434. Curry in a Hurry

Preparation time: 5 minutes
Cooking time: 25 minutes
Servings: 2
Ingredients:
- 1 cup canned diced tomatoes
- 2 cups unsweetened plain oat milk
- 2 tablespoons freshly squeezed lime juice
- 1 tablespoon No-Salt Spice Blend
- 1 tablespoon curry powder
- 1 teaspoon ground ginger
- 1/2 teaspoon ground cumin
- 1 (12-ounce) bag frozen cauliflower, thawed
- 1/2 (16-ounce) block extra-firm tofu, cubed
- 1/4 cup finely chopped fresh cilantro

Directions:
1. In a large metal baking pan, mix the diced tomatoes with their juices, oat milk, lime juice, spice blend, curry powder, ginger, and cumin together until well combined. Add the cauliflower and tofu cubes to the pan and stir to coat.
2. Bring the pan in the air fryer and roast at 375F for 15 minutes. Then give the curry a good stir and continue roasting for 10 minutes more or until the curry is bubbly.
3. Detach the pan from the air fryer and stir in the fresh cilantro. Serve warm.

Nutrition:
Calories: 253 Fat: 10g Carbohydrates: 26g Fiber: 10g Proteins: 22g

435. Plant-Based Paella

Preparation time: 15 minutes
Cooking time: 35 minutes
Servings: 3
Ingredients:
- 1/2 cup roughly chopped artichoke hearts
- 1/2 cup red bell peppers
- 4 medium white mushrooms, thinly sliced
- 1/2 cup canned diced tomatoes
- 1/2 cup canned chickpeas
- 3 tablespoons No-Salt Hot Sauce
- 2 tablespoons freshly squeezed lemon juice
- 2 tablespoons nutritional yeast
- 1 tablespoon No-Salt Spice Blend
- 1 teaspoon dulse granules
- 1 cup uncooked rice
- 2 cups boiling water

Directions:
1. In a metal baking pan, mix the artichoke hearts, bell peppers, mushrooms, diced tomatoes with their juices, chickpeas, hot sauce, lemon juice, nutritional yeast, spice blend, and dulse granules.
2. Bring the pan in the air fryer and roast at 400F for 10 minutes.
3. Add the uncooked rice and boiling water to the pan and stir. Carefully cover the pan tightly with aluminum foil and roast for 22 minutes. Then remove the foil cover, stir, and continue roasting the paella for an additional 3 minutes, or until the top is crisped.
4. Let the paella cool slightly. Stir once more and serve warm.

Nutrition:
Calories: 318 Fat: 1g Carbohydrates: 68g Fiber: 8g Proteins: 9g

436. Crispy Tofu Buddha Bowls

Preparation time: 15 minutes
Cooking time: 30 minutes
Servings: 2
Ingredients:
- 1/2 cup uncooked quinoa, washed and drained
- 1 cup boiling water
- 1 medium sweet potato
- 1 (12-ounce) bag frozen broccoli florets, thawed
- 3/4 cup panko breadcrumbs
- 1/4 cup chickpea flour
- 1/4 cup No-Salt Hot Sauce
- 1/2 (16-ounce) block super-firm tofu, cut into 1-inch cubes
- 1/4 cup Lemon-Tahini Dressing
- 2 scallions, green parts only, thinly sliced
- 1 tablespoon sesame seeds

Directions:
1. Place the quinoa in a small metal baking pan and pour the boiling water over it. Carefully cover the pan tightly with aluminum foil. Bring the pan in the air fryer and fry at 400F for 10 minutes. Detach the pan from the air fryer and set aside. Leave the foil on so the quinoa will continue to steam while you prepare the rest of the meal.
2. Set the sweet potatoes in the air fryer basket or on the rack and fry for 2 minutes. Then add the broccoli and continue to fry for an additional 5 minutes. Shake up the basket and fry for 3 minutes more. Set the sweet potatoes and broccoli aside.
3. Pour the breadcrumbs onto a plate. In a medium bowl, merge together the chickpea flour and hot sauce. Attach the tofu cubes to the bowl and toss to coat. Then toss the tofu in the breadcrumbs until the tofu cubes are fully coated. Set the tofu in the air fryer basket or on the rack in a single layer and fry for 10 minutes, or until crispy.

4. Divide the quinoa, sweet potatoes, and broccoli evenly between 2 bowls. When the tofu is processed add it to the bowls. Drizzle the lemon-tahini dressing over each bowl and sprinkle the scallions and sesame seeds on top. Enjoy warm.

437. Shakshuka

Preparation time: 10 minutes
Cooking time: 35 minutes
Servings: 4
Ingredients:

- 1 red bell pepper, seedless and finely chopped
- 1 small red onion, finely chopped
- 1 (28-ounce) can diced tomatoes
- 2 tablespoons balsamic vinegar
- 1 tablespoon No-Salt Spice Blend
- 1 teaspoon ground cumin
- 1 cup fresh baby spinach
- 1/2 cup Almond Ricotta

Directions:

438. Grilled Tofu with Chimichurri Sauce

Preparation time: 10 minutes
Cooking time: 12 minutes
Servings: 4
Ingredients:

- 2 tablespoons plus 1 teaspoon olive oil
- 1 teaspoon dried oregano
- 1 cup parsley leaves
- 1/2 cup cilantro leaves
- 2 chili peppers, seeded and chopped
- 2 tablespoons white wine vinegar
- 2 tablespoons water
- 1 tablespoon fresh lime juice
- Salt and black pepper to taste
- 1 cup couscous, cooked
- 1 teaspoon lime zest
- 1/4 cup toasted pumpkin seeds
- 1 cup fresh spinach, chopped
- 1(15.5-ounce) can kidney beans, washed and drained
- 1(14 to 16-ounce) block tofu, diced
- 2 summer squashes, diced

439. Grilled Seitan with Creole Sauce

Preparation time: 10 minutes
Cooking time: 14 minutes
Servings: 4
Ingredients:
Grilled seitan kebabs:

- 4 cups seitan, diced
- 2 medium onions, diced into squares
- 8 bamboo skewers
- 1 can coconut milk
- 2(1/2) tablespoons creole spice
- 2 tablespoons tomato paste
- 2 cloves of garlic

Creole spice mix:

- 2 tablespoons paprika
- 12 dried Peri chili peppers
- 1 tablespoon salt

Nutrition:
Calories: 564 Fat: 18g Carbohydrates: 76g Fiber: 14g Proteins: 30g

1. In a large metal baking pan, mix the bell pepper, red onion, diced tomatoes with their juices, balsamic vinegar, spice blend, and cumin. Set the pan in the device and roast at 400F for 25 minutes, stirring after 10 and 20 minutes.
2. Attach the baby spinach to the pan and carefully stir it in. Roast for 5 minutes more.
3. Use a spoon to create 3 wells in the Shakshuka. Place one-third of the almond ricotta in each well. Roast for an additional 5 minutes; then serve warm.

Nutrition:
Calories: 168 Fat: 8g Carbohydrates: 19g Fiber: 9g Proteins: 6g

- 3 spring onions, quartered

Directions:

1. In a saucepan, heat 2 tbsp. of oil and add oregano over medium heat.
2. After 30 seconds add parsley, chili pepper, cilantro, and lime juice, 2 tablespoons of water, vinegar, salt, and black pepper.
3. Mix well, and then blend in a blender.
4. Add the remaining oil, pumpkin seeds, beans, and spinach and cook for 3 minutes.
5. Stir in couscous and adjust seasoning with salt and black pepper.
6. Prepare and set up a grill on medium heat.
7. Thread the tofu, squash, and onions on the skewer in an alternating pattern.
8. Grill these skewers for 4 minutes per side while basting with the green sauce.
9. Serve the skewers on top of the couscous with green sauce.
10. Enjoy.

Nutrition:
Calories: 813 Fat: 83g Carbohydrates: 25g Net Carbohydrates: 11g Fiber: 1g Proteins: 7g

- 1 tablespoon freshly ground pepper
- 2 teaspoons dried thyme
- 2 teaspoons dried oregano

Directions:

1. Prepare the creole seasoning by blending all the ingredients and preserve them in a sealable jar.
2. Thread seitan and onion on the bamboo skewers in an alternating pattern.
3. On a baking sheet, mix coconut milk with creole seasoning, tomato paste, and garlic.
4. Soak the skewers in the milk marinade for 2 hours.
5. Prepare and set up a grill over medium heat.
6. Grill the skewers for 7 minutes per side.
7. Serve.

Nutrition:
Calories: 407 Fat: 42g Carbohydrates: 13g Fiber: 1g Proteins: 4g

440. Lemon Broccoli Rabe

Preparation time: 10 minutes
Cooking time: 10 minutes
Servings: 4
Ingredients:

- 8 cups water
- Sea salt to taste
- 2 bunches broccoli rabe, chopped
- 3 tablespoons olive oil
- 3 garlic cloves, minced
- Pinch of cayenne pepper
- Zest of 1 lemon

441. Spicy Swiss chard

Preparation time: 10 minutes
Cooking time: 10 minutes
Servings: 4
Ingredients:

- 2 tablespoons olive oil
- 1 onion, chopped
- 2 bunches Swiss chard
- 3 garlic cloves, minced
- 1/2 tsp. red pepper flakes (or to taste)
- Juice of 1/2 lemon

Directions:

442. Red Peppers and Kale

Preparation time: 5 minutes
Cooking time: 15 minutes
Servings: 4
Ingredients:

- 2 bunches kale
- 3 tablespoons olive oil
- 1/2 onion, chopped
- 2 red bell peppers, cut into strips
- 3 garlic cloves, minced
- 1/4 teaspoon red pepper flakes

Directions:

443. Mashed Cauliflower with Roasted Garlic

Preparation time: 5 minutes
Cooking time: 10 minutes
Servings: 4
Ingredients:

- 2 heads cauliflower, cut into small florets
- 1 tablespoon olive oil
- 8 jarred roasted garlic cloves
- 2 teaspoons chopped fresh rosemary
- Sea salt to taste
- Freshly ground black pepper to taste

444. Steamed Broccoli with Walnut Pesto

Preparation time: 5 minutes
Cooking time: 10 minutes
Servings: 4
Ingredients:

- 1-pound broccoli florets
- 2 cups chopped fresh basil
- 1/4 cup olive oil
- 4 garlic cloves
- 1/2 cup walnuts
- Pinch of cayenne pepper

Directions:
1. Boil 8 cups of water. Sprinkle a pinch of salt and the broccoli rabe. Cook until the broccoli rabe is slightly softened, about 2 minutes. Drain.
2. Heat olive oil over medium-high heat. Cook the garlic for 30 seconds. Stir in the broccoli rabe, cayenne, and lemon zest. Season with salt and black pepper. Serve immediately.

Nutrition:
Calories: 120 Fat: 5g Carbohydrates: 18g Fiber: 4g Proteins: 5g

1. In a big pot, cook olive oil over medium-high heat until it shimmers. Cook the onion and chard stems for 5 minutes.
2. Cook chard leaves for 1 minute. Stir in the garlic and pepper flakes. Cover and cook for 5 minutes. Stir in the lemon juice. Season with salt and serve immediately.

Nutrition:
Calories: 215 Proteins: 8.7g Carbohydrates: 18g Fat: 11.5g Fiber: 2.3g

1. In a steamer basket in a pan, steam the kale until it softens, 5 to 10 minutes. Remove from the heat and set aside.
2. Meanwhile, in a sauté pan, heat the olive oil over medium-high heat until it shimmers. Cook onion and bell peppers for 5 minutes. Cook garlic for 30 seconds. Take out from heat and stir in the kale and red pepper flakes. Season and serve immediately.

Nutrition:
Calories: 166 Fat: 2g Total Carbohydrates: 31g Fiber: 10g Proteins: 9g

- 1 tablespoon chopped fresh chives

Directions:
1. Boil cauliflower florets for 9 minutes, then drain.
2. In a blender or food processor, merge the cauliflower, olive oil, garlic, and rosemary and process until smooth. Season with salt and pepper. Stir in the chives and serve hot.

Nutrition:
Calories: 151 Fat: 3.9g Fiber: 3.3g Carbohydrates: 23.6g Proteins: 4.9g

Directions:
1. Put the broccoli in a large pot and cover it with water. Bring to a parboil and cook until the broccoli is tender about 5 minutes.
2. Process basil, olive oil, garlic, walnuts, and cayenne for ten 1-second pulses, scraping down the bowl halfway through processing.
3. Drain and put again to the pan. Toss with the pesto. Serve immediately.

Nutrition:
Calories: 431 Fat: 28.5g Carbohydrates: 42.7g Proteins: 6.6g

445. Roasted Asparagus with Balsamic Reduction

Preparation time: 10 minutes.
Cooking time: 25 minutes.
Servings: 4
Ingredients:

- 1(1/2) pounds asparagus, trimmed
- 2 tablespoons olive oil
- 1/2 teaspoon sea salt
- 1/4 teaspoon freshly ground black pepper
- 1/3 cup balsamic vinegar
- Juice and zest of 1 Meyer lemon

Directions:

1. Preheat the oven to 375F. On a large rimmed baking sheet, throw the asparagus with the olive oil, salt, and pepper, and then spread the asparagus out into a single layer. Roast for 23 minutes.
2. While roasting, put the vinegar in a small saucepan and bring it to a boil over medium-high heat. Decrease the heat to low.
3. When the asparagus is roasted, remove the baking sheet from the oven. Stir lemon juice and zest to coat. Drizzle the balsamic reduction over the top. Serve immediately.

Nutrition:
Calories: 322 Fat: 5g Carbohydrates: 58g Fiber: 4g

446. Sweet and Sour Tempeh

Preparation time: 10 minutes
Cooking time: 8 minutes
Servings: 4
Ingredients:

- 1 cup pineapple juice
- 1 tablespoon unseasoned rice vinegar
- 1 tablespoon soy sauce
- 1 tablespoon cornstarch
- 2 tablespoons coconut oil
- 1-pound tempeh, cut into thin strips
- 6 green onions
- 1 green bell pepper, diced
- 4 garlic cloves, minced
- 2 cups prepared brown or white rice

Directions:

1. Blend pineapple juice, rice vinegar, soy sauce, and cornstarch and set aside.
2. In a wok or large sauté pan, warmth the coconut oil over medium-high heat until it shimmers. Add the tempeh, green onions, and bell pepper, and cook until vegetables soften about 5 minutes.
3. Cook garlic. Set in sauce and cook until it thickens. Serve over rice.

Nutrition:
Calories: 244 Fat: 2g Proteins: 11g Carbohydrates: 50g Fiber: 10g

447. Fried Seitan Fingers

Preparation time: 15 minutes
Cooking time: 10 minutes
Servings: 4
Ingredients:

- 1 cup all-purpose flour
- 1 teaspoon garlic powder
- 1 teaspoon onion powder
- Pinch of cayenne pepper
- 1 teaspoon dried thyme
- 1/2 teaspoon sea salt
- 1/2 teaspoon freshly ground black pepper
- 1 cup soy milk
- 1 tablespoon lemon juice
- 2 tablespoons baking powder
- 2 tablespoons olive oil
- 8 ounces Seitan

Directions:

1. In a shallow dish, incorporate the flour, garlic powder, onion powder, cayenne, thyme, salt, and black pepper, whisking to mix thoroughly. In another shallow dish, whisk together the soy milk, lemon juice, and baking powder.
2. In a sauté pan, cook the olive oil over medium-high heat. Set each piece of seitan in the flour mixture, tapping off any excess flour. Next, dip the seitan in the soymilk mixture and then back into the flour mixture.
3. Fry for 4 minutes per side. Blot on paper towels before serving.

Nutrition:
Calories: 388 Fat: 19g Carbohydrates: 45g Fiber: 12g Sugar: 13g

448. Crusty Grilled Corn

Preparation time: 10 minutes
Cooking time: 15 minutes
Servings: 4
Ingredients:

- 2 corn cobs
- 1/3 cup Vegenaise
- 1 small handful cilantro
- 1/2 cup breadcrumbs
- 1 teaspoon lemon juice

Directions:

1. Preheat the gas grill on high heat.
2. Add corn grill to the grill and continue grilling until it turns golden-brown on all sides.
3. Mix the Vegenaise, cilantro, breadcrumbs, and lemon juice in a bowl.
4. Add grilled corn cobs to the crumbs mixture.
5. Toss well then serve.

Nutrition:
Calories: 253 Fat: 13g Proteins: 31g Fiber: 0g Carbohydrates: 3g

449. Grilled Carrots with Chickpea Salad

Preparation time: 10 minutes.
Cooking time: 10 minutes.
Servings: 8
Ingredients:

- 8 large carrots
- 1 tablespoon oil
- 1(1/2) teaspoon salt
- 1 teaspoon dried oregano
- 1 teaspoon dried thyme
- 2 teaspoons paprika powder
- 1(1/2) tablespoon soy sauce
- 1/2 cup of water
- Chickpea salad:
- 14 ounces canned chickpeas
- 3 medium pickles
- 1 small onion
- A big handful of lettuce

450. Grilled Avocado Guacamole

Preparation time: 10 minutes
Cooking time: 20 minutes
Servings: 4
Ingredients:

- 1/2 teaspoon olive oil
- 1 lime, halved
- 1/2 onion, halved
- 1 serrano chili, halved, stemmed, and seeded
- 3 Haas avocados, skin on
- 2-3 tablespoons fresh cilantro, chopped
- 1/2 teaspoon smoked salt

Directions:

1. Preheat the grill over medium heat.

451. Spinach and Dill Pasta Salad

Preparation time: 5 minutes
Cooking time: 0 minutes
Servings: 4
Ingredients:
For the salad:

- 3 cups cooked whole-wheat fusilli
- 2 cups cherry tomatoes, halved
- 1/2 cup vegan cheese, shredded
- 4 cups spinach, chopped
- 2 cups edamame, thawed
- 1 large red onion, finely chopped

For the dressing:

- 2 tablespoons white wine vinegar

452. Italian Veggie Salad

Preparation time: 10 minutes
Cooking time: 0 minutes
Servings: 8
Ingredients:
For the salad:

- 1 cup fresh baby carrots, quartered lengthwise
- 1 celery rib, sliced
- 3 large mushrooms, thinly sliced
- 1 cup cauliflower florets, bite-sized, blanched
- 1 cup broccoli florets, blanched

- 1 teaspoon apple cider vinegar
- 1/2 teaspoon dried oregano
- 1/2 teaspoon salt
- Ground black pepper to taste
- 1/2 cup vegan cream

Directions:

1. Toss the carrots with all the ingredients in a bowl.
2. Thread one carrot on a stick and place it on a plate.
3. Preheat the grill over high heat.
4. Grill the carrots for 2 minutes per side on the grill.
5. Toss the ingredients for the salad in a large salad bowl.
6. Slice grilled carrots and add them on top of the salad.
7. Serve fresh.

Nutrition:
Calories: 661 Fat: 68g Carbohydrates: 7g Fiber: 2g Proteins: 4g

2. Brush the grilling grates with olive oil and place chili, onion, and lime on them.
3. Grill the onion for 10 minutes, chili for 5 minutes, and lime for 2 minutes.
4. Transfer the veggies to a large bowl.
5. Now cut the avocados in half and grill them for 5 minutes.
6. Mash the flesh of the grilled avocado in a bowl.
7. Chop the other grilled veggies and add them to the avocado mash.
8. Stir in the remaining ingredients and merge well. Serve.

Nutrition:
Calories: 165 Fat: 17g Carbohydrates: 4g Fiber: 1g Proteins: 1g

- 1/2 teaspoon dried dill
- 2 tablespoons extra-virgin olive oil
- Salt to taste
- Pepper to taste

Directions:

1. To make the dressing: Attach all the ingredients for dressing into a bowl and whisk well. Set aside for a while for the flavors to set in.
2. To make the salad: Add all the ingredients of the salad to a bowl. Toss well. Drizzle dressing on top. Toss well. Divide into 4 plates and serve.

Nutrition:
Calories: 684 Fat: 33.6g Carbohydrate: 69.5g

- 1 cup thinly sliced radish
- 4–5 ounces hearts of romaine salad mix to serve
- For the dressing:
- 1/2 package Italian salad dressing mix
- 3 tablespoons white vinegar
- 3 tablespoons water
- 3 tablespoons olive oil
- 3-4 pepperoncino, chopped

Directions:

1. To make the salad: Add all the ingredients of the salad except hearts of romaine to a bowl and toss.
2. To make the dressing: Attach all the ingredients of the dressing in a small bowl. Whisk well. Pour dressing over salad and toss well. Refrigerate for a

couple of hours. Place romaine in a large bowl. Place the chilled salad over it and serve.

Nutrition:
Calories: 84 Fat: 6.7g Carbohydrate: 5g

453. Spinach and Mashed Tofu Salad

Preparation time: 20 minutes
Cooking time: 0 minutes
Servings: 4
Ingredients:
- 2(8-ounces) blocks firm tofu, drained
- 4 cups baby spinach leaves
- 4 tablespoons cashew butter
- 1(1/2) tablespoon soy sauce
- 1 tablespoon ginger, chopped
- 1 teaspoon red miso paste
- 2 tablespoons sesame seeds
- 1 teaspoon organic orange zest
- 1 teaspoon nori flakes
- 2 tablespoons water

Directions:
1. In a bowl, merge the mashed tofu with the spinach leaves.
2. Merge the remaining ingredients in another small bowl and, if desired, add the optional water for a smoother dressing.
3. Spill this dressing over the mashed tofu and spinach leaves.
4. Set the bowl to the fridge and allow the salad to chill. Enjoy!

Nutrition:
Calories: 623 Fat: 30.5g Carbohydrate: 48g

454. Super Summer Salad

Preparation time: 10 minutes.
Cooking time: 0 minutes.
Servings: 2
Ingredients:
Dressing:
- 1 tablespoon olive oil
- 1/4 cup chopped basil
- 1 teaspoon lemon juice
- 1/4 teaspoon salt
- 1 medium avocado, halved, diced
- 1/4 cup water

Salad:
- 1/4 cup dry chickpeas
- 1/4 cup dry red kidney beans
- 4 cups raw kale, shredded
- 2 cups Brussels sprouts, shredded
- 2 radishes, thinly sliced
- 1 tablespoon walnuts, chopped
- 1 teaspoon flaxseeds
- Salt and pepper to taste

Directions:
1. Prepare the chickpeas and kidney beans according to the method.
2. Soak the flaxseeds according to the method and then drain excess water.
3. Attach the olive oil, basil, lemon juice, salt, and half of the avocado to a food processor or blender, and pulse at low speed. Set the dressing to a small bowl and set it aside.
4. Combine the kale, Brussels sprouts, cooked chickpeas, kidney beans, radishes, walnuts, and the remaining avocado in a large bowl and mix thoroughly.
5. Store the mixture, or serve with the dressing and flaxseeds, and enjoy!

Nutrition:
Calories: 266 Fat: 26.6g Carbohydrates: 8.8g Fiber: 6.8g
Proteins: 2g

455. Roasted Almond Protein Salad

Preparation time: 30 minutes
Cooking time: 0 minutes
Servings: 4
Ingredients:
- 1/2 cup dry quinoa
- 1/2 cup dry navy beans
- 1/2 cup dry chickpeas
- 1/2 cup raw whole almonds
- 1 teaspoon extra-virgin olive oil
- 1/2 teaspoon salt
- 1/2 teaspoon paprika
- 1/2 teaspoon cayenne
- Dash of chili powder
- 4 cups spinach, fresh or frozen
- 1/4 cup purple onion, chopped

Directions:
1. Prepare the quinoa according to the recipe. Store in the fridge for now. Prepare the beans according to the method. Store in the fridge for now. Set the almonds, olive oil, salt, and spices in a large bowl, and stir until the ingredients are evenly coated.
2. Set a skillet over medium-high heat and transfer the almond mixture to the heated skillet.
3. Roast while stirring. Stir frequently to prevent burning.
4. Set off the heat and toss the cooked and chilled quinoa and beans, onions, spinach, or mixed greens in the skillet. Stir well and set the roasted almond salad to a bowl.
5. Enjoy!

Nutrition:
Calories: 347 Fat: 10.5g Carbohydrate: 49.2g Fiber: 14.7g

456. Lentil, Lemon and Mushroom Salad

Preparation time: 10 minutes
Cooking time: 0 minutes
Servings: 2
Ingredients:

- 1/2 cup dry lentils of choice
- 2 cups vegetable broth
- 3 cups mushrooms, thickly sliced
- 1 cup sweet or purple onion, chopped
- 4 teaspoons extra-virgin olive oil
- 2 tablespoons garlic powder
- 1/4 teaspoon chili flakes
- 1 tablespoon lemon juice
- 2 tablespoons cilantro, chopped
- 1/2 cup arugula
- 1/4 teaspoon salt
- 1/4 teaspoon pepper

Directions:

1. Sprout the lentils according to the method. (Don't cook them).
2. Place the vegetable stock in a deep saucepan and bring it to a boil.

3. Add the lentils to the boiling broth, cover the pan, and cook for about 5 minutes over low heat until the lentils are a bit tender.
4. Remove the pan from heat and drain the excess water.
5. Set a frying pan over high warmth and attach 2 tablespoons of olive oil.
6. Add the onions, garlic, and chili flakes, and cook until the onions are almost translucent, around 5 to 10 minutes while stirring.
7. Attach the mushrooms to the frying pan and mix in thoroughly. Continue cooking until the onions are completely translucent and the mushrooms have softened; remove the pan from the heat.
8. Mix the lentils, onions, mushrooms, and garlic in a large bowl.
9. Attach the lemon juice and the remaining olive oil. Toss or stir to combine everything thoroughly.
10. Serve the mushroom/onion mixture over some arugula in a bowl, adding salt and pepper to taste, or store and enjoy later!

Nutrition:
Calories: 365 Fat: 11.7g Carbohydrates: 45.2g Proteins: 22.8g

457. Sweet Potato and Black Bean Protein Salad

Preparation time: 15 minutes.
Cooking time: 0 minutes.
Servings: 2
Ingredients:

- 1 cup dry black beans
- 4 cups of spinach
- 1 medium sweet potato
- 1 cup purple onion, chopped
- 2 tablespoons olive oil
- 2 tablespoons lime juice
- 1 tablespoon minced garlic
- 1/2 tablespoon chili powder
- 1/4 teaspoon cayenne
- 1/4 cup parsley
- 1/4 teaspoons salt
- 1/4 teaspoons pepper

Directions:

1. Prepare the black beans according to the method.
2. Preheat the oven to 400F.
3. Cut the sweet potato into 1/4-inch cubes and put these in a medium-sized bowl. Add the onions, 1 tablespoon of olive oil, and salt to taste.

4. Toss the ingredients until the sweet potatoes and onions are completely coated.
5. Transfer the ingredients to a baking sheet lined with parchment paper and spread them out in a single layer.
6. Bring the baking sheet in the oven and roast until the sweet potatoes start to turn brown and crispy, around 40 minutes.
7. Meanwhile, combine the remaining olive oil, lime juice, garlic, chili powder, and cayenne thoroughly in a large bowl, until no lumps remain.
8. Detach the sweet potatoes and onions from the oven and transfer them to the large bowl.
9. Add the cooked black beans, parsley, and a pinch of salt.
10. Toss everything until well combined.
11. Then mix in the spinach and serve in desired portions with additional salt and pepper.
12. Store or enjoy!

Nutrition:
Calories: 558 Fat: 6.2g Carbohydrate: 84g Fiber: 20.4g

458. Lentil Radish Salad

Preparation time: 15 minutes
Cooking time: 0 minutes
Servings: 3
Ingredients:
Dressing:

- 1 tablespoon extra-virgin olive oil
- 1 tablespoon lemon juice
- 1 tablespoon maple syrup
- 1 tablespoon water
- 1/2 tablespoon sesame oil
- 1 tablespoon miso paste, yellow or white
- 1/4 teaspoon salt

- 1/4 teaspoons Pepper

Salad:

- 1/2 cup dry chickpeas
- 1/4 cup dry green
- 1 (14-ounce) pack of silken tofu
- 5 cups mixed greens, fresh or frozen
- 2 radishes, thinly sliced
- 1/2 cup cherry tomatoes, halved
- 1/4 cup roasted sesame seeds

Directions:

1. Prepare the chickpeas according to the method.
2. Prepare the lentils according to the method.

3. Set all the ingredients for the dressing in a blender or food processor. Mix on low until smooth, while adding water until it reaches the desired consistency.
4. Add salt, pepper (to taste), and optionally more water to the dressing; set aside.
5. Cut the tofu into bite-sized cubes.
6. Combine the mixed greens, tofu, lentils, chickpeas, radishes, and tomatoes in a large bowl.

459. Jicama and Spinach Salad Recipe

Preparation time: 10 minutes
Cooking time: 20 minutes
Servings: 4
Ingredients:
Salad:
- 10 ounces baby spinach, washed and dried
- 16 grape or cherry tomatoes
- 1 jicama
- Green or Kalamata olives, chopped
- 8 teaspoons walnuts, chopped
- 1 teaspoon raw or roasted sunflower seeds

Dressing:
- 1 heaping tablespoon Dijon mustard
- Dash cayenne pepper to taste
- 2 tablespoons maple syrup
- 2 garlic cloves, minced

460. High-Protein Salad

Preparation time: 5 minutes.
Cooking time: 5 minutes.
Servings: 4
Ingredients:
Salad:
- 1(15-ounces) can green kidney beans
- 4 tablespoons capers
- 4 handfuls arugula
- 4(15-ounces) can lentils

Dressing:
- 1 tablespoon caper brine
- 1 tablespoon tamari
- 1 tablespoon balsamic vinegar

461. Mussels in Red Wine Sauce

Preparation time: 5 minutes
Cooking time: 5 minutes
Servings: 2
Ingredients:
- 800g mussels
- 2 x 400g tins of chopped tomatoes
- 25g butter
- 1 fresh chives, chopped
- 1 fresh parsley, chopped
- 1 bird's-eye chili, finely chopped
- 4 cloves of garlic, crushed
- 400mls red wine

462. Roast Balsamic Vegetables

Preparation time: 10 minutes
Cooking time: 45 minutes
Servings: 4
Ingredients:
- 4 tomatoes, chopped 2 red onions, chopped

7. Add the dressing and mix everything until it is coated evenly.
8. Top with the optional roasted sesame seeds, if desired.
9. Refrigerate before serving and enjoy, or store for later!

Nutrition:
Calories: 621 Fat: 19.6g Carbohydrates: 82.7g Fiber: 26.1g

- 1 to 2 tablespoons water
- 1/4 teaspoons sea salt

Directions:
1. For the salad: Divide the baby spinach onto 4 salad plates. Set each serving with 1/4 of the jicama, 1/4 of the chopped olives, and 4 tomatoes. Sprinkle 1 teaspoon of the sunflower seeds and 2 teaspoons of the walnuts.
2. For the dressing: In a small mixing bowl, whisk all the ingredients together until emulsified. Check the taste and add more maple syrup for sweetness. Drizzle 1(1/2) tablespoon of the dressing over each salad and serve.

Nutrition:
Calories: 196 Fat: 2g Proteins: 7g Carbohydrates: 28g Fiber: 12g

- 2 tablespoons peanut butter
- 2 tablespoons hot sauce
- 1 tablespoon tahini

Directions:
1. For the dressing: In a bowl, spill together all the ingredients until they come together to form a smooth dressing.
2. For the salad: Mix the beans, arugula, capers, and lentils. Top with the dressing and serve.

Nutrition:
Calories: 205 Fat: 2g Proteins: 13g Carbohydrates: 31g Fiber: 17g

- Juice of 1 lemon

Directions:
1. Wash the mussels, remove their beards, and set them aside. Warmth the butter in a large saucepan and add in the red wine. Reduce the heat and add the parsley, chives, chili, and garlic whilst stirring. Add in the tomatoes, lemon juice, and mussels. Cover the saucepan and cook for 2-3 minutes.
2. Remove the saucepan from the heat and take out any mussels which haven't opened and discard them. Serve and eat immediately.

Nutrition:
Calories: 364 Carbohydrates: 3.3g Fat: 4.9g Proteins: 8g

- 3 sweet potatoes, peeled and chopped
- 100g red chicory (or if unavailable, use yellow)
- 100g kale, finely chopped
- 300g potatoes, peeled and chopped
- 5 stalks of celery, chopped

- 1 bird's-eye chili, de-seeded and finely chopped
- 2g fresh parsley, chopped
- 2gs fresh coriander (cilantro) chopped
- 3 teaspoons olive oil
- 2 teaspoons balsamic vinegar
- 1 teaspoon mustard Sea salt
- Freshly ground black pepper

Directions:

463. Vegan Caesar Salad

Preparation time: 20 minutes
Cooking time: 1 hours 50 minutes
Servings: 4
Ingredients:

- 1 15-oz can chickpeas
- 1/2 tsp. grated lemon zest
- 1 tbsp. olive oil
- Salt and pepper
- 1/4 c. olive oil
- 1 tsp. grated lemon zest plus 1/3 cup lemon juice
- 1/4 c. tahini
- 2 tsp. capers plus 1 tsp caper brine
- 1 small clove garlic, finely grated
- 1 tbsp. nutritional yeast
- 1 tbsp. Dijon mustard
- 3 tbsp. olive oil
- 4 thick slices bread
- 2 small red onions, cut into thick rounds
- 2 heads gem lettuce or romaine hearts, leaves separated
- 2 bunches small radishes
- 1 clove garlic, cut in half

Directions:
Crispy Chickpeas:
1. Preheat the oven to 425 degrees Fahrenheit. Rinse the chickpeas and pat them dry with paper towels, removing any loose skins.

464. Steak and Mushroom Noodles

Preparation time: 10 minutes
Cooking time: 20 minutes
Servings: 4
Ingredients:

- 100g shitake mushrooms, halved, if large
- 100g chestnut mushrooms, sliced
- 150g udon noodles
- 75g kale, finely chopped
- 75g baby leaf spinach, chopped
- 2 sirloin steaks
- 2 teaspoons miso paste
- 2.5cm piece fresh ginger, finely chopped
- 1 star anise
- 1 red chili, finely sliced
- 1 red onion, finely chopped
- 1 fresh coriander (cilantro) chopped
- 1 liter (11/2 pints) warm water

Directions:

1. Place the olive oil, balsamic, mustard, parsley, and coriander (cilantro) into a bowl and mix well.
2. Toss all the remaining ingredients into the dressing and season with salt and pepper.
3. Transfer the vegetables to an ovenproof dish and cook in the oven at 200C/400F for 45 minutes.

Nutrition:
Calories: 98 Fiber: 2g Proteins: 3g Carbohydrates: 3.1g

2. Toss chickpeas with olive oil and 1/4 teaspoon salt and pepper on a rimmed baking sheet. Roast for 30 to 40 minutes, tossing occasionally, until crisp.
3. Remove from the oven and stir with lemon zest in a mixing basin. As the chickpeas cool, they will crisp up even more.

Dressing And Salad:
1. Preheat the grill to medium heat. To make the dressing, purée all dressing ingredients in a small blender or food processor until smooth, adding 1 tablespoon water at a time to modify consistency and seasoning with salt and pepper to taste. Set aside the dressing.
2. To make the salad, follow these steps: 1 1/2 tablespoons oil, brushed on the bread 1 tablespoon oil, 1/4 teaspoon salt, and 1/4 teaspoon pepper, brushed on onion slices Season radishes with a pinch of salt and the remaining 1/2 tbsp oil. Using small skewers, thread radishes. 2 to 3 minutes per side on the grill, until toasted; immediately massage with garlic. Onions and radishes should be grilled until soft, about 5 minutes per side for onions and 6–8 minutes for radishes.
3. Separate the onion rings and tear the bread into pieces. Toss half of the dressing with the lettuce to coat it. Fold in the grilled croutons and onion rings gently. Serve with radish skewers, crispy chickpeas, and any leftover dressing for dipping or drizzling.

Nutrition:
Calories: 70 Carbohydrates: 5.8g Fiber: 1g Proteins: 2.9g

1. Spill the water into a saucepan and add in the miso, star anise, and ginger. Bring it to the boil, reduce the heat, and simmer gently. In the meantime, cook the noodles then drain them.
2. Warmth the oil in a saucepan, add the steak and cook for around 2-3 minutes on each side. Remove the meat and set aside.
3. Place the mushrooms, spinach, coriander (cilantro), and kale into the miso broth and cook for 5 minutes.
4. Warmth the remaining oil in a separate pan and fry the chili and onion for 4 minutes, until softened.
5. Serve the noodles into bowls and pour the soup on top.
6. Thinly slice the steaks and add them to the top. Serve immediately.

Nutrition:
Calories: 296 Carbohydrates: 24g Fat: 13g Proteins: 32g

465. Masala Scallops
Preparation time: 10 minutes
Cooking time: 20 minutes
Servings: 4
Ingredients:

- 2 jalapenos, chopped
- 1 pound sea scallops
- A pinch of salt and black pepper
- 1/4 teaspoon cinnamon powder
- 1 teaspoon garam masala
- 1 teaspoon coriander, ground
- 1 teaspoon cumin, ground
- 2 tablespoons cilantro

Directions:

1. Warmth up a pan with the oil over medium heat, add the jalapenos, cinnamon, and the other ingredients except for the scallops and cook for 10 minutes.

Nutrition:
Calories: 251 Fat: 4g Carbohydrates: 11g Proteins: 17g

466. Lemongrass and Ginger Mackerel
Preparation time: 10 minutes
Cooking time: 25 minutes
Servings: 4
Ingredients:

- 4 mackerel fillets, skinless and boneless
- 1 tablespoon ginger, grated
- 2 lemongrass sticks, chopped
- 2 red chilies, chopped
- Juice of 1 lime
- A handful parsley, chopped

Directions:

1. In a roasting pan, combine the mackerel with the oil, ginger, and the other ingredients, toss and bake at 390F for 25 minutes.
2. Divide everything between plates and serve.

Nutrition:
Calories: 251 Fat: 3g Carbohydrates: 14g Proteins: 8g

467. Mashed Potatoes
Preparation time: 10 minutes
Cooking time: 12 minutes
Servings: 2
Ingredients:

- 4 potatoes, halved
- 1/4 tablespoons chives, chopped
- 1 teaspoon minced garlic
- 3/4 teaspoon sea salt
- 2 tablespoons butter, unsalted
- 1/4 teaspoon ground black pepper

Directions:

1. Take a medium pot, place it over medium-high heat, add potatoes, cover with water and boil until cooked and tender.
2. When done, drain the potatoes, let them cool for 10 minutes, peel them and return them to the pot.
3. Mash the potatoes by using a hand mixer until fluffy, add remaining ingredients except for chives, and then stir until mixed.
4. Sprinkle chives over the top and then serve.

Nutrition:
Calories:396 Fat: 5g Carbohydrates: 10g Proteins: 23g

468. Quinoa with Vegetables
Preparation time: 10 minutes
Cooking time: 5 to 6 hours
Servings: 8
Ingredients:

- 2 cups quinoa, rinsed and drained
- 2 onions, chopped
- 2 carrots, peeled and sliced
- 1 cup sliced cremini mushrooms
- 3 garlic cloves, minced
- 4 cups low-sodium vegetable broth
- 1/2 teaspoon salt
- 1 teaspoon dried marjoram leaves
- 1/8 teaspoon freshly ground black pepper

Directions:

1. In a 6-quart slow cooker, mix all the ingredients.
2. Cover and cook on low heat for 5 to 6 hours, or until the quinoa and vegetables are tender.
3. Stir the mixture and serve.

Nutrition:
Calories: 204 Carbohydrates: 35g Fiber: 4g Fat: 3g Proteins: 7g

469. Cold Cauliflower-Coconut Soup
Preparation time: 7 minutes
Cooking time: 20 minutes
Servings: 3-4
Ingredients:

- 1 pound (450g) new cauliflower
- 1 1/4 cup (300ml) unsweetened coconut milk
- 1 cup of water (best: antacid water)
- 2 tbsp. new lime juice
- 1/3 cup cold squeezed additional virgin olive oil
- 1 cup new coriander leaves, slashed
- Spot of salt and cayenne pepper
- 1 bunch of unsweetened coconut chips

Directions:

1. Steam cauliflower for around 10 minutes.
2. At that point, set up the cauliflower with coconut milk and water in a food processor and get it started until extremely smooth.
3. Include new lime squeeze, salt and pepper, a large portion of the cleaved coriander, and the oil and blend for an additional couple of moments.
4. Pour in soup bowls and embellishment with coriander and coconut chips. Appreciate!

Nutrition:
Calories: 190 Fat: 1g Carbohydrates: 21g Proteins: 6g

470. Lettuce Bean Burritos

Preparation time: 10 minutes
Cooking time: 5 minutes
Servings: 4
Ingredients:

- 1 can white beans
- Head of romaine lettuce
- 1 red onion
- 1/2 cup basil
- 1 organic tomato
- 2 tbsp. lemon juice
- Himalayan pink salt
- Black pepper

Directions:

1. Rinse and drain the beans.

471. Mango Chutney Wraps

Preparation time: 10 minutes
Cooking time: 8 minutes
Servings: 8
Ingredients:

- 3 ripe mangoes
- 1 avocado
- 4 tbsp. lime juice
- 2 tbsp. coconut oil
- 2 tbsp. tahini
- 1 tsp. chili flakes
- 1/2 cup coriander leaves
- Sea salt
- 1 tbsp. fresh ginger
- 16 sheets of rice paper
- 3 carrots
- 2 bell peppers
- 1 cucumber
- Black pepper

Directions:

1. Set the mango meat and cut the avocado in half, dash the pit, and scoop out the flesh.

472. Chickpea Fajitas

Preparation time: 10 minutes
Cooking time: 30 minutes
Servings: 4
Ingredients:

- For the Chickpea Fajitas:
- 1 1/2 cups cooked chickpeas
- 1 medium white onion, peeled, sliced
- 2 medium green bell peppers, cored, sliced
- 1 tablespoon fajita seasoning
- 2 tablespoons olive oil

For the Cream:

- 1/2 cup cashews, soaked
- 1 clove of garlic, peeled
- 1/2 teaspoon salt
- 1/2 teaspoon ground cumin
- 1/4 cup lime juice
- 1/4 cup water
- 1 tablespoon olive oil

To serve:

- Sliced avocado for topping

2. Pull off 8 of the largest lettuce leaves and chop the hard stem off the bottom and set aside. Finely chop the onion and basil. Core and dice the tomato.
3. Mix the beans, onion, tomato, basil, lemon juice, and a pinch of salt and pepper.
4. To shape the wraps, spread a spoonful of the white bean mix down the middle of each lettuce leaf and roll the leaf like a burrito.
5. Se seam-side down on a platter and serve.

Nutrition:
Calories: 244 Fat: 2g Proteins: 11g Carbohydrates: 50g Fiber: 10g

2. Add the mango flesh of 2 mangos to a blender along with the avocado, 2 tbsp. lime juice, oil, tahini, chili, coriander leaves, and a pinch of salt.
3. Slice the ginger before adding to the blender. Pulse then blend until smooth.
4. Pour the blended mango into a bowl and refrigerate until serving.
5. Chop the remaining mango flesh into slices.
6. To prepare the wraps, carefully dip the rice paper into hot water for no more than 10 seconds, then lay them flat and let dry for 2 minutes.
7. While you wait, thinly slice your carrots, peppers, and cucumber.
8. After the wraps have dried, spread a tbsp. of mango dip down the middle of each sheet of rice paper. Put the dried mango slices and vegetable slices in the middle. Dribble some lime juice on top and a smidge of salt and pepper, then roll up like a burrito.
9. Serve with more mango dip on the side!

Nutrition:
Calories: 362 Fat: 13g Carbohydrates: 52.5g Fiber: 3g Proteins: 8g

- Chopped lettuce for topping
- 4 flour tortillas
- Chopped tomatoes for topping
- Salsa for topping
- Chopped cilantro for topping

Directions:

1. Prepare chickpeas and for this, whisk together seasoning and oil until combined, add onion, pepper, and chickpeas, toss until well coated, then spread them in a baking sheet and roast for 30 minutes at 400F until crispy and browned, stirring halfway.
2. Meanwhile, prepare the cream and for this, place all its ingredients in a food processor and pulse until smooth, set aside until required.
3. When chickpeas and vegetables have roasted, top them evenly on tortillas, then top them evenly with avocado, lettuce, tomatoes, salsa, and cilantro and serve.

Nutrition:
Calories: 300 Carbohydrates: 46g Proteins: 5.3g Fat: 10.6g

473. Garlic and White Bean Soup

Preparation time: 15 minutes
Cooking time: 10 minutes
Servings: 4
Ingredients:

- 45 ounces cooked cannellini beans
- 1/4 teaspoon dried thyme
- 2 teaspoons minced garlic
- 1/8 teaspoon crushed red pepper
- 1/2 teaspoon dried rosemary
- 1/8 teaspoon ground black pepper
- 2 tablespoons olive oil
- 4 cups vegetable broth

Directions:

474. Quinoa and Chickpeas Salad

Preparation time: 10 minutes
Cooking time: 0 minute
Servings: 4
Ingredients:

- 3/4 cup chopped broccoli
- 1/2 cup quinoa, cooked
- 15 ounces cooked chickpeas
- 1/2 teaspoon minced garlic
- 1/3 teaspoon ground black pepper
- 2/3 teaspoon salt

475. Pecan Rice

Preparation time: 5 minutes
Cooking time: 10 minutes
Servings: 4
Ingredients:

- 1/4 cup chopped white onion
- 1/4 teaspoon ground ginger
- 1/2 cup chopped pecans
- 1/4 teaspoon salt
- 2 tablespoons minced parsley
- 1/4 teaspoon ground black pepper
- 1/4 teaspoon dried basil

476. Barley Bake

Preparation time: 10 minutes
Cooking time: 98 minutes
Servings: 6
Ingredients:

- 1 cup pearl barley
- 1 medium white onion, peeled, diced
- 2 green onions, sliced
- 1/2 cup sliced mushrooms
- 1/8 teaspoon ground black pepper
- 1/4 teaspoon salt
- 1/2 cup chopped parsley
- 1/2 cup pine nuts
- 1/4 cup vegan butter
- 29 ounces vegetable broth

477. Black Beans, Corn, and Yellow Rice

Preparation time: 10 minutes
Cooking time: 25 minutes
Servings: 8
Ingredients:

- 8 ounces yellow rice mix

---

1. Place one-third of white beans in a food processor, then pour in 2 cups broth and pulse for 2 minutes until smooth.
2. Set a pot over medium heat, attach oil and when hot, add garlic and cook for 1 minute until fragrant. Add pureed beans into the pan along with remaining beans, sprinkle with spices and herbs, pour in the broth, stir until combined, and bring the mixture to boil over medium-high heat.
3. Switch heat to medium-low level, simmer the beans for 15 minutes, and then mash them with a fork. Taste the soup to adjust seasoning and then serve.

Nutrition:
Calories: 221 Fat: 2g Carbohydrates: 1g Proteins: 3g

- 1 teaspoon dried tarragon
- 2 teaspoons mustard
- 1 tablespoon lemon juice
- 3 tablespoons olive oil

Directions:

1. Take a large bowl, place all the ingredients in it, and stir until well combined. Serve straight away.

Nutrition:
Calories: 311 Fat: 2g Carbohydrates: 64g Fiber: 13g Proteins: 11g

- 2 tablespoons vegan margarine
- 1 cup brown rice, cooked

Directions:

1. Take a skillet pan, place it over medium heat, add margarine and when it melts, add all the ingredients except for rice and stir until mixed.
2. Cook for 5 minutes, then stir in rice until combined and continue cooking for 2 minutes.
3. Serve straight away

Nutrition:
Calories: 432 Fat: 12g Carbohydrates: 6g Proteins: 4g

Directions:

1. Place a skillet pan over medium-high heat, add butter and when it melts, stir in onion and barley, add nuts and cook for 5 minutes until light brown.
2. Add mushrooms, green onions and parsley, sprinkle with salt and black pepper, cook for 1 minute and then transfer the mixture into a casserole dish.
3. Pour in broth, stir until mixed and bake for 90 minutes until barley is tender and has absorbed all the liquid.
4. Serve straight away

Nutrition:
Calories: 126 Fat: 4g Carbohydrates: 4g Proteins: 13g

- 15.25 ounces cooked kernel corn
- 1 1/4 cups water
- 15 ounces cooked black beans
- 1 teaspoon ground cumin
- 2 teaspoons lime juice

- 2 tablespoons olive oil

Directions:
1. Place a saucepan over high heat, add oil, water, and rice, bring the mixture to a bowl, and then switch heat to medium-low level.
2. Parboil for 25 minutes until rice is tender and all the liquid has been absorbed and then set the rice to a large bowl.

478. Black Beans and Rice

Preparation time: 10 minutes
Cooking time: 30 minutes
Servings: 4
Ingredients:
- 3/4 cup white rice
- 1 medium white onion, peeled, chopped
- 3 1/2 cups cooked black beans
- 1 teaspoon minced garlic
- 1/4 teaspoon cayenne pepper
- 1 teaspoon ground cumin
- 1 teaspoon olive oil
- 1 1/2 cups vegetable broth

479. Vegetable and Chickpea Loaf

Preparation time: 10 minutes
Cooking time: 15 minutes
Servings: 4
Ingredients:
- 1 tsp. Salt
- 3.5tsp. Dried sage
- 1tsp. Dried savory
- 1tbsp. Soy sauce
- 3.25cup Parsley
- 4.5cup Breadcrumbs
- 1.75cup Oats 1.75
- 2.75cup Chickpea flour
- 1.5cup cooked chickpeas
- 2Minced garlic cloves
- 1Chopped yellow onion

480. Thyme and Lemon Couscous

Preparation time: 5 minutes
Cooking time: 10 minutes
Servings: 4
Ingredients:
- 3.25cup Chopped parsley
- 1.5cup Couscous
- 2tbsp. Chopped thyme
- Juice and zest of a lemon
- 2.75cup Vegetable stock

Directions:

481. Pesto and White Bean Pasta

Preparation time: 10 minutes
Cooking time: 10 minutes
Servings: 4
Ingredients:
- 2.5cup Chopped black olives
- 2.25Diced red onion
- 1cup Chopped tomato
- 2.5cup Spinach pesto
- 1.5cup Cannellini beans

3. Add remaining ingredients into the rice, stir until mixed and serve straight away

Nutrition:
Calories: 178 Fat: 8.1g Carbohydrates: 21.3g Proteins: 3.9g Fiber: 5.2g

Directions:
1. Take a large pot over medium-high heat, add oil and when hot, add onion and garlic and cook for 4 minutes until sauté.
2. Then stir in rice, cook for 2 minutes, pour in the broth, bring it to a boil, switch heat to the low level and cook for 20 minutes until tender.
3. Stir in remaining ingredients, cook for 2 minutes, and then serve straight away.

Nutrition:
Calories: 240 Fat: 0g Proteins: 0g Carbohydrates: 48g Fiber: 16g

- 1Shredded carrot
- 1Shredded white potato

Directions:
1. Set the oven to 350F. Take out a loaf pan and then grease it up.
2. Squeeze out the liquid from the potato and add to the food processor with garlic, onion, and carrot.
3. Add the chickpeas and pulse to blend well. Add in the rest of the ingredients here, and when it is done, use your hands to form this into a loaf and add to the pan.
4. Place into the oven to bake for a bit until it is nice and firm. Let it cool down and then slice.

Nutrition:
Calories: 351 Proteins: 16.86g Fat: 6.51g Carbohydrates: 64g

1. Take out a pot and add in the thyme, lemon juice, and vegetable stock. Stir in the couscous after it has gotten to a boil and then take off the heat.
2. Allow sitting covered until it can take in all the liquid. Then fluff up with a form.
3. Swirl in the parsley and lemon zest, then serve warm.

Nutrition:
Calories: 922 Proteins: 2.7g Fat: 101.04g Carbohydrates: 10.02g

- 8oz. Rotini pasta, cooked

Directions:
1. Bring out a bowl and toss together the pesto, beans, and pasta.
2. Add in the olives, red onion, and tomato, and toss around a bit more before serving.

Nutrition:
Calories: 544 Carbohydrates: 83g Fat: 17g Proteins: 23g

482. Baked Okra and Tomato

Preparation time: 10 minutes
Cooking time: 75 minutes
Servings: 2
Ingredients:

- 1/2cup lima beans, frozen
- 4tomatoes, chopped
- 8ounces okra, fresh and washed, stemmed, sliced into 1/2 inch thick slices
- 1onion, sliced into rings
- 1/2sweet pepper, seeded and sliced thin
- Pinch of crushed red pepper
- Salt to taste

483. Bean and Carrot Spirals

Preparation time: 10 minutes
Cooking time: 40 minutes
Servings: 2
Ingredients:

- 4 8-inch flour tortillas
- 1 1/2cups of Easy Mean White Bean dip
- 10ounces spinach leaves
- 1/2cup diced carrots
- 1/2cup diced red peppers

Directions:

1. Starts by preparing the bean dip, seen above. Next, spread out the bean dip on each tortilla, making

484. Tofu Nuggets with Barbecue Glaze

Preparation time: 10 minutes
Cooking time: 25 minutes
Servings: 2
Ingredients:

- 32 ounces tofu
- 1 cup quick vegan barbecue sauce

Directions:

1. Set the oven to 425F.
2. Next, slice the tofu and blot the tofu with clean towels. Next, slice and dice the tofu and eliminate the water from the tofu material.

485. Peppered Pinto Beans

Preparation time: 10 minutes
Cooking time: 15 minutes
Servings: 4
Ingredients:

- 1tsp. Chili powder
- 1tsp. ground cumin
- 3.5cup Vegetable
- 2cans Pinto beans
- 1Minced jalapeno
- 1Diced red bell pepper

486. Chili Fennel

Preparation time: 10 minutes
Cooking time: 8 minutes
Servings: 4
Ingredients:

- 2 fennel bulbs, cut into quarters
- 3 tablespoons olive oil
- Salt and black pepper to the taste
- 1 garlic clove, minced
- 1 red chili pepper, chopped

Directions:

1. Preheat your oven to 350 degrees Fahrenheit
2. Cook lima beans in water accordingly and drain them, take a 2quart casserole tin
3. Add all listed ingredients to the dish and cover with foil, bake for 45 minutes
4. Uncover the dish, stir well and bake for 35 more minutes
5. Stir then serve and enjoy!

Nutrition:
Calories: 55 Fat: 0g Carbohydrates: 12g Proteins: 3g

sure to leave about a 3/4 inch white border on the tortillas' surface. Next, place spinach in the center of the tortilla, followed by carrots and red peppers.

2. Roll the tortillas into tight rolls and cover every roll with plastic wrap or aluminum foil.
3. Let them chill in the fridge for twenty-four hours.
4. Afterward, remove the wrap from the spirals and remove the very ends of the rolls. Slice the rolls into six individual spiral pieces and arrange them on a platter for serving. Enjoy!

Nutrition:
Calories: 205 Proteins: 6.41g Fat: 4.16g Carbohydrates: 5.13g

3. Stir the tofu with the vegan barbecue sauce and place the tofu on a baking sheet.
4. Bake the tofu for fifteen minutes. Afterward, stir the tofu and bake the tofu for an additional ten minutes.
5. Enjoy!

Nutrition:
Calories: 311 Proteins: 19.94g Fat: 21.02g Carbohydrates: 15.55g

- 1tsp. Olive oil

Directions:

1. Take out a pot and heat the oil. Cook the jalapeno and pepper for a bit before adding in the pepper, salt, cumin, broth, and beans.
2. Place to a boil and then reduce the heat to cook for a bit. After 10 minutes, let it cool and serve.

Nutrition:
Calories: 183 Carbohydrates: 3.2g Fat: 2g Proteins: 11g

- 3/4 cup veggie stock
- Juice of 1/2 lemon

Directions:

1. Heat a pan that fits your Air Fryer with the oil over medium-high heat, add garlic and chili pepper, stir and cook for 2 minutes.
2. Add fennel, salt, pepper, stock, and lemon juice, toss to coat, introduce in your Air Fryer and cook at 350F for at least 6 minutes.
3. Divide into plates and serve as a side dish.

Nutrition:

487. Cajun and Balsamic Okra

Preparation time: 10 minutes
Cooking time: 15 minutes
Servings: 2
Ingredients:

- 1 cup okra, sliced
- 1/2 cup crushed tomatoes
- 1 teaspoon Cajun seasoning
- 2 tablespoons balsamic vinegar
- 1 teaspoon salt
- 1 teaspoon ground black pepper

488. Cashew Zucchinis

Preparation time: 10 minutes
Cooking time: 40 minutes
Servings: 4
Ingredients:

- 1 pound zucchinis, sliced
- 1/2 cup cashews, soaked and drained
- 1 cup coconut milk
- 1/4 teaspoon nutmeg, ground
- 1 teaspoon chili powder

489. Cauliflower Gnocchi

Preparation time: 10 minutes
Cooking time: 40 minutes
Servings: 4
Ingredients:

- 3 pounds of cauliflower florets
- 2 cups of marinara sauce or 2 cups of quartered tomatoes without skin
- 1 cup of whole-wheat flour
- 1 teaspoon of sea salt
- Basil, for garnishing

Cashew Cheese:

- 1 cup of raw cashews (soaked for hours)
- 1-2 tablespoons of apple cider vinegar
- 2-4 tablespoons of water
- 1/2 teaspoon of salt
- optional additions: smoked paprika, nutritional yeast, fresh or dried herbs, granulated garlic

Directions:

1. Set cauliflower florets in a large pot, pour water to cover them, and set it to a boil. Once boiled, parboil on low heat for 22 minutes until tender. Drain and set to cool.
2. After cooling, squeeze out extra water: Set some of the cauliflower on a dish towel, squeeze, and transfer to a large bowl. Repeat with the remaining cauliflower.

490. Curry Chickpea

Preparation time: 10 minutes
Cooking time: 30 minutes
Servings: 4
Ingredients:

- 1 chopped red bell pepper
- 1/2 chopped red onion
- 2 cups of cooked chickpeas
- 1 can of coconut milk

Calories: 158 Proteins: 3.57g Fat: 11.94g Carbohydrates: 11.33g

- 1 tablespoon fresh parsley, chopped
- 1 teaspoon olive oil

Directions:

1. Warmth up a pan with the oil over medium heat, add the okra, seasoning, and the remaining ingredients, toss and cook for 15 minutes.
2. Divide into bowls and serve.

Nutrition:
Calories: 162 Fat: 4.5g Fiber: 4.6g Carbohydrates: 12.6g Proteins: 3g

- A pinch of salt and black pepper

Directions:

1. In a roasting pan, mix the zucchinis with the cashews and the other ingredients, toss gently, and cook at 380 degrees F for 40 minutes.
2. Divide into bowls and serve.

Nutrition:
Calories: 200 Fat: 5g Fiber: 3g Carbohydrates: 7.1g Proteins: 6g

3. Press cauliflower with a fork. Add flour and salt in the bowl, merge all ingredients well by hand, and make a dough.
4. Set flour on a work surface, divide the prepared dough into 8 equal parts. Set each piece into a rope (10 inches long and 1/2-inch thick) and set aside.
5. Divide each rope into 13 equal gnocchi-like pieces. If the dough becomes too sticky, scatter some flour on your hands.
6. Set a skillet on medium heat and warm. Take the half of the formed gnocchi and put on the hot skillet. Let them cook for 2 minutes, then slowly flip gnocchi on another side. Sprinkle salt on the top and cook. Set aside. Redo it with the remaining part of the formed gnocchi.
7. Meantime cook the cashew cheese. Set the soaked cashews in a food processor with vinegar and salt, and pulse repeatedly. Attach water by a tablespoon at a time to get the desired consistency and blend. Taste and feel free to add any optional additions.
8. Bring everything back to the skillet, pour marinara sauce (tomatoes) on the top and stir. Take out from the heat and spread the cooked cashew cheese on the top.
9. Serve and enjoy your Cauliflower Gnocchi!

Nutrition:
Calories: 228 Carbohydrates: 42.6g Proteins: 12g Fat: 2g

- 1/4 cup of chopped fresh basil
- 1 tablespoon of minced fresh ginger
- 1 minced glove garlic
- 2 tablespoons of maple syrup
- 1 tablespoon of fresh lime juice
- 1 tablespoon of curry powder
- 1 teaspoon of sea salt

Directions:

1. Set a large deep skillet on medium heat, pour water, and warm it. Add chopped pepper with onion into it and sauté 5 minutes until softened.
2. Add in curry powder, garlic, and ginger. Continue cooking for 1 minute.
3. Add chickpeas, coconut milk, maple syrup, and salt to the vegetables and stir it. Set it to a boil, reduce to low heat and simmer, covered, for 15 minutes.

491. Grilled Margherita
Preparation time: 10 minutes
Cooking time: 20 minutes
Servings: 4
Ingredients:
- 1 cup of whole-wheat flour
- 1 cup of soy yogurt
- 1 1/2 cups of arugula
- 1/4 cup of marinara sauce
- 1 1/2 teaspoons of baking powder
- 1/2 teaspoon of sea salt
- Black pepper, to taste

Cashew Cheese:
- 1 cup of raw cashews (soaked for 3-24 hours)
- 1-2 tablespoons of apple cider vinegar
- 2-4 tablespoons of water
- 1/2 teaspoon of salt
- optional additions: smoked paprika, nutritional yeast, fresh or dried herbs, granulated garlic

Directions:
1. Attach flour, salt, and baking powder into a medium mixing bowl and mix them. Pour soy yogurt and whisk it with a fork until well mixed.

492. Vegan Moroccan Stew
Preparation time: 10 minutes
Cooking time: 30 minutes
Servings: 4
Ingredients:
- 4 cups of cubed butternut squash
- 1 cup of cooked chickpeas
- 1 cup of green lentils
- 1 cup of chopped tomatoes
- 1 chopped white onion
- 6 minced garlic cloves
- 2 1/2 cups of vegetable broth
- Juice of 1/2 a lemon
- 1/3 cup of chopped cilantro
- 2 teaspoons of cumin
- 1 teaspoon of ground turmeric

493. Lime Bean Artichoke Wraps
Preparation time: 10 minutes
Cooking time: 20 minutes
Servings: 2
Ingredients:
- Lima bean spread
- 1 cup cooked baby lima beans
- 2 tablespoons nutritional yeast
- 2 tablespoons parsley, chopped
- 1/2 teaspoon garlic, minced
- 1/2 teaspoon onion powder

4. Add lime juice with basil and stir. Cook until basil is wilted, then season according to your taste.
5. Serve warm* and enjoy your Curry Chickpea!

Nutrition:
Calories: 268 Fat: 24g Carbohydrates: 14g Proteins: 3g

2. Lightly spread some flour on your work surface and take the mixture from the bowl. Knead the dough until tacky but not sticky. It shouldn't stick to your hands.
3. Set the dough into 4 equal parts and form balls about 3 ounces each. Dust flour on the work surface and roll the dough into thin ovals using a rolling pin.
4. Preheat your grill on high heat and place the rolled dough to the grill. Cover and cook 1-1.5 minutes on each side until grill lines stay.
5. Meantime cook the cashew cheese. Set the soaked cashews in a food processor with vinegar and salt, and pulse repeatedly. Attach water by a tablespoon at a time to get the desired consistency and blend. Taste and feel free to add any optional additions.
6. Spread 1 tablespoon of marinara sauce over the grilled pizza bases and sprinkle the cooked cashew cheese on the top. Grill it for 2-3 minutes. Take it out and add arugula, black pepper, and salt.
7. Repeat steps 6 and 7 with the remaining part of the dough.
8. Serve and enjoy your Grilled Margherita!

Nutrition:
Calories: 242 Carbohydrates: 29.5g Proteins: 15.5g Fat: 7g

- 1 teaspoon of cinnamon
- 1/4 teaspoon of cayenne powder
- Pinch of sea salt and black pepper

Directions:
1. Put a large pot on medium heat. Add garlic and onion, cook until softened.
2. Add in cayenne, cinnamon, turmeric, cumin and cook for 30-60 second until fragrant.
3. Add in butternut squash, chickpeas, lentils, broth, tomatoes, pepper and salt. Bring it to a boil, reduce to lower heat, cover and simmer for 20 minutes until the vegetables are fully cooked. Stir in lemon juice. Taste and add more seasonings if desired.
4. Serve warm and enjoy Vegan Moroccan Stew!

Nutrition:
Calories: 431 Proteins: 27.4g Fat: 6g Carbohydrates: 78g

- 2 teaspoons fresh lime juice
- 2 teaspoons white balsamic vinegar
- Wraps
- 2 gluten-free vegan wraps
- 1 cup raw broccoli, sliced lengthwise
- 2 whole hearts of palm, sliced lengthwise

Directions:
1. Blend lime beans with yeast, parsley, garlic, onion powder, lime juice and vinegar in a blender until smooth.

2. Spread the beans mixture on top of the wraps and top them with broccoli and hearts of palm.
3. Roll the wraps like a burrito and cut in half.
4. Grill the wraps in the grill over high heat for 5 minutes per side.

494. Butternut Squash Lasagna

Preparation time: 10 minutes
Cooking time: 1 hour 30 minutes
Servings: 6
Ingredients:

- 2 tablespoons olive oil
- 2 pounds butternut squash, cubed
- 1/2 cup water
- 4 amaretti cookies, crumbled
- 8 ounces shiitake mushrooms, sliced
- 1/4 cup butter
- 1/4 cup whole-wheat flour
- 31/2 cups almond milk
- 1/2 teaspoon ground nutmeg
- 1 cup fresh basil leaves
- 13 ounces DeLillo no-boil lasagna noodles
- 3 cups vegan cheese, shredded
- Salt and black pepper, to taste

Directions:
1. Preheat your oven to 375F.
2. Sauté squash with black pepper, salt and oil in a skillet for 5 minutes.
3. Add water to the squash, cover and cook for about 20 minutes on medium heat. Blend the squash with amaretti in a blender until smooth. Sauté

495. Broccoli Dip

Preparation time: 10 minutes
Cooking time: 20 minutes
Servings: 2
Ingredients:

- 1 cup white beans, drained
- 1 cup cashews, soaked
- 1 tablespoon lemon juice
- 1 tablespoon tapioca starch
- 2 tablespoons nutritional yeast
- 1 teaspoon garlic powder
- 1 teaspoon onion powder
- 1/2 teaspoon paprika
- Salt, to taste

5. Serve.
Nutrition:
Calories: 432 Fat: 12g Carbohydrates: 6g Proteins: 4g

mushrooms with oil and 1/4 teaspoons salt in a skillet for 10 minutes. Mix butter with flour in a skillet for 1 minute.
4. Pour in milk, mix well until lump-free then boil the mixture.
5. Stir in black pepper, nutmeg and 1/4 teaspoons salt. Mix well then cook for about 5 minutes until the sauce thickens. Add basil and blend well with a blender.
6. Grease a 13x9 -inch baking dish with butter.
7. Spread 3/4 cup sauce in the baking dish. Arrange the lasagna noodles at the bottom of this dish.
8. Top the noodles with 1/3 squash puree and add 1/3 mushroom on top.
9. Drizzle 1 cup vegan cheese on top.
10. Repeat all the layers and cover this dish with foil sheet.
11. Bake the prepared lasagna for 40 minutes in the oven.
12. Remove the tin foil from the top and bake for another 15 minutes.
13. Serve warm.
Nutrition:
Calories: 240 Fat: 0g Proteins: 0g Carbohydrates: 48g Fiber: 16g

- 1 pinch red pepper flakes
- 11/4 cup almond milk
- 11/2 cups fresh broccoli, florets

Directions:
1. At 375 F, preheat your oven.
2. Spread broccoli in a baking sheet.
3. Blend rest of the dip ingredients in a blender until smooth.
4. Spread this mixture over the broccoli and bake for 25 minutes.
5. Serve.
Nutrition:
Calories: 455 Carbohydrates: 28g Fat: 9.8g Proteins: 20g

496. Squash Salsa

Preparation time: 10 mi0nutes
Cooking time: 3 hours
Servings: 2
Ingredients:

- 1 cup butternut squash, peeled and cubed
- 1 cup cherry tomatoes, cubed
- 1 cup avocado, peeled, pitted, and cubed
- 1/2 tablespoon balsamic vinegar
- 1/2 tablespoon lemon juice
- 1 tablespoon lemon zest, grated
- 1/4 cup veggie stock

497. Light & Creamy Garlic Hummus

Preparation time: 10 minutes
Cooking time: 40 minutes
Servings: 12
Ingredients:

- 1 1/2 cups dry chickpeas, rinsed
- 2 1/2 tbsp. fresh lemon juice
- 1 tbsp. garlic, minced
- 1/2 cup tahini

- 1 tablespoon chives, chopped
- A pinch of rosemary, dried
- A pinch of sage, dried
- A pinch of salt and black pepper

Directions:

1. In your slow cooker, mix the squash with the tomatoes, avocado, and the other ingredients, toss, set the lid on and cook on Low for 3 hours.
2. Divide into bowls and serve as a snack.

Nutrition:
Calories: 388 Fat: 6g Carbohydrates: 4g Proteins: 12g

- cups of water

Directions:

- Add water and chickpeas into the instant pot.
- Seal pot with a lid and select manual and set timer for 40 minutes.
- Once done, allow to release pressure naturally. Remove lid.

- Drain chickpeas well and reserved 1/2 cup chickpeas liquid.
- Transfer chickpeas, reserved liquid, lemon juice, garlic, tahini, pepper, and salt into the food processor and process until smooth.

498. Creamy Potato Spread

Preparation time: 10 minutes
Cooking time: 15 minutes
Servings: 6
Ingredients:
- 1 lb. sweet potatoes, peeled and chopped
- 3/4 tbsp. fresh chives, chopped
- 1/2 tsp paprika
- 1 tbsp. garlic, minced
- 1 cup tomato puree

Directions:

499. Flavorful Roasted Baby Potatoes

Preparation time: 10 minutes
Cooking time: 10 minutes
Servings: 4
Ingredients:
- 2 lbs. baby potatoes, clean and cut in half
- 1/2 cup vegetable stock
- 3/4 tsp garlic powder
- 1 tsp onion powder, paprika
- 2 tsp Italian seasoning

Directions:

500. Perfect Italian Potatoes

Preparation time: 10 minutes
Cooking time: 7 minutes
Servings: 6
Ingredients:
- 2 lbs. baby potatoes, clean and cut in half
- 3/4 cup vegetable broth
- 6 oz. Italian dry dressing mix

Directions:

501. Garlic Pinto Bean Dip

Preparation time: 10 minutes
Cooking time: 43 minutes
Servings: 6
Ingredients:
- 1 cup dry pinto beans, rinsed
- 1/2 tsp cumin
- 1/2 cup salsa
- 2 chipotle peppers in adobo sauce
- 5 cups vegetable stock

Directions:

502. Creamy Eggplant Dip

Preparation time: 10 minutes
Cooking time: 20 minutes
Servings: 4
Ingredients:
- 1 eggplant
- 1/2 tsp paprika
- 1 tbsp. fresh lime juice
- 2 tbsp. tahini
- 1 garlic clove

- Serve and enjoy.

Nutrition:
Calories: 152 Fat: 6.9g Carbohydrates: 17g

1. Add all ingredients except chives into the inner pot of instant pot and stir well.
2. Seal pot with lid and cook on high for 15 minutes.
3. When done, release pressure naturally for 10 minutes then releases remaining using quick release. Remove lid.
4. Transfer instant pot sweet potato mixture into the food processor and process until smooth.
5. Garnish with chives and serve.

Nutrition:
Calories: 108 Fat: 0.3g Carbohydrates: 25.4g

1. Pour oil into the inner pot of instant pot and set the pot on sauté mode.
2. Add potatoes and sauté for 5 minutes. Add remaining ingredients and stir well.
3. Seal pot with lid and cook on high for 5 minutes.
4. Once done, release pressure using quick release. Remove lid.
5. Stir well and serve.

Nutrition:
Calories: 175 Fat: 4.5g Carbohydrates: 29.3g

1. Incorporate all ingredients into the inner pot of instant pot and stir well.
2. Seal pot with lid and cook on high for 7 minutes.
3. Once done, allow to release pressure naturally for 3 minutes then release remaining using quick release. Remove lid.
4. Stir well and serve.

Nutrition:
Calories: 149 Fat: 0.3g Carbohydrates: 41.6g

1. Add beans, stock, 2 garlic cloves, and chipotle peppers into the instant pot.
2. Seal pot with lid and cook on high for 43 minutes.
3. Once done, release pressure using quick release. Remove lid.
4. Drain beans well and reserve 1/2 cup of stock.
5. Transfer beans, reserve stock, and remaining ingredients into the food processor and process until smooth.
6. Serve and enjoy.

Nutrition:
Calories: 129 Fat: 0.9g Carbohydrates: 23g

Directions:
1. Add 1 cup of water and eggplant into the instant pot.
2. Seal pot with the lid and select manual and set timer for 20 minutes.
3. Once done, release pressure using quick release. Remove lid.
4. Drain eggplant and let it cool.

5. Once the eggplant is cool then remove eggplant skin and transfer eggplant flesh into the food processor.
6. Pulse the remaining ingredients with food processor and process until smooth.

503. Jalapeno Chickpea Hummus

Preparation time: 10 minutes
Cooking time: 25 minutes
Servings: 4
Ingredients:
- 1 cup dry chickpeas, soaked overnight and drained
- 1 tsp ground cumin
- 1/4 cup jalapenos, diced
- 1/2 cup fresh cilantro
- 1 tbsp. tahini

Directions:

504. Creamy Pepper Spread

Preparation time: 10 minutes
Cooking time: 15 minutes
Servings: 4
Ingredients:
- 1 lb. red bell peppers, chopped and remove seeds
- 1 1/2 tbsp. fresh basil
- 1 tbsp. olive oil
- 1 tbsp. fresh lime juice
- 1 tsp garlic, minced

Directions:

505. Healthy Spinach Dip

Preparation time: 10 minutes
Cooking time: 8 minutes
Servings: 4
Ingredients:
- 14 oz. spinach
- 2 tbsp. fresh lime juice
- 1 tbsp. garlic, minced
- 2 tbsp. olive oil
- 2 tbsp. coconut cream

Directions:

506. Raisins Cinnamon Peaches

Preparation time: 10 minutes
Cooking time: 15 minutes
Servings: 4
Ingredients:
- 4 peaches, cored and cut into chunks
- 1 tsp vanilla
- 1 tsp cinnamon
- 1/2 cup raisins
- 1 cup of water

Directions:

507. Lemon Pear Compote

Preparation time: 10 minutes
Cooking time: 15 minutes
Servings: 6
Ingredients:
- 3 cups pears, cored and cut into chunks
- 1 tsp vanilla
- 1 tsp liquid stevia

7. Serve and enjoy.
Nutrition:
Calories: 108 Fat: 7.8g Carbohydrates: 9.7g

1. Add chickpeas into the instant pot and cover with vegetable stock.
2. Seal pot with lid and cook on high for 25 minutes.
3. Once done, allow to release pressure naturally. Remove lid.
4. Drain chickpeas well and transfer into the food processor along with remaining ingredients and process until smooth.
5. Serve and enjoy.
Nutrition:
Calories: 425 Fat: 30.4g Carbohydrates: 31.8g

1. Situate all ingredients into the inner pot of instant pot and stir well.
2. Seal pot with lid and cook on high for 15 minutes.
3. Once finish, let the pressure release naturally for 10 minutes then release the rest using quick release. Remove lid.
4. Transfer bell pepper mixture into the food processor and process until smooth.
5. Serve and enjoy.
Nutrition:
Calories: 41 Fat: 3.6g Carbohydrates: 3.5g

1. Add all ingredients except coconut cream into the instant pot and stir well.
2. Seal pot with lid and cook on low pressure for 8 minutes.
3. Once done, allow to release pressure naturally for 5 minutes then release remaining using quick release. Remove lid.
4. Add coconut cream and stir well and blend spinach mixture using a blender until smooth.
5. Serve and enjoy.
Nutrition:
Calories: 109 Fat: 9.2g Carbohydrates: 6.6g

1. Mix all ingredients into the inner pot of instant pot and stir well.
2. Seal pot with lid and cook on high for 15 minutes.
3. Once cooked, release pressure naturally for 10 minutes then releases the rest by quick release. Remove lid.
4. Stir and serve.
Nutrition:
Calories: 118 Fat: 0.5g Carbohydrates: 29g

- 1 tbsp. lemon zest, grated
- 2 tbsp. lemon juice

Directions:
1. Situate all ingredients into the inner pot of instant pot and stir well.
2. Seal pot with lid and cook on high for 15 minutes.

3. When cooked, let the pressure naturally release for 10 minutes then release remaining using quick release. Open it.

508. Strawberry Stew

Preparation time: 10 minutes
Cooking time: 15 minutes
Servings: 4
Ingredients:

- 12 oz. fresh strawberries, sliced
- 1 tsp vanilla
- 1 1/2 cups water
- 1 tsp liquid stevia
- 2 tbsp. lime juice

Directions:

509. Brussels Sprouts and Pistachios

Preparation time: 15 minutes
Cooking time: 15 minutes
Servings: 4
Ingredients:

- 1-pound Brussels sprouts, trimmed and halved lengthwise
- 4 shallots, peeled and quartered
- 1 tablespoon extra-virgin olive oil
- ½ cup roasted pistachios, chopped
- ½ lemon juice and zest

Directions:

1. Pre-heat your oven to 400 degrees Fahrenheit.

510. Spiced Up Kale Chips

Preparation time: 10 minutes
Cooking time: 25 minutes
Servings: 4
Ingredients:

- 3 cups kale, stemmed and thoroughly washed, torn into 2-inch pieces
- 1 tablespoon extra-virgin olive oil
- ½ teaspoon chili powder
- ¼ teaspoon sea salt

Directions:

1. Pre-heat your oven to 300 degrees Fahrenheit.

511. Ultra-Spicy Almonds

Preparation time: 15 minutes
Cooking time: 2 hours & 30 minutes
Servings: 32
Ingredients:

- 2½ tablespoons coconut oil
- cups of raw almonds
- garlic cloves, minced
- 1 teaspoon smoked paprika
- 2 teaspoons red chili powder
- 1 teaspoon ground cumin
- 1 teaspoon onion powder
- Salt

512. Perfect Eggplant Tapenade

Preparation time: 15 minutes
Cooking time: 9 hours
Servings: 2
Ingredients:

- cups eggplants, chopped
- 1 cup tomatoes, chopped

4. Stir and serve.

Nutrition:
Calories: 50 Fat: 0.2g Carbohydrates: 12.7g

1. Mix all ingredients into the inner pot of instant pot and stir well.
2. Seal pot with lid and cook on high for 15 minutes.
3. Once cooked, release pressure naturally for 10 minutes then by using quick release, let the remaining pressure out. Remove lid.
4. Stir and serve.

Nutrition:
Calories: 36 Fat: 0.3g Carbohydrates: 8.5g

2. Wrap baking sheet with aluminum foil and keep aside.
3. Take a large bowl and add Brussels sprouts, shallots with olive oil and coat well.
4. Season sea salt, pepper, spread veggies evenly on sheet.
5. Bake for 15 minutes until lightly caramelized.
6. Remove oven and transfer to a serving bowl.
7. Toss with lemon zest, pistachios, lemon juice.
8. Serve warm and enjoy!

Nutrition:
Calories: 126 Fat: 7g Carbohydrates: 6g

2. Cover 2 baking sheets using parchment paper and keep aside.
3. Dry kale entirely and transfer to a large bowl.
4. Add olive oil and toss.
5. Make sure each leaf is covered.
6. Season kale with chili powder and salt, toss again.
7. Divide kale between baking sheets and spread into a single layer.
8. Bake for 25 minutes.
9. Cool the chips for 5 minutes and serve.

Nutrition:
Calories: 56 Fat: 4g Carbohydrates: 2g

- ground black pepper

Directions:

1. Set a slow cooker on high and preheat for about 25 minutes.
2. Add all Ingredients and stir to combine.
3. Cook on low, uncovered, for about 2 hours, stirring occasionally.
4. Then, in high and cook, uncovered, within 30 minutes.
5. Cool before serving.

Nutrition:
Calories: 80 Carbohydrates: 2.9g Proteins: 2.6g Fat: 7.1g Fiber: 1.6g

- garlic cloves, minced
- 2 teaspoons capers
- 2 teaspoons fresh lemon juice
- 1 teaspoon dried basil
- Salt, to taste

- Pinch of ground black pepper

Directions:
1. In a slow cooker, add eggplant, tomatoes, garlic, and capers and mix well.
2. Cook on low, covered, for about 7-9 hours.

513. Trail Mix

Preparation time: 5 minutes
Cooking time: 0 minute
Servings: 4
Ingredients:
- ¼ cup of almonds
- ¼ cup of cashews
- ¼ cup of dried apricots

514. Veggie Crisps

Preparation time: 5 minutes
Cooking time: 20 minutes
Servings: 4
Ingredients:
- 2 medium carrots
- 1 medium beetroot
- 1 medium baby marrow
- 1 small sweet potato
- 1 small turnip
- 1-2 tsp of olive oil
- ½ tsp of black pepper
- ½ tsp of Himalayan salt

Directions:

515. Tamari Almonds

Preparation time: 5 minutes
Cooking time: 20 minutes
Servings: 4
Ingredients:
- 400g of raw almonds
- ¼ cup of tamari sauce
- ¼ tsp of sea salt

Directions:

516. Sweet Tiffin

Preparation time: 15 minutes
Cooking time: 2 hours
Servings: 4
Ingredients:
- 1 cup of dark chocolate (vegan)
- 2/3 cups of macadamia nuts
- 1/3 cup of dried cranberries
- 1/3 cup of coconut oil
- ¼ cup of pistachios
- 2 tbsp of maple syrup

Directions:
1. Spray a brownie tin with cooking spray. Layer the tin with a single sheet of parchment paper.

517. Black Bean Balls

Preparation time: 20 minutes
Cooking time: 0 minute
Servings: 3
Ingredients:
- 420g can black beans
- 80g raw cacao powder
- 30g almond butter

3. Uncover the slow cooker and stir in the remaining Ingredients
4. Serve hot.

Nutrition:
Calories: 46 Carbohydrates: 10.1g Proteins: 2g Fat: 0.4g Fiber: 4.2g

- ¼ cup of dried cranberries
- ¼ cup of pitted dates

Directions:
1. Combine the almonds, cashews, cranberries, apricots, and dates in a bowl.

Nutrition:
Calories: 130 Carbohydrates: 14.2g Proteins: 3.4g

1. Preheat the oven to 350-400 degrees-Fahrenheit. In a baking tray, lay out parchment paper.
2. Slice the vegetables each into 1-inch slices with a sharp knife and place them in a bowl.
3. Mix in olive oil and season the vegetables, coat well.
4. Arrange vegetables onto the baking sheet and bake them for 10 minutes on one side. Then, turn over, and bake them for 6-8 minutes.
5. Remove the vegetable crisps from the oven and allow them to cool down.

Nutrition:
Calories: 78 Carbohydrates: 34g Proteins: 2.4g

1. Heat the oven to 180 degrees-Fahrenheit and line a baking tray with parchment paper.
2. Spread the almonds onto the baking tray, drizzle the tamari sauce over the nuts, and add the sea salt.
3. Bake the almonds in the oven for 25 minutes, moving them around every 5 to 10 minutes until the tamari sauce is absorbed by the nuts.

Nutrition:
Calories: 115 Carbohydrates: 2.1g Proteins: 4.4g

2. Add the chocolate and maple syrup to a microwaveable bowl, and microwave it for 30 seconds or until you reach a smooth consistency.
3. Crush the nuts into smaller pieces in a bowl. Add the cranberries and pistachios. Mix the ingredients to combine and add the chocolate mixture to the bowl. Mix once more, then pour the mixture into the brownie tin.
4. Press the mixture with the back of a spoon to ensure it creates a flat, even layer. Refrigerate it for 2 hours, before cutting it into squares, about 4-inches in length and width.

Nutrition:
Calories: 130 Carbohydrates: 10g Proteins: 1.1g

- 15ml maple syrup

Directions:
1. In a food processor, combine 420g black beans, 60g cacao powder, almond butter, and maple syrup.
2. Process until the mixture is well combined.
3. Shape the mixture into 12 balls.

4. Roll the balls through remaining cacao powder.
5. Place the balls in a refrigerator for 10 minutes.
6. Serve.

518. Chia Soy Pudding

Preparation time: 5 minutes
Cooking time: 0 minute
Servings: 2
Ingredients:

- 45g almond butter
- 15ml maple syrup
- ¼ teaspoon vanilla paste
- 235ml soymilk
- 45g chia seeds
- 1 small banana, sliced
- 10g crushed almonds

519. Blueberry Ice Cream

Preparation time: 10 minutes
Cooking time: 0 minute
Servings: 4
Ingredients:

- 140g raw cashews
- 125g silken tofu
- 230g fresh blueberries
- 5g lemon zest
- 100ml maple syrup
- 100ml coconut oil
- 15g almond butter

Directions:
1. Rinse and drain cashews.

520. Chickpea Choco Slices

Preparation time: 10 minutes
Cooking time: 50 minutes
Servings: 2
Ingredients:

- 400g can chickpeas
- 250g almond butter
- 70ml maple syrup
- 15ml vanilla paste
- 1 pinch salt
- 2g baking powder
- 2g baking soda
- 40g vegan chocolate chips

Directions:
1. Preheat oven to 180C/350F.

521. Sweet Green Cookies

Preparation time: 10 minutes
Cooking time: 30 minutes
Servings: 3
Ingredients:

- 165g green peas
- 80g chopped Medjool dates
- 60g silken tofu, mashed
- 100g almond flour
- 1 teaspoon baking powder
- 12 almonds

Directions:
1. Preheat oven to 180C/350F.

Nutrition:
Calories: 245 Carbohydrates: 17g Proteins: 13.1g

Directions:
1. Combine almond butter, maple syrup, vanilla, and soymilk in a jar.
2. Stir in chia seeds.
3. Cover and refrigerate 3 hours.
4. After 3 hours, open the jar.
5. Top the chia pudding with banana and crushed almonds.
6. Serve.

Nutrition:
Calories: 298 Carbohydrates: 10g Proteins: 10g

2. Place the cashews, blueberries, pale syrup, coconut oil, and almond butter in a food processor.
3. Process until smooth.
4. Transfer the mixture into the freezer-friendly container.
5. Seal with plastic foil and freeze for 4 hours.
6. Remove the ice cream from the fridge 15 minutes before serving.

Nutrition:
Calories: 544
Carbohydrates: 2.6g
Proteins: 8.1g

2. Grease large baking pan with coconut oil.
3. Combine chickpeas, almond butter, maple syrup, vanilla, salt, baking powder, and baking soda in a food blender.
4. Blend until smooth. Stir in half the chocolate chips-
5. Arrange batter into the prepared baking pan.
6. Sprinkle with reserved chocolate chips.
7. Bake for 45-50 minutes.
8. Set aside on wire rack for 20 minutes. slice and serve.

Nutrition:
Calories: 426 Fiber: 4.9g Proteins: 10g

2. Combine peas and dates in a food processor.
3. Process until the thick paste is formed.
4. Transfer the pea mixture into a bowl. Stir in tofu, almond flour, and baking powder.
5. Shape the mixture into 12 balls.
6. Arrange balls onto baking sheet, lined with parchment paper. Flatten each ball with oiled palm.
7. Insert an almond into each cookie. Bake the cookies for 25-30 minutes.

Nutrition:
Calories: 221 Fiber: 6g Proteins: 8.2g

522. Chocolate Orange Mousse

Preparation time: 10 minutes
Cooking time: 0 minute
Servings: 4
Ingredients:

- 450g can black beans
- 55g dates
- 30ml coconut oil
- 110ml maple syrup
- 60ml soymilk
- 1 orange

Directions:

1. Place the black bean in a food processor.
2. Add drained dates and process until smooth.
3. Add coconut oil, maple syrup, and soymilk. Process for 1 minute.
4. Finally, stir in lemon zest.
5. Spoon the mixture into four dessert bowls.
6. Chill for 1 hour before serving.

Nutrition:
Calories: 375 Fiber: 12g Proteins: 11.3g

523. Easy Mango Tofu Custard

Preparation time: 5 minutes
Cooking time: 0 minute
Servings: 2
Ingredients:

- 100g mango puree
- 300g soft tofu
- 15ml lime juice
- 15ml maple syrup

Directions:

1. Combine all ingredients in a food blender.
2. Divide among two serving bowls.
3. Refrigerate 30 minutes. Serve.

Nutrition:
Calories: 148 Fiber: 1.1g Proteins: 10.2g

524. Chickpea Cookie Dough

Preparation time: 10 minutes
Cooking time: 0 minute
Servings: 4
Ingredients:

- 400g can chickpeas
- 130g smooth peanut butter
- 10ml vanilla extract
- ½ teaspoon cinnamon
- 10g chia seeds
- 40g quality dark Vegan chocolate chips

Directions:

1. Drain chickpeas in a colander.
2. Remove the skin from the chickpeas.
3. Place chickpeas, peanut butter, vanilla, cinnamon, and chia in a food blender.
4. Stir in chocolate chips and divide among four serving bowls.

Nutrition:
Calories: 376 Fiber: 7.3g Proteins: 14.2g

525. Cacao Thin Mints

Preparation time: 10 minutes
Cooking time: 0 minute
Servings: 2
Ingredients:

- 60g rice Proteins: powder
- 35g cacao powder
- 5ml vanilla extract
- 5ml peppermint extract
- ½ teaspoon liquid stevia
- 90ml melted and cooled coconut oil
- 40g ground almonds

Directions:

1. Combine protein powder and cacao powder in a bowl.
2. Mix vanilla, peppermint extract, stevia, and coconut oil.
3. Mix in liquid ingredients into the dry ones.
4. Line small cookie sheet with parchment paper.
5. Drop 10 mounds of prepared batter onto the cookie sheet.
6. Sprinkle the cookies with ground almonds.
7. Place in a freezer for 20 minutes.
8. Serve.

Nutrition:
Calories: 251 Fiber: 4g Proteins: 12g

526. Banana Bars

Preparation time: 10 minutes
Cooking time: 30 minutes
Servings: 8
Ingredients:

- 130g smooth peanut butter
- 60ml maple syrup
- 1 banana, mashed
- 45ml water
- 15g ground flax seeds
- 95g cooked quinoa
- 25g chia seeds
- 5ml vanilla
- 90g quick cooking oats
- 55g whole-wheat flour
- 5g baking powder
- 5g cinnamon
- 1 pinch salt

Topping:

- 5ml melted coconut oil
- 30g vegan chocolate, chopped

Directions:

1. Preheat oven to 180C/350F.
2. Line 16cm baking dish with parchment paper.
3. Mix flax seeds and water. Place aside 10 minutes.
4. In a separate bowl, incorporate peanut butter, maple syrup, and banana. Fold in the flax seed's mixture.

5. Once smooth, stir in quinoa, chia seeds, vanilla extract, oat, whole-wheat flour, baking powder, cinnamon, and salt.
6. Pour the batter into prepared baking dish. Cut into 8 bars.
7. Bake the bars for 30 minutes.

527. Pumpkin Pudding
Preparation time: 5 minutes
Cooking time: 0 minute
Servings: 4
Ingredients:
- 470ml soymilk
- 245g organic pumpkin puree
- 30ml maple syrup
- ½ teaspoon cinnamon
- ¼ teaspoon ground ginger

528. Sweet Hummus
Preparation time: 10 minutes
Cooking time: 0 minute
Servings: 4
Ingredients:
- 60ml vanilla soymilk
- 30ml maple syrup
- 400g can chickpeas
- 125g pumpkin puree
- 5ml vanilla extract

529. Lentil Balls
Preparation time: 10 minutes
Cooking time: 0 minute
Servings: 2
Ingredients:
- 150g cooked green lentils
- 10ml coconut oil
- 5g coconut sugar
- 180g quick cooking oats
- 40g unsweetened coconut
- 40g raw pumpkin seeds
- 110g peanut butter

530. Homemade Granola
Preparation time: 10 minutes
Cooking time: 24 minutes
Servings: 8
Ingredients:
- 270g rolled oats
- 100g coconut flakes
- 40g pumpkin seeds
- 80g hemp seeds
- 30ml coconut oil
- 70ml maple syrup

531. Peanut Butter Quinoa Cups
Preparation time: 10 minutes
Cooking time: 0 minute
Servings: 6
Ingredients:
- 120g puffed quinoa
- 60g smooth peanut butter
- 40g coconut butter

8. In the meantime, make the topping; combine chocolate and coconut oil in a heat-proof bowl. Set over simmering water, until melted.
9. Remove the bars from the oven. Cool on wire rack for 15 minutes.
10. Drizzle with chocolate topping. Serve.
Nutrition:
Calories: 278 Fiber: 5.8g Proteins: 9.4g

- ¼ teaspoon ground nutmeg
- 55g vanilla flavored brown rice Proteins: powder

Directions:
1. Blend all ingredients, until smooth.
2. Divide between four dessert glasses and chill for 30 minutes before serving.
Nutrition:
Calories: 163 Fiber: 4g Proteins: 15g

- 200g fresh blueberries
- 2 carrots, finely grated

Directions:
1. Combine soymilk, maple syrup, chickpeas, pumpkin puree, vanilla, and carrots in a food processor.
2. Serve, topped with fresh blueberries.
Nutrition:
Calories: 252 Fiber: 10.5g Proteins: 10.3g

- 40ml maple syrup

Directions:
1. Combine all ingredients.
2. Shape the mixture into 16 balls.
3. Arrange the balls onto a plate, lined with parchment paper.
4. Refrigerate 30 minutes.
5. Serve.
Nutrition:
Calories: 305 Fiber: 9.5g Proteins: 12.6g

- 50g Goji berries

Directions:
1. Incorporate all ingredients on baking sheet.
2. Preheat oven to 180C/350F.
3. Bake the granola for 12 minutes. Remove from the oven and stir.
4. Bake an additional 12 minutes.
5. Serve at room temperature.
Nutrition:
Calories: 344 Fiber: 5.8g Proteins: 9.9g

- 30ml coconut oil
- 25ml maple syrup
- 5ml vanilla extract

Directions:
1. Combine peanut butter, coconut butter, and coconut oil in a microwave-safe bowl.

2. Microwave on high until melted, in 40-second intervals.
3. Stir in the puffed quinoa. Stir gently to combine.

532. Flavory Beans Spread
Preparation time: 10 minutes
Cooking time: 6 hours
Servings: 2
Ingredients:
- 1 cup canned black beans, drained
- 2 tablespoons tahini paste
- 1/2 teaspoon balsamic vinegar
- 1/4 cup veggie stock
- 1/2 tablespoon olive oil

533. Rice Bowls
Preparation time: 10 minutes
Cooking time: 6 hours
Servings: 2
Ingredients:
- 1/2 cup wild rice
- 1 red onion, sliced
- 1/2 cup brown rice
- 2 cups veggie stock
- 1/2 cup baby spinach
- 1/2 cup cherry tomatoes, halved
- 2 tablespoons pine nuts, toasted
- 1 tablespoon raisins

534. Cauliflower Spread
Preparation time: 10 minutes
Cooking time: 7 hours
Servings: 2
Ingredients:
- 1 cup cauliflower florets
- 1 tablespoon mayonnaise
- 1/2 cup vegetable cream
- 1 tablespoon lemon juice
- 1/2 teaspoon garlic powder
- 1/4 teaspoon smoked paprika
- 1/4 teaspoon mustard powder

535. Flavory Mushroom Dip
Preparation time: 10 minutes
Cooking time: 5 hours
Servings: 2
Ingredients:
- 4 ounces white mushrooms, chopped
- 1 eggplant, cubed
- 1/2 cup vegetable cream
- 1/2 tablespoon tahini paste
- 2 garlic cloves, minced
- A pinch of salt and black pepper
- 1 tablespoon balsamic vinegar

536. Chickpeas Spread
Preparation time: 10 minutes
Cooking time: 8 hours
Servings: 2
Ingredients:
- 1/2 cup chickpeas, dried
- 1 tablespoon olive oil
- 1 tablespoon lemon juice

4. Divide the mixture among 12 paper cases. Freeze for 1 hour
Nutrition:
Calories: 231 Fiber: 3g Proteins: 6.3g

Directions:
1. In your slow cooker, mix the beans with the tahini paste and the other ingredients, toss, set the lid on and cook on Low for 6 hours.
2. Transfer to your food processor, blend well, divide into bowls, and serve.
Nutrition:
Calories: 432 Fat: 12g Carbohydrates: 6g Proteins: 4g

- 1 tablespoon chives, chopped
- 1 tablespoon dill, chopped
- 1/2 tablespoon olive oil
- A pinch of salt and black pepper
Directions:
1. In your slow cooker, mix the rice with the onion, stock, and the other ingredients, toss, set the lid on, and cook on Low for 6 hours.
2. Divide into bowls and serve as a snack.
Nutrition:
Calories: 211 Fat: 3g Carbohydrates: 3g Proteins: 10g

- A pinch of salt and black pepper
Directions:
1. In your slow cooker, combine the cauliflower with the cream, mayonnaise, and the other ingredients, toss, set the lid on and cook on Low for 7 hours.
2. Transfer to a blender, pulse well, into bowls, and serve as a spread.
Nutrition:
Calories: 407 Fat: 42g Carbohydrates: 13g Fiber: 1g Proteins: 4g

- 1/2 tablespoon basil, chopped
- 1/2 tablespoon oregano, chopped
Directions:
1. In your slow cooker, mix the mushrooms with the eggplant, cream, and the other ingredients, toss, set the lid on and cook on High for 5 hours.
2. Divide the mushroom mix into bowls and serve as a dip.
Nutrition:
Calories: 189 Fat: 3g Carbohydrates: 4g Proteins: 3g

- 1 cup veggie stock
- 1 tablespoon tahini
- A pinch of salt and black pepper
- 1 garlic clove, minced
- 1/2 tablespoon chives, chopped
Directions:

1. In your slow cooker, combine the chickpeas with the stock, salt, pepper, and garlic, stir cook on Low heat for 8 hours.

537. Spinach Dip
Preparation time: 10 minutes
Cooking time: 1 hour
Servings: 2
Ingredients:
- 2 tablespoons vegetable cream
- 1/2 cup Coconut yogurt
- 1/2 pound baby spinach
- 2 garlic cloves, minced
- Salt and black pepper to the taste

538. Potato Salad
Preparation time: 10 minutes
Cooking time: 8 hours
Servings: 2
Ingredients:
- 1 red onion, sliced
- 1 pound gold potatoes, peeled and roughly cubed
- 2 tablespoons balsamic vinegar
- 1/2 cup vegetable cream
- 1 tablespoons mustard
- A pinch of salt and black pepper

539. Stuffed Peppers
Preparation time: 10 minutes
Cooking time: 4 hours
Servings: 2
Ingredients:
- 1 red onion, chopped
- 1 teaspoons olive oil
- 1/2 teaspoon sweet paprika
- 1/2 tablespoon chili powder
- 1 garlic clove, minced
- 1 cup white rice, cooked
- 1/2 cup corn
- A pinch of salt and black pepper

540. Tamari Toasted Almonds
Preparation time: 2 minutes
Cooking time: 8 minutes
Servings: 1/2cup
Ingredients:
- 1/2 cup raw almonds, or sunflower seeds
- 2 tablespoons tamari, or soy sauce
- 1 teaspoon toasted sesame oil
Directions:

541. Avocado and Tempeh Bacon Wraps
Preparation time: 10 minutes
Cooking time: 8 minutes
Servings: 4
Ingredients:
- 2 tablespoons extra-virgin olive oil
- 8 ounces tempeh bacon, homemade or store-bought
- 4 (10-inch) soft flour tortillas or lavash flat bread

2. Drain chickpeas, transfer them to a blender, add the rest of the ingredients, pulse well, divide into bowls and serve as a party spread.
Nutrition:
Calories: 109 Fat: 2g Carbohydrates: 2g Proteins: 12g

Directions:
1. In your slow cooker, mix the spinach with the cream and the other ingredients, toss, set the lid and processed on High heat for 1 hour.
2. Blend using an immersion blender, set into bowls and serve as a party dip.
Nutrition:
Calories: 221 Fat: 2g Carbohydrates: 1g Proteins: 3g

- 1 tablespoon dill, chopped
- 1/2 cup celery, chopped
Directions:
1. In your slow cooker, mix the potatoes with the cream, mustard, and the other ingredients, toss, set the lid on and cook on Low for 8 hours.
2. Divide salad into bowls and serve as an appetizer.
Nutrition:
Calories: 218 Fat: 8g Carbohydrates: 2g Proteins: 4g

- 2 colored bell peppers, tops, and insides scooped out
- 1/2 cup tomato sauce
Directions:
1. In a bowl, mix the onion with the oil, paprika, and the other ingredients except for the peppers and tomato sauce, stir well and stuff the peppers with this mix.
2. Put the peppers in the slow cooker, add the sauce, put the lid on, and cook on Low for 4 hours.
3. Set the peppers to a platter and serve as an appetizer.
Nutrition:
Calories: 309 Fat: 188g Carbohydrates: 3g Proteins: 18g

1. Warmth a dry skillet to medium-high heat, and then add the almonds, stirring frequently to keep them from burning.
2. Once the almonds are toasted; 7-8 minutes for almonds, or 34 minutes for sunflower seeds; pour the tamari and sesame oil into the hot skillet and stir to coat.
Nutrition:
Calories: 89 Fat: 8g Carbohydrates: 3g Fiber: 2g Proteins: 4g

- 1/4cup vegan mayonnaise, homemade or store-bought
- 4 large lettuce leaves
- 2 ripe Hass avocados, pitted, peeled, and cut into 1/4-inch slices
- 1 large ripe tomato, cut into 1/4-inch slices
Directions:

1. In a large skillet, warmth the oil over medium heat. Attach the tempeh bacon and cook until browned on both sides, about 8 minutes. Remove from the heat and set aside.
2. Place 1 tortilla on a work surface. Spread with some of the mayonnaise and one-fourth of the lettuce and tomatoes.

542. Kale Chips

Preparation time: 5 minutes
Cooking time: 25 minutes
Servings: 2
Ingredients:
- 1 large bunch kale
- 1 tablespoon extra-virgin olive oil
- 1/2 teaspoon chipotle powder
- 1/2 teaspoon smoked paprika
- 1/4 teaspoon salt

Directions:
1. Preheat the oven to 275F.

543. Tempeh Pimiento Cheese Ball

Preparation time: 5 minutes
Cooking time: 30 minutes
Servings: 8
Ingredients:
- 8 ounces tempeh, cut into 1/2 -inch pieces
- 1 (2-ounce) jar chopped pimientos, drained
- 1/4 cup nutritional yeast
- 1/4 cup vegan mayonnaise, homemade or store-bought
- 2 tbsp. soy sauce
- 3/4 cup chopped pecans

Directions:
1. In a saucepan of boiled water, cook the tempeh for 30 minutes. Set aside to cool. In a food processor,

544. Peppers and Hummus

Preparation time: 15 minutes
Cooking time: 0 minutes
Servings: 4
Ingredients:
- 15-ounce can chickpeas, drained and rinsed
- juice of 1 lemon, or 1 tablespoon prepared lemon juice
- 1/4 cup tahini
- 3 tablespoons extra-virgin olive oil
- 1/2 teaspoon ground cumin
- 1 tablespoon water
- 1/4 teaspoon paprika
- 1 red bell pepper, sliced

545. Savory Roasted Chickpeas

Preparation time: 5 minutes
Cooking time: 25 minutes
Servings: 1
Ingredients:
- 1 (14-ounce) can chickpeas, rinsed and drained, or 11/2 cups cooked
- 2 tablespoons tamari, or soy sauce
- 1 tablespoon nutritional yeast

3. Pit, peel, and thinly slice the avocado and place the slices on top of the tomato. Add the reserved tempeh bacon and roll up tightly. Repeat with remaining Ingredients and serve.

Nutrition:
Calories: 165 Fat: 17g Carbohydrates: 4g Fiber: 1g Proteins: 1g

2. Set a large baking sheet with parchment paper. In a large bowl, stem the kale and tear it into bite-size pieces. Add the olive oil, chipotle powder, smoked paprika, and salt.
3. Toss the kale with tongs or your hands, coating each piece well.
4. Spread the kale over the parchment paper in a single layer.
5. Bake for 25 minutes.
6. Cool for 10 to 15 minutes before dividing and storing in 2 airtight containers.

Nutrition:
Calories: 318 Carbohydrates: 68g Fiber: 8g Proteins: 9g

merge the cooled tempeh, pimientos, nutritional yeast, mayo, and soy sauce. Set until smooth.
2. Set the tempeh mixture to a bowl and refrigerate until firm and chilled for at least 2 hours or overnight.
3. In a skillet, toast the pecans until lightly toasted. Set aside to cool.
4. Set the tempeh mixture into a ball, and set it in the pecans, pressing the nuts slightly into the tempeh mixture so they stick. Set it cool for at least 1 hour before serving. If not using right away, sure and keep refrigerated until needed. Properly stored, it will keep for 2-3 days.

Nutrition:
Calories: 379 Fat: 5g Carbohydrates: 66g Fiber: 4g Proteins: 17g

- 1 green bell pepper, sliced
- 1 orange bell pepper, sliced

Directions:
1. In a food processor, merge chickpeas, lemon juice, and tahini, 2 tablespoons of the olive oil, the cumin, and water.
2. Process on high speed until blended for about 30 seconds. Scoop the hummus into a bowl and drizzle with the remaining tablespoon of olive oil. Dust with paprika and serve with sliced bell peppers.

Nutrition:
Calories: 427 Carbohydrates: 67.5g Proteins: 14.2g Fat: 14.6g

- 1 teaspoon smoked paprika, or regular paprika
- 1 teaspoon onion powder
- 1/2 teaspoon garlic powder

Directions:
1. Preheat the oven to 400F.
2. Set the chickpeas with all the other ingredients and spread them out on a baking sheet.
3. Bake for 20-25 minutes, tossing halfway through.

4. Bake these at a lower temperature until fully dried and crispy if you want to keep them longer.

Nutrition:

546. Savory Seed Crackers

Preparation time: 5 minutes
Cooking time: 50 minutes
Servings: 5
Ingredients:

- 3/4 cup pumpkin seeds (pepitas)
- 1/2 cup sunflower seeds
- 1/2 cup sesame seeds
- 1/4 cup chia seeds
- 1 teaspoon minced garlic (about 1 clove)
- 1 teaspoon tamari or soy sauce
- 1 teaspoon vegan Worcestershire sauce
- 1/2 teaspoon ground cayenne pepper
- 1/2 teaspoon dried oregano
- 1/2 cup water

Directions:

1. Preheat the oven to 325F.

547. Tomato and Basil Bruschetta

Preparation time: 10 minutes
Cooking time: 6 minutes
Servings: 12
Ingredients:

- 3 tomatoes, chopped
- 1/4 cup chopped fresh basil
- 1 tablespoon extra-virgin olive oil
- pinch of sea salt
- 1 baguette, cut into 12 slices
- 1 garlic clove, sliced in half

Directions:

548. Refried Bean and Salsa Quesadillas

Preparation time: 5 minutes
Cooking time: 6 minutes
Servings: 4
Ingredients:

- 1 tbsp. canola oil, plus more for frying
- 11/2 cups cooked pinto beans, drained and mashed
- 1 teaspoon chili powder
- 4 (10-inch) whole-wheat flour tortillas
- 1 cup tomato salsa, homemade or store-bought
- 1/2 cup minced red onion (optional)

Directions:

1. In a medium saucepan, warmth the oil over medium heat. Add the mashed beans and chili

549. Jicama and Guacamole

Preparation time: 15 minutes
Cooking time: 0 minutes
Servings: 4
Ingredients:

- juice of 1 lime, or 1 tbsp. prepared lime juice
- 2 hash avocados, peeled, pits removed, and cut into cubes
- 1/2 teaspoon sea salt
- 1/2 red onion, minced

Calories: 121 Fat: 2g Carbohydrates: 20g Fiber: 6g Proteins: 8g

2. Set a rimmed baking sheet with parchment paper.
3. In a large bowl, combine the pumpkin seeds, sunflower seeds, sesame seeds, chia seeds, garlic, tamari, Worcestershire sauce, cayenne, oregano, and water.
4. Bring to the prepared baking sheet and spread it out to all sides.
5. Bake for 25 minutes. Detach the pan from the oven and flip the seed "dough" over so the wet side is up. Bake for another 20-25 minutes until the sides are browned.
6. Cool completely before breaking up into 20 pieces. Divide evenly among 4 glass jars and close tightly with lids.

Nutrition:
Calories: 339 Fat: 29g Proteins: 14g Carbohydrates: 17g Fiber: 8g

1. In a small bowl, merge the tomatoes, basil, olive oil, and salt and stir to mix. Set aside. Preheat the oven to 425F.
2. Bring the baguette slices in a single layer on a baking sheet and toast in the oven until brown for about 6 minutes.
3. Flip the bread slices over once during cooking. Detach from the oven and rub the bread on both sides with the sliced clove of garlic.
4. Top with the tomato-basil mixture and serve immediately.

Nutrition:
Calories: 288 Fat: 11.11g Carbohydrates: 45.3g Proteins: 4.4g

powder and cook, stirring, until hot, about 5 minutes. Set aside.

2. To assemble, place 1 tortilla on a work surface and spoon about 1/4cup of the beans across the bottom half. Top the beans with the salsa and onion, if using. Fold top half of the tortilla over the filling and press slightly.
3. In large skillet heat a thin layer of oil over medium heat. Place folded quesadillas, 1 or 2 at a time, into the hot skillet and heat, turning once, about 1 minute per side.
4. Cut quesadillas into 3 or 4 wedges and arrange on plates. Serve immediately.

Nutrition:
Calories: 253 Fat: 13g Proteins: 31g Fiber: 0g Carbohydrates: 3g

- 1 garlic clove, minced
- 1/4 cup chopped cilantro (optional)
- 1 jicama bulb, peeled and cut into matchsticks

Directions:

1. In a medium bowl, squeeze the lime juice over the top of the avocado and sprinkle with salt.
2. Lightly mash the avocado with a fork. Stir in the onion, garlic, and cilantro, if using.

3. Serve with slices of jicama to dip in guacamole. To store, set plastic wrap over the bowl of guacamole and refrigerate. The guacamole will keep for about 2 days.

550. Sesame- Wonton Crisps

Preparation time: 10 minutes
Cooking time: 10 minutes
Servings: 12
Ingredients:
- 12 Vegan Wonton Wrappers
- 2 tablespoons toasted sesame oil
- 12 shiitake mushrooms
- 4 snow peas
- 1 teaspoon soy sauce
- 1 tablespoon fresh lime juice
- 1/2 teaspoon brown sugar
- 1 medium carrot
- Toasted sesame seeds or black sesame seeds

Directions:

551. Macadamia-Cashew Patties

Preparation time: 10 minutes
Cooking time: 10 minutes
Servings: 4
Ingredients:
- 3/4 cup chopped macadamia nuts
- 3/4 cup chopped cashews
- 1 medium carrot, grated
- 1 small onion, chopped
- 1 garlic clove, minced
- 1 jalapeño or another green chili, seedless and minced
- 3/4 cup old-fashioned oats
- 3/4 cup dry unseasoned breadcrumbs
- 2 tablespoons minced fresh cilantro
- 1/2 teaspoon ground coriander
- Salt and freshly ground black pepper
- 2 teaspoons fresh lime juice

552. Lemon Coconut Cilantro Rolls

Preparation time: 30 minutes
Cooking time: 30 minutes
Servings: 16
Ingredients:
- 1/2 cup fresh cilantro
- 1 cup sprouts
- 1 garlic clove, pressed
- 2 tbsp. ground Brazil nuts or almonds
- 2 tbsp. flaked coconut
- 1 tbsp. coconut oil
- Pinch cayenne pepper
- Pinch of salt
- Pinch of ground black pepper
- Zest and juice of 1 lemon
- 2 tbsp. ground flaxseed

553. Stuffed Cherry Tomatoes

Preparation time: 15 minutes
Cooking time: 0 minutes
Servings: 6

Nutrition:
Calories: 379 Fat: 5g Carbohydrates: 66g Fiber: 4g Proteins: 17g

1. Preheat the oven to 350F. Set oil a baking sheet and set aside. Garnish the wonton wrappers with 1 tablespoon of the sesame oil and arrange on the baking sheet. Bake until golden brown and crisp. Set aside to cool.
2. In a large skillet, heat the extra olive oil over medium heat. Add the mushrooms and cook until softened. Set in the snow peas and the soy sauce and cook for 30 seconds. Set aside to cool.
3. In a large bowl, merge the lime juice, sugar, and remaining 1 tbsp. sesame oil. Set in the carrot and cooled shiitake mixture.
4. Set each wonton crisp with a spoonful of the shiitake mixture. Dust with sesame seeds and arrange on a platter to serve.

Nutrition:
Calories: 388 Fat: 19g Carbohydrates: 45g Fiber: 12g

- Canola or grape seed oil, for frying
- 4 sandwich rolls
- Lettuce leaves and condiment of choice

Directions:
1. In a food processor, merge the macadamia nuts, cashews, carrot, onion, garlic, chili, oats, breadcrumbs, cilantro, coriander, and salt and pepper. Process until well mixed. Attach the lime juice and process until well blended. Taste, adjusting the seasonings if necessary. Shape the mixture into 4 equal patties.
2. In a large skillet, warmth a thin layer of oil over medium heat. Attach the patties and cook until golden brown on both sides, turning once, for about 10 minutes in total.
3. Serve with lettuce and condiments of choice.

Nutrition:
Calories: 364 Carbohydrates: 3.3g Fat: 4.9g Proteins: 8g

- 1 to 2 tbsp. water
- 2 whole-wheat wraps, or corn wraps

Directions:
1. Set everything but the wraps in a food processor and pulse to combine. Attach the water, if needed, to help the merge come together.
2. Spread the mixture out over each wrap, wrap it up, and place it in the fridge for 30 minutes to set.
3. Detach the rolls from the fridge and slice each into 8 pieces to serve as appetizers or sides with a soup.
4. Take the best flavor by buying whole raw Brazil nuts or almonds, toasting them lightly in a dry skillet or toaster oven, then grinding them in a coffee grinder.

Nutrition:
Calories: 66 Fat: 4g Carbohydrates: 6g Fiber: 1g Proteins: 2g

Ingredients:
- 2 pints cherry tomatoes, tops detached, and centers scooped out

- 2 avocados, mashed
- juice of 1 lemon
- 1/2 red bell pepper
- 4 green onions finely minced
- 1 tbsp. fresh tarragon
- salt

Directions:

554. Spicy Black Bean Dip

Preparation time: 10 minutes
Cooking time: 0 minutes
Servings: 2
Ingredients:

- 1 (14-ounce) can black beans, drained and washed, or 11/2 cups cooked
- Zest and juice of 1 lime
- 1 tablespoon tamari or soy sauce
- 1/4 cup water
- 1/4 cup fresh cilantro
- 1 teaspoon ground cumin

555. French Onion Pastry Puffs

Preparation time: 10 minutes
Cooking time: 35 minutes
Servings: 24
Ingredients:

- 2 tablespoons extra-virgin olive oil
- 2 medium sweet yellow onions
- 1 garlic clove, minced
- 1 tsp. chopped fresh rosemary
- Salt and freshly ground black pepper
- 1 tbsp. capers
- 1 sheet frozen vegan puff pastry, thawed
- 18 pitted black olives, quartered

Directions:

1. In a medium skillet, warmth the oil over medium heat. Attach the onions and garlic, season with

556. Cheesy Cashew–Roasted Red Pepper Toasts

Preparation time: 15 minutes
Cooking time: 0 minutes
Servings: 16-24
Ingredients:

- 2 jarred roasted red peppers
- 1 cup unsalted cashews
- 1/4 cup water
- 1 tablespoon soy sauce
- 2 tablespoons chopped green onions
- 1/4 cup nutritional yeast
- 2 tbsp. balsamic vinegar
- 2 tbsp. olive oil

Directions:

1. Set canapé or cookie cutters to cut the bread into desired shapes about 2 inches wide. Roast the bread and set aside to cool.

557. Baked Potato Chips

Preparation time: 10 minutes
Cooking time: 30 minutes
Servings: 4
Ingredients:

- 1 large Russet potato
- 1 teaspoon paprika

1. Set the cherry tomatoes open-side up on a platter. In a small bowl, merge the avocado, lemon juice, bell pepper, scallions, tarragon, and salt.
2. Stir until well -merged. Set into the cherry tomatoes and serve immediately.

Nutrition:
Calories: 621 Fat: 19.6g Carbohydrate: 82.7g

- Pinch cayenne pepper

Directions:

1. Set the beans in a food processor (best choice) or blender, along with the lime zest and juice, tamari, and about 1/4 cup of water.
2. Blend and then merge in the cilantro, cumin, and cayenne.

Nutrition:
Calories: 190 Fat: 1g Carbohydrates: 35g Fiber: 12g Proteins: 13g

rosemary, salt and pepper. Secure and cook until very soft, stirring occasionally for about 20 minutes. Stir in the capers and set aside.
2. Preheat the oven to 400F. Wrap out the puff pastry and cut into 2- to 3-inch circles using a lightly floured pastry cutter or drinking glass.
3. Set the pastry circles on baking sheets and top each with a heaping teaspoon of onion mixture, patting down to smooth the top.
4. Set with 3 olive quarters, arranged decoratively—either like flower petals emanating from the center or parallel to each other like 3 bars.
5. Bake for about 15 minutes. Serve hot.

Nutrition:
Calories: 126 Fat: 4g Carbohydrates: 4g Proteins: 13g

2. Coarsely chop 1 red pepper and reserved. Divide the remaining pepper into thin strips or decorative shapes and set aside for garnish.
3. In a blender, merge the cashews to a fine powder. Attach the water and soy sauce and process until smooth. Attach the chopped red pepper and purée. Attach the green onions, nutritional yeast, vinegar, and oil and process until smooth and well blended.
4. Set a spoonful of the pepper mixture onto each of the toasted bread pieces and top decoratively with the reserved pepper strips. Set on a platter or tray and serve.

Nutrition:
Calories: 189 Fat: 3g Carbohydrates: 4g Proteins: 3g

- 1/2 teaspoon garlic salt
- 1/4 teaspoon vegan sugar
- 1/4 teaspoon onion powder
- 1/4 tsp. chipotle powder or chili powder
- 1/8 teaspoon salt

- 1/8 teaspoon ground mustard
- 1/8 teaspoon ground cayenne pepper
- 1 teaspoon canola oil
- 1/8 tsp. liquid smoke

Directions:
1. Wash and peel the potato. Cut into thin, 1/10-inch slices.
2. Set a large bowl with enough very cold water to cover the potato. Set the potato slices to the bowl and soak for 20 minutes.
3. Warmth the oven to 400F. Set a baking sheet with parchment paper.
4. In a small bowl, merge the paprika, garlic salt, sugar, onion powder, chipotle powder, salt, mustard, and cayenne.
5. Drain and wash the potato slices and pat dry with a paper towel.
6. Transfer to a large bowl.
7. Attach the canola oil, liquid smoke, and spice mixture to the bowl. Toss to coat.
8. Set the potatoes to the prepared baking sheet.
9. Bake for 15 minutes. Bend the chips over and bake for 15 minutes longer until browned.
10. Set the chips to 4 storage containers or large glass jars.
11. Let it cool before closing the lids tightly.

Nutrition:
Calories: 89 Fat: 1g Proteins: 2g Carbohydrates: 18g Fiber: 2g

558. Mushrooms Stuffed with Spinach and Walnuts

Preparation time: 10 minutes
Cooking time: 6 minutes
Servings: 4-6
Ingredients:
- 2 tablespoons extra-virgin olive oil
- 8 ounces white mushroom, lightly washed, patted dry, and stems set aside
- 1 garlic clove, minced
- 1 cup cooked spinach
- 1 cup finely chopped walnuts
- 1/2 cup unseasoned dry breadcrumbs
- Salt and freshly ground black pepper

Directions:

1. Preheat the oven to 400F. Set oil on a baking pan and set aside. In a skillet, warmth the oil over medium heat. Attach the mushroom caps and cook to soften slightly. Detach from the skillet and set aside.
2. Cut the mushroom stems and attach to the same skillet. Attach the garlic and cook until softened. Swirl in the spinach, walnuts, breadcrumbs, and salt and pepper to taste. Cook, stirring well to combine.
3. Set the reserved mushroom caps with the stuffing mixture and set in the baking pan. Bake the mushrooms are tender and the filling is hot. Serve hot.

Nutrition:
Calories: 126 Fat: 4g Carbohydrates: 4g Proteins: 13g

559. Salsa Fresca

Preparation time: 15 minutes
Cooking time: 0 minute
Servings: 4
Ingredients:
- 3 large tomatoes or other fresh tomatoes, sliced
- 1/2 red onion, finely sliced
- 1/2 bunch cilantro
- 2 garlic cloves, minced
- 1 jalapeño, minced
- Juice of 1 lime, or 1 tbsp. prepared lime juice
- 1/4 cup extra-virgin olive oil
- Sea salt
- Whole-grain tortilla chips, for serving

Directions:
1. In a small bowl, merge the tomatoes, onion, cilantro, garlic, jalapeño, lime juice, and olive oil and mix well. Allow to sit. Season with salt.
2. Serve with tortilla chips.

Nutrition:
Calories: 219 Fat: 12g Carbohydrates: 2g Proteins: 5g

560. Guacamole

Preparation time: 10 minutes
Cooking time: 0 minutes
Servings: 2
Ingredients:
- 2 avocados
- 2 garlic cloves
- Zest and juice of 1 lime
- 1 teaspoon ground cumin
- Pinch of salt
- Pinch freshly ground black pepper
- Pinch cayenne pepper (optional)

Directions:
1. Mash the avocados in a large bowl. Attach the rest of the ingredients and stir to merge.
2. You may try adding diced tomatoes (cherry are divine), sliced scallions or chives, minced fresh cilantro or basil, lemon rather than lime, paprika, or whatever you think would taste good!

Nutrition:
Calories: 258 Fat: 22g Carbohydrates: 18g Fiber: 11g Proteins: 4g

561. Veggie Hummus Pinwheels

Preparation time: 10 minutes
Cooking time: 0 minutes
Servings: 3
Ingredients:
- 3 whole-grain, spinach, flour, or gluten-free tortillas
- 3 large Swiss chard leaves
- 3/4 cup Edamame Hummus or prepared hummus
- 3/4 cup shredded carrots

Directions:
1. Set 1 tortilla on a cutting board.

2. Set 1 Swiss chard leaf over the tortilla. Spill 1/4 cup of hummus over the Swiss chard. Spread 1/4 cup of carrots over the hummus. Starting at one end of the tortilla, wrap tightly toward the opposite side.
3. Slice each roll up into 6 pieces. Place in a single-serving storage container.

562. Asian Lettuce Rolls

Preparation time: 15 minutes
Cooking time: 5 minutes
Servings: 4
Ingredients:

- 2 ounces rice noodles
- 2 tablespoons chopped Thai basil
- 2 tablespoons chopped cilantro
- 1 garlic clove, minced
- 1 tablespoon minced fresh ginger
- juice of 1/2 lime, or 2 tsp. prepared lime juice
- 2 tablespoons soy sauce
- 1 cucumber, julienned

563. Lemon and Garlic Marinated Mushrooms

Preparation time: 15 minutes
Cooking time: 0 minutes
Servings: 4
Ingredients:

- 3 tablespoons extra-virgin olive oil
- 2 tablespoons fresh lemon juice
- 2 garlic cloves, crushed
- 1 teaspoon dried marjoram
- 1/2 teaspoon coarsely ground fennel seed
- 1/2 teaspoon salt
- 1/4 teaspoon freshly ground black pepper
- 8 ounces small white mushrooms, lightly rinsed, patted dry, and stemmed

564. Pinto-Pecan Fireballs

Preparation time: 5 minutes
Cooking time: 30 minutes
Servings: 24
Ingredients:

- 1-1/2 cups cooked or 1 (15.5-ounce) can pinto beans, drained and rinsed
- 1/2cup chopped pecans
- 1/4 cup green onions
- 1 garlic clove
- 3 tbsp. wheat gluten flour (vital wheat gluten)
- 3 tablespoons unseasoned dry breadcrumbs
- 4 tablespoons Tabasco or other hot sauce
- 1/4 teaspoon salt
- 1/8 teaspoon ground cayenne
- 1/4 cup vegan margarine

Directions:

565. Sweet Potato Biscuits

Preparation time: 60 minutes
Cooking time: 10 minutes
Servings: 12
Ingredients:

- 1 medium sweet potato
- 3 tablespoons melted coconut oil, divided
- 1 tablespoon maple syrup

4. Redo with the remaining tortillas and filling and seal the lids.

Nutrition:
Calories: 254 Fat: 8g Proteins: 10g Carbohydrates: 39g Fiber: 8g

- 2 carrots, peeled and julienned
- 8 leaves butter lettuce

Directions:
1. Cook the rice noodle.
2. In a small bowl, set together the basil, cilantro, garlic, ginger, lime juice, and soy sauce. Set with the cooked noodles, cucumber, and carrots.
3. Set the mixture evenly among lettuce leaves and wrap.
4. Secure with a toothpick and serve immediately.

Nutrition:
Calories: 210 Fat: 7g Carbohydrates: 5g Proteins: 18g

- 1 tablespoon minced fresh parsley

Directions:
1. Cook the rice noodles.
2. In a small bowl, spill together the basil, cilantro, garlic, ginger, lime juice, and soy sauce. Set with the cooked noodles, cucumber, and carrots.
3. Set the mixture evenly among lettuce leaves and roll.
4. Serve immediately.

Nutrition:
Calories: 661 Fat: 68g Carbohydrates: 7g Fiber: 2g Proteins: 4g

1. Preheat the oven to 350F. Set oil a 9 x 13-inch baking pan and set aside. Blot the absorbed beans well with a paper towel. In a food processor, merge the pinto beans, pecans, green onions, garlic, flour, breadcrumbs, and 2 tablespoons of tabasco, salt, and cayenne. Pulse until well merged, leaving some texture. Set your hands to roll the mixture firmly into 1-inch balls.
2. Set the balls in the prepared baking pan and bake until nicely browned.
3. Meanwhile, in small saucepan, merge the remaining 2 tbsp. tabasco and the margarine and melt over low heat. Spill the sauce over the fireballs and bake 10 minutes. Serve immediately.

Nutrition:
Calories: 322 Fat: 23.7g Carbohydrates: 8.1g Proteins: 21.6g

- 1 cup whole-wheat flour
- 2 teaspoons baking powder
- Pinch sea salt

Directions:
1. Bake the sweet potato at 350F until tender.
2. Allow it to cool, and then detach the flesh and mash.

3. Turn the oven up to 375F and line a baking sheet with parchment paper or lightly grease it. Set out 1 cup potato flesh.
4. In a medium bowl, merge the mashed sweet potato with 11/2 tablespoons of the coconut oil and the maple syrup. Merge together the flour and baking powder in a separate bowl, then attach the flour mixture to the potato mixture and merge.
5. On a floured board, set the mixture out into a 1/2-inch-thick circle and cut out 1-inch rounds, or

566. Garlic Toast

Preparation time: 5 minutes
Cooking time: 5 minutes
Servings: 1
Ingredients:

- 1 tsp. coconut oil, or extra-virgin olive oil
- Pinch sea salt
- 1 to 2 teaspoons nutritional yeast
- 1 small garlic clove, pressed, or 1/4 teaspoon garlic powder
- 1 slice whole-grain bread

Directions:

567. Vietnamese-Style Lettuce Rolls

Preparation time: 15 minutes
Cooking time: 0 minutes
Servings: 4
Ingredients:

- 2 green onions
- 2 tablespoons soy sauce
- 2 tablespoons rice vinegar
- 1 teaspoon sugar
- 1/8 teaspoon crushed red pepper
- 3 tablespoons water
- 3 ounces rice vermicelli
- 4 to 6 soft green leaf lettuce leaves
- 1 medium carrot, shredded
- 1/2medium English cucumber, peeled, seeded, and cut lengthwise into 1/4-inch strips
- 1/2 medium red bell pepper
- 1 cup loosely packed fresh cilantro or basil leaves

Directions:

568. Crispy Roasted Chickpeas

Preparation time: 5 minutes
Cooking time: 20 minutes
Servings: 1
Ingredients:

- 1 (14-ounce / 397-g) can chickpeas, rinsed and drained, or 11/2 cups cooked
- 2 tablespoons tamari or soy sauce
- 1 tablespoon nutritional yeast
- 1 teaspoon onion powder
- 1 teaspoon paprika
- 1/2 teaspoon garlic powder

569. Easy Baked Sweet Potato Fries

Preparation time: 10 minutes
Cooking time: 20 minutes
Servings: 4
Ingredients:

- 1 medium sweet potato, peel off and cut into thin sticks

simply drop spoonsful of dough and pat them into rounds.

6. Set the rounds onto the prepared baking sheet. Garnish the top of each with some of the remaining 11/2 tablespoons of melted coconut oil. Bake until lightly golden on top. Serve hot.

Nutrition:
Calories: 116 Fat: 4g Carbohydrates: 19g Fiber: 3g Proteins: 3g

1. In a small bowl, merge together the oil, salt, nutritional yeast, and garlic.
2. You can either toast the bread and spread it with the seasoned oil or brush the oil on the bread and set it in a toaster oven to bake for 5 minutes.
3. If you're using fresh garlic, it's best to spread it onto the bread, and then bake it.

Nutrition:
Calories: 138 Fat: 6g Carbohydrates: 16g Fiber: 4g Proteins: 7g

1. Cut the green part off the green onions and cut them lengthwise into thin slices, then set them aside. Set the white part of the green onions and transfer to a small bowl. Add the soy sauce, rice vinegar, sugar, crushed red pepper, and water. Stir to blend and set aside.
2. Soak the vermicelli in medium bowl of hot water until softened. Drain the noodles well and slice them into 3-inch lengths. Set aside.
3. Place a lettuce leaf on a work surface and arrange a row of noodles in the center of the leaf, followed by a few strips of scallion greens, carrot, cucumber, bell pepper, and cilantro. Bring the bottom edge of the leaf over the filling and fold in the two short sides. Roll up gently but tightly. Repeat with remaining ingredients. Serve with the dipping sauce.

Nutrition:
Calories: 318 Carbohydrates: 68g Fiber: 8g Proteins: 9g

Directions:
1. Preheat the oven to 400F.
2. Set the chickpeas with all the other ingredients and spread them out on a baking sheet.
3. Roast in the warmth oven for 20 to 25 minutes, tossing the chickpeas halfway through the cooking time.
4. Let rest before serving.

Nutrition:
Calories: 124 Fat: 10.3g Carbohydrates: 5.1g Proteins: 7.9g Fiber: 6.1g

- 1 teaspoon olive oil (optional)
- 1 teaspoon dried basil
- 1/4 teaspoon sea salt (optional)
- 1/2 teaspoon dried oregano

Directions:

1. Preheat the oven to 350F.
2. Toss the potato sticks with all the other ingredients and spread them out on a large baking sheet.
3. Bake flipping them halfway through the cooking time, or until crisp-tender.

570. Crisp Onion Rings

Preparation time: 5 minutes
Cooking time: 10 minutes
Servings: 2
Ingredients:

- 1 cup vegan breadcrumbs
- 1/2 teaspoon paprika
- 1/4 teaspoon garlic powder
- 1/4 teaspoon pink Himalayan salt (optional)
- 1/4 teaspoon freshly ground black pepper
- 3/4 cup water
- 1/2 cup whole wheat flour
- 2 large yellow onions

Directions:

571. Lentil Energy Bites

Preparation time: 15 minutes
Cooking time: 20 minutes
Servings: 9
Ingredients:

- 1 cup water
- 1/2 cup lentils, rinsed and drained
- 2 cups quick-cooking oats
- 1/2 cup dairy-free chocolate chips
- 1/4 cup raw shelled hemp seeds
- 1/4 cup sunflower seed kernels
- 1/4 cup unsweetened shredded coconut
- 1/2 cup maple syrup (optional)
- 1/2 cup almond butter

Directions:

572. Crunchy Maple Granola

Preparation time: 5 minutes
Cooking time: 25 minutes
Servings: 4
Ingredients:

- 2 cups rolled oats
- 1 cup maple syrup (optional)
- 1/4 cup chopped almonds
- 1/4 cup chopped walnuts
- 1/4 cup chopped pecans
- 2 tablespoons pumpkin seeds
- 2 tablespoons sunflower seeds
- 1 tablespoon hemp seeds
- 1 teaspoon vanilla extract

573. Lemony Edamame

Preparation time: 5 minutes
Cooking time: 5 minutes
Servings: 2
Ingredients:

- 2 tablespoons freshly squeezed lemon juice
- Zest of 1 lemon
- 1/4 teaspoon freshly ground black pepper
- 1/8 teaspoon pink Himalayan salt (optional)
- 2 cups edamame, unshelled

Directions:

4. Cool for 5 minutes before serving.

Nutrition:
Calories: 259 Fat: 22.3g Carbohydrates: 18.3g Proteins: 4.6g Fiber: 11.1g

1. Preheat the oven to 400F. Line a baking sheet with parchment paper.
2. Combine the breadcrumbs, paprika, garlic powder, salt (if desired), and pepper in a bowl.
3. In another bowl, whisk the water and flour to combine.
4. Dip each onion ring in the flour, then coat in the bread crumb mixture. Arrange the coated onion rings on the prepared baking sheet.
5. Bake until lightly browned.
6. Serve immediately.

Nutrition:
Calories: 328 Fat: 1.1g Carbohydrates: 72.6g Proteins: 10.2g Fiber: 8.0g

1. Combine the water and lentils in a large saucepan and bring to a boil over high heat.
2. Cook for 20 to 25 minutes until the lentils are softened. All the water should be absorbed. Set aside to cool.
3. Mix the oats, chocolate chips, hemp seeds, sunflower seeds, and coconut in a large bowl. Stir in the cooled lentils. Whisk in the maple syrup (if desired) and almond butter until combined. Shape the mixture into thirty-six balls and place in a glass container with a lid.
4. Let sit in the refrigerator. Serve immediately.

Nutrition:
Calories: 245 Fat: 12.9g Carbohydrates: 25.6g Proteins: 6.8g Fiber: 3.6g

Directions:

1. Preheat the oven to 350F. Line a baking sheet with parchment paper.
2. Set together all the ingredients in a bowl until completely mixed.
3. Spread out the mixture on the prepared baking sheet and bake for 25 minutes, stirring the granola halfway through, or until lightly browned.
4. Detach from the oven and let cool for 5 to 10 minutes before serving.

Nutrition:
Calories: 557 Fat: 21.5g Carbohydrates: 85.6g Proteins: 11.2g Fiber: 7.1g

1. Combine the lemon juice, lemon zest, pepper, and salt (if desired) in a small bowl. Set aside.
2. Steam the edamame for 5 minutes. Detach from the heat and place in a large bowl.
3. Pour the lemon mixture over the edamame and toss until fully coated. Serve warm.

Nutrition:
Calories: 368 Fat: 15.1g Carbohydrates: 29.6g Proteins: 30.2g Fiber: 9.2g

574. Apple Nachos
Preparation time: 10 minutes
Cooking time: 0 minutes
Servings: 4
Ingredients:

- 1 cup pitted Medjool dates
- 1/2 cup unsweetened plant-based milk
- 1 teaspoon vanilla extract
- 1/8 teaspoon pink Himalayan salt (optional)
- 4 Granny Smith apples cut into 1/4-inch slices
- 1/4 cup chopped pecans
- 2 tablespoons vegan dark chocolate chips
- 1 teaspoon hemp seeds

Directions:

1. Press the dates in a food processor until they resemble a paste. Add the milk, vanilla, and salt (if desired), and pulse until smooth. Set aside.
2. On a plate, lay out 1 sliced apple (use 1 apple per serving on individual plates). Drizzle 1 tablespoon of the date sauce over the apple. Top with 1 tablespoon of chopped pecans, 1/2 tablespoon of chocolate chips, and finish with 1/4 teaspoon of hemp seeds. Repeat with the remaining apples and toppings.
3. Serve immediately.

Nutrition:
Calories: 319 Fat: 8.6g Carbohydrates: 65.1g Proteins: 3.2g Fiber: 10.1g

575. Homemade Soft Pretzels
Preparation time: 15 minutes
Cooking time: 25 minutes
Servings: 8
Ingredients:

- 21/4 teaspoons active dry yeast
- 1 tablespoon coconut sugar (optional)
- 11/2 cups warm water
- 21/2 cups whole wheat flour
- 1/4 cup vital wheat gluten
- 10 cups water
- 2/3 cup baking soda
- Pink Himalayan salt (optional)

Directions:

1. Stir the yeast and sugar (if desired) into the warm water and let sit for 10 to 15 minutes.
2. Combine the flour and wheat gluten in a large bowl. Attach the yeast mixture and stir until well incorporated.
3. Knead the dough by hand for 5 minutes. Set the dough into a ball and place it in a clean bowl. Cover and sit for 50 to 60 minutes to allow the dough to rise.
4. Preheat the oven to 450F. Set a baking sheet with parchment paper and set aside.
5. Remove the dough from the bowl and cut it into 8 equal pieces. Roll the pieces into ropes, about 15 to 18 inches long. Shape the ropes into pretzels.
6. Pour the water into a pot over high heat and add the baking soda. Bring to a boil and cook each pretzel, one at a time, for 30 to 45 seconds.
7. Set the pretzels on the prepared baking sheet and bake for 12 to 14 minutes, or until lightly browned.
8. Season with salt, if desired. Serve warm.

Nutrition:
Calories: 159 Fat: 1.7g Carbohydrates: 31.3g Proteins: 7.2g Fiber: 5.1g

576. Chocolate and Almond Balls
Preparation time: 10 minutes
Cooking time: 0 minutes
Servings: 3
Ingredients:

- 1 cup almonds
- 11/2 tablespoons cocoa powder
- 1 tablespoon maple syrup (optional)
- 1/8 teaspoon pink Himalayan salt (optional)
- 10 Medjool dates, pitted and chopped

Directions:

1. Set the almonds in a food processor until they become a rough, grainy powder. Add the remaining ingredients and process until smoothly blended.
2. Shape the mixture into 11/2-inch balls with your hands and serve. You can store the balls in the refrigerator for up to 7 days.

Nutrition:
Calories: 518 Fat: 24.3g Carbohydrates: 75.8g Proteins: 12.2g Fiber: 11.8g

577. Five-Minute Almond Butter Bites
Preparation time: 5 minutes
Cooking time: 0 minutes
Servings: 9
Ingredients:

- 1/2 cup almond or peanut butter
- 1/2 cup rolled oats
- 3 tablespoons maple syrup (optional)
- 1/4 cup ground chia seeds
- 1 tablespoon pumpkin seeds
- 1 tablespoon ground flaxseed

Directions:

1. Bring all the ingredients in a food processor until very small bits of the seeds are still visible.
2. Set the mixture into small balls with your hands. Serve immediately.

Nutrition:
Calories: 156 Fat: 10.5g Carbohydrates: 13.3g Proteins: 6.2g Fiber: 4.1g

578. Peanut Butter Snack Squares
Preparation time: 10 minutes
Cooking time: 20 minutes
Servings: 8
Ingredients:

- 1 cup creamy peanut butter
- 1/2 cup coconut sugar (optional)
- 1 teaspoon vanilla extract
- 1/4 cup garbanzo flour

- 3/4 cup whole wheat flour
- 1 teaspoon baking soda
- 1/2 teaspoon baking powder
- 1 cup old-fashioned oats
- 1/2 cup unsweetened plant-based milk
- 1/2 cup pitted and chopped small dates
- 1/2 cup peanuts

Directions:
1. Warmth the oven to 350F. Lightly grease a baking dish and reserve.
2. Mix the peanut butter and sugar (if desired) with a hand or stand mixer on medium speed for 5 minutes. Fold in the vanilla.

579. Simple Showtime Popcorn

Preparation time: 1 minute
Cooking time: 5 minutes
Servings: 2
Ingredients:
- 1/4 cup popcorn kernels
- 1 tablespoon nutritional yeast
- 1/4 teaspoon onion powder
- 1/4 teaspoon garlic powder

Directions:
1. Set the popcorn kernels in a paper lunch bag, folding over the top of the bag so the kernels won't spill out.

580. Spinach and Artichoke Dip

Preparation time: 15 minutes
Cooking time: 25 minutes
Servings: 6
Ingredients:
- 2 cups chopped cauliflower
- 3 garlic cloves, crushed
- 1 cup cashews, set in hot water for at least 1 hour
- 1/2 cup water
- 2 teaspoons Dijon mustard
- 2 teaspoons freshly squeezed lemon juice
- 2 teaspoons pink Himalayan salt (optional)
- 1 1/2 teaspoons red pepper flakes
- 1 1/2 teaspoons freshly ground black pepper
- 1 teaspoon white vinegar
- 1 cup frozen spinach, thawed and drained
- 1 (14-ounce / 397-g) can artichoke hearts, drained and chopped

581. Roasted Red Pepper Hummus

Preparation time: 20 minutes
Cooking time: 0 minutes
Servings: 8
Ingredients:
- 1 (15-ounce / 425-g) can chickpeas, 3 tablespoons aquafaba (chickpea liquid from the can) reserved, remaining liquid drained, and rinsed
- 1/4 cup tahini
- 1 tablespoon freshly squeezed lemon juice
- 1 teaspoon paprika
- 1/2 teaspoon ground cumin
- 1/4 teaspoon freshly ground black pepper
- 2 garlic cloves, peeled and stemmed
- 2 roasted red peppers

3. Attach the flours, baking soda, and baking powder and mix on medium speed. Add the oats and mix for a few seconds until stiff. Whisk in the milk until just incorporated. Fold in the dates and peanuts and stir until well combined.
4. Lightly press the dough into the prepared dish. Bake until lightly golden brown.
5. Detach from the oven and place on a wire rack to cool. Cut into squares and serve.

Nutrition:
Calories: 420 Fat: 22.0g Carbohydrates: 41.3g Proteins: 14.7g Fiber: 7.2g

2. Microwave on high until you hear a pause of 2 seconds in between kernels popping.
3. Remove the bag from the microwave, and add the nutritional yeast, onion powder, and garlic powder. Bend the top of the bag back over and shake to thoroughly coat.
4. Pour into a bowl and serve immediately.

Nutrition:
Calories: 49 Fat: 2.1g Carbohydrates: 5.7g Proteins: 4.2g Fiber: 1.9g

Directions:
1. Preheat the oven to 350F.
2. In a pot, boil the chopped cauliflower and garlic in water for 10 minutes, or until the garlic is tender.
3. Remove from the heat, drain, and set aside to cool.
4. Once cooled, combine the cauliflower and garlic with the cashews, water, mustard, lemon juice, salt (if desired), red pepper flakes, black pepper, and vinegar in a food processor. Pulse until smooth.
5. Transfer the mixture to a bowl and attach the spinach and artichoke hearts, stirring well.
6. Set the mixture in a casserole dish and bake for 15 minutes, or until lightly browned on the top and edges.
7. Let rest for 5 minutes before serving.

Nutrition:
Calories: 263 Fat: 16.1g Carbohydrates: 24.6g Proteins: 10.2g Fiber: 6.1g

Directions:
1. Pour the chickpeas into a bowl and fill the bowl with water. Gently rub the chickpeas between your hands until you feel the skins coming off. Add more water to the bowl and let the skins float to the surface. Using your hand, scoop out the skins. Drain some of the water and repeat this step once more to remove as many of the chickpea skins as possible. Drain to remove all the water. Set the chickpeas aside.
2. In a food processor or high-speed blender, merge the reserved aquafaba, tahini, and lemon juice. Process for 2 minutes.

3. Add the paprika, cumin, black pepper, garlic, and red peppers. Purée until the red peppers are incorporated.
4. Add the chickpeas and blend for 2 to 3 minutes, or until the hummus is smooth.

582. Roasted Balsamic Beets

Preparation time: 8 minutes
Cooking time: 40 minutes
Servings: 4
Ingredients:

- 4 medium beets, peeled and diced
- 2 tablespoons balsamic vinegar
- 2 tablespoons olive oil (optional)
- 1/2 teaspoon salt (optional)
- 1/4 teaspoon freshly ground black pepper

Directions:

583. Sautéed Leeks and Tomatoes

Preparation time: 10 minutes
Cooking time: 10 minutes
Servings: 4
Ingredients:

- 3 leeks, white parts only
- 1 tablespoon olive oil (optional)
- 1 yellow onion, diced
- 4 Roma tomatoes, diced
- 1 tablespoon Dijon mustard
- Salt, to taste (optional)
- Freshly ground black pepper, to taste

Directions:

1. Divide the leeks lengthwise down the middle and wash very well to remove any dirt. Then cut them into 1/2-inch pieces.

584. Garlic Roasted Brussels sprouts

Preparation time: 10 minutes
Cooking time: 30 minutes
Servings: 5
Ingredients:

- 2 pounds (907 g) Brussels sprouts, halved
- 8 to 12 garlic cloves (1 head garlic), unpeeled
- 2 tablespoons olive oil (optional)
- 2 tablespoons balsamic vinegar
- 1/2 teaspoon salt (optional)

Directions:

1. Preheat the oven to 400F.

585. Tomato Garlic Swiss chard

Preparation time: 15 minutes
Cooking time: 10 minutes
Servings: 4
Ingredients:

- 1 bunch Swiss chard, about 18 ounces (510 g)
- 1 tablespoon olive oil (optional)
- 6 garlic cloves, diced
- 11/2 cups marinara sauce
- 1/2 teaspoon salt (optional)
- 1/4 teaspoon freshly ground black pepper

Directions:

1. Set the chard leaves from the stalks and finely dice the stalks. Slice the leaves into thin strips. (Keep the stalks and leaves separate.)

5. Serve chilled.

Nutrition:
Calories: 100 Fat: 5.1g Carbohydrates: 11.8g Proteins: 4.2g Fiber: 3.1g

1. Preheat the oven to 400F. Line a baking sheet with parchment paper.
2. Toss the beets with the olive oil (if desired), vinegar, salt (if desired), and black pepper in a medium bowl.
3. Set the beets on the prepared baking sheet and roast for 40 minutes until fork-tender.
4. Cool for 5 minutes before serving.

Nutrition:
Calories: 178 Fat: 8.1g Carbohydrates: 21.3g Proteins: 3.9g Fiber: 5.2g

2. Heat the olive oil (if desired) in a saucepan over medium heat until it shimmers.
3. Add the onion and sauté for 2 minutes until translucent.
4. Attach the leeks, stir, and cook for 5 minutes, stirring occasionally.
5. Stir in the tomatoes, mustard, salt (if desired), and pepper. Continue to cook, stirring occasionally, or until the tomatoes have broken down a little.
6. Serve warm.

Nutrition:
Calories: 168 Fat: 4.3g Carbohydrates: 28.9g Proteins: 4.2g Fiber: 5.1g

2. On a baking sheet, toss the Brussels sprouts and garlic cloves with the olive oil (if desired), vinegar, and salt (if desired) until well coated.
3. Roast in the warmth oven for 30 to 40 minutes, shaking the pan halfway through the cooking time, or until crisp.
4. Serve hot.

Nutrition:
Calories: 178 Fat: 8.6g Carbohydrates: 19.5g Proteins: 6.2g Fiber: 6.1g

2. Heat the olive oil (if desired) in a large, nonstick skillet over medium heat until shimmering.
3. Add the garlic and diced chard stalks and sauté for 2 to 3 minutes until slightly golden.
4. Add the chard leaves, stir, and cook for 3 minutes until they start to wilt.
5. Set in the marinara sauce and simmer for an additional 3 minutes, or until the leaves are fully cooked.
6. Season with salt and pepper, then serve.

Nutrition:
Calories: 128 Fat: 7.3g Carbohydrates: 10.8g Proteins: 4.2g Fiber: 3.2g

586. Buffalo Cauliflower

Preparation time: 10 minutes
Cooking time: 40 minutes
Servings: 4
Ingredients:

- 1/4 cup plus 2 tbsp. olive oil, divided (optional)
- 4 garlic cloves, roughly chopped
- 6 red chills, such as cayenne, roughly chopped (more if you like it super spicy)
- 1 yellow onion, roughly chopped
- 1 cup water
- 1/2 cup apple cider vinegar
- 1/2 teaspoon salt (optional)
- 1/2 teaspoon freshly ground black pepper
- 1 head cauliflower, cut into florets

Directions:

1. In a nonstick sauté pan, heat 1/4 cup of olive oil (if desired) over medium-high heat.
2. Once hot, add the garlic, chiles, and onion. Cook for 5 minutes, stirring occasionally, until the onions are golden brown.
3. Attach the water and bring to a boil. Let this cook for about 10 minutes until the water has almost evaporated.

4. Preheat the oven to 450F. Set a baking sheet with foil or parchment paper.
5. Spread the cauliflower florets in a single layer on the prepared baking sheet.
6. Transfer the cooked garlic mixture to a food processor or blender and blend briefly to combine.
7. Add the vinegar, salt (if desired), and pepper. Blend again for 30 seconds.
8. Using a fine-mesh sieve, strain the sauce into a bowl. Set a spoon or spatula to scrape and press all the liquid from the pulp.
9. Pour half of the sauce over the cauliflower florets and toss to coat.
10. Set the remaining sauce to an airtight container and refrigerate until ready to serve.
11. Place the cauliflower in the oven and bake for 15 minutes. Remove from the oven, drizzle the remaining 2 tablespoons of olive oil (if desired) over the top, and stir. Set back to the oven to bake for 10 minutes more.
12. Serve the baked cauliflower with extra sauce, if desired.

Nutrition:
Calories: 234 Fat: 14.5g Carbohydrates: 19.3g Proteins: 7.2g Fiber: 14.1g

587. Skillet Asparagus with Caramelized Onion

Preparation time: 5 minutes
Cooking time: 15 minutes
Servings: 4
Ingredients:

- 1 tablespoon olive oil (optional)
- 1 medium yellow onion, sliced
- Pinch of salt (optional)
- 1 bunch asparagus, about 14 ounces (397 g), trimmed and cut in half
- Splash of vinegar, any variety

Directions:

1. In a large, nonstick sauté pan, warmth the olive oil (if desired) over medium-high heat.

2. Once hot, add the sliced onions and a pinch of salt (if desired). Cook for 10 minutes, stirring occasionally, until golden brown.
3. Add the asparagus to the pan with the onions. Cover and cook for another 5 minutes.
4. Set the heat off and add a splash of vinegar to deglaze the pan. As the vinegar sizzles, use a spatula to stir the onion and asparagus, scraping the browned bits from the bottom of the pan.
5. Serve warm.

Nutrition:
Calories: 153 Fat: 11.6g Carbohydrates: 10.2g Proteins: 3.2g Fiber: 3.1g

588. Simple Mustard Greens

Preparation time: 8 minutes
Cooking time: 18 minutes
Servings: 4-6
Ingredients:

- 4 pounds (1.8 kg) mustard greens, stemmed and washed
- 1 large onion, diced
- 2 cloves garlic, minced
- Sea salt, to taste (optional)
- Black pepper, to taste

Directions:

1. Set a pot of water to a boil, add the mustard greens in batches, and let them cook for 5 minutes.

2. Remove the greens from the water and transfer them to a large bowl with ice water to stop their cooking and help them keep their color.
3. Sauté the onion in a large skillet for 7 to 8 minutes over medium heat. Attach the water, 1 to 2 tablespoons, at a time to keep the onion from sticking.
4. Set the garlic and cook for another 1 minute. Add the greens and cook for 5 minutes. Season with salt (if desired) and pepper. Serve immediately.

Nutrition:
Calories: 170 Fat: 1.9g Carbohydrates: 25.1g Proteins: 13.4g Fiber: 15.2g

589. Creamy Green Beans with Mushrooms

Preparation time: 5 minutes
Cooking time: 15 minutes
Servings: 4
Ingredients:

- 1 small yellow onion, diced
- 3 or 4 garlic cloves, minced
- 1 cup vegetable broth, divided
- 1 cup sliced mushrooms
- 1 cup unsweetened plant-based milk
- 2 tablespoons nutritional yeast
- 2 tablespoons gluten-free flour
- 3 cups fresh green beans

- Pink Himalayan salt (optional)
- Freshly ground black pepper, to taste

Directions:
1. In a nonstick pan, sauté the onion and garlic in 1/4 cup of broth until the onion is softened.
2. Add the mushrooms, milk, remaining 3/4 cup of broth, flour, and nutritional yeast, whisking until there are no clumps.

590. Creamy Garlic Cauliflower Mashed Potatoes

Preparation time: 10 minutes
Cooking time: 24 minutes
Servings: 4
Ingredients:
- 5 medium yellow potatoes, chopped
- 3/4 cup unsweetened plant-based milk
- Pink Himalayan salt (optional)
- Freshly ground black pepper, to taste
- 1/2 medium cauliflower
- 6 garlic cloves, minced
- 1/4 cup vegetable broth

Directions:
1. In a pot, boil the potatoes for 15 minutes until soft.

591. Spicy Thai Vegetables

Preparation time: 10 minutes
Cooking time: 10 minutes
Servings: 2
Ingredients:
- 5 baby bok choy
- 5 broccoli florets
- 1/2 red bell pepper
- 1/2 cup edamame, shelled
- 1/4 cup rice vinegar
- 1/4 cup plus 1 tablespoon water
- 3 garlic cloves, minced
- 4 teaspoons red pepper flakes
- 1/2 tablespoon low-sodium soy sauce
- 1 tablespoon maple syrup (optional)
- 1/4 teaspoon garlic powder
- 1 teaspoon gluten-free flour

592. Cinnamon and Hemp Seed Coffee Shake

Preparation time: 5 minutes
Cooking time: 0 minutes
Servings: 1
Ingredients:
- 1 1/2 frozen bananas, sliced into coins
- 1/8 teaspoon ground cinnamon
- 2 tablespoons hemp seeds
- 1 tablespoon maple syrup
- 1/4 teaspoon vanilla extract, unsweetened
- 1 cup regular coffee, cooled
- 1/4 cup almond milk, unsweetened

593. Green Smoothie

Preparation time: 5 minutes
Cooking time: 0 minutes
Servings: 1
Ingredients:
- 1/2 cup strawberries, frozen
- 4 leaves of kale
- 1/4 of a medium banana

3. Add the green beans, cover, and cook over medium-low heat for 10 to 15 minutes, or until the beans are tender. Attach salt (if desired) and pepper to taste. Serve warm.

Nutrition:
Calories: 103 Fat: 2.0g Carbohydrates: 19.8g Proteins: 6.2g Fiber: 7.0g

2. When cooked, drain and return the potatoes to the pot. Mash the potatoes while beating in the milk. Season with salt (if desired) and pepper.
3. In a vegetable steamer, steam the cauliflower for 10 minutes. Set it to a food processor and blend until roughly smooth.
4. In a nonstick pan, sauté the garlic in the broth for 5 minutes, or until tender.
5. Transfer the cauliflower and garlic to the large pot with the mashed potatoes. Combine by using a potato masher or stirring well. Serve warm.

Nutrition:
Calories: 170 Fat: 1.0g Carbohydrates: 37.8g Proteins: 5.9g Fiber: 5.0g

Directions:
1. Steam the bok choy, broccoli, bell pepper, and edamame for 10 minutes, or until softened.
2. In a small saucepan, combine the vinegar, 1/4 cup of water, garlic, red pepper flakes, soy sauce, maple syrup (if desired), and garlic powder.
3. In a bowl, merge the flour with the remaining 1 tablespoon of water, and then add the slurry to the saucepan. Whisk the sauce until it is thickened.
4. Detach the vegetables from the steamer and transfer to a large bowl. Pour the sauce over the vegetables and stir until thoroughly covered. Serve immediately.

Nutrition:
Calories: 150 Fat: 1.0g Carbohydrates: 25.9g Proteins: 17.1g Fiber: 2.0g

- 1/2 cup of ice cubes

Directions:
1. Pour milk into a blender, add vanilla, cinnamon, and hemp seeds and then pulse until smooth.
2. Add banana, pour in the coffee, and then pulse until smooth.
3. Add ice, blend until well combined, blend in maple syrup and then serve.

Nutrition:
Calories: 410 Fat: 19.5g Proteins: 4.9g Carbohydrates: 60.8g Fiber: 6.8g

- 2 Medjool dates, pitted
- 1 tablespoon flax seed
- 1/4 cup pumpkin seeds, hulled
- 1 cup of water

Directions:

1. Set all the ingredients in the jar of a food processor or blender and then cover it with the lid.
2. Pulse until smooth and then serve.

594. Strawberry and Banana Smoothie
Preparation time: 5 minutes
Cooking time: 0 minutes
Servings: 1
Ingredients:
- 1 cup sliced banana, frozen
- 2 tablespoons chia seeds
- 2 cups strawberries, frozen
- 2 teaspoons maple syrup
- 1/4 teaspoon vanilla extract, unsweetened

595. Orange Smoothie
Preparation time: 5 minutes
Cooking time: 0 minutes
Servings: 1
Ingredients:
- 1 cup slices of oranges
- 1/2 teaspoon grated ginger
- 1 cup of mango pieces
- 1 cup of coconut water
- 1 cup chopped strawberries

596. Pumpkin Chai Smoothie
Preparation time: 5 minutes
Cooking time: 0 minutes
Servings: 1
Ingredients:
- 1 cup cooked pumpkin
- 1/4 cup pecans
- 1 frozen banana
- 1/4 teaspoon ground cinnamon
- 1/4 teaspoon cardamom
- 1/4 teaspoon ground nutmeg
- 2 teaspoons maple syrup

597. Banana Shake
Preparation time: 5 minutes
Cooking time: 0 minutes
Servings: 1
Ingredients:
- 3 medium frozen bananas
- 1 tablespoon cocoa powder, unsweetened
- 1 teaspoon shredded coconut
- 1 tablespoon maple syrup
- 1 tablespoon peanut butter
- 1 teaspoon vanilla extract, unsweetened
- 2 cups of coconut water
- 1 cup of ice cubes

598. Summer Salsa
Preparation time: 5 minutes
Cooking time: 15 minutes
Servings: 1 1/2 cup
Ingredients:
- 1 cup cherry tomatoes, chopped
- 1/4 cup chopped cilantro
- 2 tablespoons chopped red onion
- 1 teaspoon minced garlic
- 1 small jalapeno, deseeded, chopped

Nutrition:
Calories: 204 Fat: 1.1g Proteins: 6.5g Carbohydrates: 48g Fiber: 8.3g

- 6 ounces coconut yogurt
- 1 cup almond milk, unsweetened

Directions:
1. Set all the ingredients in the jar of a food processor or blender and then cover it with the lid.
2. Pulse until smooth and then serve.

Nutrition:
Calories: 114 Fat: 2.1g Proteins: 3.7g Carbohydrates: 22.3g Fiber: 3.8g

- 1 cup crushed ice

Directions:
1. Set all the ingredients in the jar of a food processor or blender and then cover it with the lid.
2. Pulse until smooth and then serve.

Nutrition:
Calories: 198.7 Fat: 1.2g Proteins: 6.1g Carbohydrates: 34.3g Fiber: 0g

- 1 cup of water, cold
- 1/2 cup of ice cubes

Directions:
1. Place pecans in a bowl, cover with water, and then let them soak for 10 minutes.
2. Drain the pecans, add them into a blender, and then add the remaining ingredients.
3. Pulse for 1 minute until smooth, and then serve.

Nutrition:
Calories: 157.5 Fat: 3.8g Proteins: 3g Carbohydrates: 32.3g Fiber: 4.5g

Directions:
1. Add banana in a food processor, add maple syrup and vanilla, pour in water and then add ice.
2. Pulse until smooth and then pour half of the smoothie into a glass.
3. Add butter and cocoa powder into the blender, pulse until smooth, and then add to the smoothie glass.
4. Sprinkle coconut over the smoothie and then serve.

Nutrition:
Calories: 301 Fat: 9.3g Proteins: 6.8g Carbohydrates: 49g Fiber: 1.9g

- 1/2 of a lime, juiced
- 1/8 teaspoon salt
- 1 tablespoon olive oil

Directions:
1. Set all the ingredients in the jar of a food processor or blender except for cilantro and then cover with its lid.
2. Pulse until smooth and then pulse in cilantro until evenly mixed.

3. Tip the salsa into a bowl and then serve with vegetable sticks.

Nutrition:

599. Red Salsa

Preparation time: 35 minutes
Cooking time: 15 minutes
Servings: 2
Ingredients:

- 4 Roma tomatoes, halved
- 1/4 cup chopped cilantro
- 1 jalapeno pepper, deseeded, halved
- 1/2 of a medium white onion, peeled, cut into quarters
- 3 cloves of garlic, peeled
- 1/2 teaspoon salt
- 1 tablespoon brown sugar
- 1 teaspoon apple cider vinegar

Directions:

600. Pinto Bean Dip

Preparation time: 5 minutes
Cooking time: 0 minutes
Servings: 1 1/2 cup
Ingredients:

- 15 ounces canned pinto beans
- 1 jalapeno pepper
- 2 teaspoons ground cumin
- 3 tablespoons nutritional yeast
- 1/3 cup basil salsa

601. Smoky Red Pepper Hummus

Preparation time: 5 minutes
Cooking time: 0 minutes
Servings: 1 1/2 cup
Ingredients:

- 1/4 cup roasted red peppers
- 1 cup cooked chickpeas
- 1/8 teaspoon garlic powder
- 1/2 teaspoon salt
- 1/8 teaspoon ground black pepper
- 1/4 teaspoon ground cumin
- 1/4 teaspoon red chili powder

602. Roasted Tamari Almonds

Preparation time: 5 minutes
Cooking time: 15 minutes
Servings: 8
Ingredients:

- 1 pound (454 g) raw almonds
- 3 tablespoons tamari
- 1 tablespoon nutritional yeast
- 1 to 2 teaspoons chili powder

Directions:

1. Preheat the oven to 400F (205C). Set a large baking tray with parchment paper and set aside.
2. Mix the almonds and tamari in a medium bowl and toss to coat.

603. Tomatillo Salsa

Preparation time: 5 minutes
Cooking time: 20 minutes
Servings: 2 cups
Ingredients:

Calories: 51 Fat: 0.1g Proteins: 1.7g Carbohydrates: 11.4g Fiber: 3.1g

1. Switch on the oven, then set it to 425F and let it preheat.
2. Meanwhile, take a baking sheet, line it with foil, and then spread tomato, jalapeno pepper, onion, and garlic.
3. Bake the vegetables for 15 minutes until vegetables have cooked and begin to brown and then let the vegetables cool for 3 minutes.
4. Transfer the roasted vegetables into a blender, add remaining ingredients and then pulse until smooth.

Nutrition:

Calories: 240 Fat: 0g Proteins: 0g Carbohydrates: 48g Fiber: 16g

Directions:

1. Merge all the ingredients in a food processor, cover with the lid, and then pulse until smooth.
2. Tip the dip in a bowl and then serve with vegetable slices.

Nutrition:

Calories: 360 Fat: 0g Proteins: 24g Carbohydrates: 72g Fiber: 24g

- 1 tablespoon Tahini
- 2 tablespoons water

Directions:

1. Set all the ingredients in the jar of the food processor and then pulse until smooth.
2. Tip the hummus in a bowl and then serve with vegetable slices.

Nutrition:

Calories: 489 Fat: 30g Proteins: 9g Carbohydrates: 15g Fiber: 6g

3. Arrange the almonds on the prepared baking tray in a single layer.
4. Roast in the preheated oven until browned, about 10 t0 15 minutes. Set the almonds halfway through the cooking time.
5. Let the almonds cool for 10 minutes in the baking tray. Sprinkle with the nutritional yeast and chili powder. Serve immediately, or store in the fridge for up to 2 weeks.

Nutrition:

Calories: 91 Fat: 28.3g Carbohydrates: 13.2g Proteins: 12.2g Fiber: 7.4g

- 5 medium tomatillos, chopped
- 3 cloves of garlic, peeled, chopped
- 3 Roma tomatoes, chopped
- 1 jalapeno, chopped

- 1/2 of a red onion, peeled, chopped
- 1 Anaheim chili
- 2 teaspoons salt
- 1 teaspoon ground cumin
- 1 lime, juiced
- 1/4 cup cilantro leaves
- 3/4 cup of water

Directions:
1. Take a medium pot, place it over medium heat, pour in water, and then add onion, tomatoes, tomatillo, jalapeno, and Anaheim chili.

604. Arugula Pesto Couscous

Preparation time: 10 minutes
Cooking time: 20 minutes
Servings: 4
Ingredients:
- 8 ounces Israeli couscous
- 3 large tomatoes, chopped
- 3 cups arugula leaves
- 1/2 cup parsley leaves
- 6 cloves of garlic, peeled
- 1/2 cup walnuts
- 3/4 teaspoon salt
- 1 cup and 1 tablespoon olive oil
- 2 cups vegetable broth

Directions:
1. Take a medium saucepan, place it over medium-high heat, add 1 tablespoon oil and then let it heat.

605. Oatmeal and Raisin Balls

Preparation time: 40 minutes
Cooking time: 0 minutes
Servings: 12 balls
Ingredients:
- 1 cup rolled oats
- 1/4 cup raisins
- 1/2 cup peanut butter

Directions:

606. Oat Crunch Apple Crisp

Preparation time: 10 minutes
Cooking time: 35 minutes
Servings: 6
Ingredients:
- 3 medium apples, cored and cut into 1/4inch pieces
- 3/4 cup apple juice
- 1 teaspoon vanilla extract
- 1 teaspoon ground cinnamon, divided
- 2 cups rolled oats
- 1/4 cup maple syrup

Directions:
1. Warmth the oven to 375F
2. In a large bowl, merge the apple slices, apple juice, vanilla, and 1/2 teaspoon of cinnamon. Mix well to thoroughly coat the apple slices.

2. Sauté the vegetables for 15 minutes, remove the pot from heat, add cilantro and lime juice and then stir in salt.
3. Remove pot from heat and then pulse by using an immersion blender until smooth.
4. Serve the salsa with chips.

Nutrition:
Calories: 317.4 Fat: 0g Proteins: 16g Carbohydrates: 64g Fiber: 16g

2. Add couscous, stir until mixed, and then cook for 4 minutes until fragrant and toasted.
3. Pour in the broth, stir until mixed, bring it to a boil, switch heat to medium level and then simmer for 12 minutes until the couscous has absorbed all the liquid and turn tender.
4. When done, remove the pan from heat, fluff it with a fork, and then set aside until required.
5. While couscous cooks, prepare the pesto, and for this, place walnuts in a blender, add garlic, and then pulse until nuts have broken.
6. Add arugula, parsley, and salt, pulse until well combined, and then blend in oil until smooth.
7. Transfer couscous to a salad bowl, add tomatoes and prepared pesto, and then toss until mixed.
8. Serve straight away.

Nutrition:
Calories: 73 Fat: 4g Proteins: 2g Carbohydrates: 8g Fiber: 2g

1. Place oats in a large bowl, add raisins and peanut butter, and then stir until well combined.
2. Shape the mixture into twelve balls, 1 tablespoon of mixture per ball, and then arrange the balls on a baking sheet.
3. Bring the baking sheet into the freezer for 30 minutes until firm and then serve.

Nutrition:
Calories: 135 Fat: 6g Proteins: 8g Carbohydrates: 13g Fiber: 4g

3. Layer the apple slices on the bottom of a round or square baking dish. Take any leftover liquid and pour it over the apple slices.
4. In a large bowl, stir together the oats, maple syrup, and the remaining 1/2 teaspoon of cinnamon until the oats are completely coated.
5. Sprinkle the oat mixture over the apples, being sure to spread it out evenly so that none of the apple slices are visible.
6. Bake for 35 minutes, or until the oats begin to turn golden brown, and serve.

Nutrition:
Calories: 150 Fat: 1.0g Carbohydrates: 25.9g Proteins: 17.1g Fiber: 2.0g

607. Pico de Gallo

Preparation time: 5 minutes
Cooking time: 0 minutes
Servings: 3
Ingredients:

- 1/2 of a medium red onion
- 2 cups diced tomato
- 1/2 cup chopped cilantro
- 1 jalapeno pepper, minced
- 1/8 teaspoon salt
- 1/4 teaspoon ground black pepper

608. Beet Balls

Preparation time: 10 minutes
Cooking time: 0 minutes
Servings: 18
Ingredients:

- 1/2 cup oats
- 1 medium beet, cooked
- 1/2 cup almond flour
- 1/3 cup shredded coconut and more for coating
- 3/4 cup Medjool dates, pitted
- 1 tablespoon cocoa powder
- 1/2 cup peanuts

609. Cheesy Crackers

Preparation time: 10 minutes
Cooking time: 20 minutes
Servings: 3
Ingredients:

- 1 3/4 cup almond meal
- 3 tablespoons nutritional yeast
- 1/2 teaspoon of sea salt
- 2 tablespoons lemon juice
- 1 tablespoon melted coconut oil
- 1 tablespoon ground flaxseed
- 2 1/2 tablespoons water

Directions:

1. Switch on the oven, then set it to 350 degrees F and let it preheat.
2. Meanwhile, take a medium bowl, place flaxseed in it, stir in water, and then let the mixture rest for 5 minutes until thickened.

610. Chocolate Protein Bites

Preparation time: 10 Minutes
Cooking time: 20 Minutes
Servings: 12
Ingredients:

- 1/2 cup Chocolate Protein Powder
- 1 Avocado, medium
- 1 tbsp. Chocolate Chips
- 1 tbsp. Almond Butter
- 1 tbsp. Cocoa Powder
- 1 tsp. Vanilla Extract
- Dash of Salt

Directions:

611. Crunchy Granola

Preparation time: 10 Minutes
Cooking time: 20 Minutes
Servings: 1
Ingredients:

- 1/2 of a lime, juiced
- 1 teaspoon olive oil

Directions:

1. Take a large bowl, place all the ingredients in it and then stir until well mixed.
2. Serve the Pico de Gallo with chips.

Nutrition:
Calories: 790 Fat: 6.4g Proteins: 25.6g Carbohydrates: 195.2g Fiber: 35.2g

- 1/4 cup chocolate chips, unsweetened

Directions:

1. Place cooked beets in a blender and then pulse until chopped into very small pieces.
2. Add remaining ingredients and then pulse until the dough comes together.
3. Shape the dough into eighteen balls, coat them in some more coconut and then serve.

Nutrition:
Calories: 114.2 Fat: 2.4g Proteins: 5g Carbohydrates: 19.6g Fiber: 4.9g

3. Place almond meal in a medium bowl, add salt and yeast and then stir until mixed.
4. Add lemon juice and oil into the flaxseed mixture and then whisk until mixed.
5. Pour the flaxseed mixture into the almond meal mixture and then stir until dough comes together.
6. Place a piece of a wax paper on a clean working space, place the dough on it, secure with another piece of wax paper, and then roll dough into a 1/8-inch thick crust.
7. Cut the dough into a square shape, sprinkle salt over the top and then bake for 15 to 20 minutes until done.
8. Serve straight away.

Nutrition:
Calories: 30 Fat: 1g Proteins: 1g Carbohydrates: 5g Fiber: 0g

1. Begin by blending avocado, almond butter, vanilla extract, and salt in a high-speed blender until you get a smooth mixture.
2. Next, spoon in the protein powder, cocoa powder, and chocolate chips to the blender.
3. Blend again until you get a smooth dough-like consistency mixture.
4. Now, check for seasoning and add more sweetness if needed.
5. Finally, with the help of a scooper, scoop out dough to make small balls.

Nutrition:
Calories: 46 Proteins: 2g Carbohydrates: 2g Fat: 2g

- 1/2 cup Oats
- Dash of Salt
- 2 tbsp. Vegetable Oil

- 3 tbsp. Maple Syrup
- 1/3 cup Apple Cider Vinegar
- 1/2 cup Almonds
- 1 tsp. Cardamom, grounded

Directions:
1. Preheat the oven to 375F.
2. After that, mix oats, pistachios, salt, and cardamom in a large bowl.
3. Next, spoon in the vegetable oil and maple syrup to the mixture.

612. Chocolate Almond Bars

Preparation time: 10 Minutes
Cooking time: 20 Minutes
Servings: 12
Ingredients:
- 1 cup Almonds
- 1 1/2 cup Rolled Oats
- 1/3 cup Maple Syrup
- 1/4 tsp. Sea Salt
- 5 oz. Protein Powder
- 1 tsp. Cinnamon

Directions:
1. For making these delicious vegan bars, you first need to place 3/4 cup of the almonds and salt in the food processor.

613. Spicy Nut and Seed Snack Mix

Preparation time: 5 Minutes
Cooking time: 10 Minutes
Servings: 4
Ingredients:
- 1/4 tsp. garlic powder
- 1/4 tsp. nutritional yeast
- 1/2 tsp. smoked paprika
- 1/4 tsp. sea salt
- 1/4 tsp. dried parsley
- 1/2 cup slivered almonds
- 1/2 cup cashew pieces
- 1/2 cup sunflower seeds

614. Flax Crackers

Preparation time: 5 Minutes
Cooking time: 60 Minutes
Servings: 4 to 6
Ingredients:
- 1 cup Flaxseeds, whole
- 2 cups Water
- 3/4 cup Flaxseeds, grounded
- 1 tsp. Sea Salt
- 1/2 cup Chia Seeds
- 1 tsp. Black Pepper
- 1/2 cup Sunflower Seeds

Directions:

615. Chocolate and Nuts Goji Bars

Preparation time: 5 Minutes
Cooking time: 5 Minutes
Servings: 4
Ingredients:

4. Then, transfer the mixture to a parchment-paper-lined baking sheet.
5. Bake them for 13 minutes until the mixture is toasted. Tip: Check on them now and then. Spread it out well.
6. Return the sheet to the oven for further ten minutes.
7. Detach the sheet from the oven and allow it to cool completely.
8. Serve and enjoy.

Nutrition:
Calories: 763 Proteins: 12.9g Carbohydrates: 64.8g Fat: 52.4g

2. Process them for a minute or until you get them in the form of almond butter.
3. Now, swirl in the rest of the ingredients to the processor and process them again until smooth.
4. Next, transfer the mixture to a greased parchment paper-lined baking sheet and spread it across evenly.
5. Press them slightly down with the back of the spoon.
6. Chop down the remaining 1/4 cup of the almonds and top it across the mixture.
7. Finally, place them in the refrigerator for 20 minutes or until set.

Nutrition:
Calories: 166 Proteins: 12.8g Carbohydrates: 17.6g Fat: 6g

- 1/2 cup pepitas

Directions:
1. In a small bowl, merge the garlic powder, nutritional yeast, paprika, salt, and parsley. Set aside.
2. In a large skillet, add the almonds, cashews, sunflower seeds, pepitas and heat over low heat until warm and glistening, 3 minutes.
3. Set the heat off and stir in the parsley mixture.
4. Allow complete cooling and enjoy!

Nutrition:
Calories: 385 Proteins: 12g Carbohydrates: 16g Fat: 33g

1. First, place all the ingredients in a large mixing bowl and mix them well. Soak them for 10 to 15 minutes.
2. After that, transfer the mixture to a parchment paper-lined baking sheet and spread it evenly. Tip: Make sure the paper lines the edges as well.
3. Next, bake it for 60 minutes at 350F.
4. Once the time is up, flip the entire bar and take off the parchment paper.
5. Bake for half an hour or until it becomes crispy and browned.
6. Allow it to cool completely and then break it down.

Nutrition:
Calories: 251 Proteins: 9.2g Carbohydrates: 14.9g Fat: 16g

- 1 cup mixed nuts
- 1/4 cup dried goji berries
- 1/4 cup chopped pitted dates
- 2 tbsp. chocolate chips

- 1 1/2 tsp. vanilla extract
- 1/4 tsp. cinnamon powder
- 2 tbsp. vegetable oil
- 2 tbsp. golden flaxseed meal
- 1 tsp. maple syrup

Directions:
1. Attach all the ingredients to a blender and process until coarsely smooth.

616. Cranberry Protein Bars

Preparation time: 5 Minutes
Cooking time: 2 hours
Servings: 4
Ingredients:
- 11/2 cups cashew nut butter
- 3 scoops protein powder
- 4 tbsp. butter, melted
- 1 1/2 tsp. maple syrup
- 1/2 tsp. salt or to taste
- 4 tbsp. dried cranberries, chopped

Directions:

617. Onion Rings

Preparation time: 15 minutes
Cooking time: 14 minutes
Servings: 4
Ingredients:
- 1 large sweet or Vidalia onion
- 1/2 cup chickpea flour
- 1/3 cup unsweetened plain plant-based milk
- 2 tablespoons freshly squeezed lemon juice
- 2 tablespoons No-Salt Hot Sauce
- 1 teaspoon No-Salt Spice Blend
- 2/3 cup panko breadcrumbs

Directions:
1. Peel off and discard the top 1/2 inch of the root end of the sweet onion. Continue cutting the onion

618. French Fries

Preparation time: 5 minutes
Cooking time: 15 minutes
Servings: 2
Ingredients:
- 1 large russet potato
- 1/4 cup freshly squeezed lemon juice
- 3 tablespoons nutritional yeast
- 1 tablespoon No-Salt Spice Blend

Directions:
1. Cut the potato lengthwise into 1/2-inch-thick fries.
2. Pour the lemon juice onto a plate. On a second plate, mix the nutritional yeast and spice blend. Dip

619. Roasted Asparagus

Preparation time: 10 minutes
Cooking time: 5 minutes
Servings: 4
Ingredients:
- 1 tablespoon tahini
- 1 tablespoon freshly squeezed lemon juice
- 1 tablespoon water
- 1 teaspoon No-Salt Spice Blend
- 1 pound fresh asparagus, woody ends trimmed

2. Lay a large piece of plastic wrap on a flat surface and spread the batter on top. Bring another piece of plastic wrap on top and using a rolling pin, flatten the dough into a thick rectangle of about 1 1/2 -inch thickness.
3. Remove the plastic wraps and use an oiled knife to cut the dough into bars.
4. Serve immediately and freeze any extras.

Nutrition:
Calories: 679 Proteins: 25g Carbohydrates: 11g Fat: 62g

1. Line a medium, shallow loaf pan with baking paper and set aside.
2. In a medium bowl, merge all the ingredients and spread in the loaf pan. Refrigerate in for 2 hours until the batter is firm.
3. Remove the batter from the refrigerator and turn it onto a clean, flat surface. Cut the batter into bars.
4. Serve, and freeze any extras.

Nutrition:
Calories: 968 Proteins: 29g Carbohydrates: 26g Fat: 86g

into 1/2-inch-thick slices. Carefully separate the slices into individual rings and set aside.
2. In a medium bowl, mix the chickpea flour, plant-based milk, lemon juice, hot sauce, and spice blend. Spill the breadcrumbs into a separate bowl.
3. Dip each ring into the chickpea batter so that it's completely and evenly covered. Then dip the rings into the breadcrumbs and place them in the air fryer basket.
4. Fry at 380F for 14 minutes, or until the coating is browned and crispy. Be sure to flip your onion rings over halfway through cooking. Serve warm.

Nutrition:
Calories: 127 Fat: 2g Carbohydrates: 23g Fiber: 3g Proteins: 5g

the fries, one at a time, into the lemon juice. Shake off the excess juice and dip the fries into the spice mixture to completely cover them on all sides. Once covered, place the fries in a single layer in the air fryer basket or on the rack.
3. Fry at 400F for 15 minutes until the fries are crispy. Shake up the basket or turn the fries over halfway through cooking. Serve immediately.

Nutrition:
Calories: 172 Fat: 0g Carbohydrates: 36g Fiber: 3g Proteins: 6g

Directions:
1. In a large bowl, merge together the tahini, lemon juice, water, and spice blend until well combined.
2. Attach the asparagus to the bowl and toss to coat.
3. Place the coated spears in a single layer in the air fryer basket or on the rack and roast at 400F for 5 minutes, or until the tips start to brown and the insides are cooked but not mushy. Serve warm.

Nutrition:

Calories: 46 Fat: 2g Carbohydrates: 5g Fiber: 3g Proteins: 3g

620. Twice-Baked Potatoes

Preparation time: 15 minutes
Cooking time: 35 minutes
Servings: 4
Ingredients:

- 2 medium russet potatoes, halved lengthwise
- 1/2 cup No-Cheese Sauce
- 2 scallions
- 1 tablespoon nutritional yeast

Directions:

1. Place each potato, cut-side down, on a scrap of parchment paper in the air fryer basket or on the rack. Roast at 400F for 30 minutes.

2. Carefully detach the potatoes from the air fryer. Set out the middle of each potato, leaving 1/4 inch of flesh around the edges, and place the scooped parts in a medium bowl. Add the no-cheese sauce, scallions, and nutritional yeast to the bowl and mix until well combined.

3. Equally spoon the mixture into the potato skins and place them back in the air fryer. Grill at 400F for 3 to 4 minutes, or until the tops get crispy. Serve warm.

Nutrition:
Calories: 178 Fat: 21g Carbohydrates: 37g Fiber: 3g Proteins: 7g

621. Baba Ghanoush

Preparation time: 10 minutes
Cooking time: 30 minutes
Servings: 2
Ingredients:

- 1 medium eggplant
- 2 tablespoons tahini
- 2 tablespoons freshly squeezed lemon juice
- 1 teaspoon granulated garlic
- 1/4 teaspoon ground cumin
- Freshly chopped parsley, for garnish

Directions:

1. Place the whole eggplant in a pan in the air fryer. Roast at 400°F for 30 minutes, carefully turning the eggplant over halfway through cooking.

2. Let the eggplant cool for 5 to 10 minutes. Then set out the flesh and set it in a medium bowl. Drain as much water from the eggplant flesh as possible.

3. Add the tahini, lemon juice, granulated garlic, and cumin to the bowl. Mix until well combined. Garnish with the parsley.

Nutrition:
Calories: 169 Fat: 9g Carbohydrates: 22g Fiber: 10g Proteins: 6g

622. Citrus-Roasted Brussels sprouts

Preparation time: 10 minutes
Cooking time: 10 minutes
Servings: 4
Ingredients:

- 1/4 cup freshly squeezed orange juice
- 1 teaspoon pure maple syrup
- 1 tablespoon balsamic vinegar
- 1 pound Brussels sprouts, trimmed and quartered

Directions:

1. In a large bowl, set together the orange juice, maple syrup, and balsamic vinegar. Add the Brussels sprouts to the bowl and toss until well coated.

2. Place the Brussels sprouts, cut-side up, in a single layer in the air fryer basket or on the rack. Roast at 400F until they start to crisp up. Be careful not to burn them!

Nutrition:
Calories: 64 Fat: 0g Carbohydrates: 14g Fiber: 4g Proteins: 4g

623. Berry and Yogurt Smoothie

Preparation time: 5 minutes
Cooking time: 0 minutes.
Servings: 2
Ingredients:

- 2 small bananas
- 3 cups frozen mixed berries
- 1(1/2) cup cashew yogurt
- 1/2 teaspoon vanilla extract, unsweetened
- 1/2 cup almond milk, unsweetened

Directions:

1. Place all the ingredients in the order to a food processor or blender and then pulse for 2 to 3 minutes at high speed until smooth.

2. Pour the smoothie into two glasses and then serve.

Nutrition:
Calories: 326 Fat: 6.5g Carbohydrates: 65.6g Proteins: 8g Fiber: 8.4g

624. Basil Lime Green Tea

Preparation time: 5 minutes
Cooking time: 4 minutes
Servings: 8
Ingredients:

- 8 cups of filtered water
- 10 bags of green tea
- 1/4 tsp. of maple syrup
- A pinch of baking soda
- Lime slices to taste
- Lemon slices to taste
- Basil leaves to taste

Directions:

1. Add water, maple syrup, and baking soda to the pot and mix. Add the tea bags and cover. Cook on High for 4 minutes. Open and serve with lime slices, lemon slices, and basil leaves.

Nutrition:
Calories: 32 Carbohydrates: 8g Fat: 0g Proteins: 0g

625. Pineapple and Spinach Juice

Preparation time: 5 minutes
Cooking time: 0 minutes
Servings: 2
Ingredients:

- 2 medium red apples, cored, peeled, chopped
- 3 cups spinach
- 1/2 of a medium pineapple, peeled
- 2 lemons, peeled

Directions:

1. Process all the ingredients in the order in a juicer or blender and then strain it into two glasses.
2. Serve straight away.

Nutrition:
Calories: 131 Fat: 0.5g Carbohydrates: 34.5g Proteins: 1.7g Fiber: 5g

626. Strawberry and Chocolate Milkshake

Preparation time: 5 minutes
Cooking time: 0 minutes
Servings: 2
Ingredients:

- 2 cups frozen strawberries
- 3 tablespoons cocoa powder
- 1 scoop protein powder
- 2 tablespoons maple syrup
- 1 teaspoon vanilla extract, unsweetened
- 2 cups almond milk, unsweetened

Directions:

1. Place all the ingredients in the order to a food processor or blender and then pulse for 2 to 3 minutes at high speed until smooth.
2. Pour the smoothie into two glasses and then serve.

Nutrition:
Calories: 199 Fat: 4.1g Carbohydrates: 40.5g Proteins: 3.7g Fiber: 5.5g

627. Fruit Infused Water

Preparation time: 5 minutes
Cooking time: 0 minutes
Servings: 2
Ingredients:

- 3 strawberries, sliced
- 5 mint leaves
- 1/2 of orange, sliced
- 2 cups of water

Directions:

1. Divide fruits and mint between two glasses, pour in water, stir until just mixed, and refrigerate for 2 hours.
2. Serve straight away.

Nutrition:
Calories: 5.4 Fat: 0.1g Carbohydrates: 1.3g Proteins: 0.1g Fiber: 0.4g

628. Lebanese Potato Salad

Preparation time: 5 minutes
Cooking time: 10 minutes
Servings: 4
Ingredients:

- 1-pound Russet potatoes
- 1(1/2) tablespoon extra-virgin olive oil
- 2 scallions, thinly sliced
- Freshly ground pepper to taste
- 2 tablespoons lemon juice
- 1/4 tsp. salt or to taste
- 2 tablespoons fresh mint leaves, chopped

Directions:

1. Set a saucepan half-filled with water over medium heat. Add salt and potatoes and cook for 10 minutes until tender. Drain the potatoes and set them in a bowl of cold water. When cool enough to handle, peel and cube the potatoes. Place in a bowl.
2. To make the dressing: Add oil, lemon juice, salt, and pepper in a bowl and whisk well. Drizzle dressing over the potatoes. Toss well.
3. Add scallions and mint and toss well.
4. Divide into 4 plates and serve.

Nutrition:
Calories: 129 Fat: 0.9g Carbohydrates: 8.8g

629. Kale and Cauliflower Salad

Preparation time: 10 minutes
Cooking time: 0 minutes
Servings: 2
Ingredients:

- 1/2 cup lemon juice
- 1 tablespoon olive oil
- 1 teaspoon maple syrup
- 1/8 teaspoon salt
- 1/4 teaspoon ground black pepper
- 1 bunch kale, cut into bite-size pieces
- 1/2 cup roasted cauliflower
- 1/2 cup dried cranberries

Directions:

1. Whisk lemon juice, olive oil, maple syrup, salt, and black pepper in a large bowl. Add kale, cauliflower, and cranberries; toss to combine.

Nutrition:
Calories: 76 Fat: 5 g Carbohydrates: 5.9 g

630. Creamy Lentil Dip

Preparation time: 10 minutes
Cooking time: 15 minutes
Servings: 3
Ingredients:

- 21/2 cups water, divided
- 1 cup dried green or brown lentils, washed
- 1/3 cup tahini
- 1 garlic clove
- 1/2 teaspoon salt (optional)

Directions:

1. Stir together 2 cups of water and dried lentils in a medium pot and bring to a boil over high heat.

2. When it starts to heat, set the heat to low, secure, and let simmer until the lentils are soft, stirring occasionally. Drain any excess liquid.
3. Transfer the lentils to a food processor, along with the remaining 1/2 cup of water, tahini, garlic, and salt (if desired), and pulse until smooth and creamy.

631. Easy Cucumber Dip
Preparation time: 5 minutes
Cooking time: 0 minutes
Servings: 11
Ingredients:
- 1 cucumber, peeled, cut in half lengthwise, deseeded and coarsely chopped
- 3 to 4 cloves garlic, crushed
- 1 cup plain soy yogurt
- 1/4 teaspoon white pepper

Directions:

632. Ranch Cauliflower Dip
Preparation time: 15 minutes
Cooking time: 0 minutes
Servings: 8
Ingredients:
- 2 cups frozen cauliflower, thawed
- 1/2 cup unsweetened almond milk
- 2 tablespoons apple cider vinegar
- 2 tablespoons extra-virgin olive oil (Optional)
- 1 garlic clove, peeled
- 2 teaspoons finely chopped fresh parsley
- 2 teaspoons finely chopped scallions, both white and green parts
- 1 teaspoon finely chopped fresh dill

633. Sweet and Tangy Ketchup
Preparation time: 5 minutes
Cooking time: 15 minutes
Servings: 21
Ingredients:
- 1 cup water
- 1/4 cup maple syrup
- 1 cup tomato paste
- 3 tablespoons apple cider vinegar
- 1 teaspoon onion powder
- 1 teaspoon garlic powder

Directions:

634. Cilantro Coconut Pesto
Preparation time: 5 minutes
Cooking time: 0 minutes
Servings: 2
Ingredients:
- 1 (13.5-ounce / 383-g) can unsweetened coconut milk
- 2 jalapeños, seeds and ribs removed
- 1 bunch cilantro leaves only
- 1 tablespoon white miso
- 1-inch (2.5 cm) piece ginger, peeled and minced
- Water, as needed

4. Serve immediately.
Nutrition:
Calories: 101 Fat: 4.2g Carbohydrates: 10.8g Proteins: 5.0g
Fiber: 6.0g

1. In a blender, blend the cucumber until finely chopped. Remove from the blend and place in a very fine strainer. Press out as much water as possible. Return to the blender.
2. Attach the remaining ingredients and process until smooth.
3. Refrigerate for several hours before serving.
Nutrition:
Calories: 48 Fat: 1.0g Carbohydrates: 6.2g Proteins: 3.6g
Fiber: 0.4g

- 1/2 teaspoon onion powder
- 1/2 teaspoon Dijon mustard
- 1/2 teaspoon salt (optional)
- 1/4 teaspoon freshly ground black pepper

Directions:
1. Press all the ingredients in a blender until smooth and combined.
2. Serve immediately or store in a sealed container in the refrigerator for up to 3 days.
Nutrition:
Calories: 51 Fat: 4.2g Carbohydrates: 2.1g Proteins: 1.2g
Fiber: 1.1g

1. Attach the water to a medium saucepan and bring to a rolling boil over high heat.
2. Reduce the heat to low, set in the maple syrup, tomato paste, vinegar, onion powder, and garlic powder. Cover and bring to a gently simmer for about 10 minutes, stirring frequently, or until the sauce begins to thicken and bubble.
3. Let the sauce rest for 30 minutes until cooled completely. Transfer to an airtight container and refrigerate for up to 1 month.
Nutrition:
Calories: 46 Fat: 5.2g Carbohydrates: 1.0g Proteins: 1.1g
Fiber: 1.0g

Directions:
1. Set all the ingredients in a blender until creamy and smooth.
2. Thin with a little extra water as needed to reach your preferred consistency.
3. Set in an airtight bag in the fridge for up t0 2 days or in the freezer for up to 6 months.
Nutrition:
Calories: 141 Fat: 13.7g Carbohydrates: 2.8g Proteins: 1.6g
Fiber: 0.3g

635. Raw Cashew Pesto

Preparation time: 5 minutes
Cooking time: 0 minutes
Servings: 1
Ingredients:

- 1/3 red onion, about 2 ounces (57 g)
- Juice of 1 lemon
- 2 garlic cloves
- 4 cups packed basil leaves
- 1 cup wheatgrass
- 1/4 cup raw cashews soak in boiling water for 5 minutes and drained

636. Plantain Chips

Preparation time: 10 minutes
Cooking time: 20 minutes
Servings: 4
Ingredients:

- 1/4 Teaspoon Cumin
- 1/2 Teaspoon Smoked Paprika
- 1 Green Plantain, Sliced

Directions:

1. Start by setting your grill to medium heat and then get out an aluminum sheet. Grease using cooking spray, and then spread out the plantain slices.

637. Stuffed Portobello

Preparation time: 10 minutes
Cooking time: 1 hour 20 minutes
Servings: 6
Ingredients:

- 1/2 Cup Mint, Fresh
- 1/2 Cup Basil, Fresh
- 1 Cup Wild Rice
- 1/2 Cup Parsley, Fresh
- 1 Tablespoon Olive Oil
- 1 Tablespoon Nutritional Yeast
- 1 Lemon, Zested
- 1/2 Lemon, Juiced
- 1 tsp. maple syrup
- 3/4 Cup Pecans
- 6 Portobello Mushrooms, Large
- Coconut Oil to Grease
- Sea Salt and Black Pepper to Taste

Directions:

1. Get a saucepan and place three cups of water in with your wild rice. Season with sea salt, and then place the lid on.

638. Easy Collard Greens

Preparation time: 10 minutes
Cooking time: 25 minutes
Servings: 4
Ingredients:

- Black Pepper to Taste
- 1/2 Teaspoon Onion Powder
- 1/2 Teaspoon Garlic Powder
- 1 Cup Vegetable Broth
- 1 1/2 lb. Collard Greens

Directions:

- 1/4 cup water
- 1 tablespoon olive oil (optional)
- 1/4 teaspoon salt (optional)

Directions:

1. Bring all the ingredients in a food processor and merge for 2 to 3 minutes, or until fully combined.
2. Serve immediately.

Nutrition:
Calories: 98 Fat: 7.3g Carbohydrates: 6.1g Proteins: 3.2g Fiber: 1.1g

Drizzle with paprika and cumin. Place this sheet on the grill.

2. Cover your grill and cook for seven minutes. Flip the plantain slices using a tong, and then cover again.
3. Cook for an additional seven minutes before serving the dish warm.

Nutrition:
Calories: 178 Fat: 21g Carbohydrates: 37g Fiber: 3g Proteins: 7g

2. Cook your rice using a simmer for fifty minutes.
3. Drain the rice, and then spread your pecans on a baking sheet. Turn the oven to 375, and then roast for eight minutes. Shake once during this time.
4. Chop your pecans, and then set the chopped pecans to the side.
5. Blend your basil, olive oil, parsley, mint, lemon juice, zest, nutritional yeast, salt, and maple syrup in a blender.
6. Clean your mushrooms before brushing them down with coconut oil. Drizzle your mushrooms with salt and pepper, and then heat the grill to medium-high heat. Grill your mushrooms for six minutes per side, and then stuff each mushroom with pesto, wild rice, and your pecans. Garnish with lemon zest before serving.

Nutrition:
Calories: 199 Fat: 4.1g Carbohydrates: 40.5g Proteins: 3.7g Fiber: 5.5g

1. Remove the hard stems and chop your leaves roughly. Get out a saucepan and mix your garlic powder, onion powder, pepper, and vegetable broth. Bring the mix to a boil using medium-high heat. Add in the greens and lower the heat to a simmer.
2. Cover the dish and cook for twenty minutes. Stir every five to six minutes. Serve warm.

Nutrition:
Calories: 371 Fat: 42.4g Carbohydrates: 42g Proteins: 5.5g Fiber: 2g

639. Sesame Fries

Preparation time: 10 minutes
Cooking time: 35 minutes
Servings: 4
Ingredients:

- 1 lb. Gold Potatoes, Unpeeled and Sliced into Wedges
- 2 Tablespoons Sesame Seeds
- 1 Tablespoon Avocado Oil
- 1 Tablespoon Potato Starch
- 1 Tablespoon Nutritional Yeast
- Sea Salt and Black Pepper to Taste

640. French Potato Salad

Preparation time: 10 minutes
Cooking time: 25 minutes
Servings: 14
Ingredients:
Dressing:

- 1/4 Cup Dill, Fresh and Chopped
- 3 Tablespoons Olive Oil
- 1 Tablespoon Apple Cider Vinegar
- 3 Tablespoons Red Wine Vinegar
- Sea Salt and Black Pepper to Taste
- 3 Cloves Garlic, Minced
- 2 1/2 Tablespoons Spicy Brown Mustard
- Potatoes and Vegetables:
- 2 lb. Baby Yellow potatoes
- Sea Salt and Black Pepper to Taste
- 1 Tablespoon Apple Cider Vinegar

641. Vanilla Milk Steamer

Preparation time: 5 minutes
Cooking time: 5 minutes
Servings: 1
Ingredients:

- 1 cup unsweetened almond milk
- 2 teaspoons pure maple syrup (optional)
- 1/2 teaspoon pure vanilla extract
- Pinch ground cinnamon

Directions:

642. Cannellini Pesto Spaghetti

Preparation time: 5 minutes
Cooking time: 10 minutes
Servings: 4
Ingredients:

- 12 ounces (340 g) whole-grain spaghetti, cooked, drained, and kept warm,
- 1/2 cup cooking liquid reserved
- 1 cup pesto

643. Cold Orange Soba Noodles

Preparation time: 10 minutes
Cooking time: 8 minutes
Servings: 4
Ingredients:

- 3 tablespoons mellow white miso
- Zest of 1 orange and of 2 oranges
- 3 tablespoons grated ginger

Directions:
1. Heat your oven to 425, and then get out a baking tray. Line with parchment paper and put your potatoes onto the tray. Toss with remaining ingredients.
2. Bake for twenty-five minutes, tossing halfway through.

Nutrition:
Calories: 199 Fat: 4.1g Carbohydrates: 40.5g Proteins: 3.7g Fiber: 5.5g

- 1 Cup Green Onion, Diced
- 1/4 Cup Parsley, Fresh and Chopped

Directions:
1. Wash your potatoes before chopping them into 1/4 inch slices. Put the slices in a pan, preferably a saucepan, and then add the water. Add a pinch of salt.
2. Boil for fifteen minutes. Your potatoes should be soft. Drain and rinse using cold water.
3. Add the potatoes to a serving bowl, seasoning with apple cider vinegar, and then a dash of salt and pepper.
4. Set all remaining ingredients together in a separate bowl. Mix well before serving.

Nutrition:
Calories: 679 Proteins: 25g Carbohydrates: 11g Fat: 62g

1. Warmth the almond milk in a small saucepan over medium heat for 5 minutes until steaming, stirring constantly (don't allow it to boil).
2. Carefully spill the hot milk into your blender and mix in the maple syrup (if desired) and vanilla. Blend on low speed, then set the speed to high and blend until well combined and frothy.
3. Serve sprinkled with the cinnamon.

Nutrition:
Calories: 184 Fat: 7.9g Carbohydrates: 20.7g Proteins: 7.6g Fiber: 0g

- 2 cups cooked cannellini beans, drained and washed

Directions:
1. Put the cooked spaghetti in a large bowl and add the pesto.
2. Add the reserved cooking liquid and beans and toss well to serve.

Nutrition:
Calories: 549 Fat: 34.9g Carbohydrates: 45.2g Proteins: 18.3g Fiber: 10.1g

- 1/2 teaspoon crushed red pepper flakes
- 1 pound (454 g) soba noodles, cooked, drained, and rinsed until cool
- 1/4 cup chopped cilantro
- 4 green onions, white and green parts

Directions:

1. Put the miso, orange zest and juice, ginger, and crushed red pepper flakes in a large bowl and whisk well to combine.
2. Add water as needed to make the sauce pourable. Add the cooked noodles and toss to coat well.

644. Indonesia Green Noodle Salad

Preparation time: 10 minutes
Cooking time: 8 minutes
Servings: 4
Ingredients:

- 12 ounces (340 g) brown rice noodles, cooked, drained, and rinsed until cool
- 1 cup snow peas, trimmed and sliced in half on the diagonal
- 2 medium cucumbers, peeled, halved, deseeded, and sliced thinly
- 2 heads baby bok choy, trimmed and thinly sliced
- 4 green onions, green and white parts, trimmed and thinly sliced

645. Fruity Rice Pudding

Preparation time: 10 minutes
Cooking time: 30 minutes
Servings: 4
Ingredients:

- 1 cup crushed pineapple with juice, drained
- 2 cups cooked brown rice
- 2 tablespoons raisins
- 1 banana, peeled and chopped
- 1/2 cup fresh orange juice
- 1 tablespoon vanilla extract
- 3/4 cup water

Directions:

646. Oat Cookies

Preparation time: 30 minutes
Cooking time: 15 minutes
Servings: 40
Ingredients:

- 2 cups rolled oats
- 1 cup whole-wheat flour
- 1/4 cup soy flour
- 1/4 cup wheat bran
- 1/4 cup oat bran
- 1 teaspoon baking soda
- 1 tablespoon baking powder
- 2 teaspoons ground cinnamon
- 1/2 cup unsweetened pineapple juice
- 1/2 cup fresh apple juice
- 1/2 cup raisins

647. Sweet Potato Tater Tots

Preparation time: 30 minutes
Cooking time: 15 minutes
Servings: 4
Ingredients:

- 1 1/2 pounds sweet potatoes, grated
- 2 chia eggs
- 1/2 cup plain flour
- 1/2 cup breadcrumbs
- 3 tablespoons hummus
- Sea salt and black pepper, to taste

3. Set garnished with the cilantro and green onions.

Nutrition:
Calories: 166 Fat: 1.1g Carbohydrates: 34.2g Proteins: 7.9g Fiber: 1.3g

- 3 tablespoons sambal oelek
- 1/2 cup chopped cilantro
- 2 tablespoons soy sauce
- 1/4 cup fresh lime juice
- 1/4 cup finely chopped mint

Directions:
1. Merge all the ingredients in a large bowl and toss to coat well.
2. Serve immediately.

Nutrition:
Calories: 288 Fat: 1.1g Carbohydrates: 64.6g Proteins: 12.1g Fiber: 18.7g

1. Warmth the oven to 350F.
2. Merge the pineapple, rice, and raisins in a bowl.
3. Set the remaining ingredients in a food processor and process until smooth. Fold the mixture into the rice mixture.
4. Pour into a casserole dish. Secure and bake in the preheated oven for 30 minutes.
5. Serve immediately.

Nutrition:
Calories: 199 Fat: 4.1g Carbohydrates: 40.5g Proteins: 3.7g Fiber: 5.5g

- 1/2 cup chopped dates
- 2 teaspoons vanilla extract
- 3/4 cup maple syrup (optional)

Directions:
1. Warmth the oven to 350F.
2. Merge the dry ingredients in a large bowl. Fold in the remaining ingredients. Stir to mix well.
3. Drop 1 tablespoon of the mixture on a baking sheet to make a cookie. Repeat with remaining mixture.
4. Bake in the warmth oven for 15 to 20 minutes.
5. Serve immediately.

Nutrition:
Calories: 34 Carbohydrates: 4g Proteins: 45g Fat: 3g

- 1 tablespoon olive oil
- 1/2 cup salsa sauce

Directions:
1. Start by preheating your oven to 395 F. Line a baking pan with parchment paper or Silpat mat.
2. Thoroughly merge all the ingredients, except for the salsa, until everything is well incorporated.
3. Roll the batter into equal balls and place them in your refrigerator for about 1 hour.

4. Bake these balls for approximately 25 minutes, turning them over halfway through the cooking time. Bon appétit!

648. Roasted Pepper and Tomato Dip

Preparation time: 30 minutes
Cooking time: 35 minutes
Servings: 10
Ingredients:

- 4 red bell peppers
- 4 tomatoes
- 4 tablespoons olive oil
- 1 red onion, chopped
- 4 garlic cloves
- 4 ounces canned garbanzo beans, drained
- Sea salt and ground black pepper

Directions:

1. Warmth your oven to 400 F.
2. Place the peppers and tomatoes on a parchment-lined baking pan. Bake for about 30 minutes; peel

649. Seeds Crackers

Preparation time: 30 minutes
Cooking time: 35 minutes
Servings: 6
Ingredients:

- 3 tablespoons water
- 1 tablespoon chia seeds
- 3 tablespoons sunflower seeds
- 1 tablespoon quinoa flour
- 1 teaspoon ground turmeric
- Pinch of ground cinnamon
- Salt, to taste

Directions:

650. Spicy Almonds

Preparation time: 30 minutes
Cooking time: 10 minutes
Servings: 4
Ingredients:

- 2 cups whole almonds
- 1 tablespoon chili powder
- 1/2 teaspoon ground cinnamon
- 1/2 teaspoon ground cumin
- 1/2 teaspoon ground coriander
- Salt and black pepper, to taste
- 1 tablespoon olive oil

Directions:

Nutrition:
Calories: 98 Fat: 7.3g Carbohydrates: 6.1g Proteins: 3.2g Fiber: 1.1g

the peppers and transfer them to your food processor along with the roasted tomatoes.

3. Meanwhile, warmth 2 tablespoons of the olive oil in a frying pan over medium-high heat. Sauté the onion and garlic for about 5 minutes or until they've softened.
4. Add the sautéed vegetables to your food processor. Add in the garbanzo beans, salt, pepper and the remaining olive oil, process until creamy and smooth.
5. Bon appétit!

Nutrition:
Calories: 371 Fat: 42.4g Carbohydrates: 42g Proteins: 5.5g Fiber: 2g

1. Preheat your oven to 345F Line a baking sheet with parchment paper.
2. In a bowl, add the water and chia seeds and set aside for about 15 minutes.
3. Then attach the remaining ingredients and mix well.
4. Spread the mixture onto the prepared baking sheet evenly.
5. Bake for about 20 minutes.
6. Detach from the oven and place onto a wire rack to cool completely before serving.
7. Break into pieces and serve.

Nutrition:
Calories: 34 Carbohydrates: 4g Proteins: 45g Fat: 3g

1. Preheat your oven to 375F.
2. Line a suitable baking pan with parchment paper.
3. Toss almonds with all the spices and oil.
4. Spread the almond mixture into the prepared baking dish in a single layer.
5. Roast for about 10 minutes, flipping twice.
6. Detach from the oven and let it cool completely before serving.

Nutrition:
Calories: 456 Fat: 33g Carbohydrates: 37g Proteins: 8.3g Fiber: 5g

651. Berries Pie

Preparation time: 10 minutes
Cooking time: 25 minutes
Servings: 12
Ingredients:

- 2 cups coconut flour
- 1 cup coconut butter, soft
- 1 cup pecans, chopped
- 1 and 1/4 cup coconut sugar
- 4 cups rhubarb, chopped
- 1 cup strawberries, sliced
- 8 ounces coconut cream

Directions:

1. In a bowl, merge the flour with the butter, pecans and 1/4 cup of sugar and mix well.
2. Transfer this to a cake pan, press firmly into the pan, place in the oven and bake at 350F for 20 minutes.
3. In a pan combine the strawberries with the remaining ingredients mix well and cook over medium heat for 4 minutes.
4. Spread it on the crust of the cake and keep it in the fridge for a few hours before slicing and serving.

Nutrition:
Calories: 332 Fat: 5g Fiber: 5g Carbohydrates: 15g Proteins: 6.3g

652. Tomato Jam

Preparation time: 10 minutes
Cooking time: 3 hours
Servings: 2
Ingredients:

- ½ pound tomatoes, chopped
- 1 green apple, grated
- tablespoons red wine vinegar
- tablespoons sugar

Directions:

- In your slow cooker, mix the tomatoes with the apple with the other ingredients, put the lid on and cook on Low for 3 hours.
- Whisk the jam well, blend a bit using an immersion blender, divide into bowls and serve cold.

Nutrition:
Calories: 70 Fat: 1g Fiber: 1g Carbohydrates: 18g Proteins: 1g

653. Green Tea Pudding

Preparation time: 10 minutes
Cooking time: 1 hour
Servings: 2
Ingredients:

- ½ cup coconut milk
- 1 and ½ cup avocado, pitted and peeled
- tablespoons green tea powder
- teaspoons lime zest, grated

654. Candied Lemon

Preparation time: 20 minutes
Cooking time: 4 hours
Servings: 4
Ingredients:

- lemons, peeled and cut into medium segments
- cups white sugar
- cups water

655. Dates and Rice Pudding

Preparation time: 10 minutes
Cooking time: 3 hours
Servings: 2
Ingredients:

- 1 cup dates, chopped
- ½ cup white rice
- 1 cup almond milk
- tablespoons brown sugar
- 1 teaspoon almond extract

656. Berries Salad

Preparation time: 10 minutes
Cooking time: 1 hour
Servings: 2
Ingredients:

- tablespoons brown sugar
- 1 tablespoon lime juice
- 1 tablespoon lime zest, grated
- 1 cup blueberries
- ½ cup cranberries
- 1 cup blackberries

657. Pears and Apples Bowls

Preparation time: 10 minutes
Cooking time: 2 hours
Servings: 2
Ingredients:

- 1 teaspoon vanilla extract
- pears, cored and cut into wedges
- apples, cored and cut into wedges
- 1 tablespoon walnuts, chopped
- tablespoons brown sugar

658. Pears and Wine Sauce

Preparation time: 10 minutes
Cooking time: 1 hours
Servings: 6
Ingredients:

- green pears
- 1 vanilla pod
- 1 clove
- A pinch of cinnamon
- oz. sugar

- 1 tablespoon sugar

Directions:

1. In your slow cooker, mix coconut milk with avocado, tea powder, lime zest and sugar, stir, cover and cook on Low for 1 hour.
2. Divide into cups and serve cold.

Nutrition:
Calories: 107 Fat: 5g Fiber: 3g Carbohydrates: 6g Proteins: 8g

Directions:

1. In your slow cooker,
2. mix lemons with sugar and water,
3. cover, cook on Low for 4 hours,
4. transfer them to bowls and serve cold.

Nutrition:
Calories: 62 Fat: 3g Fiber: 5g Carbohydrates: 3g Proteins: 4g

Directions:

1. In your slow cooker, mix the rice with the milk and the other ingredients, whisk, put the lid on and cook on Low for 3 hours.
2. Divide the pudding into bowls and serve.

Nutrition:
Calories: 152 Fat: 5g Fiber: 2g   Carbohydrates: 6g Proteins: 3g

- 1 cup strawberries
- ½ cup heavy cream

1. **Directions:**
2. In your slow cooker, mix the berries with the sugar and the other ingredients, toss, put the lid on and cook on High for 1 hour.
3. Divide the mix into bowls and serve.

Nutrition:
Calories: 262 Fat: 7g Fiber: 2g   Carbohydrates: 5g Proteins: 8g

- ½ cup coconut cream

Directions:

1. In your slow cooker, mix the pears with the apples, nuts and the other ingredients, toss, put the lid on and cook on Low for 2 hours.
2. Divide the mix into bowls and serve cold.

Nutrition:
Calories: 120 Fat: 2g Fiber: 2g Carbohydrates: 4g Proteins: 3g

- 1 glass red wine

Directions:

1. In your slow cooker, mix wine with sugar, vanilla and cinnamon.
2. Add pears and clove, cover slow cooker and cook on High for 1 hour and 30 minutes.
3. Transfer pears to bowls and serve with the wine sauce all over.

Nutrition:
Calories: 162 Fat: 4g Fiber: 3g Carbohydrates: 6g Proteins: 3g

659. Creamy Rhubarb and Plums Bowls

Preparation time: 10 minutes
Cooking time: 2 hours
Servings: 2
Ingredients:

- 1 cup plums, pitted and halved
- 1 cup rhubarb, sliced
- 1 cup coconut cream
- ½ teaspoon vanilla extract
- ½ cup sugar
- ½ tablespoon lemon juice
- 1 teaspoon almond extract

Directions:

1. In your slow cooker, mix the plums with the rhubarb, and other ingredients, toss, put the lid on and cook on High for 2 hours.
2. Divide the mix into bowls and serve.

Nutrition:
Calories: 162 Fat: 2g Fiber: 2g Carbohydrates: 4g Proteins: 5g

660. Bananas Foster

Preparation time: 5 minutes
Cooking time: 5 minutes
Servings: 4
Ingredients:

- 2/3 cup dark brown sugar
- 1/2 teaspoons vanilla extract
- 1/2 teaspoon of ground cinnamon
- bananas, peeled and cut lengthwise and broad
- 1/4 cup chopped nuts, butter

Directions:

1. Melt the butter in a deep-frying pan over medium heat. Stir in sugar, 3 ½ tbsp. of rum, vanilla, and cinnamon.
2. When the mixture starts to bubble, place the bananas and nuts in the pan. Bake until the bananas are hot, 1 to 2 minutes. Serve immediately with vanilla ice cream.

Nutrition:
Calories: 534 Fat: 23.8g Proteins: 4.6g

661. Rhubarb Strawberry Crunch

Preparation time: 15 minutes
Cooking time: 45 minutes
Servings: 18
Ingredients:

- 3 tablespoons all-purpose flour
- 3 cups of fresh strawberries, sliced
- 3 cups of rhubarb, cut into cubes
- 1/2 cup flour
- 1 cup butter

Directions:

1. Preheat the oven to 190 ° C.
2. Combine 1 cup of white sugar, 3 tablespoons flour, strawberries and rhubarb in a large bowl. Place the mixture in a 9 x 13-inch baking dish.
3. Mix 1 1/2 cups of flour, 1 cup of brown sugar, butter, and oats until a crumbly texture is obtained. You may want to use a blender for this. Crumble the mixture of rhubarb and strawberry.
4. Bake in the preheated oven for 45 minutes or until crispy and light brown.

Nutrition:
Calories: 253 Fat: 10.8g Proteins: 2.3g

662. Caramel Popcorn

Preparation time: 30 minutes
Cooking time: 1 hour
Servings: 20
Ingredients:

- 2 cups brown sugar
- 1/2 cup of corn syrup
- 1/2 teaspoon baking powder
- teaspoon vanilla extract
- 5 cups of popcorn

Directions:

1. Preheat the oven to 95° C (250° F). Put the popcorn in a large bowl.
2. Melt 1 cup of butter in a medium-sized pan over medium heat. Stir in brown sugar, 1 tsp. of salt, and corn syrup. Bring to a boil, constantly stirring — Cook without stirring for 4 minutes. Then remove from heat and stir in the soda and vanilla. Pour in a thin layer on the popcorn and stir well.
3. Place in two large shallow baking tins and bake in the preheated oven, stirring every 15 minutes for an hour. Remove from the oven and let cool completely before breaking into pieces.

Nutrition:
Calories: 253 Fat: 14g Carbohydrates: 32.8g

663. Chocolate, Almond, and Cherry Clusters

Preparation time: 15 minutes
Cooking time: 3 minutes
Servings: 5
Ingredients:

- 1 cup dark chocolate (60% cocoa or higher), chopped
- 1 tablespoon coconut oil
- ½ cup dried cherries
- 1 cup roasted salted almonds

Directions:

1. Line a baking sheet with parchment paper.
2. Melt the chocolate and coconut oil in a saucepan for 3 minutes. Stir constantly.
3. Turn off the heat and mix in the cherries and almonds.
4. Drop the mixture on the baking sheet with a spoon. Place the sheet in the refrigerator and chill for at least 1 hour or until firm.
5. Serve chilled.

Nutrition:
Calories: 197 Fat: 13.2g Proteins: 4.1g

664. Chocolate and Avocado Mousse

Preparation time: 40 minutes
Cooking time: 5 minutes
Servings: 5
Ingredients:

- 8 ounces (227 g) dark chocolate (60% cocoa or higher), chopped
- ¼ cup unsweetened coconut milk
- 2 tablespoons coconut oil
- 2 ripe avocados, deseeded

Directions:

1. Put the chocolate in a saucepan. Pour in the coconut milk and add the coconut oil.
2. Cook for 3 minutes or until the chocolate and coconut oil melt. Stir constantly.
3. Put the avocado in a food processor and melted chocolate. Pulse to combine until smooth.
4. Pour the mixture in a serving bowl, then sprinkle with salt. Refrigerate to chill for 30 minutes and serve.

Nutrition:
Calories: 654 Fat: 46.8g Proteins: 7.2g

665. French Lover's Coconut Macaroons

Preparation time: 15 minutes
Cooking time: 25 minutes
Servings: 6
Ingredients:

- 1/3 cup agave nectar
- ½ cup coconut cream
- 1 cup shredded coconut
- ½ tsp. salt
- 1/3 cup chocolate chips

Directions:

1. Begin by preheating your oven to 300 degrees Fahrenheit.
2. Next, mix the coconut cream, the agave, and the salt. Next, fold in the chocolate chips and the coconut. Stir well and create cookie balls. Place the balls on a baking sheet and bake the cookies for twenty-five minutes. Enjoy.

Nutrition:
Calories: 118 Fat: 6g Proteins: 9g

666. Elementary Party Vegan Oatmeal Raisin Cookies

Preparation time: 15 minutes
Cooking time: 35 minutes
Servings: 12
Ingredients:

- 1 cup whole wheat flour
- ½ tsp. salt
- ½ tsp. baking soda
- 1 tsp. cinnamon
- ½ cup brown sugar
- 2 tbsp. maple syrup
- ½ cup sugar
- 1/3 cup applesauce
- ½ tsp. vanilla
- 1/3 cup olive oil
- ½ cup raisins
- 1 ¾ cup oats

Directions:

1. Begin by preheating the oven to 350 degrees Fahrenheit.
2. Next, mix all the dry ingredients. Place this mixture to the side.
3. Next, mix all the wet ingredients in a large mixing bowl. Add the dry ingredients to the wet ingredients slowly, stirring as you go. Add the oats next, stirring well. Lastly, add the raisins.
4. Allow the batter to chill in the refrigerator for twenty minutes. Afterwards, drop the cookies onto a baking sheet and bake them for thirteen minutes. Enjoy after cooling.

Nutrition:
Calories: 114 Fat: 6g Proteins: 10g

667. Zucchini Chocolate Crisis Bread

Preparation time: 15 minutes
Cooking time: 25 minutes
Servings: 8
Ingredients:

- 1 cup sugar
- 2 tbsp. flax seeds
- 6 tbsp. water
- 1 cup applesauce
- 1/3 cup cocoa powder
- 2 cups all-purpose flour
- 2 tsp. vanilla
- 1 tsp. baking soda
- ½ tsp. baking powder
- 1 tbsp. cinnamon
- 1 tsp. salt
- 2 1/3 cup grated zucchini
- 1 cup nondairy chocolate chips

Directions:

1. Begin by preheating your oven to 325 degrees Fahrenheit.
2. First, mix the water and the flax seeds and allow the mixture to thicken to the side for five minutes.
3. Mix all the dry ingredients together. Next, add the wet ingredients to the dry ingredients, including the flax seeds. Next, add the chocolate chips and the zucchini. Stir well and spread the batter out into your bread loaf pan. Bake the creation for thirty minutes. Afterward it cools, enjoy!

Nutrition:
Calories: 116 Fat: 4g Proteins: 8g

668. Banana Blueberry Bread

Preparation time: 15 minutes
Cooking time: 35 minutes
Servings: 8

Ingredients:

- 3 tbsp. lemon juice
- 4 bananas

- ½ cup agave nectar
- ½ cup vegan milk
- 1 ¾ cup all-purpose flour
- 1 tsp. baking soda
- 1 tsp. baking powder
- 1 tsp. salt
- 2 cups blueberries

Directions:
1. Begin by preheating your oven to 350 degrees Fahrenheit.

669. Vegan Apple Cobbler Pie

Preparation time: 15 minutes
Cooking time: 25 minutes
Servings: 3
Ingredients:
- 3 cups sliced apples
- 6 cups sliced peaches
- 2 tbsp. arrowroot powder
- ½ cup white sugar
- 1 tsp. cinnamon
- 1 tsp. vanilla
- ½ cup water

Biscuit Topping **Ingredients:**
- ½ cup almond flour
- 1 cup gluten-free ground-up oats
- ½ tsp. salt
- 2 tsp. baking powder
- 2 tbsp. white sugar
- 1 tsp. cinnamon
- ½ cup soymilk

670. Vegan Vanilla Ice Cream

Preparation time: 15 minutes
Cooking time: 45 minutes
Servings: 3
Ingredients:
- 3 vanilla pods
- 1 ½ tsp. vanilla bean paste
- 400 ml soymilk
- 600 grams light coconut milk
- 200 grams agave syrup

Directions:

671. Watermelon Lollies

Preparation time: 15 minutes
Cooking time: 35 minutes
Servings: 5
Ingredients:
- ½ cup watermelon, cubed
- 2 tablespoons lemon juice, freshly squeezed
- ½ cup water
- 1 tablespoon stevia

Directions:

672. Lemon Bars

Preparation time: 15 minutes
Cooking time: 25 minutes
Servings: 5
Ingredients:
- 3/4 cup melted butter

2. Next, mix the dry ingredients in a large bowl and your wet ingredients in a different, smaller bowl. Make sure to mash up the bananas well.
3. Stir the ingredients together in the large bowl, making sure to assimilate the ingredients together completely. Add the blueberries last, and then pour the mixture into a bread pan. Allow the bread to bake for fifty minutes and enjoy.

Nutrition:
Calories: 119 Fat: 7g Proteins: 11g

- 4 tbsp. vegan butter

Directions:
1. Begin by preheating your oven to 400 degrees Fahrenheit.
2. Next, coat the peaches and the apples with the sugar, arrowroot, the cinnamon, the vanilla, and the water in a large bowl. Allow the mixture to boil in a saucepan. After it begins to boil, allow the apples and peaches to simmer for three minutes. Remove the fruit from the heat and add the vanilla.
3. You've created your base.
4. Now, add the dry ingredients together in a small bowl. Cut the biscuit with the vegan butter to create a crumble. Add the almond milk and cover the fruit with this batter.
5. Bake this mixture for thirty minutes. Serve warm and enjoy!

Nutrition:
Calories: 116 Fat: 7g Proteins: 16g

1. Begin by slicing the vanilla pods and removing the seeds. Place the seeds in a big mixing bowl and toss out the pods. Next, add the rest of the ingredients, and position the ingredients into an ice cream maker. Churn the ice cream for forty-five minutes. Next, place the mixture into a freezer container, and allow the ice cream to freeze for three hours. Serve, and enjoy!

Nutrition:
Calories: 115 Fat: 3g Proteins: 12g

1. In a food processor, put cubed watermelon. Process until smooth. Divide an equal amount of the mixture into an ice pop container. Place inside the freezer for 1 hour.
2. Meanwhile, in a small bowl, put together lemon juice, water, and stevia. Mix well. Pour over frozen watermelon lollies. Add in pop sticks. Freeze for another hour.
3. Pry out watermelon lollies. Serve.

Nutrition:
Calories: 114 Fat: 8g Proteins: 12g

- 3/4 cup almond flour
- 1 1/2 cups boiling water
- 2/3 cup lemon gelatin mix, no sugar added
- 3 Tbsp freshly squeezed lemon juice

Directions:

1. Set the oven to 350 degrees F.
2. Combine the melted butter and flour together in a bowl, then pour the mixture into a baking pan, pressing down to create a crust.
3. Bake for 10 minutes then set on a cooling rack. Cool completely before use.

673. Orange Blueberry Blast

Preparation time: 30 minutes
Cooking time: 0 minute
Servings: 1
Ingredients:

- 1 cup almond milk
- 1 scoop plant-based protein powder
- 1 cup blueberries
- 1 orange, peeled

674. Chocolate Coconut Almond Tart

Preparation time: 15 minutes
Cooking time: 25 minutes
Servings: 9
Ingredients:
For crust:

- 1 cup almonds
- 2 tbsp. maple syrup
- 1 cup almond flour
- 3 tbsp. coconut oil

Filling & topping:

- 3 oz. bittersweet chocolate bars
- 1 tbsp. maple syrup
- oz. coconut milk
- Coconut, almonds
- Sea salt a pinch

Directions:

675. Peanut Butter and Celery

Preparation time: 5 minutes
Cooking time: 5 minutes
Servings: 2
Ingredients:

- 4 stalks celery
- 1 cup peanut butter

Directions:

676. Tangy Heirloom Carrot

Preparation time: 10 minutes
Cooking time: 45 minutes
Servings: 6
Ingredients:

- 1 bunch heirloom carrots
- 1 tablespoon fresh thyme leaves
- ½ tablespoon coconut oil
- 1 tablespoon date paste
- 1/8 cup freshly squeezed orange juice
- 1/8 teaspoon salt
- Extra salt if needed

677. Just Apple Slices

Preparation time: 10 minutes
Cooking time: 10 minutes
Servings: 4
Ingredients:

- 1 cup of coconut oil

4. In a large mixing bowl, mix the gelatin and boiling water. Stir until the gelatin completely dissolves.
5. Stir in the lemon juice

Nutrition:
Calories: 119 Fat: 6g Proteins: 8g

- 1 teaspoon nutmeg
- 1 tablespoon shredded coconut

Directions:
1. Add all ingredients to a blender.
2. Hit the pulse button and blend till it is smooth.
3. Chill well to serve.

Nutrition:
Calories: 117 Fat: 4g Proteins: 9g

1. In a blender mix the almond flour and almonds until chopped and mix evenly. Pour maple syrup and coconut oil or mix well. Pour the batter into a baking pan and press it with a spoon to set its edges.
2. Bake the pie for 10 to 1 minutes in a preheated oven at 300 degrees until golden brown. Take a medium bowl, add chocolate and melt it over the boiling water. Add maple syrup on the top of the chocolate.
3. In a pan, add coconut milk and boil on a flame, pour the chocolate in boiling coconut milk and stir well until smooth. Now pour the filling on the crust and top with almonds, coconut and sea salt. Store in a refrigerator for 2 hours or leave over the night. Serve the tart when completely set.

Nutrition:
Calories: 118 Fat: 5g Proteins: 13g

1. Take 4 stalks of celery, clean them well and let it dry.
2. Now cut one stalk in 3 equal parts.
3. Apply the peanut butter with the knife on every stalk piece. Serve it with a cold glass of milk or enjoy a crunchy peanut butter celery.

Nutrition:
Calories: 115 Fat: 4g Proteins: 9g

Directions:
1. Preheat your oven to 350 degrees Fahrenheit
2. Wash carrots and discard green pieces
3. Take a small-sized bowl and add coconut oil, orange juice, salt, and date paste
4. Pour mixture over carrots and spread on a large baking sheet
5. Sprinkle thyme and roast for 45 minutes
6. Sprinkle salt on top and enjoy!

Nutrition:
Calories: 106 Fat: 2g Proteins: 2g

- ¼ cup date paste
- 2 tablespoons ground cinnamon
- 4 granny smith apples, peeled and sliced, cored

Directions:

1. Take a large-sized skillet and place it over medium heat
2. Add oil and allow the oil to heat up
3. Stir in cinnamon and date paste into the oil

678. The Classic Rice Pudding

Preparation time: 10 minutes
Cooking time: 30 minutes
Servings: 4
Ingredients:

- 1 cup of brown rice (uncooked)
- 1 teaspoon vanilla extract
- ½ teaspoon salt
- ½ teaspoon cinnamon
- ¼ teaspoon nutmeg
- 3 cups coconut milk, light

679. Cinnamon and Pumpkin Fudge

Preparation time: 25 minutes
Cooking time: 0 minute
Servings: 4
Ingredients:

- 1 teaspoon ground cinnamon
- 1 cup pumpkin puree
- ¼ teaspoon nutmeg, ground
- 1 ¾ cups of coconut butter, melted
- 1 tablespoon coconut oil

Directions:

680. Blueberry and Pecan Bake

Preparation time: 10 minutes
Cooking time: 30 minutes
Servings: 4
Ingredients:

- ounces blueberries
- 1 tablespoon lemon juice, fresh
- 1 ½ teaspoons Stevia powder
- tablespoons chia seeds
- cups almond flour, blanched
- ¼ cup pecans, chopped
- tablespoons coconut oil
- tablespoons cinnamon

Directions:

681. Fantastic Sticky Mango Rice

Preparation time: 10 minutes
Cooking time: 25 minutes
Servings: 4
Ingredients:

- 1/2 cup sugar
- 1 mango, sliced
- ounces coconut milk, canned
- 1/2 cup basmati rice

Directions:

682. Sesame Cookies

Preparation time: 10 minutes
Cooking time: 75 minutes
Servings: 20
Ingredients:

- 1 cup sesame seeds
- 1 cup sunflower seeds

4. Add cut up apples and cook for 5-8 minutes until crispy
5. Serve and enjoy!

Nutrition:
Calories: 368 Fat: 23g Proteins: 19g

- 2 cups brown rice, cooked

Directions:

1. Take a bowl and mix in all ingredients, stir well
2. Preheat your oven to 300 degrees Fahrenheit
3. Transfer mixture to a baking dish and put the dish into the oven
4. Bake for 90 minutes
5. Serve and enjoy!

Nutrition:
Calories: 330 Fat: 20g Proteins: 5g

1. Take a bowl and mix in pumpkin spices, coconut butter, coconut oil and whisk well
2. Spread mixture into pan and cover with foil, press it down well
3. Discard the foil
4. Let it chill for 2 hours
5. Chop into squares, serve and enjoy!

Nutrition:
Calories: 110 Fat: 10g Proteins: 12g

1. Take a bowl and mix in blueberries, Stevia, chia seeds, lemon juice, and stir
2. Take an iron skillet and place it overheat, add mixture and stir
3. Take a bowl and mix in remaining ingredients, spread mixture over blueberries
4. Preheat your oven to 400 degrees Fahrenheit
5. Transfer baking dish to your oven, bake for 30 minutes
6. Serve and enjoy!

Nutrition:
Calories: 380 Fat: 32g Proteins: 10g

1. Cook the rice according to the package instructions and add half of the sugar while cooking rice. Make sure to substitute half of the required water with coconut milk
2. Take another skillet and boil remaining coconut milk with sugar. Once the mixture is thick, add rice and gently stir
3. Add mango slices and serve
4. Enjoy!

Nutrition:
Calories: 550 Fat: 30g Proteins: 6g

- 1 cup flaxseeds
- ½ cup hulled hemp seeds
- 3 tablespoons Psyllium husk
- 1 teaspoon salt
- 1 teaspoon baking powder

- 2 cups of water

Directions:
1. Pre-heat your oven to a temperature of 350 degrees Fahrenheit
2. Take your blender and add seeds, baking powder, salt, and Psyllium husk
3. Blend well until a sand-like texture appears
4. Stir in water and mix until a batter form
5. Allow the batter to rest for 10 minutes until a dough-like thick mixture forms

683. Cool Avocado Pudding

Preparation time: 3 hours
Cooking time: 0 minute
Servings: 4
Ingredients:
- 1 cup almond milk
- 2 avocados, peeled and pitted
- ¾ cup cocoa powder
- 1 teaspoon vanilla extract
- 2 tablespoons Stevia
- ¼ teaspoon cinnamon

684. Gingerbread Muffins

Preparation time: 10 minutes
Cooking time: 15 minutes
Servings: 6
Ingredients:
- 1 tablespoon ground flaxseed
- 6 tablespoons coconut milk
- 1 tablespoon apple cider vinegar
- ½ cup peanut butter
- 2 tablespoons gingerbread spice blend
- 1 teaspoon baking powder
- 1 teaspoon vanilla extract
- 2 tablespoons Swerve

685. Cashew Roasted Cauliflower

Preparation time: 5 minutes
Cooking time: 30 minutes
Servings: 8
Ingredients:
- 1 large cauliflower head
- 2 tablespoons melted coconut oil
- 2 tablespoons fresh thyme
- 1 teaspoon Celtic sea salt
- 1 teaspoon fresh ground pepper
- 1 head roasted garlic
- 2 tablespoons fresh thyme for garnish

Directions:

686. Bake-Free Fudge

Preparation time: 15 minutes
Cooking time: 5 minutes
Servings: 25
Ingredients:
- 1 ¾ cups of coconut butter
- 1 cup pumpkin puree
- 1 teaspoon ground cinnamon
- ¼ teaspoon ground nutmeg
- 1 tablespoon coconut oil

Directions:

6. Pour the dough onto a cookie sheet lined with parchment paper
7. Spread it evenly, making sure that it has a ¼ inch thickness all around
8. Bake for 75 minutes in the oven
9. Remove and cut up into 20 pieces
10. Allow them to cool for 30 minutes and enjoy!

Nutrition:
Calories: 156 Fat: 13g Proteins: 5g

- Walnuts, chopped for serving

Directions:
1. Add avocados to a blender and pulse well
2. Add cocoa powder, almond milk, Stevia, vanilla bean extract and pulse the mixture well
3. Pour into serving bowls and top with walnuts
4. Chill for 2-3 hours and serve!

Nutrition:
Calories: 221 Fat: 8g Proteins: 3g

Directions:
1. Preheat your oven to 350 degrees Fahrenheit
2. Take a bowl and add flaxseed, salt, vanilla, sweetener, spices, and non-dairy milk
3. Keep it on the side
4. Add peanut butter, baking powder and keep mixing
5. Stir well
6. Spoon batter into muffin liners and bake for 30 minutes
7. Let them cool and serve

Nutrition:
Calories: 283 Fat: 23g Proteins: 11g

1. Preheat your oven to 425 degrees Fahrenheit
2. Rinse cauliflower and trim, core and slice
3. Lay cauliflower evenly on a rimmed baking tray
4. Drizzle coconut oil evenly over cauliflower, sprinkle thyme leaves
5. Season with a pinch of salt and pepper
6. Squeeze roasted garlic
7. Roast cauliflower until slightly caramelized for about 30 minutes, making sure to turn once
8. Garnish with fresh thyme leaves

Nutrition:
Calories: 129 Fat: 11g Proteins: 7g

1. Take an 8x8 inch square baking pan and line it with aluminum foil
2. Take a spoon and scoop out coconut butter into a heated pan and allow the butter to melt
3. Keep stirring well and remove the heat once fully melted
4. Add spices and pumpkin and keep straining until you have a grain-like texture
5. Add coconut oil and keep stirring to incorporate everything
6. Scoop the mixture into your baking pan and evenly distribute it

7 Place wax paper on top of the mixture and press gently to straighten the top
8 Remove the paper and discard
9 Allow it to chill for 1-2 hours

687. Tasty Zucchini Brownies

Preparation time: 5 minutes
Cooking time: 45 minutes
Servings: 4
Ingredients:

- 2 cups flour
- 1 ½ cups vegan sugar
- 1 teaspoon baking soda
- 1 teaspoon salt
- ½ cup cocoa, unsweetened
- 2 tablespoons vanilla extract
- ½ cup oil
- 2 cups zucchini, peeled and grated

688. Great Chia and Blackberry Pudding

Preparation time: 45 minutes
Cooking time: 0 minute
Servings: 2
Ingredients:

- ¼ cup chia seeds
- ½ cup blackberries, fresh
- 1 teaspoon liquid sweetener
- 1 cup coconut milk, full fat and unsweetened
- 1 teaspoon vanilla extract

Directions:

689. Choco-Avocado Truffles

Preparation time: 1 hour and 10 minutes
Cooking time: 1 minute
Servings: 18
Ingredients:

- 1 medium avocado, ripe
- 2 tablespoons cocoa powder
- 10 ounces of dark chocolate chips

Directions:

1. Remove the avocado pulp, put it in a bowl, and then mash it with a fork until smooth and mix in 1/2 cup of chocolate chips.

690. Mango Ice Cream

Preparation time: 5 minutes
Cooking time: 0 minute
Servings: 1
Ingredients:

- 2 frozen bananas, sliced
- 1 cup diced frozen mango

Directions:

691. Snickers Pie

Preparation time: 4 hours
Cooking time: 0 minute
Servings: 16
Ingredients:
For the Crust:

- 12 Medjool dates, pitted
- 1 cup dried coconut, unsweetened
- 5 tablespoons cocoa powder
- 1/2 teaspoon sea salt
- 1 teaspoon vanilla extract, unsweetened

10 Once chilled, take it out and slice it up into pieces
Nutrition:
Calories: 120 Fat: 10g Proteins: 1.2g

Directions:

1 Pre-heat your oven to 350 degrees Fahrenheit
2 Take a bowl and sift in cocoa, salt, flour, sugar, and baking soda
3 Stir well
4 Add oil, vanilla, zucchini mix well until you have a nice batter
5 Pour mixture into a baking dish and transfer to the oven
6 Bake for 30-45 minutes until done

Nutrition:
Calories: 138 Fat: 5g Proteins: 1.5g

1 Take the vanilla, liquid sweetener and coconut milk and add to blender
2 Process until thick
3 Add in blackberries and process until smooth
4 Divide the mixture between cups and chill for 30 minutes
5 Serve and enjoy!

Nutrition:
Calories: 437 Fat: 38g Proteins: 8g

2. Set the remaining chocolate chips in a heat resistant bowl and microwave for 1 minute until the chocolate has melted, stirring halfway.
3. Attach the melted chocolate to the avocado mixture, mix well until blended, and then refrigerate for 1 hour.
4. Then shape the mixture into balls, 1 tablespoon of the mixture per ball and roll in the cocoa powder until covered.
5. Serve immediately.

Nutrition:
Calories: 59 Fat: 4g Carbohydrates: 7g Proteins: 0g Fiber: 1g

1. Put the whole ingredients in a food processor and blend for 2 minutes until smooth.
2. Spread the ice cream mixture between two bowls and serve immediately.

Nutrition:
Calories: 74 Fat: 0g Carbohydrates: 17g Proteins: 0g Fiber: 4g

- 1 cup almonds

For the Caramel Layer:

- 10 Medjool dates, pitted, soaked for 10 minutes in warm water, drained
- 2 teaspoons vanilla extract, unsweetened
- 3 teaspoons coconut oil
- 3 tablespoons almond butter, unsalted

For the Peanut Butter Mousse:

- 3/4 cup peanut butter
- 2 tablespoons maple syrup

- 1/2 teaspoon vanilla extract, unsweetened
- 1/8 teaspoon sea salt
- 28 ounces coconut milk, chilled

Directions:
1. Prepare the crust and, for this, put all ingredients in a food processor and blend for 3-5 minutes until the thick dough comes together.
2. Take a baking sheet, line it with parchment paper, put the crust mixture in it, roll it out and press it evenly to the bottom, and freeze until required.
3. Prepare the caramel layer and for this put your entire ingredients in a food processor and blend for 2 minutes until smooth.

692. Ice Cream with Peanut Butter

Preparation time: 5 minutes
Cooking time: 0 minute
Servings: 2
Ingredients:
- 21/2 tablespoons peanut butter
- 2 bananas frozen, sliced
- 11/2 tablespoons maple syrup

Directions:

693. Rainbow Fruit Salad

Preparation time: 10 minutes
Cooking time: 0 minute
Servings: 4
Ingredients:
For the Fruit Salad:
- 1 pound strawberries, hulled, sliced
- 1 cup kiwis, halved, cubed
- 1 1/4 cups blueberries
- 1 1/3 cups blackberries
- 1 cup pineapple chunks

For the Maple Lime Dressing:
- 2 teaspoons lime zest

694. Brownie Batter

Preparation time: 5 minutes
Cooking time: 0 minute
Servings: 4
Ingredients:
- 4 Medjool dates, pitted, soaked in warm water
- 1.5ounces chocolate, unsweetened, melted
- 2 tablespoons maple syrup
- 4 tablespoons tahini
- 1/2 teaspoon vanilla extract, unsweetened
- 1 tablespoon cocoa powder, unsweetened

695. Orange Compote

Preparation time: 10 minutes
Cooking time: 15 minutes
Servings: 6
Ingredients:
- 5 tablespoons stevia
- 1-ounce orange juice
- 1 pound oranges, peeled and sliced

Directions:

696. Fruit Protein Energy Balls

Preparation time: 1 hour and 10 minutes
Cooking time: 3 minutes
Servings: 4

4. Pour the caramel over the prepared crust, smooth the top and freeze for 30 minutes until solidified.
5. Prepare the mousse and for this, separate the coconut milk and its solid, then add the solid from the coconut milk in a food processor, add the remaining ingredients and then blend for 1 minute until smooth.
6. Coat the prepared mousse on top of the caramel layer, and then freeze for 3 hours until it solidifies.
7. Serve immediately.

Nutrition:
Calories: 456 Fat: 33g Carbohydrates: 37g Proteins: 8.3g Fiber: 5g

1. Put the whole ingredients in a food processor and blend for 2 minutes until smooth.
2. Spread the ice cream mixture between two bowls and serve immediately.

Nutrition:
Calories: 190 Fat: 11g Carbohydrates: 20g Proteins: 4g Fiber: 0g

- 1/4 cup maple syrup
- 1 tablespoon lime juice

Directions:
- Prepare the salad, and for this, take a bowl, place all ingredients and mix until amalgamated.
- Prepare the sauce and for this take a small bowl, put all ingredients and beat well.
- Spill the dressing over the salad, stir until coated and serve.

Nutrition:
Calories: 88.1 Fat: 0.4g Carbohydrates: 22.6g Proteins: 1.1g Fiber: 2.8g

- 1/8 teaspoon sea salt
- 1/8 teaspoon espresso powder
- 2 to 4 tablespoons almond milk, unsweetened

Directions:
1. Put the whole ingredients in a food processor and cook for 2 minutes until combined.
2. Set aside until needed.

Nutrition:
Calories: 44 Fat: 1g Carbohydrates: 6g Proteins: 2g Fiber: 0g

1. In a pot combine the oranges with the stevia and the other shopping list: mix, bring to a boil, cook for 15 minutes, divide into bowls and serve cold.

Nutrition:
Calories: 120
Fat: 2g
Fiber: 3g
Carbohydrates: 6g
Proteins: 9g

Ingredients:
- 1 cup rolled oats
- 1/2 cup maple syrup

- 2 1/2 scoops of vanilla powder
- 1 cup almond butter
- Chia seeds for rolling

Directions:
1. Take a pan, set it on medium heat, add butter and maple syrup, stir and cook for 2 minutes until hot.
2. Set the mixture to a bowl, set in the protein powder until blended, and then stir in the oatmeal until well blended.

697. Chocolate Raspberry Ice Cream

Preparation time: 5 minutes
Cooking time: 0 minute
Servings: 2
Ingredients:
- 2 frozen bananas, sliced
- 1/4 cup fresh raspberries
- 2 tablespoons cocoa powder, unsweetened
- 2 tablespoons raspberry jelly

Directions:

698. Chocolate Raspberry Brownies

Preparation time: 4 hours
Cooking time: 0 minute
Servings: 4
Ingredients:
For the Chocolate Brownie Base:
- 12 Medjool Dates, pitted
- 3/4 cup oat flour
- 3/4 cup almond meal
- 3 tablespoons cacao
- 1 teaspoon vanilla extract, unsweetened
- 1/8 teaspoon sea salt
- 3 tablespoons water
- 1/2 cup pecans, chopped

For the Raspberry Cheesecake:
- 3/4 cup cashews, soaked, drained
- 6 tablespoons agave nectar
- 1/2 cup raspberries
- 1 teaspoon vanilla extract, unsweetened
- 1 lemon, juiced
- 6 tablespoons liquid coconut oil

For the Chocolate Coating:
- 2 1/2 tablespoons cacao powder

699. Coconut Oil Cookies

Preparation time: 10 minutes
Cooking time: 10 minutes
Servings: 15
Ingredients:
- 3 1/4 cup oats
- 1/2 teaspoons salt
- 2 cups coconut Sugar
- 1 teaspoon vanilla extract, unsweetened
- 1/4 cup cocoa powder
- 1/2 cup liquid Coconut Oil
- 1/2 cup peanut butter
- 1/2 cup cashew milk

Directions:

3. Set the mixture into balls, roll them in chia seeds, then place them on a baking sheet and refrigerate for 1 hour until they solidify.
4. Serve immediately

Nutrition:
Calories: 200 Fat: 10g Carbohydrates: 21g Proteins: 7g Fiber: 4g

1. Arrange all the ingredients in a food processor except the berries and blend for 2 minutes until smooth.
2. Spread the ice cream mixture between two bowls, stir in the berries until well blended and serve immediately.

Nutrition:
Calories: 104 Fat: 0g Carbohydrates: 25g Proteins: 0g Fiber: 5g

- 3 3/4 tablespoons coconut Oil
- 2 tablespoons maple syrup
- 1/8 teaspoon sea salt

Directions:
1. Prepare the crust and, for this, put his entire shopping list: in a food processor and blend for 3-5 minutes until the thick dough comes together.
2. Take a 6-inch spring form pan, grease it with oil, put the crust mixture in it and spread it and press the mixture evenly across the bottom and sides and freeze it until needed.
3. Prepare the cheesecake coating and, for this, put his entire shopping list: in a food processor and blend until the mixture is smooth.
4. Spill the filling into the prepared pan, smooth the top and freeze for 8 hours until solidified.
5. Prepare the chocolate coverture and for that, whisk her entire shopping list together: until smooth, sprinkle over the cake and then serve.

Nutrition:
Calories: 371 Fat: 42.4g Carbohydrates: 42g Proteins: 5.5g Fiber: 2g

1. Take a saucepan, put it on medium heat, and add the whole shopping list: except the oats and vanilla, mix until combined, and then bring the mixture to a boil.
2. Simmer the mixture for 4 minutes, stirring often, then remove the pan from the heat and stir in the vanilla.
3. Add the oats, mix until smooth and then pour the mixture onto a plate lined with wax paper.
4. Serve immediately.

Nutrition:
Calories: 112 Fat: 6.5g Carbohydrates: 13g Proteins: 1.4g Fiber: 0.1g

700. Cookie Dough Bites

Preparation time: 4 hours and 10 minutes
Cooking time: 0 minute
Servings: 18
Ingredients:

- 15 ounces cooked chickpeas
- 1/3 cup vegan chocolate chips
- 1/3 cup and 2 tablespoons peanut butter
- 8 Medjool dates pitted
- 1 teaspoon vanilla extract, unsweetened
- 2 tablespoons maple syrup
- 1 1/2 tablespoons almond milk, unsweetened

Directions:

701. Peach Pie

Preparatio0n time: 10 minutes
Cooking time: 20 minutes
Servings: 4
Ingredients:

- 4 peaches, peeled and sliced
- 1/2 teaspoon coconut sugar
- 2 tablespoons flaxseed mixed with 3 tablespoons water
- 1 tablespoon avocado oil
- 1/2 cup almond milk
- 1/2 cup almond flour

702. Mango Coconut Cheesecake

Preparation time: 4 hours and 10 minutes
Cooking time: 0 minute
Servings: 4
Ingredients:
For the Crust:

- 1 cup macadamia nuts
- 1 cup dates, pitted, soaked in hot water for 10 minutes

For the Filling:

- 2 cups cashews, set in warm water for 10 minutes
- 1/2 cup and 1 tablespoon maple syrup
- 1/3 cup and 2 tablespoons coconut oil
- 1/4 cup lemon juice
- 1/2 cup and 2 tablespoons coconut milk, unsweetened, chilled

For the Topping:

- 1 cup fresh mango slices

703. Matcha Coconut Cream Pie

Preparation time: 5 minutes
Cooking time: 0 minute
Servings: 4
Ingredients:
For the Crust:

- 1/2 cup ground flaxseed
- 3/4 cup shredded dried coconut
- 1 cup Medjool dates, pitted
- 3/4 cup dehydrated buckwheat grouts
- 1/4 teaspoons sea salt

For the Filling:

- 1 cup dried coconut flakes
- 4 cups of coconut meat
- 1/4 cup and 2 Tablespoons coconut nectar
- 1/2 Tablespoons vanilla extract, unsweetened

1. Set the chickpeas in a food processor along with dates, butter and vanilla and then cook for 2 minutes until smooth.
2. Add the remaining shopping list: except the chocolate chips, then pulse for 1 minute until the mixes and dough come together.
3. Add the chocolate chips, mix until blended, then form 18 balls and refrigerate for 4 hours until solidified.
4. Serve immediately

Nutrition:
Calories: 200 Fat: 9g Carbohydrates: 26g Proteins: 1g Fiber: 0g

- 1/4 cup coconut cream

Directions:

1. In a bowl, merge the peaches with the sugar and mix.
2. In another bowl, merge the rest of the Shopping List: mix well and pour into a greased cake plate.
3. Add the peach mixture above, spread, bake at 400 degrees for 20 minutes, slice and serve.

Nutrition:
Calories: 199 Fat: 4g Fiber: 3g Carbohydrates: 12g Proteins: 9g

Directions:

1. Prepare the crust and, for this, put the walnuts in a food processor and blend until the mixture resembles crumbs.
2. Drain the dates, attach them to the food processor and blend for 2 minutes until thick.
3. Take a 4-inch cheesecake, put the date mixture in it, spread and press evenly and set aside.
4. Prepare the filling and for this put all the ingredients in a food processor and blend until the mixture is smooth.
5. Pour the filling into the crust, distribute evenly and freeze for 4 hours until solidified.
6. Cover the cake with mango slices and then serve.

Nutrition:
Calories: 200 Fat: 11g Carbohydrates: 22.5g Proteins: 2g Fiber: 1g

- 1/4 teaspoons sea salt
- 2/3 cup and 2 Tablespoons coconut butter
- 1 Tablespoons Matcha powder
- 1/2 cup coconut water

Directions:

1. Prepare the crust and, for this, put all the ingredients in a food processor and blend for 3-5 minutes until the thick dough comes together.
2. Take a 6-inch spring form pan, grease it with oil, put the crust mixture in it and spread it and press the mixture evenly across the bottom and sides and freeze it until needed.
3. Prepare the filling and for this put all the ingredients in a food processor and blend until the mixture is smooth.

4. Spill the filling into the prepared pan, smooth the top and freeze for 4 hours until solidified.
5. Serve.

704. Chocolate Banana Cupcakes

Preparation time: 5 minutes
Cooking time: 45 minutes
Servings: 12
Ingredients:

- 3 Bananas
- 1 Cup Almond Milk
- 2 Tablespoons Almond Butter
- 1 Teaspoon Apple Cider Vinegar
- 1 Teaspoon Vanilla Extract, Pure
- 1 1/4 Cups Whole Grain Flour
- 1/2 Cup Rolled Oats
- 1/4 Cup Coconut Sugar
- 1 Teaspoon Baking Powder
- 1/2 Cup Cocoa Powder, Unsweetened
- 1/2 Teaspoon Baking Soda
- Pinch Sea Salt
- 1/4 Cup Chia Seeds

705. Coconut Chia Pudding

Preparation time: 15 minutes
Cooking time: 30 minutes
Servings: 4
Ingredients:

- 1 Lime, Juiced and Zested
- 14 Ounces Coconut Milk, Canned
- 2 Dates
- 2 Tablespoons Chia Seeds, Ground

706. Mango Cream Pie

Preparation time: 15 minutes
Cooking time: 25 minutes
Servings: 8
Ingredients:
Crust:

- 1/2 Cup Rolled Oats
- 1 Cup Cashews
- 1 Cup Dates, Pitted

Filling:

- 2 Mangos, Large, Peeled and Chopped
- 1/2 Cup Water
- 1 Cup Coconut Milk, Canned

707. Avocado Blueberry Cheesecake

Preparation time: 15 minutes
Cooking time: 1 hour 25 minutes
Servings: 8
Ingredients:
Crust:

- 1 Cup Rolled Oats
- 1 Cup Walnuts
- 1 Teaspoon Lime Zest
- 1 Cup Soft Pitted Dates

Filling:

- 2 Tablespoons Maple Syrup
- 1 Cup Blueberries, Frozen

Nutrition:
Calories: 209 Fat: 18g Carbohydrates: 10g Proteins: 1g Fiber: 2g

- 1/4 Cup Dark Chocolate Chips

Directions:
1. Heat the oven to 350 and get out a muffin pan. Grease it. Place your almond butter, vinegar, milk, bananas, and vanilla together. Puree until smooth.
2. Place the flour, sugar, oats, baking soda, baking powder, chia seeds, cocoa powder, chocolate chips, and salt together in a bowl. Mix well.
3. Mix your wet and dry ingredients, and make sure there are no lumps.
4. Spoon into muffin cups and bake for twenty to twenty-five minutes.
5. Allow them to cool before serving. They should be moist.

Nutrition:
Calories: 317.4 Fat: 0g Proteins: 16g Carbohydrates: 64g Fiber: 16g

- 2 Teaspoons Matcha Powder

Directions:
1. Get out a blender and blend everything until smooth. Chill for twenty minutes before serving.

Nutrition:
Calories: 100 Fat: 5.1g Carbohydrates: 11.8g Proteins: 4.2g Fiber: 3.1g

- 1/2 Cup Coconut, Shredded and Unsweetened

Directions:
1. Get out a food processor and pulse all your crust ingredients together. Press into an eight-inch pie pan.
2. Blend all filling ingredients. It should be thick and make sure it's smooth.
3. Pour it into the crust, and smooth out. Allow it to set in the freezer.
4. Allow it to rest before slicing.

Nutrition:
Calories: 127 Fat: 2g Carbohydrates: 23g Fiber: 3g

- 2 Avocados, Peeled and Pitted
- 2 Tablespoons Basil, Fresh and Minced Fine
- 4 Tablespoons Lime Juice

Directions:
1. Pulse all crust ingredients together in your food processor, and then press into a pie pan.
2. Blend all filling ingredients until smooth and pour it into the crust. Smooth out and freeze for two hours before serving.

Nutrition:
Calories: 73 Fat: 4g Proteins: 2g Carbohydrates: 8g Fiber: 2g

708. Spice Cake

Preparation time: 15 minutes
Cooking time: 40 minutes
Servings: 6
Ingredients:

- 1 Sweet Potato, Cooked and Peeled
- 1/2 Cup Applesauce, Unsweetened
- 1/2 Cup Almond Milk
- 1/4 Cup Maple Syrup, Pure
- 1 Teaspoon Vanilla Extract, Pure
- 2 Cups Whole Wheat Flour
- 1/2 Teaspoon Ground Cinnamon
- 1/2 Teaspoon Baking Soda

709. Lemon Cake

Preparation time: 15 minutes
Cooking time: 4 hours 40 minute
Servings: 10
Ingredients:
Crust:

- 1 Cup Dates, Pitted
- 2 Tablespoons Maple Syrup
- 2 1/2 Cups Pecans

Filling:

- 1 Lemon, Juiced and Zested
- 3/4 Cup Maple Syrup
- 1 1/2 Cups Pineapple, Crushed
- 3 Cups Cauliflower Rice, Prepared
- 3 Avocados, Halved and Pitted
- 1/2 Teaspoon Vanilla Extract, Pure
- 1/2 Teaspoon Lemon Extract
- 1 Pinch Cinnamon

Topping:

- 1 Teaspoon Vanilla Extract, Pure

710. Butterscotch Tart

Preparation time: 5 minutes
Cooking time: 45 minutes
Servings: 10
Ingredients:
Crust:

- 1/2 Cup Sugar
- 1/4 Cup Coconut Oil
- 1 Teaspoon Vanilla Extract, Pure
- 1/2 Teaspoon Sea Salt
- 2 Cups Almond Meal Flour

Filling:

- 2/3 Cup Light Brown Sugar, Packed
- 1 Teaspoon Kosher Salt
- 1/2 Cup Coconut Oil
- 2/3 Cup Coconut Cream, Canned
- Flaked Sea Salt, As Needed

711. Easy Brownies

Preparation time: 5 minutes
Cooking time: 25 minutes
Servings: 12
Ingredients:

- 2 Tablespoons Coconut Oil, Melted
- 1/2 Cup Peanut Butter, Salted
- 1/4 Cup Warm Water

- 1/4 Teaspoon Ground Ginger

Directions:

1. Turn your oven to 350, and then get a large bowl out. Mash your sweet potatoes and then mix in the vanilla, milk, and maple syrup. Mix well.
2. Stir in the baking soda, cinnamon, flour, and ginger. Mix well.
3. Pour this batter into a baking dish that's been lined with parchment paper. Bake the batter for forty-five minutes.
4. Allow it to cool before slicing to serve.

Nutrition:
Calories: 219 Fat: 12g Carbohydrates: 2g Proteins: 5g

- 1 1/2 Cups Coconut Yogurt, Plain
- 3 Tablespoons Maple Syrup

Directions:

1. Get a nine-inch spring form pan out, lining it with parchment paper.
2. Put your pecans in a food processor, grinding until fine. Stir in the maple syrup and dates, blending for a minute more. Spread this into your pan to make the crust.
3. Blend your maple syrup, pineapple, lemon juice, lemon zest, cauliflower rice, and avocados in a food processor. Add in the lemon extract, cinnamon, and vanilla. Mix well.
4. Top your crust with this mixture and freeze for five hours.
5. To make your topping whisk all ingredients together, spreading it over your prepared cake.

Nutrition:
Calories: 221 Fat: 2g Carbohydrates: 1g Proteins: 3g

- 1 Green Apple, Sliced

Directions:

1. Turn the oven to 375, and then get out a bowl. Prepare your crust ingredients by mixing everything until smooth. Spread this into a tart pan that's nine inches. Spread it as evenly as possible. Freeze for ten minutes, and then bake for fifteen. It should be golden brown.
2. Prepare the filling by cooking it all in a saucepan for twenty-five minutes. It should thicken and allow it to cool. You will need to stir often to keep it from burning.
3. Add this to the tart, and then chill for two hours before serving.

Nutrition:
Calories: 114 Fat: 2.1g Proteins: 3.7g Carbohydrates: 22.3g
Fiber: 3.8g

- 2 Cups Dates, Pitted
- 1/3 Cup Dark Chocolate chips
- 1/3 Cup Cocoa Powder
- 1/2 Cup Raw Walnuts, Chopped

Directions:

1. Heat the oven to 350, and then get out a loaf pan. Place parchment paper in it, and then get out a

food processor. Blend your dates until it's a fine mixture. Add in some hot water and blend well until the mixture becomes an as smooth batter.

2. Add in the coconut oil, cacao powder, and peanut butter. Blend more, and then fold in the chocolate and walnuts. Spread this into your loaf pan.

712. Eggplant and Zucchini Snack

Preparation time: 10 minutes
Cooking time: 8 minutes
Servings: 4
Ingredients:
- 1 eggplant, cubed
- 3 zucchinis, cubed
- 2 tablespoons lemon juice
- 1 teaspoon oregano, dried
- 3 tablespoons olive oil
- 1 teaspoon thyme, dried
- Salt and black pepper to taste

713. Artichokes with Mayo Sauce

Preparation time: 10 minutes
Cooking time: 6 minutes
Servings: 4
Ingredients:
- 2 artichokes, trimmed
- 1 tablespoon lemon juice
- 2 garlic cloves, minced
- A drizzle olive oil

For the Sauce:
- 1 cup vegan mayonnaise
- 1/4 cup olive oil
- 1/4 cup coconut oil
- 3 garlic cloves

Directions:

714. Fried Mustard Greens

Preparation time: 10 minutes
Cooking time: 11 minutes
Servings: 4
Ingredients:
- 2 garlic cloves, minced
- 1 tablespoon olive oil
- 1/2 cup yellow onion, sliced
- 3 tablespoons vegetable stock
- 1/4 teaspoon dark sesame oil
- 1-pound mustard greens, torn
- Salt and black pepper to the taste

Directions:

715. Cheese Brussels sprouts

Preparation time: 10 minutes
Cooking time: 8 minutes
Servings: 4
Ingredients:
- 1-pound Brussels sprouts, washed
- 3 tablespoons vegan parmesan, grated
- Juice from 1 lemon
- 2 tablespoons vegan butter
- Salt and black pepper to the taste

Directions:
1. Spread the Brussels sprouts in the air fryer basket.

3. Bake for fifteen minutes, and then chill before serving.

Nutrition:
Calories: 360 Fat: 0g Proteins: 24g Carbohydrates: 72g Fiber: 24g

Directions:
1. Take a baking dish suitable to fit in your air fryer.
2. Combine all ingredients in the baking dish.
3. Place the eggplant dish in the air fryer basket and seal it.
4. Cook at 360 degrees F on air fryer mode.
5. Enjoy warm.

Nutrition:
Calories: 210 Fat: 4g Carbohydrates: 16g Proteins: 3g Fiber: 9g

1. Toss artichokes with lemon juice, oil and 2 garlic cloves in a large bowl.
2. Place the seasoned artichokes in the air fryer basket and seal it.
3. Cook the artichokes for 6 minutes at 350 degrees on air fryer mode.
4. Blend coconut oil with olive oil, mayonnaise and 3 garlic cloves in a food processor.
5. Place the artichokes on the serving plates.
6. Pour the mayonnaise mixture over the artichokes.
7. Enjoy fresh.

Nutrition:
Calories: 230 Fat: 11g Carbohydrates: 24g Proteins: 6g Fiber: 11g

1. Take a baking dish suitable to fit in your air fryer.
2. Add oil and place it over the medium heat and sauté onions in it for 5 minutes.
3. Stir in garlic, greens, salt, pepper, and stock.
4. Mix well then place the dish in the air fryer basket.
5. Seal it and cook them for 6 minutes at 350 degrees F on air fryer mode.
6. Drizzle sesame oil over the greens.
7. Devour.

Nutrition:
Calories: 210 Fat: 8g Carbohydrates: 24g Proteins: 4g Fiber: 10g

2. Seal it and cook them for 8 minutes at 350 degrees F on air fryer mode.
3. Place a nonstick pan over medium high heat and add butter to melt.
4. Stir in pepper, salt, lemon juice, and Brussels sprouts.
5. Mix well then add parmesan.
6. Serve warm.

Nutrition:
Calories: 160 Fat: 7g Carbohydrates: 18g Proteins: 5g Fiber: 12g

716. Mushroom Stuffed Poblano

Preparation time: 10 minutes
Cooking time: 20 minutes
Servings: 10
Ingredients:

- 10 Poblano peppers, tops cut off and seeds removed
- 2 teaspoons garlic, minced
- 8 ounces mushrooms, chopped
- 1/2 cup cilantro, chopped
- 1 white onion, chopped
- 1 tablespoon olive oil
- Salt and black pepper to taste

Directions:

1. Arrange a nonstick pan over medium heat and add oil.
2. Stir in mushrooms and onion, sauté for 5 minutes.
3. Add salt, black pepper, cilantro and garlic.
4. Stir while cooking for 2 additional minutes then take it off the heat.
5. Divide this mixture in the Poblano peppers and stuff them neatly.
6. Set the peppers in the air fryer basket and seal it.
7. Cook them for 15 minutes at 350 degrees F on air fryer mode. Enjoy.

Nutrition:
Calories: 220 Fat: 2g Carbohydrates: 20g Proteins: 4g Fiber: 6g

717. Mushroom Stuffed Tomatoes

Preparation time: 10 minutes
Cooking time: 15 minutes
Servings: 4
Ingredients:

- 4 tomatoes, tops removed and pulp removed (reserve for filling)
- 1 yellow onion, chopped
- 1/2 cup mushrooms, chopped
- 1 tablespoon breadcrumbs
- 1 tablespoon vegan butter
- 1/4 teaspoon caraway seeds
- 1 tablespoon parsley, chopped
- 2 tablespoons celery, chopped
- 1 cup vegan cheese, shredded
- Salt and black pepper to the taste

Directions:

1. Arrange a pan over medium heat, add butter.
2. When it melts, add onion and celery to sauté for 3 minutes.
3. Stir in mushrooms and tomato pulp. Cook for 1 minute then add crumbled bread, pepper, salt, cheese, parsley, and caraway seeds.
4. Cook while stirring for 4 minutes then remove from the heat. After cooling the mixture, stuff it equally in the tomatoes.
5. Set the tomatoes in the air fryer basket and seal it. Cook them for 8 minutes at 350 degrees F on air fryer mode. Enjoy.

Nutrition:
Calories: 280 Fat: 9g Carbohydrates: 35g Proteins: 11g Fiber: 11g

718. Banana Cinnamon Muffins

Preparation time: 10 minutes
Cooking time: 22 minutes
Servings: 12
Ingredients:

- 3 very ripe bananas, mashed
- 1/2 cup vanilla almond milk
- 1 cup sugar
- 2 cups flour
- 1 teaspoon baking soda
- 1/2 teaspoon cinnamon
- 1/4 teaspoon salt

Directions:

1. Preheat your oven to 350F.
2. Separately, whisk together the dry ingredients in one bowl and the wet ingredients in another bowl.
3. Beat the two mixtures together until smooth.
4. Set a muffin tray with muffin cups and evenly divide the muffin batter among the cups.
5. Bake for 22 minutes and serve.

Nutrition:
Calories: 320 Fat: 4g Carbohydrates: 55g Proteins: 8g Fiber: 4g

719. Cashew Oat Muffins

Preparation time: 10 minutes
Cooking time: 22 minutes
Servings: 12
Ingredients:

- 3 cups rolled oats
- 3/4 cup raw cashews
- 1/4 cup maple syrup
- 1/4 cup sugar
- 1 teaspoon vanilla extract
- 1/2 teaspoon salt
- 11/2 teaspoon baking soda
- 2 cups water

Directions:

1. Preheat your oven to 375F.
2. Separately, whisk together the dry ingredients in one bowl and the wet ingredients in another bowl.
3. Beat the two mixtures together until smooth.
4. Fold in cashews and give it a gentle stir.
5. Set a muffin tray with muffin cups and evenly divide the muffin batter among the cups.
6. Bake for 22 minutes and serve.

Nutrition:
Calories: 300 Fat: 4g Carbohydrates: 50g Proteins: 4g Fiber: 6g

720. Banana Walnut Muffins

Preparation time: 10 minutes
Cooking time: 18 minutes
Servings: 12
Ingredients:

- 4 large pitted dates, boiled
- 1 cup almond milk
- 2 tablespoons lemon juice
- 21/2 cups rolled oats
- 1 teaspoon baking powder
- 1 teaspoon baking soda
- 1 teaspoon cinnamon
- 1/4 teaspoon nutmeg
- 1/8 teaspoon salt
- 11/2 cups mashed banana
- 1/4 cup maple syrup
- 1 tablespoon vanilla extract
- 1 cup walnuts, chopped

Directions:

1. Preheat your oven to 350F.
2. Separately, whisk together the dry ingredients in one bowl and the wet ingredients in another bowl.
3. Beat the two mixtures together until smooth. Fold in walnuts and give it a gentle stir.
4. Set a muffin tray with muffin cups and evenly divide the muffin batter among the cups.
5. Bake for 18 minutes and serve.

Nutrition:
Calories: 330 Fat: 4g Carbohydrates: 55g Proteins: 6g Fiber: 4g

721. Carrot Flaxseed Muffins

Preparation time: 10 minutes
Cooking time: 20 minutes
Servings: 12
Ingredients:

- 2 tablespoons ground flax
- 5 tablespoons water
- 3/4 cup almond milk
- 3/4 cup applesauce
- 1/2 cup maple syrup
- 1 teaspoon vanilla extract
- 11/2 cups whole wheat flour
- 1/2 cup rolled oats
- 1 cup grated carrot

Directions:

1. Whisk flaxseed with water in a bowl and leave it for 10 minutes
2. Separately, whisk together the dry ingredients in one bowl and the wet ingredients in another bowl.
3. Beat the two mixtures together until smooth. Fold in flaxseed and carrots, give it a gentle stir.
4. Set a muffin tray with muffin cups and evenly divide the muffin batter among the cups.
5. Bake for 20 minutes and serve.

Nutrition:
Calories: 320 Fat: 4g Carbohydrates: 50g Proteins: 4g Fiber: 6g

722. Chocolate Peanut Fat Bombs

Preparation time: 10 minutes
Cooking time: 1 hour 1 minute
Servings: 12
Ingredients:

- 1/2 cup coconut butter
- 1 cup plus 2 tablespoons peanut butter
- 5 tablespoons cocoa powder
- 2 teaspoons maple syrup

Directions:

1. In a bowl, combine all the ingredients. Dissolve them in the microwave for 1 minute.
2. Mix well then divide the mixture into silicone molds. Freeze them for 1 hour to set.

Nutrition:
Calories: 350 Fat: 15g Carbohydrates: 45g Proteins: 8g Fiber: 4g

723. Protein Fat Bombs

Preparation time: 10 minutes
Cooking time: 1 hour
Servings: 12
Ingredients:

- 1 cup coconut oil
- 1 cup peanut butter, melted
- 1/2 cup cocoa powder
- 1/4 cup plant-based protein powder
- 1 pinch of salt
- 2 cups unsweetened shredded coconut

Directions:

1. In a bowl, attach all the ingredients except coconut shreds. Merge well then make small balls out of this mixture and place them into silicone molds. Freeze for 1 hour to set. Roll the balls in the coconut shreds. Serve.

Nutrition:
Calories: 340 Fat: 14g Carbohydrates: 35g Proteins: 12g Fiber: 3g

724. Mojito Fat Bombs

Preparation time: 10 minutes
Cooking time: 1 hour and 1 minute
Servings: 12
Ingredients:

- 3/4 cup hulled hemp seeds
- 1/2 cup coconut oil
- 1 cup fresh mint
- 1/2 teaspoon mint extract
- Juice and zest of two limes
- 1/4 teaspoon stevia

Directions:

1. In a bowl, combine all the ingredients. Melt in the microwave for 1 minute. Mix well then divide the mixture into silicone molds. Freeze them for 1 hour to set. Serve.

Nutrition:

Calories: 290 Fat: 12g Carbohydrates: 35g Proteins: 6g Fiber: 2g

725. Key Lime Pie

Preparation time: 10 minutes
Cooking time: 3 hours 15 minutes
Servings: 4
Ingredients:
For the Crust:

- 3/4 cup coconut flakes, unsweetened
- 1 cup dates, set in warm water for 10 minutes in water, drained

For the Filling:

- 3/4 cup of coconut meat
- 1 1/2 avocado, peeled, pitted
- 2 tablespoons key lime juice
- 1/4 cup agave

Directions:

1. Prepare the crust, and for this, place all its ingredients in a food processor and pulse until the thick paste comes together.
2. Take an 8-inch pie pan, grease it with oil, pour crust mixture in it and spread and set the mixture evenly in the bottom and along the sides, and freeze until required.
3. Prepare the filling and for this, place all its ingredients in a food processor, and pulse for 2 minutes until smooth.
4. Pour the filling into prepared pan, smooth the top, and freeze for 3 hours until set.
5. Cut pie into slices and then serve.

Nutrition:
Calories: 310 Fat: 9g Carbohydrates: 45g Proteins: 4g Fiber: 2g

726. Chocolate Mint Grasshopper Pie

Preparation time: 10 minutes
Cooking time: 4 hours 15 minutes
Servings: 4
Ingredients:
For the Crust:

- 1 cup dates, set in warm water for 10 minutes in water, drained
- 1/8 teaspoons salt
- 1/2 cup pecans
- 1 teaspoons cinnamon
- 1/2 cup walnuts

For the Filling:

- 1/2 cup mint leaves
- 2 cups of cashews, soaked in warm water for 10 minutes in water, drained
- 2 tablespoons coconut oil
- 1/4 cup and 2 tablespoons of agave
- 1/4 teaspoons spirulina

- 1/4 cup water

Directions:

1. Prepare the crust, and for this, place all its ingredients in a food processor and pulse until the thick paste comes together.
2. Take a 6-inch spring form pan, grease it with oil, place crust mixture in it and spread and set the mixture evenly in the bottom and along the sides and freeze until required.
3. Prepare the filling and for this, place all its ingredients in a food processor, and pulse for 2 minutes until smooth.
4. Pour the filling into prepared pan, smooth the top, and freeze for 4 hours until set.
5. Cut pie into slices and then serve.

Nutrition:
Calories: 340 Fat: 9g Carbohydrates: 45g Proteins: 4g Fiber: 3g

727. Strawberry Mousse

Preparation time: 5 minutes
Cooking time: 15 minutes
Servings: 4
Ingredients:

- 8 ounces coconut milk, unsweetened
- 2 tablespoons maple syrup chili
- 5 strawberries

Directions:

1. Place berries in a blender and pulse until the smooth mixture comes together.
2. Place milk in a bowl, whisk until whipped, and then add remaining ingredients and stir until combined. Refrigerate the mousse for 10 minutes and then serve.

Nutrition:
Calories: 140 Fat: 1g Carbohydrates: 25g Proteins: 1g Fiber: 6g

728. Blueberry Mousse

Preparation time: 10 minutes
Cooking time: 15 minutes
Servings: 2
Ingredients:

- 1 cup wild blueberries
- 1 cup cashews, soaked for 10 minutes, drained
- 1/2 teaspoon berry powder
- 2 tablespoons coconut oil, melted
- 1 tablespoon lemon juice

- 1 teaspoon vanilla extract, unsweetened
- 1/4 cup hot water

Directions:

1. S all the ingredients in a food processor and process for 2 minutes until smooth. Set aside until required.

Nutrition:
Calories: 150 Fat: 4g Carbohydrates: 24g Proteins: 4g Fiber: 10g

729. Olive Kabobs

Preparation time: 10 minutes
Cooking time: 20 minutes
Servings: 16
Ingredients:

- 16 large low-sodium olives, pitted
- 2 bell peppers, seedless and cut in 1-inch pieces
- 16 cherry tomatoes

Directions:

1. Thread 1 olive, 1 piece of pepper, and 1 tomato on a toothpick, and repeat with the remaining ingredients.
2. Swap It: Try adding onions, radishes, or cucumbers.
3. Flavor Boost: Add a splash of lemon juice.

Nutrition:
Calories: 58 Fat: 2g Carbohydrates: 10g Fiber: 2g Proteins: 2g

730. Crunchy Veggies with Peanut Sauce

Preparation time: 5 minutes
Cooking time: 5 minutes
Servings: 1
Ingredients:

- 4 baby carrots
- 2 broccoli florets
- 1 tablespoon Sweet Peanut Butter Dipping Sauce

Directions:

1. Dip the carrots and broccoli florets into the Sweet Peanut Butter Dipping Sauce and enjoy.
2. Swap It: If the peanut dipping sauce isn't available, use 1 tablespoon of nut butter instead. Alternatively, quarter regular carrots instead of using baby carrots. Also try celery or snap peas for variety.

Nutrition:
Calories: 81 Fat: 3g Carbohydrates: 11g Fiber: 3g Proteins: 3g

731. Salsa with Mushrooms and Olives

Preparation time: 10 minutes
Cooking time: 30 minutes
Servings: 3
Ingredients:

- 1/2 cup chopped white button mushrooms
- 1 tablespoon chopped fresh parsley
- 1 tablespoon chopped fresh basil
- 2 Roma tomatoes, finely chopped
- 1 tablespoon finely chopped scallions
- 1/3 cup chopped marinated artichoke hearts
- 1/2 cup chopped olives
- 1 tablespoon balsamic vinegar
- 3 slices sourdough toast

Directions:

1. Combine the mushrooms, parsley, basil, tomatoes, scallions, artichoke hearts, and olives in a medium mixing bowl.
2. Dress with the balsamic vinegar. Let marinate at room temperature about 20 minutes to blend flavors. Alternatively, refrigerate until serving time.
3. Serve the salsa with the slices of sourdough toast.

Nutrition:
Calories: 205 Fat: 3g Carbohydrates: 41g Fiber: 4g Proteins: 9g

732. Watermelon with Coconut-Lime Yogurt

Preparation time: 10 minutes
Cooking time: 15 minutes
Servings: 1
Ingredients:

- 3/4 cup unsweetened coconut milk yogurt, plain or vanilla
- 1 teaspoon maple syrup
- Zest and juice of 1 lime, plus 1 lime cut into wedges for garnish
- 11/4 cups cubed seedless watermelon

Directions:

1. Arrange the yogurt in a small bowl and add the maple syrup.
2. Zest 1 lime on top of the yogurt; then halve the lime and squeeze the juice into the yogurt. Mix well.
3. Serve the watermelon cubes with the coconut-lime yogurt.
4. Garnish with the lime wedges.

Nutrition:
Calories: 120 Fat: 2g Fiber: 3g Carbohydrates: 6g Proteins: 9g

733. Baby Potatoes with Dill, Chives, and Garlic

Preparation time: 5 minutes
Cooking time: 20 minutes
Servings: 2
Ingredients:

- 2 cups water
- 12 baby potatoes
- 2 garlic cloves, minced
- 2 tablespoons chopped fresh dill
- 2 tablespoons chopped fresh chives
- Pinch freshly ground black pepper (optional)

Directions:

1. Combine the water and potatoes in a medium saucepan and bring to a boil over medium-high heat. Cook.
2. Drain the liquid and add the garlic; then mix well.
3. Serve warm and top each portion with 1 tablespoon of dill, 1 tablespoon of chives, and pepper (if using).

Nutrition:
Calories: 155 Fat: 1g Carbohydrates: 34g Fiber: 6g Proteins: 4g

734. Green Beans with Almonds

Preparation time: 5 minutes
Cooking time: 10 minutes
Servings: 2
Ingredients:

- 10 ounces cut green beans
- 4 garlic cloves, minced
- 1/4 cup Flavorful Vegetable Broth
- 1 small red jalapeño pepper, seeded, ribs removed, and diced
- 1/2 cup sliced almonds, toasted

Directions:

1. Combine the green beans, garlic, vegetable broth, and jalapeño pepper in a large nonstick skillet over medium heat. Secure with a lid and steam for 5 to 7 minutes.
2. Remove the lid, add the almonds, and cook on low for 2 minutes more.

Nutrition:
Calories: 188 Fat: 12g Carbohydrates: 17g Fiber: 7g Proteins: 8g

735. Spicy Carrots with Coriander

Preparation time: 10 minutes
Cooking time: 15 minutes
Servings: 2
Ingredients:

- 3 cups shredded carrots
- 4 garlic cloves, minced
- 1/4 cup rice vinegar
- 1 tablespoon maple syrup
- 1 tablespoon ground coriander
- 1 teaspoon red pepper flakes
- 1/2 teaspoon freshly ground black pepper
- 1/4 tablespoon cayenne pepper
- 1 teaspoon dried dill (optional)
- 1 teaspoon dried parsley (optional)

Directions:

1. Mix the carrots, garlic, rice vinegar, maple syrup, red pepper flakes, coriander, cayenne pepper, and black pepper in a large mixing bowl.
2. Add the dried dill and parsley (if using).
3. Let sit then enjoy.

Nutrition:
Calories: 101 Fat: 0g Carbohydrates: 23g Fiber: 4g Proteins: 2g

736. Flavorful Brown Rice Pilaf

Preparation time: 5 minutes
Cooking time: 40 minutes
Servings: 3
Ingredients:

- 1 cup brown basmati rice, uncooked and rinsed
- 3 cups Flavorful Vegetable Broth
- 1 cup chopped fresh flat-leaf parsley

Directions:

1. Merge the rice and vegetable broth in a medium pot and bring to a boil. Cover with a lid, reduce the heat to low, and simmer for 40 minutes or until the liquid is absorbed.
2. Detach from the heat and let sit covered for 5 minutes.
3. Stir in the parsley. Use immediately or store in an airtight container in the refrigerator for up to 7 days.

Nutrition:
Calories: 235 Fat: 2g Carbohydrates: 49g Fiber: 2g Proteins: 5g

737. Homemade Applesauce with Raisins and Nuts

Preparation time: 10 minutes
Cooking time: 25 minutes
Servings: 6
Ingredients:

- 6 medium apples, peeled, cored, and chopped
- 1/3 cup water
- 1/4 cup maple syrup
- 1/2 cup golden raisins
- 1/2 cup chopped pecans, toasted

Directions:

1. Combine the apples, water, and maple syrup in a large saucepan and bring to a boil. Set the heat to a low simmer, cover, and cook for 15 to 20 minutes, or until the apples are very tender.
2. Remove the lid; add the raisins, mix, and simmer for 5 minutes more to thicken.
3. Mash the apples slightly with a potato masher until they reach a chunky consistency.
4. Set each portion with a quarter of the chopped pecans. Serve warm or chilled.

Nutrition:
Calories: 233 Fat: 7g Carbohydrates: 46g Fiber: 6g Proteins: 2g

738. Thick and Chewy Oatmeal and Cherry Cookies

Preparation time: 10 minutes
Cooking time: 15 minutes
Servings: 12
Ingredients:

- 6 medium Medjool dates, pitted
- 1 ripe banana, mashed
- 1/4 cup molasses
- 2 tablespoons almond butter
- 1/2 cup all-purpose flour, sifted
- 1/2 cup old-fashioned oats
- 1/2 cup dried cherries
- 1 teaspoon baking powder
- 1/2 teaspoon baking soda

Directions:

1. Warmth the oven to 350F and line a baking sheet with nonstick foil or parchment paper.
2. Combine the dates, banana, molasses, almond butter, and flour in a food processor. Combine until smooth.

3. Spill the mixture into a large mixing bowl; then add the oats, cherries, baking powder, and baking soda. Mix well.
4. Set about 2 tablespoons of the dough and roll it into a ball. Repeat with the remaining dough. Set dough balls 2 inches apart on the prepared baking

sheet and bake for 15 minutes, or until brown around the edges.
5. Let cool and enjoy.

Nutrition:
Calories: 133 Fat: 2g Carbohydrates: 28g Fiber: 2g Proteins: 2g

739. Caramelized Banana with Yogurt and Toasted Coconut

Preparation time: 5 minutes
Cooking time: 5 minutes
Servings: 1
Ingredients:
*   1 tablespoon maple syrup
*   1 small banana, cut into 1/4-inch-thick slices
*   1/4 cup plain unsweetened cashew milk yogurt
*   1 tablespoon toasted shredded coconut
*   Pinch ground cinnamon

Directions:

1. Spill the maple syrup into a small skillet and heat over medium-low heat. Add the bananas and caramelize for 3 to 5 minutes.
2. Put the yogurt on a small plate or in a small bowl. Place the caramelized bananas on top of the yogurt, and sprinkle with the shredded coconut and cinnamon.

Nutrition:
Calories: 196 Fat: 3g Carbohydrates: 43g Fiber: 3g Proteins: 3g

740. Almond Truffles with Toasted Coconut

Preparation time: 5 minutes
Cooking time: 10 minutes
Servings: 8
Ingredients:
*   1/4 cup almond meal
*   1/4 cup toasted shredded coconut
*   2 tablespoons cacao powder
*   2 tablespoons maple syrup

Directions:

1. In a medium bowl, merge the almond meal, coconut, cacao, and maple syrup. Using a fork or by hand, mix the ingredients to a smooth consistency.
2. Scoop about 1 tablespoon of dough and roll it into a small ball. Redo with the remaining dough to make 8 truffles.
3. Enjoy immediately or refrigerate for 10 to 20 minutes before serving.

Nutrition:
Calories: 42 Fat: 3g Carbohydrates: 5g Fiber: 1g Proteins: 1g

741. Homemade Caramel with Dates and Peanut Butter

Preparation time: 20 minutes
Cooking time: 30 minutes
Servings: 8
Ingredients:
*   5 Medjool dates, pitted
*   1 tablespoon peanut butter (no sugar or salt added)
*   2 teaspoons molasses
*   8 small apples, cored and sliced into 8 wedges

Directions:
1. Soak the dates in hot water.

2. Drain the dates and set them in a food processor. Add the peanut butter and molasses and blend to a smooth consistency.
3. Refrigerate the caramel mixture for 20 to 30 minutes.
4. Serve 1 tablespoon of the caramel mixture with each sliced apple. Refrigerate the remaining caramel mixture for up to 5 days.

Nutrition:
Calories: 145 Fat: 1g Carbohydrates: 36g Fiber: 6g Proteins: 1g

742. Baked Pear with Muesli

Preparation time: 5 minutes
Cooking time: 25 minutes
Servings: 1
Ingredients:
*   1 small pear, halved and pitted (use spoon to remove pit to create a small hole)
*   1 teaspoon maple syrup
*   2 tablespoons Simple Homemade Muesli
*   Pinch ground cinnamon (optional)
*   1/4 cup unsweetened cashew milk yogurt

Directions:

1. Preheat the oven to 375F.
2. Set a baking sheet with nonstick foil or parchment paper. Place the pear halves on the baking sheet, cut-side up.
3. Drizzle the pear halves with the maple syrup. Top with the muesli and cinnamon (if using).
4. Bake for 20 to 25 minutes.
5. Serve with the cashew milk yogurt.

Nutrition:
Calories: 174 Fat: 2g Carbohydrates: 37g Fiber: 5g Proteins: 3g

743. Apple Pie Bites

Preparation time: 10 minutes
Cooking time: 0 minutes
Servings: 6
Ingredients:
*   1 cup walnuts, chopped
*   1/2 cup coconut oil
*   1/4 cup ground flax seeds

*   1/2 ounce freeze-dried apples
*   1 teaspoon vanilla extract
*   1 teaspoon cinnamon
*   Liquid stevia, to taste

Directions:
1. In a bowl, add all the ingredients.
2. Mix well, and then roll the mixture into small balls.

3. Freeze them for 1 hour to set.
4. Serve.

Nutrition:

744. Peach Popsicles

Preparation time: 10 minutes
Cooking time: 0 minutes
Servings: 6
Ingredients:

- 2 1/2 cups peaches, peeled and pitted
- 2 tablespoons agave
- 3/4 cup coconut cream

Directions:

745. Green Popsicles

Preparation time: 10 minutes
Cooking time: 0 minutes
Servings: 4
Ingredients:

- 1 ripe avocado, peeled and pitted
- 1 cup fresh spinach
- 1 can (13.5-ounce) full fat coconut milk
- 1/4 cup lime juice
- 2 tablespoons maple syrup
- 1 teaspoon vanilla extract

746. Strawberry Coconut Popsicles

Preparation time: 10 minutes
Cooking time: 0 minutes
Servings: 4
Ingredients:

- 2 medium bananas, sliced
- 1 can coconut milk
- 1 cup strawberries
- 3 tablespoons maple syrup

Directions:

747. Crunchy Chocolate Brownies

Preparation time: 1 hour 15 minutes
Cooking time: 1 minutes
Servings: 4
Ingredients:
Filling:

- 2 cups dates, pitted
- 2 cups walnuts
- Pinch of sea salt
- 2 tablespoons water

Topping:

- 1 dark chocolate bar, chopped
- 1/2 cup peanut butter
- 1 tablespoon coconut oil

Directions:

1. Add pitted dates to water in a bowl and soak for 10 minutes, then drain.

748. Chickpea Meringues

Preparation time: 10 minutes
Cooking time: 2 hours
Servings: 6
Ingredients:

- 1 (15-ounce) can chickpeas
- 1/4 teaspoon cream of tartar
- Kosher salt

Calories: 217 Fat: 12g Carbohydrates: 28g Fiber: 1.1g
Proteins: 5g

1. Blend peaches with cream and agave in a blender until smooth.
2. Divide the Popsicle blend into the Popsicle molds.
3. Insert the Popsicle sticks and close the molds.
4. Place these molds in the freezer for 2 hours to set.
5. Serve.

Nutrition:
Calories: 195 Fat: 3g Carbohydrates: 17g Fiber: 1g Proteins: 1g

Directions:

1. Blend vanilla, maple, lime juice, spinach, coconut milk and avocado in a blender until smooth.
2. Divide the Popsicle blend into the Popsicle molds.
3. Insert the Popsicle sticks and close the molds.
4. Place these molds in the freezer for 2 hours to set.
5. Serve.

Nutrition:
Calories: 203 Fat: 8.9g Carbohydrates: 22g Fiber: 1.2g
Proteins: 5.3g

1. Blend coconut milk, maple, strawberries and bananas in a blender until smooth.
2. Divide the Popsicle blend into the Popsicle molds.
3. Insert the Popsicle sticks and close the molds.
4. Place these molds in the freezer for 2 hours to set.
5. Serve.

Nutrition:
Calories: 153 Fat: 1g Carbohydrates: 16g Fiber: 0.8g Proteins: 1g

2. Add walnuts to a blender and pulse until it forms a crumble.
3. Stir sea, salt, cacao powder, dates, and 1 tablespoon water to the blender.
4. Blend again until it forms thick date dough.
5. Spread this mixture in an 8-inch baking pan lined with a parchment sheet.
6. Press the dough in the pan, and then freeze for 1 hour.
7. Meanwhile, melt peanut butter, coconut oil, and chocolate chips in a glass bowl by heating in the microwave.
8. Pour this chocolate melt over the date's batter.
9. Allow it to sit, and then slice.
10. Serve.

Nutrition:
Calories: 198 Fat: 14g Carbohydrates: 17g Fiber: 1g Proteins: 1.3g

- 3/4 cup of sugar

Directions:

1. Layer 2 baking sheets with parchment sheet and preheat the oven to 250F.
2. Drain the chickpeas and reserve 3/4 cup of its liquid.
3. Blend the chickpeas with cream of tartar, a pinch of salt, and the reserved liquid in the blender.

4. Attach this mixture to a piping bag and pipe the mixture drop by drop on the baking sheet.
5. Bake these meringue drops for 2 hours in the preheated oven until firm.

749. Watermelon Coconut Sorbet

Preparation time: 15 minutes
Cooking time: 0 minutes
Servings: 6
Ingredients:
- 5 cups seedless watermelon, peeled and diced
- 4 cups coconut milk
- 1/4 cup coconut syrup
- Juice from 1/2 lemon

Directions:
1. Blend watermelon with the rest of the ingredients in a blender until smooth.
2. Spread this mixture in a baking dish and cover it with plastic wrap.

750. Dates and Almonds Cake

Preparation time: 5 hours
Cooking time: 0 minutes
Servings: 6
Ingredients:
For the crust:
- 1/2 cup dates, pitted
- 1 tablespoon water
- 1/2 teaspoon vanilla extract
- 1/2 cup almonds

For the cake:
- 3 cups almonds, soaked for 8 hours
- 1 cup blueberries
- 4 tablespoons stevia

751. Grape Cream

Preparation time: 10 minutes
Cooking time: 0 minutes
Servings: 2
Ingredients:
- 1 pound grapes
- 1/2 pound coconut cream
- 1 teaspoon vanilla extract
- 1 tablespoon stevia

752. Lime Parfait

Preparation time: 10 minutes
Cooking time: 0 minutes
Servings: 6
Ingredients:
- 4 cups coconut cream
- 3 tablespoons stevia
- 2 tablespoons lime juice
- 2 teaspoons lime zest, grated
- 2 avocados, peeled and chopped

753. Coconut and Cocoa Brownies

Preparation time: 10 minutes
Cooking time: 30 minutes
Servings: 8
Ingredients:
- 4 tablespoons cocoa powder
- 2 tablespoons flaxseed mixed with 3 tablespoons water

6. Cool and serve.
Nutrition:
Calories: 159 Fat: 3g Carbohydrates: 39g Fiber: 1g Proteins: 2g

3. Freeze the watermelon mixture for 4 hours.
4. Cut the frozen mixture into cubes and blend in a food processor.
5. Spread this mixture in the baking dish and freeze again for 2 hours.
6. Scoop out and serve.
Nutrition:
Calories: 245
Fat: 14g
Carbohydrates: 28g
Fiber: 1.2g
Proteins: 4.3g

- 1 tbsp. coconut oil, melted
Directions:
1. In your food processor, merge dates with water, vanilla, and almonds and pulse well. Bring the dough to a work surface and roll it out then transfer to a lined cake pan.
2. In your blender, mix the almonds and the other ingredients for the cake and blend well.
3. Spread evenly on the crust and place cake in the freezer for 5 hours, slice, and serve.
Nutrition:
Calories: 330 Fat: 7.2g Fiber: 5g Carbohydrates: 12g Proteins: 4g

Directions:
1. In your food processor, puree the grapes with the cream and the other ingredients, divide them into small cups and serve.
Nutrition:
Calories: 120 Fat: 9g Fiber: 3g Carbohydrates: 10g Proteins: 3g

- 1 tablespoon mint, chopped
Directions:
1. In a bowl, combine the cream with stevia and the other ingredients except for the avocados and stir.
2. Divide the avocado pieces into small cups, add the coconut mix in each and serve.
Nutrition:
Calories: 200 Fat: 3g Fiber: 4g Carbohydrates: 15g Proteins: 10g

- 1/2 cup hot water
- 1 teaspoon vanilla extract
- 2/3 cup coconut sugar
- 1 and 1/2 cups almond flour
- 1/2 cup walnuts, chopped
- Cooking spray
- 1 teaspoon baking soda

Directions:
1. In a bowl, mix the cocoa with the flaxseed and the other ingredients stir well, spill this into a pan with cooking spray, spread well, bake in the oven for 30 minutes, cool down, slice, and serve.

754. Mango and Cranberries Tart
Preparation time: 10 minutes
Cooking time: 25 minutes
Servings: 8
Ingredients:
- 2 mangoes, peeled and cubed
- 1/4 cup natural apple juice
- 1/2 cup cranberries, dried
- 2 teaspoons coconut sugar
- 1 teaspoon vanilla extract
- 1/4 teaspoon almond extract

For the crust:
- 1 and 1/4 cup almond flour
- 2 teaspoons stevia
- 3 tablespoons coconut oil, melted

755. Avocado Cake
Preparation time: 10 minutes
Cooking time: 25 minutes
Servings: 10
Ingredients:
- 3 cups almond flour
- 4 tablespoons stevia
- 1 tablespoon vanilla extract
- 3 tablespoons cocoa powder
- 1 cup avocado, peeled, pitted, and mashed
- 2 and 1/2 teaspoons baking soda
- 2 cups coconut cream

756. Blueberry Pancakes
Preparation time: 10 minutes
Cooking time: 10 minutes
Servings: 4
Ingredients:
- 1 cup coconut flour
- 1/4 cup almond flour
- 1 teaspoon baking soda
- 1 teaspoon baking powder
- 2 tablespoons flaxseeds
- 1/2 teaspoon nutmeg, ground
- 2 tablespoons stevia
- 1/2 cup natural orange juice
- 1/2 cup blueberries
- 1/4 cup water

757. Avocado Fudge
Preparation time: 2 hours
Cooking time: 7 minutes
Servings: 12
Ingredients:
- 1 cup almond milk
- 1/2 cup coconut butter, soft
- 2 cups coconut sugar
- 2 cups avocado, peeled, pitted, and mashed
- 1 teaspoon vanilla extract

Directions:

Nutrition:
Calories: 244 Fat: 5.5g Fiber: 4g Carbohydrates: 9g Proteins: 8.2g

- 1/4 cup cold water

Directions:
1. In a bowl, merge the flour with stevia and the other ingredients for the crust, stir and knead until you obtain dough, flatten it, roll into a circle and transfer to a tart pan.
2. In a separate bowl, combine the mangoes with the apple juice and the rest of the ingredients for the filling stir and spread over the crust.
3. Introduce the pan in the oven, bake at 375 degrees F for 25 minutes, cool it down, slice, and serve.

Nutrition:
Calories: 182 Fat: 5g Fiber: 4g Carbohydrates: 15g Proteins: 5.7g

- 1/2 cup coconut oil, melted

Directions:
1. In a bowl, merge the flour with the stevia and the other ingredients, stir well and pour into a cake pan.
2. Introduce in the oven at 350F, bake for 25 minutes, and leave the cake to cool down, slice, and serve.

Nutrition:
Calories: 200 Fat: 4.7g Fiber: 2.7g Carbohydrates: 12g Proteins: 6g

- Cooking spray

Directions:
1. In a bowl, merge the flour with the baking soda, powder, and the other ingredients except for the cooking spray and stir well.
2. Warmth up a pan over medium-high heat, grease with cooking spray, drop some of the batter, spread, cook the pancake until it's golden on both sides, and transfer to a plate.
3. Redo with the rest of the batter and serve your pancakes warm.

Nutrition:
Calories: 232 Fat: 5.1g Fiber: 6g Carbohydrates: 5.2g Proteins: 4g

1. Warmth up a pan with the milk over medium heat, add the coconut butter and the other ingredients, stir and cook for 7 minutes.
2. Pour this into a lined square pan, spread well, keep in the fridge for 2 hours, cut into small squares and serve.

Nutrition:
Calories: 214 Fat: 5.3g Fiber: 5g Carbohydrates: 16g Proteins: 3g

758. Watermelon Salad

Preparation time: 10 minutes
Cooking time: 0 minutes
Servings: 8
Ingredients:

- 1 watermelon, peeled and chopped
- 1 teaspoon almond extract
- 1 cup avocado, peeled, pitted, and cubed
- 1 cup mango, peeled and cubed
- 1 cup blueberries
- 1 teaspoon stevia
- 2 cups coconut cream
- Juice of 1 lime

Directions:

1. In a bowl, merge the watermelon with the avocado, mango, and the other ingredients, toss, divide into small cups and serve cold.

Nutrition:

Calories: 143 Fat: 4g Fiber: 6g Carbohydrates: 12g Proteins: 5g

759. Vanilla and Apple Brownies

Preparation time: 10 minutes
Cooking time: 20 minutes
Servings: 12
Ingredients:

- 1 and 1/2 cups apples, cored and cubed
- 2 tablespoons stevia
- 1/2 cup quick oats
- 2 tablespoons cocoa powder
- 1/3 cup coconut cream
- 1/4 cup coconut oil, melted
- 1/2 teaspoon baking powder
- 2 teaspoons vanilla extract
- Cooking spray

Directions:

1. In your food processor, combine the apples with the stevia and the other ingredients except for the cooking spray and blend well.
2. Grease a square pan with cooking spray, add the apples mix, spread, introduce in the oven, and bake at 350F for 20 minutes, leave aside to cool down, slice, and serve.

Nutrition:

Calories: 200 Fat: 3g Fiber: 3g Carbohydrates: 14g Proteins: 4g

760. Banana Cake

Preparation time: 10 minutes
Cooking time: 25 minutes
Servings: 8
Ingredients:

- 2 cups almond flour
- 1/4 cup cocoa powder
- 1 banana, peeled and mashed
- 1/2 teaspoon baking soda
- 1/2 cup coconut sugar
- 3/4 cup almond milk
- 1/4 cup coconut oil, melted
- 2 tablespoons flaxseed mixed with 3 tablespoons water
- 1 teaspoon vanilla extract
- 1 tablespoon lemon juice
- Cooking spray

Directions:

1. In a bowl, merge the flour with the cocoa powder, banana, and the other ingredients except for the cooking spray and stir well.
2. Grease a cake pan with cooking spray, pour the cake mix, spread, bake in the oven at 350F for 25 minutes, cool down, slice, and serve.

Nutrition:

Calories: 245 Fat: 5.6g Fiber: 4g Carbohydrates: 17g Proteins: 4g

761. Coconut Mousse

Preparation time: 10 minutes
Cooking time: 0 minutes
Servings: 12
Ingredients:

- 2 and 3/4 cup almond milk
- 2 tablespoons cocoa powder
- 1 teaspoon coconut extract
- 1 teaspoon vanilla extract
- 4 teaspoons stevia
- 1 cup coconut, toasted

Directions:

1. In a bowl, merge the almond milk with cocoa powder and the other ingredients, whisk well, divide into small cups and serve cold.

Nutrition:

Calories: 352 Fat: 5.4g Fiber: 5.4g Carbohydrates: 11g Proteins: 3g

762. Mango Coconut Pudding

Preparation time: 10 minutes
Cooking time: 50 minutes
Servings: 4
Ingredients:

- 1 cup coconut, shredded
- 1 cup coconut cream
- 1 mango, peeled and chopped
- 1 cup coconut milk
- 2 tablespoons coconut sugar
- 1 teaspoon vanilla extract
- 1/2 teaspoon cinnamon powder

Directions:

1. In a pan, mix the coconut with the cream and the other ingredients, stir, simmer for 50 minutes over medium heat, divide into bowls and serve cold.

Nutrition:

Calories: 251 Fat: 3.6g Fiber: 4g Carbohydrates: 16g Proteins: 7.1g

763. Rhubarb and Berries Pie

Preparation time: 10 minutes
Cooking time: 25 minutes
Servings: 12
Ingredients:

- 2 cups coconut flour
- 1 cup coconut butter, soft
- 1 cup pecans, chopped
- 1 and 1/4 cup coconut sugar
- 4 cups rhubarb, chopped
- 1 cup strawberries, sliced
- 8 ounces coconut cream

Directions:

1. In a bowl, merge the flour with the butter, pecans, and 1/4 cup sugar and stir well.
2. Transfer this to a pie pan, press well into the pan, introduce in the oven and bake at 350F for 20 minutes.
3. In a pan, combine the strawberries with the remaining ingredients, stir well and cook over medium heat for 4 minutes.
4. Spread this over the pie crust and keep it in the fridge for a few hours before slicing and serving.

Nutrition:
Calories: 332 Fat: 6g Fiber: 5g Carbohydrates: 15g Proteins: 6.3g

764. Banana Salad

Preparation time: 10 minutes
Cooking time: 0 minutes
Servings: 2
Ingredients:

- 1/4 cantaloupe, cubed
- 3 bananas, cut into chunks
- 1 apple, cored and cut into chunks
- 1 tablespoon stevia
- 1 teaspoon vanilla extract
- Juice of 1 lime

Directions:

1. In a bowl, merge the cantaloupe with the bananas and the other ingredients, toss and serve.

Nutrition:
Calories: 126 Fat: 3.3g Fiber: 1g Carbohydrates: 1.2g Proteins: 2g

765. Lemon Berries

Preparation time: 10 minutes
Cooking time: 10 minutes
Servings: 6
Ingredients:

- 2 teaspoons lemon juice
- 2 teaspoons lemon zest, grated
- Juice of 1 apple
- 1 teaspoon vanilla extract
- 1 pound blackberries
- 1 pound strawberries
- 4 tablespoons stevia

Directions:

1. In a pan, mix the berries with the stevia and the other ingredients, stir and cook over medium heat for 10 minutes.
2. Divide into cups and serve cold.

Nutrition:
Calories: 170 Fat: 3.4g Fiber: 3g Carbohydrates: 4g Proteins: 4g

766. Peach Stew

Preparation time: 10 minutes
Cooking time: 10 minutes
Servings: 6
Ingredients:

- 1 pound peaches, peeled and chopped
- 2 tablespoons water
- 2 tablespoons stevia
- 2 tablespoons lemon juice
- 1/4 teaspoon almond extract

Directions:

1. In a pot, combine the peaches with the water and the other ingredients, toss well, cook over medium heat for 10 minutes, divide into bowls and serve.

Nutrition:
Calories: 160 Fat: 3.8g Fiber: 2g Carbohydrates: 6g Proteins: 6g

767. Apple Stew

Preparation time: 10 minutes
Cooking time: 15 minutes
Servings: 6
Ingredients:

- 6 apples, cored and roughly chopped
- 4 tablespoons stevia
- 2 teaspoons vanilla extract
- 2 teaspoons lime juice
- 2 teaspoons cinnamon powder

Directions:

1. In a small pan, combine the apples with the stevia and the other ingredients, heat up and cook for about 10-15 minutes, divide between small dessert plates and serve.

Nutrition:
Calories: 210 Fat: 7.3g Fiber: 3g Carbohydrates: 8g Proteins: 5g

768. Minty Apricots

Preparation time: 10 minutes
Cooking time: 10 minutes
Servings: 4
Ingredients:

- 1/3 cup water
- 2 pounds apricots, chopped
- 3 tablespoons stevia
- 1 tablespoon mint, chopped

Directions:

1. In a pot, mix the apricots with the stevia and the other ingredients, stir, cook for 10 minutes, divide into bowls and serve.

769. Mango Mix

Preparation time: 10 minutes
Cooking time: 10 minutes
Servings: 8
Ingredients:
- 1 and 1/2 pounds mango, peeled and cubed
- 3 tablespoons stevia
- 1 cup orange juice
- 1/2 tablespoon lime juice
- 1 teaspoon vanilla extract

770. Blueberry Stew

Preparation time: 10 minutes
Cooking time: 10 minutes
Servings: 4
Ingredients:
- 2 tablespoons lemon juice
- 3 tablespoons stevia
- 12 ounces blueberries
- 1 cup orange juice

771. Lime Cream

Preparation time: 10 minutes
Cooking time: 15 minutes
Servings: 4
Ingredients:
- 3 cups coconut milk
- Juice of 2 limes
- Lemon zest of 2 limes, grated
- 3 tablespoons stevia
- 3 tablespoons coconut oil
- 2 tablespoons gelatin
- 1 cup water

772. Vanilla Peach Mix

Preparation time: 10 minutes
Cooking time: 10 minutes
Servings: 4
Ingredients:
- 4 cups water
- 3 peaches, chopped
- 2 cups rolled oats
- 1 teaspoon vanilla extract

773. Pear Stew

Preparation time: 10 minutes
Cooking time: 10 minutes
Servings: 4
Ingredients:
- 3 pears, cored and chopped
- 2 tablespoons stevia
- 1/4 cup coconut, shredded
- 1/2 teaspoon cinnamon powder
- 3 tablespoons coconut oil, melted

774. Mango Shake

Preparation time: 5 minutes
Cooking time: 0 minutes
Servings: 2
Ingredients:
- 2 medium mangoes, peeled

Nutrition:
Calories: 160 Fat: 5.1g Fiber: 4g Carbohydrates: 8g Proteins: 5.2g

Directions:
1. In a small pot, combine the mango with the stevia, orange juice, and the other ingredients, toss, bring to a parboil over medium heat, cook for 10 minutes, divide into bowls and serve.

Nutrition:
Calories: 160 Fat: 5.4g Fiber: 4g Carbohydrates: 8g Proteins: 3.4g

- 1 teaspoon vanilla extract

Directions:
1. In a pot, mix the blueberries with the stevia and the other ingredients, stir, cook over medium heat for 10 minutes, divide into small cups and serve cold.

Nutrition:
Calories: 201 Fat: 3g Fiber: 2g Carbohydrates: 6g Proteins: 3.8g

Directions:
1. In your blender, mix coconut milk with lime juice and the other ingredients except for the water and blend well.
2. Divide this into small jars and seal them.
3. Put the jars in a pan, add the water, introduce in the oven and cook at 380 degrees F for 15 minutes.
4. Serve the cream cold.

Nutrition:
Calories: 161 Fat: 3.4g Fiber: 5g Carbohydrates: 6g Proteins: 4g

- 2 tablespoons flax meal

Directions:
1. In a pan, combine the peaches with the water and the other ingredients, stir, bring to a parboil over medium heat, cook for 10 minutes, divide into bowls and serve.

Nutrition:
Calories: 161 Fat: 3g Fiber: 3g Carbohydrates: 7g Proteins: 5g

- 1/4 cup pecans, chopped

Directions:
1. In a pan, combine pears with the stevia and the other ingredients, stir, cook for 8 minutes, divide into bowls and serve cold.

Nutrition:
Calories: 142 Fat: 4g Fiber: 4g Carbohydrates: 7.2g Proteins: 7g

- 2 teaspoons cocoa powder
- 1/2 big avocado, mashed
- 3/4 cup almond milk
- 1 tablespoon stevia

Directions:
1. In a blender, mix the mangoes with the cocoa powder and the other ingredients, blend, divide into glasses and serve.

775. Lime Bars

Preparation time: 30 minutes
Cooking time: 0 minutes
Servings: 4
Ingredients:
- 1 cup avocado oil
- 2 bananas, peeled and chopped
- A pinch of salt
- 3 tablespoons stevia
- 1/4 cup lime juice
- A pinch of lime zest, grated
- Cooking spray

776. Blackberry Cobbler

Preparation time: 10 minutes
Cooking time: 30 minutes
Servings: 6
Ingredients:
- 3/4 cup coconut sugar
- 6 cups blackberries
- 1/8 teaspoon baking soda
- 1 tablespoon lemon juice
- 1/2 cup almond flour
- A pinch of salt
- 1/2 cup water
- 3 and 1/2 tablespoon avocado oil
- Cooking spray

777. Black Tea Cake

Preparation time: 10 minutes
Cooking time: 35 minutes
Servings: 12
Ingredients:
- 6 tablespoons black tea powder
- 2 cups almond milk
- 1/2 cup coconut butter
- 2 cups coconut sugar
- 2 tablespoons flaxseed mixed with 3 tablespoons water
- 2 teaspoons vanilla extract
- 1/2 cup olive oil
- 3 and 1/2 cups almond flour

778. Green Tea Avocado Pudding

Preparation time: 2 hours
Cooking time: 5 minutes
Servings: 6
Ingredients:
- 2 cups almond milk
- 2 tablespoons green tea powder
- 1 cup coconut cream
- 3 tablespoons stevia
- 1 avocado, peeled, pitted, and mashed

779. Pineapple and Mango Oatmeal

Preparation time: 5 minutes
Cooking time: 0 minutes
Servings: 2
Ingredients:

Nutrition:
Calories: 185 Fat: 3.4g Fiber: 4.2g Carbohydrates: 6g Proteins: 7g

- 3 kiwis, peeled and chopped

Directions:
1. In a food processor, mix the oil with the bananas and the other ingredients except for the cooking spray pulse and spread it into a pan after you've greased it with the cooking spray.
2. Keep in the fridge for 30 minutes, slice, and serve bars.

Nutrition:
Calories: 187 Fat: 3g Fiber: 3g Carbohydrates: 4g Proteins: 4g

Directions:
1. Set a baking dish with some cooking spray and leave it aside.
2. In a bowl, mix blackberries with half of the coconut sugar, sprinkle some flour and add lemon juice, whisk and pour into the baking dish.
3. In another bowl, mix flour with remaining sugar, a pinch of salt, baking soda, 1/2 cup water, and the oil and stir well with your hands.
4. Spread over berries, bake at 375 degrees F for 30 minutes, cool down, and serve.

Nutrition:
Calories: 221 Fat: 7.3g Fiber: 3.3g Carbohydrates: 6g Proteins: 9g

- 1 teaspoon baking soda
- 3 teaspoons baking powder

Directions:
1. In a large bowl, mix the black tea powder with the almond milk, coconut butter, and the other ingredients and stir well.
2. Pour this into a lined cake pan, place in the oven at 350 degrees F and bake for 30 minutes. Leave cakes to cool down.
3. Slice and serve.

Nutrition:
Calories: 200 Fat: 6.5g Fiber: 4g Carbohydrates: 6.5g Proteins: 4.5g

- 1 teaspoon gelatin powder

Directions:
1. In a pan, mix the almond milk with green tea powder and the other ingredients, stir, cook for 5 minutes, divide into cups and keep in the fridge for 2 hours before serving.

Nutrition:
Calories: 210 Fat: 4.4g Fiber: 3g Carbohydrates: 7g Proteins: 4g

- 2 cups unsweetened almond milk
- 2 cups rolled oats
- 1/2 cup pineapple chunks, thawed if frozen

- 1/2 cup diced mango, thawed if frozen
- 1 banana, sliced
- 1 tablespoon chia seeds
- 1 tablespoon maple syrup

Directions:
1. Stir together the almond milk, oats, pineapple, mango, banana, chia seeds, and maple syrup in a large bowl until you see no clumps.

780. Breakfast Quinoa
Preparation time: 5 minutes
Cooking time: 10 minutes
Servings: 2
Ingredients:
- 1 cup unsweetened almond milk
- 2 cups cooked quinoa
- 1 tablespoon defatted peanut powder
- 1 tablespoon cocoa powder
- 1 tablespoon maple syrup

Directions:

781. Strawberry Chia Jam
Preparation time: 10 minutes
Cooking time: 20 minutes
Servings: 2
Ingredients:
- 1 pound (454 g) fresh strawberries, hulled and halved
- 1/4 cup maple syrup
- 1/4 cup water
- 3 tbsp. freshly squeezed lemon juice (from 1 lemon)
- 3 tablespoons chia seeds
- 1 teaspoon vanilla extract

Directions:
1. Add the strawberries, maple syrup, water, and lemon juice to a medium saucepan over medium

782. Sticky Rice Congee with Dates
Preparation time: 10 minutes
Cooking time: 15 minutes
Servings: 4
Ingredients:
- 2 cups water
- 4 cups cooked brown rice
- 1/2 cup chopped apricots
- 1/2 cup dates, pitted and chopped
- 1/4 teaspoon ground cloves
- 1 large cinnamon stick
- Salt, to taste (optional)

Directions:

783. Easy Apple and Cinnamon Muesli
Preparation time: 10 minutes
Cooking time: 0 minutes
Servings: 2
Ingredients:
- 1 cup rolled oats
- 1/2 cup raisins
- 3/4 cup unsweetened almond milk
- 2 tablespoons date molasses (optional)
- 1/4 teaspoon ground cinnamon
- 1 Granny Smith apple, grated

2. Secure and refrigerate to chill for at least 4 hours, preferably overnight.
3. Serve chilled with your favorite toppings.

Nutrition:
Calories: 512 Fat: 22.1g Carbohydrates: 13.1g Proteins: 14.1g Fiber: 15.2g

1. Add the almond milk to a saucepan over medium-high heat and bring to a boil.
2. Set the heat to low, and add the quinoa, peanut powder, coco powder, and maple syrup while whisking.
3. Allow to simmer for 6 minutes, stirring frequently, or until some liquid has evaporated.
4. Remove from the heat and serve warm.

Nutrition:
Calories: 340 Fat: 18.2g Carbohydrates: 3.1g Proteins: 14.2g Fiber: 7.1g

heat. Allow to parboil for about 15 minutes, stirring occasionally, or until the strawberries begin to soften and bubble. Mash the strawberries to your desired consistency.
2. Add the chia seeds and continue stirring over low heat for 5 minutes. The chia seeds will help the jam achieve a gelatinous texture.
3. Add the vanilla and stir until combined. Detach from the heat and let the jam cool to room temperature. Stir again.
4. Serve immediately.

Nutrition:
Calories: 132 Fat: 2.5g Carbohydrates: 25.7g Proteins: 1.9g Fiber: 2.5g

1. Add 2 cups water to a large saucepan over medium heat and bring to a boil.
2. Add the brown rice, apricots, dates, cloves, and cinnamon stick, and stir well.
3. Set the heat to medium-low and parboil for 15 minutes, stirring occasionally, or until the mixture is thickened. Sprinkle the salt to season, if desired.
4. Let the congee cool for 5 minutes and remove the cinnamon stick, then serve.

Nutrition:
Calories: 313 Fat: 1.9g Carbohydrates: 68.8g Proteins: 6.0g Fiber: 6.2g

Directions:
1. In a large bowl, merge the oats, raisins, almond milk, date molasses (if desired), and cinnamon. Stir until well combined and transfer the bowl to the fridge. Let the oats soak for at least 30 minutes.
2. Remove from the fridge and add the grated apple. Give it a good stir and serve immediately.

Nutrition:
Calories: 325 Fat: 4.2g Carbohydrates: 63.7g Proteins: 8.8g Fiber: 10.1g

784. Salted Caramel Oatmeal

Preparation time: 5 minutes
Cooking time: 15 minutes
Servings: 4
Ingredients:

- 4 cups water
- 16 Medjool dates, pitted and chopped
- Pinch salt (optional)
- 2 cups steel-cut oats
- Fresh berries, for topping (optional)
- Sliced almonds, for topping (optional)

Directions:

1. Put the water, dates, and salt (if desired) in a small saucepan over high heat and bring to a rapid boil.
2. Once it starts to boil. Add the oats and allow to simmer for 10 minutes, stirring frequently, or until the oats are cooked through.
3. Divide the oatmeal among four serving bowls. Serve topped with fresh berries and sliced almonds, if desired.

Nutrition:
Calories: 376 Fat: 2.1g Carbohydrates: 84.9g Proteins: 5.2g Fiber: 9.1g

785. Creamy Brown Rice Cereal with Raisins

Preparation time: 5 minutes
Cooking time: 10 minutes
Servings: 2
Ingredients:

- 2 cups water
- 1/2 cup uncooked brown rice
- 1/4 cup raisins
- 1 1/2 cups unsweetened almond milk (optional)
- 1/2 teaspoon cinnamon (optional)

Directions:

1. Add the water to a medium saucepan over medium-high heat and bring to a boil.
2. Meanwhile, pulverize the brown rice by using a high-speed blender or food processor. Grind until the rice resembles sand.
3. Once it starts to boil, gradually stir in the ground brown rice.
4. Add the raisins and set the heat to low. Secure and simmer for 5 to 8 minutes, stirring once or twice during cooking, or until the rice is tender.
5. Sprinkle with the almond milk and cinnamon, if desired.

Nutrition:
Calories: 131 Fat: 1.8g Carbohydrates: 26.5g Proteins: 2.4g Fiber: 1.3g

786. Cashew-Date Waffles

Preparation time: 20 minutes
Cooking time: 10 minutes
Servings: 2
Ingredients:

- 1 ounce (28 g) raw, unsalted cashews (about 1/4 cup)
- 1 ounce (28 g) pitted dates, chopped
- 2 cups unsweetened coconut milk
- 1 1/2 cups old-fashioned rolled oats
- 1/2 cup cornmeal
- 2 teaspoons baking powder
- 1/2 teaspoon cinnamon

Directions:

1. In a small bowl, add the cashews, dates, and coconut milk. Let the nuts and dates soak in the milk for at least 15 minutes.
2. Merge the rolled oats in a blender until it has reached a powdery consistency.
3. Place the oats in a medium bowl, along with the cornmeal, baking powder, and cinnamon. Stir well and set aside.
4. Preheat the waffle iron to medium-high heat.
5. Blend the cashews, dates, and coconut milk in a blender until completely mixed. Spill the mixture into the bowl of dry ingredients and whisk to combine. Let the batter sit for 1 minute.
6. Slowly pour 1/2 to 3/4 cup of the batter into the preheated waffle iron and cook until golden brown. Repeat with the remaining batter.
7. Divide the waffles between two plates and serve warm.

Nutrition:
Calories: 849 Fat: 13.5g Carbohydrates: 66.4g Proteins: 16.8g Fiber: 10.1g

787. Maple Sunflower Seed Granola

Preparation time: 20 minutes
Cooking time: 0 minutes
Servings: 2
Ingredients:

- 1 1/2 cups peanut butter
- 1/4 cup maple syrup
- 1 1/2 cups old-fashioned rolled oats
- 3/4 cup raw sunflower seeds
- 3/4 cup flaxseed meal

Directions:

1. Set the peanut butter and maple syrup in a microwave-safe bowl, and microwave on high, stirring well between each interval, until the mixture is completely mixed. Let it rest for a few minutes until slightly cooled.
2. Add the rolled oats, sunflower seeds, and flaxseed meal to the bowl, and whisk until well incorporated.
3. Set the mixture to a baking sheet lined with parchment paper and spread it out into an even layer.
4. Transfer the baking sheet in the freezer for at least 25 minutes until firm.
5. Remove from the freezer and break the granola into large chunks before serving.

Nutrition:
Calories: 764 Fat: 51.7g Carbohydrates: 47.8g Proteins: 27.0g Fiber: 16.0g

788. Vegan Dairy Free Breakfast Bowl

Preparation time: 20 minutes
Cooking time: 0 minutes
Servings: 2
Ingredients:

- 1/2 cup strawberries
- 1/2 cup blueberries
- 1/2 cup blackberries
- 1/2 cup raspberries
- 1 grapefruit, peeled and segmented
- 3 tbs. fresh orange juice (from 1 orange)
- 1 tablespoon pure maple syrup
- 1/4 cup chopped fresh mint
- 1/4 cup sliced almonds

Directions:

1. In a serving bowl, combine the berries and grapefruit.
2. In a bowl, stir together the orange juice and maple syrup.
3. Pour the syrup mixture over the fruit. Sprinkle with the mint and almonds. Serve immediately

Nutrition:
Calories: 199 Fat: 4g Fiber: 3g Carbohydrates: 12g Proteins: 9g

789. Hot and Healthy Breakfast Bowl with Nuts

Preparation time: 5 minutes
Cooking time: 0 minutes
Servings: 1
Ingredients:

- 1/2 cup oats, or quinoa flakes
- 1 tablespoon ground flaxseed, or chia seeds, or hemp hearts
- 1 tablespoon maple syrup or coconut sugar (optional)
- 1/4 teaspoon ground cinnamon (optional)
- 1 apple, chopped and 1 tablespoon walnuts
- 2 tablespoons dried cranberries and 1 tablespoon pumpkin seeds
- 1 pear, chopped and 1 tablespoon cashews
- 1 cup sliced grapes and 1 tablespoon sunflower seeds
- 1 banana, sliced, and 1 tablespoon peanut butter
- 2 tablespoons raisins and 1 tablespoon hazelnuts
- 1 cup berries and 1 tablespoon unsweetened coconut flakes

Directions:

1. Mix the oats, flax, maple syrup, and cinnamon (if using) together in a bowl or to-go container (a travel mug or short thermos works beautifully).
2. Pour enough cool water over the oats to submerge them and stir to combine. Leave to soak for a minimum of half an hour, or overnight.
3. Add your choice of toppings.
4. Boil about 1/2 cup water and pour over the oats. Let them soak about 5 minutes before eating.

Nutrition:
Calories: 244 Fat: 16g Carbohydrates: 10g Fiber: 6g Proteins: 7g

790. Healthy Chocolaty Oats Bites

Preparation time: 15 minutes
Cooking time: 12 minutes
Servings: 2
Ingredients:

- 1 tablespoon ground flaxseed
- 2 tbsp. almond butter or sunflower seed butter
- 2 tablespoons maple syrup
- 1 banana, mashed
- 1 teaspoon ground cinnamon
- 1/4 teaspoon ground nutmeg (optional)
- Pinch sea salt
- 1/2 cup rolled oats
- 1/4 cup raisins, or dark chocolate chips

Directions:

1. Preheat the oven to 350F. Set a large baking sheet with parchment paper. Merge the ground flax with just enough water to cover it in a small dish and leave it to sit.
2. In a large bowl, merge together the almond butter and maple syrup until creamy, then attach the banana. Add the flax-water mixture.
3. Sift the cinnamon, nutmeg, and salt into a separate bowl, and then stir into the wet mixture. Attach the oats and raisins, and fold in.
4. From 3 to 4 tbsp. batter into a ball and press lightly to flatten onto the baking sheet. Repeat, spacing the cookies 2 to 3 inches apart. Bake for 12 minutes until golden brown.
5. Set the cookies in an airtight bag in the fridge.

Nutrition:
Calories: 192 Fat: 16g Carbohydrates: 4g Fiber: 4g Proteins: 4g

791. Homemade Nutty Fruity Muffins

Preparation time: 15 minutes
Cooking time: 30 minutes
Servings: 6
Ingredients:

- 1 teaspoon coconut oil, for greasing muffin tins (optional)
- 2 tbsp. almond butter, or sunflower seed butter
- 1/4 cup non-dairy milk
- 1 orange, peeled
- 1 carrot, coarsely chopped
- 2 tbsp. chopped dried apricots, or other dried fruit
- 3 tablespoons molasses
- 2 tablespoons ground flaxseed
- 1 teaspoon apple cider vinegar
- 1 teaspoon pure vanilla extract
- 1/2 teaspoon ground cinnamon
- 1/2 teaspoon ground ginger (optional)
- 1/4 teaspoon ground nutmeg (optional)
- 1/4 teaspoon allspice (optional)

- 3/4 cup rolled oats, or whole-grain flour
- 1 teaspoon baking powder
- 1/2 teaspoon baking soda

Mix-Ins (Optional)

- 1/2 cup rolled oats
- 2 tbsp. raisins, or other chopped dried fruit
- 2 tablespoons sunflower seeds

Directions:

1. Preheat the oven to 350F. Prepare a 6-cup muffin tin by rubbing the insides of the cups with coconut oil or using silicone or paper muffin cups.
2. Purée the nut butter, milk, orange, carrot, apricots, molasses, flaxseed, vinegar, vanilla, cinnamon,

ginger, nutmeg, and allspice in a food processor until somewhat smooth.

3. Grind the oats in a clean coffee grinder until they're the consistency of flour (or use whole-grain flour). In a bowl, mix the oats with the baking powder and baking soda.
4. Mix the wet ingredients into the dry ingredients until just combined. Fold in the mix-ins (if using).
5. Set about 1/4 cup batter into each muffin cup and bake for 30 minutes.

Nutrition:
Calories: 287 Fat: 23g Carbohydrates: 11g Fiber: 6g Proteins: 8g

792. Vanilla Flavored Whole Grain Muffins

Preparation time: 15 minutes
Cooking time: 20 minutes
Servings: 12
Ingredients:

- 1 teaspoon coconut oil, for greasing muffin tins (optional)
- 2 tablespoons nut butter or seed butter
- 11/2 cups unsweetened applesauce
- 1/3 cup coconut sugar
- 1/2 cup non-dairy milk
- 2 tablespoons ground flaxseed
- 1 teaspoon apple cider vinegar
- 1 teaspoon pure vanilla extract
- 2 cups whole-grain flour
- 1 teaspoon baking soda
- 1/2 teaspoon baking powder
- 1 teaspoon ground cinnamon
- Pinch sea salt
- 1/2 cup walnuts, chopped

Toppings (Optional)

- 1/4 cup walnuts

- 1/4 cup coconut sugar
- 1/2 teaspoon ground cinnamon

Directions:

1. Preheat the oven to 350F. Prepare two 6-cup muffin tins by rubbing the insides of the cups with coconut oil or using silicone or paper muffin cups.
2. In a large bowl, mix the nut butter, applesauce, coconut sugar, milk, flaxseed, vinegar, and vanilla until thoroughly combined, or purée in a food processor or blender.
3. In bowl, sift together the flour, baking soda, baking powder, cinnamon, salt, and chopped walnuts.
4. Merge the dry ingredients into the wet ingredients until just combined.
5. Set about 1/4 cup batter into each muffin cup and sprinkle with the topping of your choice (if using).
6. Bake for 15 to 20 minutes. The applesauce creates a very moist base, so the muffins may take longer, depending on how heavy your muffin tins are.

Nutrition:
Calories: 287 Fat: 12g Carbohydrates: 8g Fiber: 6g Proteins: 8g

793. Coconut Banana Sandwich with Raspberry Spread

Preparation time: 10 minutes
Cooking time: 30 minutes
Servings: 8
Ingredients:
French toast

- 1 banana
- 1 cup coconut milk
- 1 teaspoon pure vanilla extract
- 1/4 teaspoon ground nutmeg
- 1/2 teaspoon ground cinnamon
- 11/2 Teaspoons arrowroot powder or flour
- Pinch sea salt
- 8 slices whole-grain bread

Raspberry Syrup

- 1 cup fresh or frozen raspberries
- 2 tablespoons water or pure fruit juice
- 1 to 2 tablespoons maple syrup or coconut sugar (optional)

794. Apple Toasted Sweet Sandwich

Preparation time: 5 minutes
Cooking time: 20 minutes
Servings: 2
Ingredients:

Directions:

1. Preheat the oven to 350F.
2. In a shallow bowl, purée or mash the banana well. Mix in the coconut milk, vanilla, nutmeg, cinnamon, arrowroot, and salt.
3. Dip the slices of bread in the banana mixture, and then lay them out in a 13-by-9-inch baking dish.
4. Pour any leftover banana mixture over the bread and put the dish in the oven. Bake about 30 minutes.
5. Serve topped with raspberry syrup.
6. Heat the raspberries in a small pot with the water and the maple syrup (if using) on medium heat.
7. Leave to simmer, stirring occasionally and breaking up the berries, for 15 to 20 minutes, until the liquid has reduced.

Nutrition:
Calories: 166 Fat: 15g Carbohydrates: 7g Fiber: 4g Proteins: 5g

- 1 to 2 teaspoons coconut oil
- 1/2 teaspoon ground cinnamon
- 1 tablespoon maple syrup or coconut sugar

- 1 apple, cored and thinly sliced
- 2 slices whole-grain bread

Directions:
1. In a large bowl, merge the coconut oil, cinnamon, and maple syrup together.
2. Add the apple slices and toss with your hands to coat them.
3. To panfry the toast, place the apple slices in a medium skillet on medium-high and cook for about 5 minutes.

795. Dried Cranberry Almond Bowl

Preparation time: 10 minutes
Cooking time: 0 minutes
Servings: 5
Ingredients:
Muesli:

- 1 cup rolled oats
- 1 cup spelt flakes, or quinoa flakes, or more rolled oats
- 2 cups puffed cereal
- 1/4 cup sunflower seeds
- 1/4 cup almonds
- 1/4 cup raisins
- 1/4 cup dried cranberries
- 1/4 cup chopped dried figs
- 1/4 cup unsweetened shredded coconut

796. Chocolaty Banana Breakfast Bowl

Preparation time: 5 minutes
Cooking time: 25 minutes
Servings: 4
Ingredients:

- 1 cup quinoa
- 1 tsp. ground cinnamon
- 1 cup non-dairy milk
- 1 cup water
- 1 large banana
- 2 to 3 tbsp. unsweetened cocoa powder
- 1 to 2 tbsp. almond butter, or other vegan butter
- 1 tbsp. ground flaxseed, or chia or hemp seeds
- 2 tablespoons walnuts

797. Fresh mint and coconut Fruit Salad

Preparation time: 5 minutes
Cooking time: 5 minutes
Servings: 1
Ingredients:

- 1 orange, zested and juiced
- 1/4 cup whole-wheat couscous, or corn couscous
- 1 cup assorted berries (strawberries, blackberries, blueberries)
- 1/2 cup cubed melon (cantaloupe or honeydew)
- 1 tablespoon maple syrup or coconut sugar (optional)
- 1 tablespoon fresh mint, minced (optional)
- 1 tablespoon unsweetened coconut flakes

Directions:
1. Put the orange juice in a small pot, add half the zest, and bring to a boil.

4. Cook the bread in the same skillet for 2 to 3 minutes on each side. Top the toast with the apples. Alternately, you can bake the toast.
5. Use your hands to rub each slice of bread with some of the coconut oil mixture on both sides.
6. Lay them on a small baking sheet, top with the coated apples, and put in the oven or toaster oven at 350F (180C) for 15 to 20 minutes, or until the apples have softened.

Nutrition:
Calories: 187 Fat: 18g Carbohydrates: 7g Fiber: 4g Proteins: 4g

- 1/4 cup non-dairy chocolate chips
- 1 to 3 Teaspoons ground cinnamon
- Bowl:
- 1/2 cup non-dairy milk, or unsweetened applesauce
- 3/4 cup muesli
- 1/2 cup berries

Directions:
1. Put the muesli ingredients in a container or bag and shake.
2. Combine the muesli and bowl ingredients in a bowl or to-go container.

Nutrition:
Calories: 441 Fat: 20g Carbohydrates: 13g Fiber: 13g Proteins: 10g

- 1/4 cup raspberries

Directions:
1. Bring the quinoa, cinnamon, milk, and water in a medium pot. Set to a boil over high heat, and then turn down low and simmer, secured, for 25 to 30 minutes.
2. Purée or press the banana in a bowl and stir in the cocoa powder, almond butter, and flaxseed.
3. To serve, set 1 cup cooked quinoa into a bowl, set with half the pudding and half the walnuts and raspberries.

Nutrition:
Calories: 392 Fat: 19g Carbohydrates: 9g Fiber: 10g Proteins: 12g

2. Put the dry couscous in a small bowl and pour the boiling orange juice over it. If there isn't enough juice to fully submerge the couscous, add just enough boiling water to do so.
3. Cover the bowl with a plate or seal with wrap and let steep for 5 minutes.
4. In a medium bowl, set the berries and melon with the maple syrup (if using) and the rest of the zest. You can either keep the fruit cool or heat it lightly in the small pot you used for the orange juice.
5. When the couscous is soft, remove the cover and fluff it with a fork. Top with the fruit, fresh mint, and coconut.

Nutrition:
Calories: 496 Fat: 22g Carbohydrates: 7g Fiber: 14g Proteins: 11g

798. Nutty Fruity Breakfast Bowl

Preparation time: 15 minutes
Cooking time: 30 minutes
Servings: 5
Ingredients:

- 2 cups rolled oats
- 3/4 cup whole-grain flour
- 1 tablespoon ground cinnamon
- 1 teaspoon ground ginger (optional)
- 1/2 cup sunflower seeds, or walnuts, chopped
- 1/2 cup almonds, chopped
- 1/2 cup pumpkin seeds
- 1/2 cup unsweetened shredded coconut
- 11/4 cups pure fruit juice (cranberry, apple, or something similar)
- 1/2 cup raisins, or dried cranberries
- 1/2 cup goji berries (optional)

Directions:

1. Preheat the oven to 350F.
2. Mix the oats, flour, cinnamon, ginger, sunflower seeds, almonds, pumpkin seeds, and coconut in a large bowl.
3. Dust the juice over the mixture and stir until it's just moistened. You might need a bit more or a bit less liquid, depending on how much your oats and flour absorb.
4. Scatter the granola on a large baking sheet (the more spread out it is the better) and put it in the oven. Use a spatula to turn the granola so that the middle gets dried out. Let the granola bake 30 minutes.
5. Set the granola out of the oven and stir in the raisins and goji berries (if using).
6. Set leftovers in an airtight container for up to 2 weeks.

Nutrition:
Calories: 398 Fat: 25g Carbohydrates: 9g Fiber: 8g Proteins: 10g

799. Peppery Mushroom Tomato Bowl

Preparation time: 10 minutes
Cooking time: 15 minutes
Servings: 1
Ingredients:

- 1 tsp. olive oil, or 1 tbsp. vegetable broth or water
- 1/2 cup sliced mushrooms
- Pinch sea salt
- 1/2 cup chopped zucchini
- 1/2 cup chickpeas (cooked or canned)
- 1 teaspoon smoked paprika, or regular paprika
- 1 teaspoon turmeric
- 1 tablespoon nutritional yeast (optional)
- Freshly ground black pepper
- 1/2 cup cherry tomatoes, chopped
- 1/4 cup fresh parsley, sliced

Directions:

1. Heat a large skillet to medium-high. Once the skillet is hot, attach the olive oil and mushrooms, along with the sea salt to help them soften, and sauté, stirring occasionally, 7 to 8 minutes.
2. Attach the zucchini to the skillet.
3. If you're using canned chickpeas, wash and drain them. Press the chickpeas with a potato masher, fork, or your fingers. Add them to the skillet and cook until they are heated through.
4. Set the paprika, turmeric, and nutritional yeast over the chickpeas, and stir to combine.
5. Set in the black pepper, cherry tomatoes and fresh parsley at the end.

Nutrition:
Calories: 265 Fat: 18g Carbohydrates: 7g Fiber: 12g Proteins: 16g

800. Roasted Beets and Carrot with Avocado Dip

Preparation time: 10 minutes
Cooking time: 30 minutes
Servings: 2
Ingredients:
Avocado Dip:

- 1 avocado
- 1 tablespoon apple cider vinegar
- 1/4 to 1/2 cup water
- 2 tablespoons nutritional yeast
- 1 tsp. dried dill, or 1 tablespoon fresh dill
- Pinch sea salt
- Roasted Veg:
- 1 small sweet potato, peeled and cubed
- 2 small beets, peeled and cubed
- 2 small carrots, peeled and cubed
- 1 teaspoon sea salt
- 1 teaspoon dried oregano
- 1/4 teaspoon cayenne pepper
- Pinch freshly ground black pepper

Directions:

1. In a blender, purée the avocado with the other dip ingredients, using just enough water to get a smooth, creamy texture.
2. Alternately, you can mash the avocado thoroughly in a large bowl, then stir in the rest of the dip ingredients.
3. Preheat the oven to 350F.
4. Put the sweet potato, beets, and carrots in a large pot with a small amount of water and set to a boil. Boil for 15 minutes, until they're just barely soft, and then drain.
5. Sprinkle the salt, oregano, cayenne, and pepper over them and stir gently to combine.
6. Set the vegetables on a large baking sheet and roast them in the oven 10 to 15 minutes, until they've browned around the edges.
7. Serve the veg with the avocado dip on the side.

Nutrition:
Calories: 335 Fat: 32g Carbohydrates: 11g Proteins: 11g Fiber: 16g

801. Raisin Oat Cookies

Preparation time: 10 minutes
Cooking time: 30 minutes
Servings: 2
Ingredients:

- 1/3 cup almond butter
- 1/2 cup maple sugar
- 1/4 cup unsweetened applesauce
- 1 teaspoon vanilla extract
- 1/3 cup sorghum flour
- 2/3 cups oat flour
- 1/2 teaspoon baking soda
- 1/2 cup raisins
- 1 cup rolled oats
- 1/2 teaspoon ground cinnamon
- 1/4 teaspoon salt (optional)

Directions:

1. Preheat the oven to 350F (180C). Line two baking sheets with parchment paper.
2. Whisk together the almond butter, maple sugar, and applesauce in a large bowl until smooth.
3. Mix in the remaining ingredients and keep whisking until a stiff dough form.
4. Divide and roll the dough into 24 small balls, then arrange the balls in the baking sheets. Keep a little space between each two balls. Bash them with your hands to make them form like cookies.
5. Bake in the warmth oven for 9 minutes or until crispy. Flip the cookies halfway through the cooking time.
6. Detach them from the oven and allow cooling for 10 minutes before serving.

Nutrition:
Calories: 140 Fat: 56.0g Carbohydrates: 224.1g Proteins: 45.5g Fiber: 30.5g

802. Oat Scones

Preparation time: 15 minutes
Cooking time: 22 minutes
Servings: 12
Ingredients:

- 1 teaspoon apple cider vinegar
- 1/2 cup unsweetened soy milk
- 1 teaspoon vanilla extract
- 3 cups oat flour
- 2 tablespoons baking powder
- 1/2 cup maple sugar
- 1/2 teaspoon salt (optional)
- 1/3 cup almond butter
- 1/2 cup unsweetened applesauce

Directions:

1. Preheat the oven to 350F (180C). Line a baking sheet with parchment paper.
2. Combine cider vinegar and soy milk in a bowl. Stir to mix well. Let stand for a few minutes to curdle, and then mix in the vanilla.
3. Merge the flour, baking powder, sugar, and salt (if desired) in a second bowl. Stir to mix well.
4. Combine the almond butter and applesauce in a third bowl. Stir to mix well.
5. Gently fold the applesauce mixture in the flour mixture, and then stir in the milk mixture.
6. Scoop the mixture on the baking sheet with an ice-cream scoop to make 12 scones. Drizzle them with a touch of water.
7. Bake in the warmth oven for 22 minutes or until puffed and lightly browned. Flip the scones halfway through the cooking time.
8. Remove them from the oven and allow cooling for 10 minutes before serving.

Nutrition:
Calories: 177 Fat: 6.0g Carbohydrates: 26.6g Proteins: 5.4g Fiber: 2.5g

803. Golden Milk

Preparation time: 5 minutes
Cooking time: 0 minutes
Servings: 2
Ingredients:

- 1/2 teaspoon ground cinnamon
- 1/2 teaspoon ground turmeric
- 1/2 teaspoon grated fresh ginger
- 1 teaspoon maple syrup
- 1 cup unsweetened coconut milk
- Ground black pepper, to taste
- 2 tablespoons water

Directions:

1. Combine all the ingredients in a saucepan. Stir to mix well.
2. Heat over medium heat for 5 minutes. Keep stirring during the heating.
3. Allow to cool then pour the mixture in a blender. Pulse until creamy and smooth. Serve immediately.

Nutrition:
Calories: 577 Fat: 57.3g Carbohydrates: 19.7g Proteins: 5.7g Fiber: 6.1g

804. Mango Agua Fresca

Preparation time: 5 minutes
Cooking time: 0 minutes
Servings: 2
Ingredients:

- 2 fresh mangoes, diced
- 11/2 cups water
- 1 teaspoon fresh lime juice
- Maple syrup, to taste
- 2 cups ice
- 2 slices fresh lime, for garnish
- 2 fresh mint sprigs, for garnish

Directions:

1. Put the mangoes, lime juice, maple syrup, and water in a blender. Process until creamy and smooth.

2. Divide the beverage into two glasses, and then garnish each glass with ice, lime slice, and mint sprig before serving.

805. Classic Switchel

Preparation time: 5 minutes
Cooking time: 0 minutes
Servings: 5
Ingredients:
- 1-inch piece ginger, minced
- 2 tablespoons apple cider vinegar
- 2 tablespoons maple syrup
- 4 cups water

806. Easy and Fresh Mango Madness

Preparation time: 5 minutes
Cooking time: 0 minutes
Servings: 5
Ingredients:
- 1 cup chopped mango
- 1 cup chopped peach
- 1 banana
- 1 cup strawberries
- 1 carrot, peeled and chopped

807. Blueberry Coconut Milkshake

Preparation time: 5 minutes
Cooking time: 0 minutes
Servings: 2
Ingredients:
- 1 can coconut milk
- 11/2 cups frozen blueberries
- 1 tbsp. maple syrup
- 1 tsp. vanilla extract

Nutrition:
Calories: 230 Fat: 1.3g Carbohydrates: 57.7g Proteins: 2.8g Fiber: 5.4g

- 1/4 teaspoon sea salt (optional)

Directions:
1. Combine all the ingredients in a glass. Stir to mix well.
2. Serve immediately.

Nutrition:
Calories: 110 Fat: 0g Carbohydrates: 28.0g Proteins: 0g Fiber: 0g

- 1 cup water

Directions:
1. Arrange all the ingredients in a food processor, then blitz until glossy and smooth.
2. Serve immediately.

Nutrition:
Calories: 376 Fat: 22.0g Carbohydrates: 19.0g Fiber: 14.0g Proteins: 5.0g

Directions:
1. Use a blender to mix all the ingredients until smooth. If it's too thick, add a little water. Serve immediately.

Nutrition:
Calories: 496 Fat: 22g Carbohydrates: 7g Fiber: 14g Proteins: 11g

Conclusion

Eating more vegan foods, by definition, will lead you to eat less saturated fat and overall calories than you would on a non-vegan diet. If you're a vegetarian or vegan or are just curious about the possibilities of plant-based nutrition, we hope that we've shown you that just because something is plant-based don't mean it are boring. There are so many great vegan dishes out there! Rather than being overwhelmed by everything on the market. Try to focus on the core principles of cooking with whole foods and substituting for animal products where possible. You might be amazed at how fast you gain confidence in making your recipes. Vegan food that is good for you is delicious food!

For the average adult, a diet of non-animal-based proteins and essential fats is sufficient to meet all nutritional needs.

Vegan and vegetarian diets are rich in essential fatty acids, vitamins, iron and calcium, consumed here in higher concentrations than non-vegetarian diets. Vegan foods provide all the nutrients necessary for human health. Vegan foods are entirely cholesterol-free. Vegan plant-based proteins have been shown to lower blood sugars in people with diabetes, reduce serum cholesterol levels and even alleviate arthritis symptoms.

It's radiant to get tied up in the diet trends, but if we follow the basic principles of healthy eating, we will always be on course. Consuming overflow of fruits and vegetables, whole grains, nuts, seeds and legumes, unprocessed lean protein such as beans and tofu, plenty of water and low saturated fat will be your ticket to good health. Whatever you choose to call it – vegan, vegetarian or flexitarian.

The recipes in this book are fun, delicious and inspiring! Cooking vegan is easy. The hardest part is being consistent. You'll want to choose your ingredients wisely and be prepared to cook often. I hope that my tips encourage you to continue your plant-based journey.

Printed in Great Britain
by Amazon